Lanier Golf Guides have set the standard for the industry . . .

Golf R........ ...mplete Guide ... Golf ... International™

LPGA
.......rts is a ...... points out the championship golf courses around the country and lists the various LPGA and PGA competitions held on them. But more than that, the Guide is a well-researched multi-purpose book with a special-interest index highlighting diversions such as shopping areas and suggestions for family entertainment near the resorts. This work is a comprehensive travel guide for anyone interested in planning a trip around the exhilarating sport of golf."

Washington Times
"If Golf is your game, more to your liking will be *Golf Resorts.* Just reading the description of more than 400 golf resorts is likely to persuade duffer and expert alike to head for the fairway."

Rees Jones
"This book is fantastic!"

Industry Week
"Executives who enjoy golf vacations may appreciate a new guidebook: *Golf Resorts,* by Pamela Lanier . . . details on 400 golf resorts, special facilities and the special challenge' of each course."

**Peter A. Georgescu,
President,
Young & Rubicam
Advertising**
"I loved reading *Golf Resorts*—it's about practicing the sport in style! If you're lucky to get older and a bit wiser, you learn that part of the fun is the actual physical environment."

Denver Post
"The first comprehensive guide to the more than 400 resorts nationwide. Rates, facilities and courses are described in detail."

San Diego Tribune
"If your vacations center around golf, check out *Golf Resorts*."

Orville Moody
"I think I've played at most of these courses at one time or another."

Benjamin Taber, President, Phillips Screw Company	"At last—a guide to the resorts with details for the conference planner as well as those contemplating a vacation. The narrative's refreshing, with titillating tidbits of history, local lore and useful info, such as courses that still have caddies, and where Babe Ruth might have birdied a few holes."
Golf Lifestyle	"*Golf Resorts* includes everything you need to know about resort rates and special facilities . . . and the special challenges of each course."
Barry McDermott	"Don't leave home without it."
New Orleans Times-Picayune	". . . invaluable for those who can't move without their clubs."
Meat Loaf	"I'd like to play more golf, but it always rains on my day off—now this guide lists everything you need to know, but does it tell how to hit the ball?"
Golden Years Magazine	"All the information you could want for the ideal golf vacation could be found in *Golf Resorts—The Complete Guide.*"
Homero Blancas	"This is a good book."
University of Arizona Library	"The sub-title pretty much says it all. The best places, state by state, to stay and shoot a few holes, are listed in this guide. Information on the courses, fees, room rates, reservation policies, seasons and other amenities is provided."
Stephen F. Mona, Executive Director, Georgia State Golf Association	"The Guide is most impressive and well done. You should be congratulated on your fine effort in putting together this guide."
Book Passage	". . . unique golfing guides perfect for the wandering golfer."
John Stirling, Captain, British PGA	"I hope this comprehensive book inspires you to play the courses, and that you'll get as much fun out of the game as I have."
New York Times	". . . a useful guide."

More Lanier Guides:

The Complete Guide to Bed & Breakfasts, Inns & Guesthouses in the United States and Worldwide™

Lanier Publishing International, Ltd.

Elegant Small Hotels™

Family Travel & Resorts™

Golf Resorts International™

All Suite Hotel Guide™

Condo Vacations— The Complete Guide™

Elegant Hotels of the Pacific Rim™

Bed & Breakfast: Australia's Best™

Cinnamon Mornings & Raspberry Teas™

The Back Almanac™

To contact the Guide, please write:

Golf Resorts—The Complete Guide
P.O. Box D
Petaluma, CA 94953
USA

TravelGuideS.com

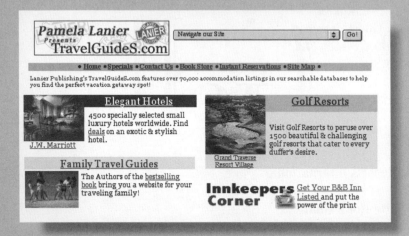

Pamela Lanier

Golf Resorts

The Complete Guide™
to 900 Resorts Nationwide
Introduction by Fuzzy Zoeller

---

*Lanier Publishing facilitates planting 9
trees for every tree used in the production
of our guides.*

A *Lanier* Guide
▲

11/01 796.352
G

Acknowledgments: I wish to acknowledge and thank the following individuals and organizations for their help with this guide: Peter Morse, Tony Morse, Carol and Don Gwaltney, Monnie Tiffany, John Fite, Golf Pro at the Claremont Country Club, Martin Calfee, Steve Cox, Barry Terjesen, David Bohn, Margaret Bollenbacher, Margaret Callahan, Marianne Barth, Mary Ellen Callahan, T and bie Vale, Lauren Elliot, Venetia Young, Seifu Haile, John Richards, Lauren Childress, John Smeck, Dona Turner, Karen Hunter, Hal Hershey, George Young, Al Heeg, Phil Wood, Michael Hendrickson, Glenna Goulet, Todd Nolan, Stephen Starbuck, Sarah Morse, Gillian Pelham, Rachel Collen and Karen Aaronson.

I especially want to thank Jack Elliot, President of the Northern California Golf Association for his assistance, the United States Golf Association, each of the states' individual golf associations and Departments of Tourism.

First edition — April 1989
Second edition — April 1990
Third edition — April 1991
Fourth edition — April 1992
Fifth edition — April 1993
Sixth edition — May 1996
Seventh edition—June 2001

Library of Congress Cataloging-in-Publication Data

Lanier, Pamela
    Golf resorts : the complete guide / by Pamela Lanier
        p.   cm.
    ISBN 1-58008-306-4
    1. Golf resorts—United States—Directories.   I. Title.
GV962.L35   1989   89-30027
796.352'06'873—oc19   CIP

Published by
Lanier Publishing International, Ltd.
P.O. Box D
Petaluma, CA 94953

Distributed by
Ten Speed Press
P.O. Box 7123
Berkeley, CA 94707

Printed in Canada

Table of Contents

Introduction

I'm amazed at the number of golf resorts that have developed recently, and I'm delighted to see a reference guide of this scope and quality.

Business travellers, especially those attending conferences, want to meet at a golf resort—one that provides service and at the same time, an enjoyable round of golf. They want to play a classic course—one that's fun and rewarding for the average player.

I like to have a good time on and off the course, and one of the things I like about Pamela's book is the number of activities—ranging from hiking in wildlife preserves to great kids' activities, shopping and quality restaurants.

Enjoy your game!

—*Fuzzy Zoeller*

2001 Resort of the Year

The Equinox
Manchester Village, VT

Nestled between the Taconic and Green Mountain ranges, The Equinox has been serving travelers and neighbors since 1769. The Equinox, a national landmark is listed in the National Register of Historic Places. This complete resort has everything for a spectacular vacation, with a myriad of one-of-a-kind activities sure to satisfy almost anyone.

The Gleneagles Golf Course at The Equinox, named after its famous sister resort in Scotland, is a repeat recipient of *Golf Magazine*'s prestigious Silver Medal Award. The course's rustic Scottish flavor also follows an environmentally friendly approach combining a dramatic blend of the past and present in a picturesque mountain setting.

Other unique activities abound at the Equinox. The first school-of-its-kind in the United States, The British School of Falconry offers the rare opportunity to learn how to handle and fly a hawk. Open year-round, the Land Rover Driving School at The Equinox teaches off-road driving techniques for all seasons and driving conditions. The Equinox Fitness Spa offers a full complement of activities and services. The facility also offers tone & stretch, aqua aerobics and fitness treks. Play tennis and croquet on the regulation courts or give volleyball a try.

This elegant resort offers a choice of culinary options and special dining events. Dine in the casual Marsh Tavern, outdoors at the Dormy Grill or in the beautifully restored Colonnade. See more on page 258.

A Good Golf Course (What Is It?)

How does one define what a "good" golf course really is? It means different things to different people. One definition might be that a "good", or successful, golf course is one that creates a desire in the golfer to return and play it again and again. He might not be able to explain why the attraction exists—it just feels good!

A good golf course is one that the real estate developer, municipality, daily fee operator, resort, or private club can afford to maintain. A golf course might be very dramatic, picturesque, and striking in its visual effect, but if it is too difficult to play, the average golfer, after playing it once or twice, will decide that he is not enjoying it and will never go back again. Income from green fees will diminish and the quality of maintenance will suffer. Poor maintenance will cause a further reduction in rounds of golf played. Also, because of excessively steep mounding and other design features, maintenance costs may be higher than usual. Can this be called a "good" golf course since it is not producing the results expected of it? Anticipated costs of maintenance *must* be considered during the design phase of the facility.

The design relationship between the parking area, the pro shop, the practice tee and green, the first and 10th tees, and the 9th and 18th greens is very important. This involves walking from the automobile to the pro shop, reaching the practice areas, starting and completing the 18 holes, and returning to the automobile. First and last impressions of the facility are developed during this process.

The design of a good 18-hole golf course first involves the development of a routing plan which takes advantage of existing topography. The goal is to have an interesting rotation of par for the course in which each hole would be followed by one of a different par, such as 4-5-4-3-4-5-4-3-4 for each nine holes. This example is not often possible because of topography and property boundary restrictions (I think it has happened to me twice in the last thirty years!), but an attempt must be made to achieve as much as possible in this regard.

Taking advantage of existing topography means using all the interesting features existing on the land in our design. Where nature has not provided interesting contours or other features, we must attempt to match nature's theme and make it appear that only clearing, floating, and planting was required to develop the golf course.

A good golf course is interesting and challenging, but not impossible or unfair, for all types of golfers, including low, middle, and high handicapper and, very importantly, the ladies. This is done mostly by having multiple tee locations, and positioning hazards so that the longer hitter is faced with the need for accuracy, while the others are provided with much more space at their drive landing area. In short, the farther one hits the ball, the more accurate he must be.

The practice fairway should face toward the north, with a southerly direction being the second choice. The first several holes on the first nine should not require hitting toward the rising sun, and the final holes on the back nine should not aim toward the west.

Each individual hole should be a complete picture within itself, with each area of the hole being a unified part of the total effect. Tee design, contouring throughout the entire length of the hole; mowing patterns at tee, fairway, and green; tree types and location; water courses and lakes; and perhaps the most important part of the whole picture, the individual design of each green, together with locations of those seemingly necessary—but oh so troublesome—cart paths; all are part of the picture to be developed.

If possible, each hole should be aimed in a somewhat different direction than the previous hole, to prevent monotony of the view from the several holes as play progresses. If it is necessary at times to have a succession of parallel holes, they should individually be of different lengths and character.

This is only a short summary of some of the items involved in designing and developing a "good" golf course. The profession of Golf Course Architecture, created out of necessity as a result of the development of the game in Scotland, requires a lifetime of study and practice. It overlaps, and require knowledge of other fields, such as agronomy, hydrology, land surveying, civil engineering, landscape architecture, arboriculture, site planning, golf course maintenance, heavy equipment operation, and others.

The education process never ends.

—Arthur Jack Snyder
  Former President
  Golf Course Architects Association

Guide Notes

In this guide we will acquaint you with the ever-expanding world of golf resorts—those special havens striving to give the traveler a memorable eighteen holes and then some. Many of these resorts are newcomers, and others are from another generation and well-established, but all have one thing in common—great golf and plenty of it!

Our descriptions are brief—just enough to tempt you and provide an overview. If you're interested in learning more, write or call the resort for brochures, and be sure to inquire about golf and promotional packages; these often include lessons and clinics for all levels and usually represent substantial savings. Also check the airlines for special promotional fares for golfers.

Our price categories reflect rates most recently quoted for the lowest priced double room. But remember, it's merely a guideline to help you establish a price range, as hotel rates are affected by seasonal demands, type of accommodation, and group rates. When inquiring, be sure to ask for details on special promotions. To deal with fluctuating prices, we've adopted symbols that we think will help you determine the approximate cost of accommodations listed in our guide. Categories are as follows:

$0–$100	are distinguished by one $
$101–$175	are distinguished by two $$
$175 and up	are distinguished by three $$$

We have noted many facilities provided by the hotels. Other services and amenities are often available. We've also given details on business facilities and conference room capacity, because we know that golf resorts are the premier venues for business conferences today.

We have indicated when a hotel will not accept pets, or when pets are accepted under special conditions. An additional deposit is often required. In establishments that do not admit pets, the concierge can make arrangements with the local kennel. Children are usually welcome at resorts, and many offer special programs and services geared to their interests. Often children may stay free in the room with parents, but this should be checked out when you make the reservation.

Most hotels have at least some rooms designed to accommodate the handicapped. We have noted the number so equipped. Hotels with only a few handicapped-accessible rooms should be booked well in advance.

America's resorts are dedicated to providing guests with the finest and most comprehensive sports facilities imaginable, and we give you information on everything from jogging trails to tennis courts, marlin fishing to wind surfing.

Nobody can golf all the time, so we have included information on a host of other diversions in the proximity of each resort, whether you fancy historic gardens and houses, amusement parks for the kids, or championship shopping; it's all there for you.

Consider the variables in determining the cost of a round of golf. Is it peak season morning, or is it off-season after 3 p.m.? On some packages, guests have unlimited golf privileges. Our green fees symbols are based on weekday play in "high" season, for a resort guest. Since rates, seasons, and promotional packages are all subject to change, be sure to verify the cost of a round of golf, as well as for carts, when you book. Categories are as follows:

Under $45— ⊺
$46 to $75— ⊺⊺
$76 and up— ⊺⊺⊺

Golf resorts are extremely popular, especially during high seasons, and tee times are often booked far in advance. We suggest you book your starting times with the pro shop when you make your room reservation. We've given local telephone numbers. The large majority of resorts have an 800 number, but it's not always accessible from every area.

Many resort courses are virtually empty in the afternoon. Green fees are often reduced, and for those who like a leisurely game, late afternoons are for you! Also, higher handicappers are urged to consider an afternoon tee time—then you can take your time.

Consider the pro shop personnel your best friends. They'll help you rent clubs, replenish your supply of tees, tell you whether the greens are fast, and be happy to sell you a shirt with a good-looking logo.

Resorts have varying policies regarding golf club storage. Often there's no charge, but be sure to inquire about this.

Every attempt has been made to provide current and complete information. Some information has been provided by the hotels' management, and management policies may change. If you feel anything in this book is even slightly inaccurate, please let us know on the reader response form in the back. This book is as complete as we can make it, but even as we go to press, information on new resorts is pouring in. If you know of a golf resort we've missed, please let us know! Happy golfing!

—Pamela Lanier
San Francisco
June, 2001

Golf Resorts

Listings by State/City

Marriott's Grand Hotel

Address: One Grand Blvd, Point Clear, 36564
Phone: 334-928-9201
800-228-9290
Web site: http://www.marriotthotels.com/PTLAL/
No. of Rooms: 308
Rates: Inquire
Restrictions: No pets allowed
Restaurant: Grand Dining Room, BayView, Lakewood Club Room
Bar: Birdcage Lounge
Business Fac.: Administrative assistance, Audio-visual, Conference rooms, capacity 900
Sports Fac.: Swimming pool, Tennis court, Croquet, Horseback riding, Sailing
Location: Gulf Coast

Courses: Dogwood (6331), Azalea
No. of Holes: 36
Guest Policy: Open to Marriott guests and club members
Club House: 334-990-6312
Reservations: May be made one week in advance
Season: Open all year

This rambling structure of weathered cypress, known as "The Queen of Southern Resorts," covers about 550 acres of aged magnolias, and moss-draped live oaks on Mobile Bay, a short drive southeast of Mobile. The first hotel appeared in 1847, and history logs reveal it has witnessed Confederate soldiers needing hospitalization, fires, replaced structures, hurricanes, and a US Marine Training School. Hospitality and a sense of tradition are maintained in the recently renovated resort, which Marriott bought in 1981, right down to daily tea, fresh mint juleps and dressing for dinner. Three separate buildings and 16 cottages house more than 300 guest rooms, which offer views of the marina, lagoon, or the bay.

The chef will prepare your catch for a sumptuous repast in the Magnolia Room. Others will want to try the Bon Secour oysters, bay shrimp and seafood gumbo, all fresh daily. The Grand's orchestra plays for dancing each evening in the Grand Dining Room, and guests will find The Bird Cage Lounge a lively spot.

You can board the resort's 53-foot Hatteras yacht for a local cruise, drop a line or crabtrap off the wharf, sail, water ski, jog, bike, stroll or ride horseback. The extensive facilities also include card rooms, a swimming beach, lawn bowling, croquet, ten tennis courts, and a 750,000 gallon swimming pool constructed from an old ship's hull.

The 40-slip marina can accommodate your dinghy, or you can rent their paddleboats, powerboats, windsurfers or skiffs. If its water-sports oriented, its here. The Grand also offers a supervised children's program during summer. If you like antiques, the area's full of irresistible shops laden with historic treasures.

Golf here is unhurried on two fine 18 hole layouts at Lakewood Golf Club which zigzag through white pines and sleepy lagoons. (Watch out for alligators!) Built in 1945, the original 27 holes played host to notables such as Julius Boros, Sam Snead and Byron Nelson, and is now home of the Women's Western Amateur Championship. What was once mosquito-ridden swampland, and later a Confederate cemetery is today 36 holes of championship pleasure with majestic tree-lined fairways. And to think you can have one of Bucky's famous mint juleps (he picks the mint from his private patch) after you've double-bogeyed Dogwood!

Weeping Trout Sports Resort

Weeping Trout Sports Resort is a vacation spot so special, even locals keep it secret. Its beauty awes guests because the location is extraordinary, service is attentive and facility is truly unique.

The main building of the resort was erected as a family cabin in 1964. The decor is fresh and natural and showcases native Tlingit and local art. The main building houses the kitchen, dining room, bar, toilet and shower facilities for all guests. It is a short walk from sleeping cabins to the main building. They offer two sleeping cabins: one with three separate sleeping rooms, shared seating area, wood heat, solar-powered electric lights, cold-water plumbing and shared toilet. The second cabin has a sleeping loft with ample space for families. There is no television, fax or email but have radio telephone communication.

Weeping Trout Sports Resort celebrates the great outdoors. Your dining enjoyment is doubled, with both fabulous food and fabulous scenery at your table. An upright grand piano brought to Alaska during the gold rush of '98 sits in the dining room for guests to play.

The Weeping Trout executive golf course is a 9 hole, par 28 course is fun and challenging as it winds through the old growth Sitka Spruce and Hemlock forest. Greens are sand-filled artificial turf. A party of four fair golfers can play nine holes in about 90 minutes, which leaves time for fishing! The resort inventories professional equipment but if you prefer your own, you'll need only a putter, a 5 iron, and a 9 iron.

Address: PO Box 129, Haines, 99827
Phone: 907-766-2827
877-94-TROUT
Fax: 907-766-2824
E-mail: trout@weepingtrout.com
Web site: http://www.weepingtrout.com
No. of Rooms: 4
Restaurant: Dining Room—with delicious gourmet meals
Bar: Bar with wine, beers and distilled spirits
Sports Fac.: fishing in Chilkat Lake for Sockeye, Coho Salmon, and Trout
Location: Remotely located near Haines in northern southeast Alaska, adjacent to the Chilkat Bald Eagle Preserve

Course: Weeping Trout (1000, par 28)
No. of Holes: 9
Guest Policy: Open to public
Club House: 907-766-2827
Reservations: Call to make a reservation
Carts: You only need a 5 and 9 iron and putter

Boulders Resort

Address: 34631 N. Tom Darlington, Carefree, 85377
Phone: 602-488-9009
800-553-1717
Fax: 602-488-4118
Web site: http://www.wyndham.com/Boulders/default.cfm
No. of Rooms: 160
Rates: $$$
Restrictions: Children under 16 free in same room with parents
Restaurant: The Palo Verde, The Latilla, The Boulders Club, Cantina del Pedregal, The Bakery Cafe, Pool Pavilion
Bar: Discovery Lounge, The Pool Pavilion
Business Fac.: 12,000 sq. ft Tohono Center, Audio-visual, Full-service kitchen, Boardroom
Sports Fac.: Golf school, 6 tennis courts, Spa and fitness center, Walking and jogging trails, Nature walks—guided,
Location: 16 miles northeast of Scottsdale in the Sonoran Desert foothills

Courses: South Course (6589), North Course (6731)
No. of Holes: 36
Guest Policy: Members and hotel guests only
Club House: 602-488-9028
Fees: ꭲꭲ
Reservations: With hotel reservations or any time available
Season: September 14–June 15

You have to like a place called Carefree, where asterisks on your scorecard denote saguaros, huge boulders harbor cottontails, and your cocktail comes with blue corn tortillas. The adobe buildings of the Main lodge and 120 casitas blend harmoniously with the Sonoran desert north of Scottsdale, it could be a mirage. From austere desert topography, lies an opulent oasis, where nature has been left untouched. The Boulders is truly an experience; contemporary in feeling, yet a place to unwind amid Indian handicrafts, and regional art. Even the main door is made of natural woods.

Dining here is definitely au courant, whether its in the formal, subtly colored Latilla Room, or the more casual Palo Verde Room. The menus reflect a style of cuisine focusing on innovative dishes using natural ingredients, plenty of fresh fish and regional specialties. The wine list here is impressive—not only will you recognize the traditional renowned vintages, but some of Napa Valley's finest premium wines are to be found here, such as the intense Duckhorn Merlot.

You can be as active or as lazy as your spirit moves you. The free-form turquoise pool evokes the feeling of a natural desert water-hole, or maybe you'd prefer cruising over the clear desert air in a balloon, airplane or on horseback. Six all-weather tennis courts, and a fitness center round out sporting facilities.

If you'd like to visit another desert habitat, venture out to nearby Taliesin West, Frank Lloyd Wright's studio and home, or head for Paolo Soleri's prototype in urban architecture, Arcosanti. Feeling energetic? You could play golf in the morning, helicopter through the Grand Canyon in the afternoon, and sip a margarita in front of a fiery sunset at the Boulders. Three tough golf courses await you, with tees, fairways and greens framed by and often virtually a part of the dramatic, time-carved scenery. The courses roll gently with undulating greens, grass bunkers and beautiful desert specimens which often make it difficult to concentrate on one's game. Boulders #9 is a post-card scenic par 5, 583 yard gem which requires over a 200 yard carry to the fairway from the back tees. Your second shot has to favor the left, and the approach shot, if played from the left will keep you out of the lake. This is assuming you didn't slice into the 300 year old saguaro near the tee and lose your ball.

Wigwam Resort

Built in 1919 as an organization house for executives visiting the Goodyear Tire & Rubber Company's cotton plantations, The Wigwam has become a favorite winter vacation resort. Its low-rise casitas are architecturally faithful to the original building which still stands as part of the lobby. Stately palms, ornamental orange trees, and annually replanted flower gardens complete the Southwestern atmosphere of the beautiful 75-acre oasis.

Groups can arrange to have a desert steak broil at Sunset Point, where you'll witness the spectacular beauty of an Arizona sunset. A horse-drawn hay wagon, complete with banjo players and cold drinks, will transport you to Sunset Point. There, you'll find The Wigwam chefs at work over an old-fashioned barbecue grilling steaks to perfection, a buffet laden with hearty Western-style dishes and a full bar.

In addition to golf, other sports activities are naturally suited to the desert surroundings, including tennis, trap and skeet shooting, bicycling, shuffleboard, lawn sports and, of course, swimming.

You'll enjoy shopping or simply visiting the 14,000-acre ranch surrounding the resort and village with crops of cotton, alfalfa, grains, citrus, vegetables, melons and other fruits.

There are three championship courses here. The most challenging is Robert Trent Jones' Gold Course, matured to perfection and offering a wide variety of play with the many tee and pin placements that are possible. For instance, the 10th tee can be stretched out to play 605 yards (from the normal tees it is a mere 555 yards). Even the exceptional golfer will find that this long course requires a high degree of skill and accuracy. This is a par 72, with 7,074 yards of wicked traps, undulating greens and long lakes.

Jones also was responsible for the Blue Course thirty-three years later, a par 70 with many water holes, tree-lined fairways and the famous Trent Jones tricky greens. The Red Course, by Robert "Red" Lawrence, designed around a meandering stream and five lakes, is a par 72, extremely fine test of golfing skill.

Address: 300 Wigwam Blvd, Litchfield Park, 85340
Phone: 623-935-3811
800-327-0396
Fax: 623-535-1309
E-mail: wigwam@primenet.com
Web site: http://www. wigwamresort.com
No. of Rooms: 331
Rates: $$
Restrictions: Pets limited to small with deposit
Restaurant: Terrace Dining Room, The Arizona Kitchen, Grill on the Greens, Pool Cabana Grill
Bar: Arizona Bar, Kachina Bar, Pool Cabana
Business Fac.: 25 meeting rooms, 6 Executive boardrooms, Built-in screen projection, In-house Audio Visual Dept., Satellite check-in, Private registration, In-house Props & Decor Dept., Outdoor function areas
Sports Fac.: 3 18-hole golf courses, 2 swimming pools, Waterslide, Health club, Spa services, Bike trails, 9 tennis courts, Shuffle board, Basketball, Ping-pong, Croquet, Sand & water volleyball, Camp Pow Wow, Stables
Location: Twenty minutes west of downtown Phoenix in Village of Litchfield Park

Courses: Gold Course (7200), Blue Course (6112), Red Course (6861)
No. of Holes: 54
Guest Policy: Resort guests have priority
Club House: 623-272-4653
Fees: ↑
Reservations: Call for reservations
Season: Open all year
Carts: Walking allowed on Blue Course

Arizona Golf Resort & Conference Center

Address: 425 S. Power Rd, Mesa, 85206
Phone: 480-832-3202
800-528-8282
Fax: 480-981-0151
E-mail: info@azgolfresort.com
Web site: http://www.azgolfresort.com
No. of Rooms: 186
Rates: $
Restaurant: Annabelle's-breakfast, lunch and dinner, Anna's-lunch and dinner, Sunrise Cafe-breakfast and lunch
Business Fac.: 8,000 sq. ft with capacity to 400, Complete catering and conference staff
Sports Fac.: Swimming pool, 4 spas, Tennis courts, Fitness center, Bicycling, Jogging
Location: 150 lush acres 30 minutes from Phoenix Airport

Course: Championship course (6574, par 73)
No. of Holes: 18
Guest Policy: Has Golf school too, Open to public
Club House: 480-832-0003
Fees: ⌐
Reservations: Call for reservations
Season: Open all year

One of Arizona's best golf resorts, 30 minutes from Phoenix Airport. The resort features distinctively styled guest accommodations, ranging from deluxe rooms to fully appointed suites, with panoramic views of the golf course. A complete range of activities—golf, tennis, spas, swimming, bicycling and volleyball. In the line of hotel dining, we offer Anabelle's Restaurant and Lounge with the finest dining and entertainment.

Embassy Suites Paradise Valley

The Embassy Suites Paradise Valley offers a casual contemporary atmosphere. Each of the 270 one-bedroom suites features a separate living and sleeping area, galley kitchen with microwave, wet bar, refrigerator and coffee maker. Also included are two TVs with remote controls, two phones with data port, a dressing area, and in-room safes. All suites have spectacular views of the golf course or surrounding community. A full cooked-to-order breakfast is included each morning and room service is available from 11:00 a.m. to 11:00 p.m.

The new Embassy Suites Paradise Valley is ideally situated on Stonecreek Golf Club, and a taste of the old country awaits you. A traditional Scottish links style golf course, it plays up to 6,800 yards and features a slope of 134. Five sets of tees can accommodate golfers of all skill levels, but the formidable opponent lies within the creek itself that comes into play on fifteen holes. With rolling fairways and elevated greens, a round of golf at Stonecreek is a trip to Scotland with the Arizona sun, and the weather in general is a definite double eagle.

The Suites are also close to The Raven, Wildfire, Legend Trails, Kierland, TPC, Scottsdale Country Club, Orangetree and Ancala just to name a few.

Address: 4415 E Paradise Village Pkwy S, Paradise Valley, 85032
Phone: 602-765-5800
800-EMBASSY
Fax: 602-765-5890
E-mail: info@embassysuitesaz.com
Web site: http://www.embassysuitesaz.com/suites.html
No. of Rooms: 270
Rates: Inquire
Restaurant: Tatum's
Bar: Complimentary evening beverages—wine, beer, cocktails, soft drinks and light snacks 5:30-7:30 p.m.
Business Fac.: 11 meeting rooms, 3 executive boardrooms, capacity 10-400, Complete catering and conference staff, Banquets, Receptions, Trade shows, Classrooms
Sports Fac.: Swimming pool, 10 golf courses within a few miles, Fitness center
Location: 6 miles from Scottsdale, 10 miles from downtown Phoenix
Course: Stonecreek Golf Club (6839)
No. of Holes: 18
Guest Policy: Open to public
Club House: 602-953-9110
Fees: ↑↑
Reservations: 7 days in advance, 60 days in advance with $7 charge
Season: Open all year
Carts: Price includes cart

Arizona Biltmore

Address: 24th St & Missouri, Phoenix, 85016
Phone: 602-955-6600
800-950-0086
Fax: 602-381-7600
E-mail: azbres@ arizonabiltmore.com
Web site: http:// www.arizonabiltmore.com
No. of Rooms: 730
Rates: $$$
Restrictions: No pets allowed
Restaurant: Wright's, The Cafe, The Biltmore Grill, Cabana Club, Afternoon Tea, Squaw Peak Lounge
Bar: Squaw Peak Lounge
Business Fac.: On-site facilities, Secretarial services, Computer rental, Cellular phones, Pagers, Advanced sound systems, Screen projectors, Pin spotlighting capabilities
Sports Fac.: Bicycling, Putting course, Golf, Jogging paths, Lawn games, Swimming pools, Tennis, Water sports, Kids Kabana
Location: Center of Phoenix

Courses: The Adobe (6400), The Links
No. of Holes: 36
Guest Policy: Call for tee times
Club House: 800-950-0086
Reservations: Reservations may be made 7 days in advance
Season: Open all year

Inspired by the patterns, geometric shapes and textures of Frank Lloyd Wright, this "Jewel of the Desert," on 39 lushly landscaped acres offers today's guests a tradition of service and grandeur from a classic era. The resort has never looked better—thanks to a recent improvement and expansion program. The original system of hand-cast, patterned concrete blocks has been retained in the additions, stained glass windows dazzle, new roofs are gleaming Arizona copper, the famous Dixon/Hamlin murals are enhanced by contemporary new lighting, all harmonizing with the Wright conception of a dream resort destination. Many rooms have private patios or balconies with views of gardens, Squaw Peak, Camelback Mountain or the pool area.

Experience one of the most highly awarded restaurants at Orangerie. Striking architectural ambiance provides the perfect setting for breakfast, lunch and dinner. The seasonal menu is accompanied by an extensive wine list. Cafe Sonora offers southwestern specialties and American favorites in a casual atmosphere. Cocktails and lively entertainment can be enjoyed in the Lobby Lounge. For conferences, the hotel's professional conference facilities can accommodate 1,250 people.

Resort activities include bicycling, an exercise salon, five heated pools, eight tennis courts, badminton, croquet, horseshoes, a putting green, and lawn chess. A complimentary shuttle will whisk you to Biltmore Fashion Park, truly a shopper's paradise, while the Concierge can direct you to just about any diversion in the area, ranging from Grand Canyon Tours to the A's and Giant's Spring Training.

Golfers will want to play one or both of the PGA-rated championship courses. Try flat Adobe, built in 1930, where Clark Gable lost his wedding ring, with 6900 yards of tree-lined fairways, streams and lakes. Or play the long, narrow Links, with its unusual rolling terrain, five lakes and scenic views of the resort. #15, a par 3, is straight downhill with a clear shot of Phoenix.

The Kids Kabana follows a 64-year tradition of children's activities by offering arts and crafts, bike rides, games, movies, sports, storytime, and snacks. The Biltmore Nanny Pool offers babysitting services. The fees are $25 for half day, $50 for full day and lunches for and additional $5.

Pointe Hilton Tapatio Cliffs Resort

An extraordinary escape from the ordinary. Whether you are spending a day or the week, the Pointe Hilton Tapatio Cliffs Resort has something for everyone. The award-winning Lookout Mountain Golf Club, Tocaloma Spa & Salon, horseback riding and The Falls water oasis allow for a restful or invigorating retreat. Adults and children alike will find plenty to do with a 138-ft. waterslide and Vacation Station™ with a wide assortment of games and activities for family fun at its fullest.

Elegantly appointed, the fabrics and furnishings of the rooms combine bold hues and patterns that embrace the spirit of the surrounding Sonoran landscape.

Five restaurants will meet every expectation. Different Pointe of View has innovative cuisine and Pointe In Tyme is a contemporary grille and tavern. There also is the Cascades Café and La Cantina.

Pamper yourself with a soothing session at the Tocaloma Spa & Salon. Enjoy massage therapy, body treatments, manicures and whirlpool pedicures. Complete hair services are available. Steeped into the mountainside is the state-of-the-art fitness centre.

The Lookout Mountain Golf Club at Tapatio Cliffs is a magnificent par-72 course, home of the Skills Challenge, won quick PGA approval as the site of the Arizona Classic and was christened the "Champagne Stop" by visiting pros on the Senior Tour. It features lush greens entwined by carefully preserved Sonoran Desert.

Address: 11111 N. 7th St, Phoenix, 85020
Phone: 602-866-7500
800-876-4683
Fax: 602-993-0276
Web site: http://www.pointehilton.com
No. of Rooms: 585
Rates: Inquire
Restaurant: Different Pointe of View, Pointe In Tyme Grille & Tavern, La Cantina, Cascade Cafe
Business Fac.: Boardroom suites, 65,000 sq. ft. of meeting and outdoor garden function space, capacity 20-1500
Sports Fac.: The Falls—swimming pools, waterfalls, water slide, private cabanas, kids activities, Tocaloma Spa & Salon, Fitness Centre, Nature hikes, Riding Stables, Jeep tours, Golf School
Location: Nestled into the the rugged terrain of the Phoenix North Mountains just outside of Phoenix.

Course: Lookout Mountain (6653, par 72)
No. of Holes: 18
Guest Policy: Open to public
Club House: 602-866-6356
Fees: Inquire
Reservations: Reservations available 7-30 days in advance
Season: Open all year
Carts: Cart included in fees

The Pointe Hilton Resort at Squaw Peak

Address: 7677 North 16th Street, Phoenix, 85020
Phone: 602-997-2626
800-876-4683
Fax: 602-993-0276
Web site: http://www.pointehilton.com
No. of Rooms: 563
Rates: Inquire
Restaurant: Hole-in-the-Wall Eatin' and Drinkin' Place, Lantana Grille, Aunt Chilada's
Business Fac.: Flexible meeting space, 2 complete business centers, Meeting planners, Events staff, State-of-the-art audio/visual equipment
Sports Fac.: Lagoon pool, Sport pool, Tennis, Water volleyball, 18 hole putting greens, Aerobics, Aqua aerobics, Massage therapist, Cardio equipment, Weight machines, Bobby Eldridge Golf School
Location: In the Valley of the Sun, nestled into the slopes of the Phoenix North Mountains

Course: Lookout Mountain (6617, par 72)
No. of Holes: 18
Guest Policy: Open to public
Club House: 602-866-6356
Fees: Inquire
Reservations: Call for reservations
Season: Open all year
Carts: Cart included in fees

Pointe Hilton, Squaw Valley Resort, is home to the River Ranch—a water wonderland of family fun activities, acres of cool pools, a lazy river for tubing, a winding waterslide, tennis, fitness and spa delights. The ultimate in luxurious accommodations awaits guests in the spacious 430 two-room suites and 133 luxury Casitas, and unique settings create a memorable dining experience at Lantana Grill, Hole-in-the-Wall, and Aunt Chilada's Hideaway.

At the heart of the resort is the Hole-in-the-Wall River Ranch. Nine acres of shimmering pools and cascading waterfalls are just the beginning of an unforgettable resort experience. Set beside the world-class tennis courts, the spacious sports pool is the place for water volleyball games. Remarkable exercise facilities offer aerobics and aqua-aerobic classes, a complete range of cardiovascular equipment and weight machines, as well as a variety of massage therapists and diagnostic services.

The Pointe Hilton Resorts have become renowned as golf resorts. They have three championship courses to choose from and all three are available to guests no matter which resort they stay at during their visit. The resort offers a variety of golf packages that enable guests to play more than 30 other courses in the Valley of the Sun. They are also home to the Bobby Eldridge Golf School, located at the Pointe Hilton Tapatio Cliffs Resort.

Hyatt Regency Scottsdale at Gainey Ranch

Set against the majestic McDowell mountains, the 493-room Hyatt Regency Scottsdale combines the beauty of the Sonoran desert with all the amenities of a luxury resort. Here, swaying palm trees overlook cook refreshing pools, emerald green golf courses and ruby sunsets … the feeling is relaxed, and the service, unparalleled.

Cast in soothing desert tones, the accommodations are elegant, yet comfortable, having all the luxurious comforts for which Hyatt is famous. Balconies and decks have views of mountains, fairways and that unforgettable pool of pools with its swim-up bar, a water slide and a subterranean grotto whirlpool. You'll find seven casitas, a Regency Club, VIP suites and one Presidential Suite. Two restaurants and a lobby bar provide refreshing outlets for meeting and relaxing. Conference planners will find a full range of meeting rooms and facilities for just about any type of gathering.

A full health spa, 8 Laykold tennis courts, lawn tennis, croquet, and bicycle, jogging and walking paths will help keep you in shape. If you're bringing the kids, you can enroll them in Kamp Kachina, the children's program for ages 3–12.

Excellent shopping adjacent to the resort awaits the non-golfer as well as numerous other area adventures.

There are three separate individually designed nine hole courses that make up a 27 hole championship course. Benz and Poellot designed this 6,800-yard masterpiece of rolling desert terrain. Dunes, first of the three, is characterized by sand dunes amidst rolling greens. Golfers will find five lakes cropping up on the next nine, oddly enough called Lakes. The most difficult of the three is Arroyo, with a winding dry river bed and two lakes. Beware—its three finishing holes were designed to be particularly challenging, for that's where the game is frequently decided.

Address: 7500 E. Doubletree Ranch Rd, Scottsdale, 85258
Phone: 480-991-3388
Fax: 480-483-5550
Web site: http://www.hyatt.com/pages/s/scotta.html
No. of Rooms: 493
Rates: Inquire
Restaurant: Golden Swan, Ristorante Sandolo, Squash Blossom
Bar: Two poolside bars
Business Fac.: Native American Learning Center, 23 meeting rooms, Master controls, Heat/AC, Sound–280V 1-3 phase electricity, Special lighting effects, Music, Telephones, Microphone outlets, In-house vendors
Sports Fac.: Ten swimming pools, Water slide, Sand beach, Whirlpool spa, Cold plunges, Jogging & bike paths, Golf, 8 tennis courts, Complimentary bikes
Location: North Scottsdale

Courses: Arroyo (3424, par 36), Dunes (3376, par 36), Lakes (3376, par 36)
No. of Holes: 27
Guest Policy: Private, hotel guests only
Club House: 480-951-0022
Fees: ↑↑↑
Reservations: Call for reservations
Season: Open all year

Marriott's Camelback Inn Resort

Address: 5402 E. Lincoln Dr,
Scottsdale, 85253
Phone: 480-948-1700
800-24-CAMEL
Fax: 480-951-8469
Web site: http://www.
marriothotels.com/PHXCB
No. of Rooms: 453
Rates: $$
Restaurant: The Chaparral, The
Navajo, Golf Grille, Sprouts, Hoppin'
Jack's, Kokopelli Cafe
Bar: Oasis Lounge
Business Fac.: 40,000 sq ft of
meeting space, with several confer-
ence facilities with state-of-the-art
audio/visual equipment.
Sports Fac.: Sand volleyball,
Basketball, Pitch n' putt golf, 3
heated swimming pools, Horseback
riding, Jeep tours, White water
rafting, Hot air balloon rides, 6
tennis courts, Hopalong College for
kids, fitness center and spa, table
tennis, shuffleboard
Location: Paradise Valley—20
minutes from airport

Courses: Padre Course (6559),
Indian Bend Course (7014)
No. of Holes: 36
Club House: 800-244-9995
Reservations: Call for reservations
Season: Open all year

Camelback Inn, situated on 125 scenic desert
acres in prestigious Paradise Valley, has become a
respected landmark as generations have enjoyed
the rustic Southwestern charm created by Jack
Stewart in 1936. In the shadow of majestic Camel-
back mountain, the Inn radiates from a main
lodge, where for fifty years, lettering on the tower
has declared the resort to be a place "Where Time
Stands Still."

Dining is as memorable as the unsurpassed
beauty of the desert backdrop. The elegant Chap-
arral Dining Room, a Mobile Four-Star Award win-
ner and Fine Dining Award recipient from the
International Gourmet Society, offers its cele-
brated rack of lamb, topped off with a decadent
chocolate truffle cake. Less formal meals are
served in the authentic southwestern decor of the
Navajo Room, The North Garden Buffet terrace,
or Sprouts Restaurant in The Spa at Camelback
Inn.

Tennis enthusiasts will thrill to discover ten
all weather courts, five of which are illuminated
for night play. Three huge outdoor heated pools
with adjacent whirlpool baths beckon guests, and
surrounding the property are well maintained
paths—ideal for jogging, walking or bicycling.
Indulge yourself with pampering body- and skin-
care treatments at the hacienda inspired, Euro-
pean Spa at Camelback Inn, the only resort spa of
its kind in the southwest. At The Spa, you can
rejuvenate in the fitness center and revitalize in
daily exercise classes. You'll also have the option
of playing volleyball, table tennis or shuffleboard.
A pitch-and-putt course, as well as a nine-hole
putting green are but a short distance from your
"casita."

Camelback Golf Club, offering 36 holes of
USGA championship golf, awaits you. The long
and open Indian Bend Course was designed by
Jack Snyder, and lies within a verdant natural
wash basin. Its links-type layout provides the
golfer with stretches of gently-rolling terrain and
incredible mountain vistas. Camelback's original
18-hole Padre course is short but tight—but don't
be lulled into thinking it's a snap—there's plenty
of challenge here. Sweeping eucalyptus and
stately palms line the well-manicured fairways,
and for most of the year, you'll be invigorated by
the desert air.

Orange Tree Golf & Conference Resort

Here's a good-looking, unique resort in the heart of Scottsdale. What sets it apart is that it's all suites with the feeling of a private club. The course was here first, followed by a resort built around golf. It's a 30-foot putt from one end of your suite to the other, and of course every amenity possible is here. Living and sleeping areas are well defined; computer modems await your command; you can relax in the spa or turn on the VCR. French doors open onto your own patio, the perfect place to sip a tall cool one and watch golfers hit straight down the fairway.

Joe's Restaurant, with views of the course, offers breakfast, lunch and dinner, as well as fine spirits. Nearby is a sports lounge featuring memorabilia of golf's greats, a big screen TV, and live music.

A heated pool for a few laps, or a few moments in the therapy spa might be perfect before tennis (off property), racquetball or a workout in the weight room. Should you need to conference, you'll find 8 rooms, able to accommodate up to 500, and secretarial services available. Unless you absolutely need a car, have the resort's van meet you at the airport, so you can spend your days enjoying the warm desert air, on and off the course.

The course here dates back to 1957 with some very large trees, mostly eucalyptus, pines, bottle trees, and some palms. Water comes into play on eight holes, with #18 being our favorite. It's a par 4, 388-yard stretch with a lake guarding the green. You won't be in the drink on your tee shot if you hit it over 250 yards, but everyone has to face it to get up on the green. Most big hitters want to lay up short with 3 wood or a 2 iron to avoid that kerplunk sound. Slope rating for the Men's Regular tees is 111.

Address: 10601 N. 56th St, Scottsdale, 85254
Phone: 480-948-3730
E-mail: info@orangetree.com
Web site: http://www.orangetreegolfresort.com
No. of Rooms: 160
Rates: $
Business Fac.: Business services
Sports Fac.: Tennis, Golf
Location: 1 mile north of Shea Blvd. on 56th street

Course: Orange Tree (6762, par 72)
No. of Holes: 18
Guest Policy: Open to public
Club House: 480-948-6100
Fees: ↑
Reservations: Call for reservations
Season: Open all year
Carts: Price includes cart

Phoenician

Address: 6000 E. Camelback Rd,
Scottsdale, 85251
800-888-8234
Fax: 480-947-4311
Web site: http://www.
thephoenician.com
No. of Rooms: 654
Rates: $$$
Restaurant: Terrace Dining Room,
Windows on the Green, Mary
Elaine's, Oasis, Lobby Tea Court
Bar: The Praying Monk, The Thirsty
Camel Lounge
Business Fac.: Convention Banquet
& Catering Services, Full service
Business Center, Destination
services, Corporate gifts, Floral
design, Audio/visual production
dept., Photography service, Full
service special event & theme party
production
Sports Fac.: Tennis Garden, 9
heated pools, Water slide, Center of
Well-Being Spa, Funicians Kids
Club, Archery, Basketball, Bicycling,
Croquet, Health & fitness classes,
Hiking, Jogging, Lawn bowling,
Water sports, Horseback riding
Location: Base of Camelback
Mountain in Scottsdale's Valley

Course: Canyon (3008), Oasis/
Desert (6310, par 71)
No. of Holes: 27
Guest Policy: Open to public
Club House: 602-423-2449
Fees: ↑↑↑
Reservations: Reservations
available 30 days in advance
Season: Open all year

By any measure, the Phoenician is one of those outstanding deluxe resorts, with marble floors and walls, exquisite furnishings, gardens, fountains, and state-of-the-art facilities, heightened by art treasures everywhere. This five-year-old resort is situated at the base of Camelback Mountain, and pampers you as if you were at a private club. Rooms in the main hotel are spacious (600 square feet), with computer hookup lines, wool berber carpeting, and an oversized bathroom sheathed in Italian marble. Sybarites wishing more privacy and luxury can opt for a casita, many with parlor suites embellished with handcarved travertine fireplaces.

No need to search for the "right" restaurant—there are three distinctively different dining areas. Windows On The Green features Southwestern comestibles, while The Terrace, complete with a terrazo dance floor, specializes in Continental favorites. For an intoxicating view of palms, mountains and lengthening shadows across the valley, try Mary Elaine's for Contemporary fare and a very attractive wine list. Peek into The Praying Monk, a lovely, isolated eatery in a wine cellar, can accommodate a dinner party for 16 of your best companions.

Strolling the grounds is like being in a large gallery—gigantic bronze sculptures pop up, swimming pools shimmer, boutiques beckon, and even the jogging trails are manicured. Children can participate in a supervised program while adults play tennis or take advantage of the automated practice court. The Centre for Well-Being with a full service spa, croquet lawn, and an 18-hole putting green. Tally ho! Even an afternoon English tea is served.

Golf is king here. The championship 18-hole course, designed by Homer Flint in 1988, is like a verdant jewel because it's seeded every year, even in winter. The front nine is more tropical with lakes, lush fairways and stately queen palms. The back side winds around the base and onto Camelback Mountain's mammoth shoulders. Slope rating (Men's Regular) is 128. As you pass between the 14th green and the 15th tee, you'll see a large cactus garden resplendent with 350 varieties of desert foliage; you'll no doubt rejoice that you are not faced with looking for a lost ball.

Scottsdale Princess Resort

This is the first resort in this country for Princess Hotels International, and it's made a big splash. Part Mexican Colonial, part ultra-chic, and pure Southwestern in style, the 600 rooms and suites blend unobtrusively into the 450 acres. The largest ballroom in Arizona, a constellation of outstanding restaurants, a major spa, and close proximity to Horseworld, with its 480 stables and polo field, are big attractions. Guest rooms and suites feature the earthy subtle patterns of desert country, phones in oversized bathrooms, and many have fireplaces, wet bars and defined living and work areas.

Restaurants run the gamut from casual to elegant La Hacienda with its garden atrium and golf course view. Recreational amenities are nothing short of spectacular. Among the ten tennis courts is a 10,000 seat stadium court, site of the annual WCT Scottsdale Open. Other diversions include swimming, water volleyball, racquetball and squash and aerobics.

The lure of Scottsdale's shopping tempts most visitors, and you'll want to visit the Borgata and Biltmore shops. How about seeing the Grand Canyon from the air?

As a guest here, you're guaranteed a starting time on one of the two 18 hole, Tournament Players Courses. Designed by Tom Weiskopf and Jay Moorish to facilitate more than seventy thousand spectators, you'll have a chance to go for par on the fifteenth—the one with the island green. This is the home of the Phoenix Open, remembered by many as the spot where Scottish-born Sandy Lyle walked away with the winner's check in gorgeous shirtsleeve weather while most of the country shivered.

Address: 7575 E. Princess Dr, Scottsdale, 85255
Phone: 480-585-4848
800-344-4758
Fax: 480-585-0086
E-mail: scottsdale@fairmont.com
Web site: http://www.fairmont.com/Hotels/Index_SC.html
No. of Rooms: 650
Rates: $$$
Restaurant: 5 restaurants
Bar: 7 Bars & Lounges
Business Fac.: 29 meeting rooms, Complete conference facilities
Sports Fac.: Fitness center, Swimming pool, Spa, Tennis courts
Location: Where the McDowell Mountains frame the Sonoran Desert

Courses: TPC Stadium Course (6992, par 71), TPC Desert Course (6552, par 70)
No. of Holes: 36
Guest Policy: Open to public
Club House: 480-585-3600
Fees: ↑↑↑
Reservations: Reservations available 90 days in advance
Season: Open all year
Carts: Carts available

Enchantment Resort

Address: 525 Boynton Canyon Rd, Sedona, 86336
Phone: 520-282-2900
800-826-4180
Fax: 520-282-9249
E-mail: info@ enchantmentresort.com
Web site: http://www. enchantmentresort.com
No. of Rooms: 222
Rates: $$$
Restaurant: Tii Gavo, Yavapai Restaurant
Business Fac.: The Village meeting pavilion includes a complex of meeting spaces as well as a 5,000 sq ft ballroom
Sports Fac.: tennis, spa and fitness center, steam and sauna rooms,croquet
Location: Nestled within the breathtaking panorama of Boynton Canyon in Sedona

Courses: Oak Creek (5352, par 70), Sedona (6642, par 71)
No. of Holes: 27
Guest Policy: Open to public
Reservations: Oak—520-529-0674, Sedona—520-284-9355
Season: Open all year

Nestled within the breathtaking panorama of Boynton Canyon in Sedona lies Enchantment Resort. We offer world class accommodations, a full service conference center, spa services, fine dining, swimming and tennis.

The Adobe Casitas, Haciendas and Guest Rooms are set against towering red rocks, among juniper and pine trees. You'll find all the comforts of home, decorated in a Southwest theme, with private decks viewing Boynton Canyon. Enchantment Resort's versatile guest rooms, studios and parlors can be enjoyed separately or joined to create one or two bedroom Casitas or Haciendas.

For those wanting a fine dining experience, the Yavapai Restaurant, is graced by a Randy Hedden mural and elegant Southwest interiors. A breakfast buffet is served daily with a Jazz Brunch on Sundays. Tii Gavo is a second restaurant at Enchantment Resort that provides a more relaxed atmosphere with casual entertainment on weekends.

Enchantment Resort's Healing Spa & Fitness Center is founded on restorative body treatments and gentle massages that help you rest, rejuvenate, and nourish yourself. Enchantment Resort has expanded its offerings to more than two dozen regimens including massage, facials & aesthetics, connecting with spirit, and nature's restorative treatments.

Two 18-hole championship courses designed by R.H. Trent Jones and Gary Panks, respectively welcome Enchantment guests. Oakcreek Country Club is a beautiful golf course located in the Red Rock grandeur of Sedona, Arizona. Designed by Robert Trent Jones, Oakcreek Country Club offers both challenge and beauty. Nestled in one of the most picturesque regions of America's Southwest, the new Sedona Golf Resort was masterfully, planned with a commitment to quality and a deep regard for the fragile environment of the Coconino National Forest. These unique settings provide the golfing enthusiast-high and low handicapper alike-breathtaking views at every turn.

Loews Ventana Canyon Resort

Loews Ventana Canyon Resort is nestled on 93 acres in Tucson's Catalina Mountain foothills with spectacular city and mountain views. It features 398 luxurious guest rooms, including 27 suites. The resort houses five restaurants and lounges, eight lighted tennis courts, two 18-hole Fazio-designed PGA championship golf courses, a croquet green, 2.5 miles of fitness trails, two swimming pools, a health club, new spa, beauty salon and several retail outlets. Group meeting space includes three ballrooms, six breakout rooms, five hospitality suites and outdoor function areas. The entire staff is trained in the highest standards of guest service.

Address: 7000 North Resort Drive, Tucson, 85715
Phone: 520-299-2020
800-234-5117
Fax: 520-299-6832
E-mail: kguggino@loews.com
Web site: http://www.
loewshotels.com
No. of Rooms: 398
Rates: $
Restrictions: based on availability
Restaurant: Ventana Room:, Canyon Cafe, Flying V Bar & Grill, Bill's Grill
Bar: Flying Bar & Grill, Cascade Lounge
Business Fac.: Onsight conference facilities, 37,000 sq ft of meeting space, along with a full service business center.
Sports Fac.: 8 tennis courts, golf, croquet, par course fitness trails, 2 heated pools with jacuzzis, a full service fitness facility including aerobic studios, weights, personal trainers, saunas, steam room and a full service spa.
Location: On 93 desert acres at the foothills of the Catalina Mountains
Courses: Canyon Course (from back tees—6819), 72, Mountain Course (from back tees—6926), 72
No. of Holes: 36
Guest Policy: Private
Club House: 520-299-2020
Fees: ↑↑↑
Reservations: Call for reservations
Season: Open all year
Carts: Golf carts are included in fees, driving range and balls included

Omni Tucson National Resort & Spa

Address: 2727 West Club Dr,
Tucson, 85742
Phone: 520-297-2271
Fax: 520-297-7544
E-mail: tucsonnational@
omnihotels.com
Web site: http://www.
tucsonnational.com
No. of Rooms: 167
Rates: Inquire
Restaurant: Catalina Grill, Fiesta
Room, Guest Dining Room
Bar: Legends
Business Fac.: Thirteen function
rooms, Ten conference style rooms
Sports Fac.: Tennis, Sand volley-
ball, Basketball, Indoor/outdoor
shuffleboard, Badminton, Croquet,
Horshoes, Two outdoor heated pools
and whirlpools, Fitness center,
Personal trainers, Aerobic & yoga
classes, Mountain biking & jogging
paths
Location: Northwest side of Tucson

Courses: Orange Course, Gold
Course, Green Course
No. of Holes: 27
Club House: 520-575-7540
Fees: ↑↑
Reservations: Call for reservations
Season: Open all year
Carts: Cart included in fee

You'll think you've gone to heaven after a few days in the sunny dry foothills at one of the country's leading spas, which also happens to be a fantastic golf facility. The resort is a low, rambling, and comfortable newish-looking group of buildings accented by a pleasing combination of arches, colonnades and fountains that appear to be jet-propelled. Gardens, weeping willows and loung-ing areas are everywhere, and you get the idea that you're here to be pampered.

167 villa suites constitute lodgings, and you'll have your own patio, refrigerator/wet bar and stunning view. Many have fireplaces, kitchens and other extras. You won't have to leave the premises for fine dining—two good restaurants and three cocktail lounges cater to guests' appetites.

Two separate, divisible ballrooms, and nine meeting rooms offer 15,000 square feet of meeting space, and outdoor areas can expand meeting capabilities to more than 30,000 square feet.

Few European spas can surpass the variety of services and amenities available here. You can opt for a spa plan, or pick and choose what appeals to you, sort of a salad bar approach. Not to be missed are the Scotch water massage, Orthian equip-ment massages, loofah rubdown, and the renowned salt glow scrub. The Russian bath in the men's spa is guaranteed to loosen you up, and the Finnish sauna for women is one you'll want to repeat.

Tennis lovers will have four hard-surfaced courts, with two lighted, and that wonderful sound of the ball popping off the racket in the quiet desert air. Naturally, there's a gorgeous swimming pool to complete the picture. Tucson is not a desert wasteland when it comes to the arts. It's one of only 14 U.S. cities claiming its own sym-phony, theatre, ballet, and opera company. Not too shabby for a golf town that maintains a cool, dry average yearly temperature around 70.

Golf is taken seriously here. Consisting of three nines, it's hosted the NBC Tucson Open for 15 years, and the Arizona Amateur. This is a von Hagge/Devlin redesign on gently rolling terrain sprinkled with the occasional saguaro—pocked with gashes and holes from nesting birds and errant shots. As a permanent site for the Golf Digest Schools, anyone wanting putting pointers or intensive instruction will be in good hands. Tees and fairways resemble a lush carpet—they're Tifway pollen-free Bermudagrass.

Sheraton Tucson El Conquistador

As you turn onto El Conquistador Way the mesquite-tree-lined drive leads you to the resort's porte cochere. Step into the lobby and your eyes are immediately drawn to the high copper-encased dome. And behind the front desk, two 12 x 20 murals painted on; pure copper sheets by Dutch-born Tucson artist Anke Van Dun blend perfectly with the hotel's Spanish and Indian inspired decor.

Dining at El Conquistador brings alive that Southwestern flair. Dos Locos Cantina features Mexican cuisine in a casual setting, while The Last Territory serves up mesquite-grilled steaks, ribs, chicken and fish with a live Country-Western band. For a special evening of fine dining, The White Dove provides the intimate and elegant atmosphere you're looking for. Savor the creations of Chef Molly McCall's swordfish, veal and beef dishes covered with her famed gourmet sauces.

From your spacious room, decorated in either turquoise or rose color schemes, you'll enjoy a glorious view of the grassy courtyard or the natural desert and mountain scenery that surrounds the 150-acre site, nestled beneath the dramatic 2,000-feet Pusch Ridge cliffs at the western end of the Santa Catalina Mountain range.

Plenty of sports activities will let you experience the great outdoors, including 16 lighted Laykold tennis courts, horseback riding, and swimming.

45 holes await the golfer staying at El Conquistador. Nine holes are at the resort itself, with another 36 at Oro Valley's Canada Hills Country Club. These are desert courses, with a spectacular backdrop of jagged mountain peaks and seemingly cloudless azure skies, gullies, dry washes, and a variety of cacti.

Six miles away, at Canada Hills, the fairways are tight with rolling hills, large, undulating double-tiered greens, clustered sand traps, and plenty of mesquite and palo verdes to avoid. #6 is a stickler—a difficult par three of 167 yards. You'll need a straight tee shot, because only the front third of the green is visible from the tee, and hooks and slices will be penalized. The green has 100 feet of putting surface behind the left front bunker that can't be seen. Events hosted here have been the 1985 Southwest Section PGA Match Play Championship, the 1987 Oldsmobile Scramble, and numerous mini-tour events.

Address: 10000 North Oracle Rd, Tucson, 85737
Phone: 520-544-5000
800-325-7832
Fax: 520-544-1228
E-mail: jay_larsen@ittsheraton.com
Web site: http://www.sheratonelconquistador.com
No. of Rooms: 428
Rates: $$
Restaurant: The Last Territory, Dos Locos, Sundance, La Vista
Bar: Dos Locos
Business Fac.: Flexible meeting spaces with state-of-the-art equipment
Sports Fac.: 31 tennis courts, 2 fitness centers, 4 swimming pools, Volleyball, Basketball, Mountain bike rentals, Horseback riding, Jeep tours, Hot air balloons, Jogging/hiking trails, Nature walks
Location: Base of Santa Catalina Mountains, 30 minutes north of Tucson

Courses: Sunset Course (6763), Sunrise Course (6619), Pusch Ridge Course (2788)
No. of Holes: 45
Club House: 520-544-1800
Reservations: Call for reservations
Season: Open all year

Westin La Paloma

Address: 3800 E. Sunrise Dr,
Tucson, 85718
Phone: 520-742-6000
888-625-5144
Fax: 520-577-5886
E-mail: tucso@westin.com
No. of Rooms: 487
Rates: $$
Restaurant: Four restaurants
Bar: Lounge and swim-up bar
Business Fac.: On-site business
center, Administrative support, 23
meeting rooms, Cell phone rental,
Conference center, Westin One Call
Sports Fac.: Tennis, Golf, Volleyball,
Waterslide, Health club, Fitness
center, 3 outdoor swimming pools,
Raquetball
Location: North of Tucson in
Sonora Desert

Courses: Canyon Course (3554, par
36), Hill Course (3081, par 36),
Ridge Course (3534, par 36)
No. of Holes: 27
Club House: 520-577-4061
Fees: ↑↑↑
Reservations: Can make reserva-
tions 7 days in advance
Season: Open all year
Carts: Carts included in fees

Reverence for the desert's natural gifts was the
primary concern of landscape architects Rogers,
Gladwin and Harmony in designing this resort
complex which earned them an Award of Merit
from the American Society of Landscape Archi-
tects. Over 7,000 Saguaros were transplanted and
saved, and environmental zones were planted
with drought-resistant brittlebush, desert mari-
gold, Arizona poppies and Chochise lovegrass to
create the unspoiled setting for this 487 room
resort in the foothills of the Santa Catalina Moun-
tains.

Jack Nicklaus' 27-hole championship layout
encircles the resort which is conveniently located
just 10 miles from downtown. 24 two-story com-
plexes in a village setting give each guest a patio
or balcony with private exterior entrance, and
inside, shades of dusty rose, sage, cobalt, mauve
and muted grey are echoed in nubby cottons,
woven raffia and copper accents. Restaurants
emphasize healthy fare for the active life. If the
tennis, (on competition-calibre lighted courts),
hiking, volleyball, croquet and bicycling have
tired you out, why not try Room Service with its
motorized carts, specially outfitted with heating
and refrigeration units to bring you fresh selec-
tions 24 hours a day?

Other amenities include an aerobics room and
weight room with Lifecycle and Nautilus equip-
ment, and a Personal Services Center for skin and
hair pampering, and massages. Shoppers and
browsers have the option of exploring the ten on-
premises stores or heading for nearby Old Tucson.

Not only are the three challenging 9 hole
courses in excellent condition, the putting greens
and driving ranges are worthy of note. Each
course is a par 36, but each has a different rating.
Built in 1984, the combined yardage is 9776 yards,
with 4-5 tees for varying expertise on each green.
Nicklaus has designed a desert course with large
bunkers, no water, but plenty of grassy hollows,
swales and mounds, with the mountains forming
a magnificent backdrop to the lush greens and
desert fairways. Hill Course's #5, a 465-yard, par 4
is a beauty. From the back tee it takes two big
shots to "get home." The approach to this green—
which is guarded on the left by a grassy swale and
to the right by a sand trap—is through a long val-
ley that opens up behind the green with views of
the entire city of Tucson several miles away.

Rancho De Los Caballeros

Rediscover a less complicated era when time was measured, not by the tyranny of clocks but, by soft shadows darkening against majestic mountainsides. Stroll amid flowering gardens and emerald green lawns and watch keen-eyed hawks soar above rugged Vulture Peak. Escape into the rapidly vanishing past and encounter the sheer pleasures of 20,000 acres of the unspoiled southwest when you stay at Rancho de los Caballeros.

Bring your family, your sense of adventure, and most of all, bring along your healthiest appetite. The outdoor activities and the clean desert air will make you hungry for fabulous "home cookin" prepared over glowing mesquite. Sample Rancho's breakfast of griddle cakes, a leisurely buffet luncheon on the poolside patio, or an intimate and elegant dinner of thoughtfully prepared cuisine.

Besides golf, there's also tennis on four acrylic courts, trap and skeet shooting, swimming at the teardrop-shaped pool, and of course, riding over miles of open countryside, an old favorite here. Their 60 horse stable is one of the finest collections in Arizona.

Spend a day exploring The Vulture Mine, the source of $30 million in gold bullion during Wickenburg's heyday. Visit Heard Museum, a notable hacienda housing the finest collection of Indian arts and artifacts in the Southwest. Then simply relax and enjoy a quiet moment with other guests in the ranch living room.

Golf is at a private club for members and their guests, and guests at Rancho de los Caballeros. *Golf Digest* in 1987 rated Los Caballeros Golf Course in the Top 10 golf courses in Arizona. There are three sets of tees, a driving range, putting green and a clubhouse featuring men's and ladies' locker rooms, pro shop, and kitchen with bar and grill room. The course was completed in 1981, and was designed so that there are no crossing fairways. Undulating greens of "tif" are elevated and the lush bermudagrass fairways are overseeded with perennial rye to insure a deep green playing area all year. Three lakes and a variety of cacti (preferably to admire) will test your skill and concentration on this demanding course.

Address: 1551 S. Vulture Mine, PO Box 1148, Wickenberg, 85390
Phone: 520-684-5484
800-684-5030
Fax: 520-684-2267
E-mail: home@SunC.com
Web site: http://www.
ranchweb.com/caballeros
No. of Rooms: 150
Rates: $$$
Business Fac.: Conference facilites
Sports Fac.: Horseback riding, Trap & Skeet, Nature hikes, Massage, Mountain bike rental, Swimming pool
Location: One hour north of Phoenix

Course: Los Caballeros Golf Club (7025, par 72)
No. of Holes: 18
Guest Policy: Open to public
Club House: 520-684-2704
Fees: ⫯ ⫯
Reservations: Can make reservations 2 days in advance
Season: Open all year

Rio Bravo Resort

Address: 11200 Lake Ming Rd,
Bakersfield, 93306
Phone: 805-872-5000
888-517-5500
E-mail: relax@riobravoresort.com
Web site: http://www.
riobravoresort.com
No. of Rooms: 105
Rates: $
Restaurant: Club Rio, Club Rio Bar
& Grill, Rio Bravo Roasting Company
Bar: Rio Bravo Bar & Grill, Club-
house Grill
Business Fac.: State of the art
services & technical support,
Catering, Special event coordination
Sports Fac.: 19 lighted tennis
courts, Fitness center & spa, Sand
volleyball, Whitewater rafting,
Wind-surfing, Sailing, Power
boating, Kayaking, Fishing, Hiking
Location: Minutes from downtown
Bakersfield

Course: Rio Bravo (7018, par 72)
No. of Holes: 18
Guest Policy: Open to public
Club House: 805-871-4653
Reservations: Call for reservations
Season: Open all year

"You go there not to see Bakersfield, but to play
golf and tennis" is the description of a Rio Bravo
devotee. Rooms are in two-story cedar building
scattered among gardens, with ponds and landscaped walkways and vistas of neighboring mountains. Bring your windsurfer and your water skiis
so you can head for Lake Ming, right next to the
resort. If kayaking is your sport, you can tackle
the rapids on Kern River, where Olympic hopefuls
practice.

Nineteen tennis courts, several swimming
pools, a gym, and volleyball are all yours. The
resort's restaurant, Godfreys, is a favorite with
locals for juicy steaks.

The course, by Robert Muir Graves in 1982,
plays long and has excellent greens. The back
nine holes are hilly, while the front nine is flat,
just like most of the surrounding terrain. This is
the west coast regional qualifying course for the
PGA tour, and the site of the Southern California
Open. Slope rating is 122 Regular.

Borrego Springs Resort & Country Club

Borrego Springs Resort is a lushly landscape nestled between the Santa Rosa Mountains in the Anza-Borrego Desert and offers an attractive variety of amenities and recreation.

The resort features 100 rooms, each with it's own terrace and unique view. Every room includes a refrigerator with icemaker, microwave oven, in-room coffee, satellite TV, alarm clock radio, hair dryer, in-room phone with voice mail, and our specialty developed line of personal care amenities. Suites are equipped with kitchenettes including stoves. Standard furnishings include handsome oak cabinetry. Rooms have individually controlled thermostats. Second floor rooms have panoramic views of the mountains.

For group functions, the resort offers 5,000 square feet of meeting and banquet space including four separate meeting rooms. Group services include catering, barbecue, and hospitality suites. Borrego Springs Resort also offers six-lighted tennis courts, two heated swimming pools and spa, a state-of-the-art fitness center, and therapeutic massage.

Our 18-hole championship golf course, par three warm-up holes, three practice greens and driving range make the resort a golfer's paradise. Designed by La Jolla-based Golf Course Architect Cary Bickler, the course offers four sets of tees to challenge any player. Four lakes are in play in the 1,160-acre course. Doglegs and sloping greens make for a very playable course that is "no pushover." Landscaped with native desert vegetation, the course includes 354 mature date palms.

With its magnificent location just 76 miles northeast of San Diego and 60 miles south of Palm Springs, the resort is convenient to the entire southwest. For worry-free traveling, guests of the resort enjoy shuttle service from the Borrego Valley Airport.

Address: 1112 Tilting T Dr, Borrego Springs, 92004
Phone: 760-767-5700
888-826-7734
Fax: 760-767-5710
E-mail: bsr@znet.com
Web site: http://www.
borregospringsresort.com
No. of Rooms: 100
Rates: $
Business Fac.: 5000 sq ft of meeting/banquet facilities including 4 separate meeting rooms. Catering, barbeque and hospitality suites available
Sports Fac.: 6 lighted tennis courts, 2 heated swimming pools and spa, fitness center, and therapeutic massage
Location: 76 miles northeast of San Diego and 60 miles south of Palm Springs

Course: Borrego Springs (6982, par 71)
No. of Holes: 18
Guest Policy: Open to public
Club House: 760-767-3330
Fees: ⊺
Reservations: Call to make reservations
Season: Open all year

Boulder Creek Golf Club

Address: 16901 Big Basin Hwy,
Boulder Creek, 95006
Phone: 831-338-2111
Fax: 831-338-7862
Web site: http://www.
bouldercreekgolf.com
Restaurant: Full service open for
breakfast and lunch daily, dinner
Friday through Monday
Business Fac.: For business confer-
ences large and small, full facilities
and staff
Sports Fac.: Tennis and Swimming
Location: Amid the majestic
redwoods of the Santa Cruz Moun-
tains

Course: Boulder Creek (par 65 men,
67 women)
No. of Holes: 18
Club House: 831-338-2121
Reservations: Call for reservations
Season: Open all year
Carts: Carts available

Boulder Creek Golf & Country Club, located amid
the majestic redwoods of the Santa Cruz Mountains, offers a scenic and challenging 18 hole golf
course, a conference and meeting facility, overnight condominium lodging and vacation rental
packages, a full service restaurant and bar, tennis, and swimming in a resort setting. Whether
you come for the day or stay for the week- the
Boulder Creek Golf & Country Club experience is
one you won't forget.

Spend a perfect weekend in one of the comfortable condominiums complete with fireplace,
fully equipped kitchen and spacious decks overlooking the scenic golf course. While staying at
Boulder Creek Country Club: Take a scenic walk
and gaze at the majestic redwood trees, bridged
ponds and bubbling creeks. Take a short drive
and explore Santa Cruz City and the Beach
Boardwalk. Or simply stay and relax by swimming,
playing golf or tennis.

The full service restaurant overlooking the
golf course at Boulder Creek is open for breakfast
and lunch daily and serves dinner Friday, Saturday, Sunday and Monday. Banquets are available
for tournaments and special events.

Whether yours is a large or a small company,
business conferences and seminars are probably
very important to you. A truly productive business
conference should be held away from the telephones, the interruptions and the pressures of
the office. When you select a site for your business conference, you want a quiet location, pleasant surroundings, a competent staff and ample
leisure facilities.

Opened in 1961, this scenic course, set among
the redwoods, lakes and creeks, offers a challenging and memorable golfing experience. Designed
by Jack Fleming, this demanding par 65 for men
and par 67 for women course features superb
medium wooded rolling terrain undulating
greens. Group and company tournaments are
available at Boulder Creek. The complete tournament service and facilities include luxury condominium rentals, deluxe banquet and barbecue
facilities, power carts, tennis and swimming.

Four Seasons Resort Aviara

Just up the road from La Costa in the Costa Brava hills lies the most luxurious golf resort in all of Southern California—The Four Seasons Aviara Resort. Three hundred and thirty-one oversized guestrooms each offer elegant comfort, a private patio and a superb view. Five choice restaurants, 24-hour room service and concierge service are just a few of the many amenities awaiting your arrival.

A full-service spa and fitness center includes steam, spa treatments, saunas, 2 whirlpools, weight training, aerobics and cardiovascular equipment. The resort pool features deck-side whirlpools and a children's play pool. There are also six tennis courts, including a stadium court and two clay courts. Recreation abounds. Take your choice of hot air ballooning, hang gliding and sailplanes, surfing, jet skiing, water skiing, whale watching, in-line skating, biplane and helicopter coastline tours.

Golf Digest named the four-star 18-hole championship course one of the best new resort courses in the United States. Rolling valleys and the Pacific Ocean cradle a famed wildlife sanctuary and an Arnold Palmer signature golf course. From the tippy-tips, it stretches out to 7,007 yards, providing a great challenge to low handicappers and all the way down to 5,007 yards for players not quite ready for the PGA Tour.

Address: 7100 Four Seasons Point, Carlsbad, 92009
Phone: 760-603-6800
Fax: 760-603-6801
Web site: http://www.fourseasons.com/locations/Aviara/
No. of Rooms: 331
Rates: Inquire
Restaurant: Vivace, California Bistro, The Ocean Grill and Bar, Golf Clubhouse Argyle
Bar: The Lobby Lounge
Business Fac.: Flexible, outdoor-oriented meeting spaces including Grand Ballroom, 24 hour business service center
Sports Fac.: 6 tennis courts, Full service spa and fitness center, Outdoor swimming pool with whirlpools, Biking, Volleyball, Sauna/steam, Massage
Location: On the Southern California coast

Course: Aviara (7007, par 72)
No. of Holes: 18
Guest Policy: Open to public
Club House: 760-929-0077
Fees: ↑↑↑
Reservations: Reservations available 6 days in advance
Season: Open all year
Carts: Carts included in fees

La Costa Hotel & Spa

Address: Costa Del Mar Rd,
Carlsbad, 92009
Phone: 760-438-9111
800-854-5000
E-mail: info@lacosta.com
Web site: http://www.
lacosta.com/lacosta.htm
No. of Rooms: 479
Rates: $$$
Restaurant: Pisces, Ristorante
Figaro, Brasserie La Costa
Bar: Lobby Lounge
Business Fac.: Conference
facilities, Audio/visual equipment,
Experienced staff, Rear screen
projection theatre.
Sports Fac.: 21 tennis courts,
Croquet, Bicycles, Heated pools,
Massage Aerobics, Water aerobics,
Water toning, Step, Stretch, Interval
circuit.
Location: 30 minutes north of San
Diego

Courses: North Course (7021, par
72), South Course (7004, par 72)
No. of Holes: 36
Guest Policy: Open to public
Club House: 760-438-9111
Fees: ↑↑↑
Reservations: Can make reserva-
tions 7 days in advance
Season: Open all year
Carts: Carts included in fees

One of the world's leading resorts, La Costa Hotel
& Spa features extensive spa facilities. The men's
and women's Spas at La Costa serve as twin cen-
terpieces for this 400-acre private world of resort
pleasures. Here the natural scenic splendor of
Southern California's Costa Brava combine with
world-class golf and countless other amenities
that make La Costa living an experience of time-
less elegance.

Enjoy tennis on your choice of the Racquet
Club's 21 courts—including two grass, four clay
and 15 hardcourt surfaces—and swim in heated
pools featuring a lovely aquatic center overlook-
ing the golf course. But, the Spa that will keep
you coming back. Relax in a sauna, rock steam
bath, Swiss shower, Roman pool, whirlpool or a
solarium. Schedule yourself for a facial, massage,
herbal wrap or loofah scrub.

The pros who competed for 30 years in La
Costa's Tournament of Champions have dubbed
the last 4 holes of the South Course "the longest
mile in golf." What they find so tough isn't their
length, but hitting into the head winds which
come off the ocean. You'll no doubt want to tackle
both of these highly-acclaimed eighteen-hole
courses, which are surrounded on three sides by
towering hills. The South Course is a true test of
driving skill and shot-making at every stroke,
while the North Course consists of classic holes
with a variety of intriguing water hazards.

Carmel Valley Ranch Resort

For anyone who enjoys a sunny, warm climate, splendid golf and tennis facilities, and an exclusive resort featuring graciously appointed guest suites, the Carmel Valley Ranch Resort is the answer. Based in Carmel, Oak Tree Hotels, Inc., also operate Mission Hills Country Club Resort Condominiums, and Palm Beach Polo and Country Club, among other properties.

The 100 suites are set in clusters among old oak trees and gardens, and are individually decorated with rustic textures and soft natural colors. Against a backdrop of the Santa Lucia Mountains and clear blue skies, the cathedral ceilings, private decks, wood burning fireplaces and fairway views lend an air of country refinement. Many have private outdoor spas.

The Lodge, housing an intimate dining room specializing in fresh fish from Monterey Bay, and local produce, changes its menu every other day. The cozy lounge is a showpiece of local craftsmen whose talents are displayed in the weavings, art, and a massive stone fireplace. A pianist and freshly cut flowers add to the ambience of this informal gathering place.

Meeting and banquet rooms are designed to accommodate a group of 10, or one as large as 250, and the sweeping Oak Tree Courtyard along with the terrace area offers ample space for an outdoor conference or dining. Golf is superb here. The Club is private, and available only to resort guests and club members. There are tennis courts, an inviting freeform pool a full spa, and a choice of scenic walks in the valley.

If your goal is to play a Pete Dye creation, especially after watching the 1988 PGA Tournament at Oak Tree, and you can't make it to Ponte Verda Beach to the TPC course, here's your chance! As one of the courses in the Spalding Pro-Am featuring PGA stars such as Greg Norman, Craig Stadler and Johnny Miller, this championship design has the Carmel River bordering several holes on the north, and luxurious mountain greenery on the south. Test your prowess on some of Dye's trademarks here—a layout dappled with numerous deep sand and grass bunkers, undulating greens, and railroad ties and telephone pole bulkheading which are deemed an integral part of the course. Five of the holes climb the mountainside affording some incredible views of the valley, and the cooling fog banks that hover over the coast.

Address: One Old Ranch Rd, Carmel, 93923
Phone: 831-625-9500
888-GRAN-BAY
Fax: 831-624-2858
Web site: http://www.wyndham.com/Carmel_Valley_Ranch/default.cfm
No. of Rooms: 44
Rates: Inquire
Restaurant: The Oaks, Ranch House Cafe, Club Grill
Bar: The lounge
Business Fac.: Several onsight facilities with state-of-the-art technology
Sports Fac.: Fitness center, Power walks, Bike tours, Nature hikes, Massage, 13 tennis courts, Pool, Whirlpool spa
Location: Just minutes east of Carmel-by-the-sea

Course: Pete Dye's 18-Hole Championship Golf Course (6234, par 70)
No. of Holes: 18
Guest Policy: Open to public
Club House: 831-626-2510
Fees: ⌐⌐⌐
Reservations: Can make reservations 60 days in advance
Season: Open all year
Carts: Carts included in fees

Quail Lodge Resort & Golf Club

Address: 8205 Valley Greens Drive, Carmel, 93923
Phone: 831-624-2888
888-828-8787
Fax: 831-624-3726
E-mail: info@
quail-lodge-resort.com
Web site: http://www.
quail-lodge-resort.com
No. of Rooms: 100
Rates: $$$
Restaurant: Covey, The Deck,
Business Fac.: Function rooms adapt to anything from an official board meeting to banquets
Sports Fac.: Golf, 4 tennis courts, 2 pools, Hiking, Biking
Location: Minutes from Carmel-by-the-Sea, California

Course: Quail Lodge (6515, par 71)
No. of Holes: 18
Guest Policy: Open to public
Club House: 831-614-2770
Fees: ↑↑↑
Reservations: Accept reservations one year in advance
Season: Open all year
Carts: Carts included in green fees

In a peaceful country setting, located in the sunny part of Carmel, Quail Lodge Resort & Golf Course is nestled among 850 scenic acres of lush fairways, oak-studded meadows, sparkling lakes, and green hills. The lodge's low profile, cedar-siding and heavy shake roofs exude rustic charm. The three-story lobby features timbered redwood and cedar, Spanish tile and oak flooring. The Resort conveys a casual elegance throughout, with a passion for quality. Quail Lodge has won the Mobil Travel Guide 5 Star Award, a distinction the resort has enjoyed for 17 years.

Along with the beauty of nature, guests enjoy a host of civilized pleasures, such as an 18-hole championship golf course, 4 tennis courts, 2 swimming pools, and miles of jogging and hiking trails. An additional enticement is the award-winning Covey Restaurant, which features refined European cuisine. It overlooks a lake with panoramic views of a lighted fountain and arched bridge.

The beautifully decorated guest rooms and suites offer a multitude of comforting amenities, while overlooking the golf course, lakes and lush gardens from their private decks and patios. They are decorated in bright Southwest colors and accented by contemporary furnishings. The Resort also offers Executive Villas, representing the ultimate in luxury.

This is peaceful California golf at its best. The course is a meticulously maintained 71 par course with 2 practice putting greens and a 17-acre practice range. It is also home of the annual Women's California Amateur Division and the Men's California State Handicap Division. The slope rating is 122 regular.

Cimarron Golf Resort

The Cimarron Resort is not for golf alone. The golf operations share a unique relationship with a high-profile vacation ownership development consisting of 242 villas adjacent to the golf courses. Owners of the villas will receive membership-type rights at Cimarron during the time of their stay and will also have privileges along the OB Sports Trail, a collection of high-end golf properties.

The Vacation Villas will offer tennis, pools, recreation and fitness as well. And the location is the best in the valley to enjoy everything Palm Springs has to offer. The Cimarron Resort is only minutes from the shopping, dining and nightlife of Palm Springs, yet with a desert location providing excellent views of the surrounding mountains and the celebration of what desert living is all about.

The true showpiece at Cimarron is two world-class golf courses. Golf course architect John Fought has fashioned a masterful variety of bunkers with flat tongues and jagged edges, while incorporating sod into the walls of others. All of the bunkers at Cimarron are filled with brilliant white sand, creating a spectacular contrast to the immaculate green fairways, light-brown native wash areas, multi-colored displays of landscaping and the San Jacinto Mountains.

Address: 67-603 30th Avenue, Cathedral City, 92234
Phone: 760-324-9911
877-286-0888
E-mail: info@cimarronresorts.com
Web site: http://www.cimarronresorts.com
No. of Rooms: 242
Rates: Inquire
Restaurant: Leapin' Lizards Bistro
Sports Fac.: Outdoor swimming pool
Location: At the foot of the San Jacinto Mountains

Courses: The Long Course (6857, par 71), The Short Course (3164, par 56)
No. of Holes: 36
Guest Policy: Open to public
Club House: 760-770-6060
Fees: ⊤
Reservations: Call for reservations
Season: Open all year

Doubletree Resort at Desert Princess Country Club

Address: Vista Chino at Landau, PO Box 1644, Cathedral City, 92234
Phone: 760-322-7000
800-222-TREE
Fax: 760-322-6853
Web site: http://www.
desertresorts.com/dbletree/
No. of Rooms: 289
Rates: Inquire
Restrictions: No pets allowed
Restaurant: Princess
Bar: Oasis
Business Fac.: Full conference facilities
Sports Fac.: Tennis courts, Swimming pool, Bicycle rental
Location: 10 minutes from airport

Course: 3 Nine hole courses
No. of Holes: 27
Club House: 760-322-2280
Reservations: May be made in advance
Season: Open all year

This is a 345-acre golf resort just two hours driving from Los Angeles. Spacious guest rooms and elegant condominium, meeting facilities and recreational facilities are what you'll find here just 10 minutes from the Palm Springs airport. All accommodations feature built-in refrigerators, remote-control TV, computerized sages and spacious dressing areas. You really will want to be seen in the Princess Restaurant, where elegant dining is the name of the game. There's also nightly entertainment and dancing in the Oasis Lounge, and cocktails and quiet conversation in the Vista Lounge. Maybe Sonny Bono will be conversing quietly near you.

The countryside is flat, so why not rent a bicycle and pedal it all over town? There are ten tennis courts, five of which are lighted, and two swimming pools and whirlpools. Racquetball courts, and a state-of-the-arts fitness center are guaranteed to keep you in shape.

If you'd like to roam around the Palm Springs area, check out the Joshua Tree National Monument, the Palm Springs Desert Museum, or the Moorten Botanical Garden.

The Desert Princess Country Club has recently opened a third nine. By re-configuration, you can play some old holes and some new ones. If you tee up on the Vista nine and go to Cielo nine, the Slope is 113 (Men's Regular), but if you play Cielo and Lagos, it's 111. Lagos and Vista are rated 112, and it all adds up to a pleasant game. The new nine resembles a links layout—it traverses a wash where no trees can be planted, and it's hilly with parts of it almost barren.

Industry Hills Sheraton Resort

With a name like City of Industry, you might wonder what sort of resort could be there. Centrally located means 25 minutes to downtown L.A., 30 minutes to Disneyland, 40 minutes to the Hollywood Bowl, and 45 minutes to Beverly Hills. Now add a reasonable price, two golf courses, seventeen tennis courts, 15 miles of riding trails, 2 swimming pools, 3 restaurants and rooms large enough to be called oversized.

The swimming complex boasts a true Olympic size pool (17 feet deep), separate warmup pool and NCAA rated diving platform. Health spas have virtually everything. The equestrian center with show rings, polo grounds, western shore and riding academy is top-notch, and is the answer to a horseless afternoon.

Take time to browse in the Ralph W. Miller Golf Library and Museum, which contains over 5,000 books, 5,000 photos and 1,600 bound periodicals in addition to golf videos, clubs and balls, and other golf memorabilia. Bobby Jones' irons, Dwight Eisenhower's hickory shafted clubs and Babe Zaharias' putter are among the interesting exhibits.

You can play the Babe Zaharias Course or the adjacent Eisenhower Course. Touted as one of the nation's best public courses, the Eisenhower is a long, wide open championship course featuring high rough and plenty of hills. You can't get away with a lot of mistakes here. This is a beautifully maintained property, and from its heights you'll have great views of the Pasadena, the San Gabriel Valley, and even Los Angeles.

Address: 1 Industry Hills Pkwy, City of Industry, 91744
Phone: 626-810-4455
800-524-4557
Fax: 626-964-9535
Web site: http://www.sheraton.com/property.taf?prop=604&lc=en
No. of Rooms: 294
Rates: Inquire
Business Fac.: Complete conference and exhibition center
Sports Fac.: 17 tennis courts, Olympic swimming complex, Fitness center, Horseback riding, Watersports
Location: 23 miles from downtown Los Angeles

Courses: Babe Didrikson Zaharias (6600), Dwight D. Eisenhower (6735)
No. of Holes: 36
Guest Policy: Open to public
Club House: 626-965-0861
Fees: ↑
Reservations: Can make reservations 3 days in advance
Season: Open all year
Carts: Carts included in fees

Ritz Carlton Laguna Niguel

Address: One Ritz-Carlton Dr, Dana Point, 92629
Phone: 949-240-2000
800-241-3333
Fax: 949-240-0829
Web site: http://www. ritzcarlton.com
No. of Rooms: 393
Rates: $$$
Restaurant: The Dining Room, Club Grill & Bar, The Terrace Restaurant, The Library, The Ocean Terrace
Bar: The Lounge, The Wine Room
Business Fac.: Full-service meeting facilities, Full-service Business Center
Sports Fac.: Golf, 4 tennis courts, Fitness Center, Sauna, Steam, Massages, 2 outdoor swimming pools/Jacuzzis, Volleyball, Croquet, Jogging/bike trails
Location: 35 minutes from John Wayne Airport in Orange County

Course: Monarch Beach (6224, 70)
No. of Holes: 18
Guest Policy: Open to public
Club House: 949-240-8247
Fees: ↑↑↑
Reservations: Reservations available 7 days in advance
Season: Open all yar
Carts: Carts included in fees

The Laguna Niguel is set on a high bluff overlooking the Pacific Ocean, and takes full advantage of the spectacular views of the ocean from its public rooms and well as the guest rooms. The resort is California's only five star, five diamond resort, and it shows in the meticulous attention to details. The Mediterranean-style buildings are enhanced by the courtyard and pool areas that are palm filled and lushly landscaped.

The hotel is filled with beautiful growing flora and a magnificent art collection graces the walls in most of the public rooms. The chef is Paris-born and a true artist, the fare is exceptional and uses only the freshest produce and finest meats while offering many menu selections for the fitness conscious. Your dining experiences here will be sure to please the eye as well as the palate. The fitness center not only has the latest in equipment, but offers an assessment program called "Personal Best," which is well worth the trip on its own merit.

Located between Los Angeles and San Diego makes it easy to see the attractions in both areas and still enjoy the resort. Be sure to visit the artists' colony in Laguna Beach and world-class shopping in Newport Beach is another must do! The Ritz was Ernest Hemingway's favorite place to stay, and it's sure to become yours too.

The golfing at Monarch Beach is set along the ocean, which can be seen from all points on the course. The bunkers here are sand, and sure to give you plenty to think about. An elevated triple-tiered green set right above the ocean is magnificent and a truly challenging moment for your round of golf.

Furnace Creek Inn and Ranch Resort

If you've never visited the driest, lowest, hottest area of the United States, you're in for a real treat—for in its foreboding isolation, between October through May, it's also starkly beautiful. Most of the action today centers around Furnace Creek, site of a visitor's center, a small airport and the resort.

Consisting of the Inn and the Ranch, guests can choose between a luxurious 66 room Inn, and a more family oriented Ranch complete with old wagon wheels, three restaurants, a General Store and Borax Museum. The rambling adobe brick Inn welcomed its first guests in 1927, and became a destination for the well-heeled who came to be pampered. The atmosphere at the Inn is relaxed, unpretentious and intriguing because of its quiet surroundings. Desert colors, oasis gardens, ceiling fans, wicker furniture and Afternoon Tea characterize the Inn, which caters to many repeat guests.

Maybe you'll want to explore the canyons and nearby sights on horseback, or play tennis, or you can bicycle or jog on meandering paths, and there are miles of scenic trails to hike. The golf course is fun to play and surprisingly verdant for an area whose average rainfall is 1.7 inches yearly. Tamarisk trees and stands of date palms line the fairways, but you'll probably want to use every club in your bag, as the out of bounds areas are unexpected and numerous. Water comes into play on several holes. This tough course with its outstanding layout was designed by William Bell.

Address: Highway 190, P.O. Box 1, Death Valley, 92328
Phone: 760-786-2345
Fax: 760-786-2307
E-mail: reserv@ furnacecreekresort.com
Web site: http://www. furnacecreekresort.com
No. of Rooms: 290
Rates: $
Restrictions: No pets allowed, deposit required
Restaurant: Inn Dining Room(dress code), 19th Hole Grill, Forty Niner Cafe, Wrangler Buffet, Wrangler Steakhouse
Bar: Inn Lobby Bar, Inn Pool Bar, Corkscrew Saloon, 19th Hole Bar
Business Fac.: Meeting and banquet facilites, capacity 120, Boardroom, Conference rooms, Executive retreats.
Sports Fac.: 2 Spring-fed swimming pools, 6 lighted tennis courts, Horseback riding, Hiking.
Location: Death Valley National Park, 120 miles northeast of Las Vegas

Course: The Furnace Creek Golf Course (yardage 6215, par 70)
No. of Holes: 18
Guest Policy: Open to public
Club House: 760-786-2301
Fees: ||
Reservations: Call for reservations
Season: Open all year
Carts: $25

Hyatt Grand Champions Resort

Address: 44-600 Indian Wells Ln, Indian Wells, 92210
Phone: 760-341-1000
800-55-HYATT
Fax: 760-568-2236
Web site: http://www.grandchampions.hyatt.com/champ/
No. of Rooms: 338
Rates: $$$
Restaurant: Santa Rosa Grille, Hamilton's
Bar: Sports Gallery
Business Fac.: 20,000 sq ft
Sports Fac.: 12 tennis courts, 5 swimming pools, fitness center and spa
Location: 16 miles West of Palm Springs

Courses: East (6700, par 72), West (6500, par 72)
No. of Holes: 36
Guest Policy: Open to public
Club House: 760-346-4653
Fees: ⏐⏐
Reservations: Call for reservations
Season: Open all year
Carts: Fee includes electric cart

Just outside Palm Springs, where the resorts are endless and the Rolls Royces long, sits this Hyatt. On 34 acres of natural desert terrain, this European-style resort houses 336 all-suite guest rooms, including 289 split-level suites, penthouse suites and garden villas. Twelve suites are equipped for handicapped, and garden suites have butler service in case you forgot to bring yours. Dining rooms, snack bars, lounges and bars are not in short supply. Naturally, you can be served by the pool as you gaze at the cloudless sky. This is one of the few places in North America where you can play golf in 80-degree temperature and (in January and February) see snow-capped peaks of the Santa Rosa Mountains beyond.

Everything is here—from boutiques and modern spa, to babysitting services and a Japanese translator. This is a major resort for meetings, 7,000 square feet of it. After the meetings are over, guests can partake of the resorts recreational facilities. There are four pools and two spas, twelve tennis courts, including grass, clay and hard surfaces, a 10,500-seat stadium court with private enclosed boxes for tournaments, and all sorts of electronic devices to aid your game.

And the golf rates high. Two 18-hole championship courses designed by Ted Robinson, dubbed East and West courses are adjacent to the Hyatt. The property was owned by members of Bob Hope's family. Though the course lacks mature trees, Ted Robinson routed the holes over mad-made lakes and through palm groves. Remember that this is a seasonal resort, with some great golf packages available during the warmer months.

Indian Wells Resort Hotel

Surrounded by panoramic views of the Santa Rosa Mountains, the Indian Wells Resort Hotel prides itself on providing all the elegance expected from a full service resort including ultimate service. With numerous guestrooms, three golf courses, many activities, and meeting and banquet facilities, the resort is an ideal vacation or meeting place.

The Indian Wells offers 155 rooms, and on and off site meeting accommodations. Suites offer spacious rooms, private balconies, and large marble bathrooms. Deluxe rooms feature pool views or desert panoramas and have a private patio or balcony, mini-bar, and custom amenities in an elegant environment. Or, stay in the Presidential Suite, with 4 bedrooms, two floors with private elevator, bar, full kitchen, and 1,000 sq. ft. of entertaining space.

When not golfing, enjoy the heated pool and hot therapy pool, salon, tennis courts, state-of-the-art fitness center and nearby casinos, shopping, and outdoor adventures.

The concept of the Indian Wells Country Club was first discussed in 1956, the original founders, including Desi Arnaz, envisioned a nine-hole private club. It has since grown into 27 holes of golf winding their way through the mountains. Associated with the Bob Hope Chrysler Classic since its 1960 inception, the club course has been played by numerous people including President Bill Clinton, President George Bush and President Gerald Ford.

The resort features three golf courses, two of which are Ted Robinson designed courses, a driving range, and a year-round golf school. Robinson designed the course with rolling fairways, contoured greens, dazzling water hazards and views of the surrounding Santa Rosa Mountains.

Address: 44-500 Indian Wells Lane, Indian Wells, 92210
Phone: 760-346-6466
800-248-3220
E-mail: info@indianwellsresort.com
Web site: http://www.indianwellsresort.com
No. of Rooms: 155
Rates: $
Restaurant: Loren, Palm Terrace, Jake's Lounge, Vicky's of Santa Fe
Bar: Jake's Lounge
Business Fac.: Ballroom, Club 100, Country Club, Banquet facilities
Sports Fac.: State-of-the-art fitness center, Heated pool, Hot therapy pool, 3 golf courses, Tennis courts
Location: Located in the heart of Indian Wells

Courses: West Course (6643), East Course (6631, par 72)
No. of Holes: 27
Guest Policy: Open to public
Club House: 760-346-4653
Fees: ↑↑↑
Reservations: Reservations available 3 days in advance
Season: Open all year
Carts: Carts included in fees

Renaissance Esmeralda Resort

Address: 44-400 Indian Wells Ln, Indian Wells, 92210
Phone: 760-773-4444
800-552-4386
Fax: 760-773-9250
Web site: http://www.desertresorts.com/esmerald/
No. of Rooms: 560
Rates: $
Restaurant: Sirocco, Charisma
Bar: Las Estrellas lounge
Business Fac.: 56,000 sq ft total, includes: 15,000 sq ft Crystal Ballroom, 32 meeting rooms, 25,000 sq ft of outdoor space.
Sports Fac.: 4 tennis courts, Full health spa, Steam room, Sauna, Massage, 3 swimming pools, Aerobics, Sandy beach in pool, 2 outdoor whirlpools, Beach volleyball, Basketball
Location: 18 miles from Palm Springs

Courses: East Course (6631, par 72), West Course (6500, par 72)
No. of Holes: 36
Guest Policy: Open to public
Club House: 760-346-4653
Fees: ↑ ↑ ↑
Reservations: Can make reservations 3 days in advance
Season: Open all year
Carts: Carts included in fees

At the base of the Santa Rosa Mountains in Indian Wells you'll find this 560-room effort by Stouffer to join the ranks of the major golf resorts in the desert. Rising up seven stories in clusters, the rooms and suites, each with a balcony, face the man-made lake, the lush golf course, or the moutains.

Non-golfers will find plenty of recreation and amusements, ranging from tickets to the venerable Valley Players, the McCallum Theater, Sunday afternoon concerts at the Desert Museum's Annenberg Theater, or a tour of some of the area's best art galleries. Tennis and golf are such big attractions here that it's impossible to miss this celebrity event. You can choose from the Vintage Invitational where you might see Chi Chi, to the Newsweek Champions Cup for a $1 million purse. Have you thought about how much fun the Sled Dog Classic would be? Or how about the polo matches here in the "Winter Polo Capital of the West"?

Seven tennis courts, a full health spa, and three swimming pools (one with a sandy beach entrance) deserve your attention. There are golf and tennis pros eager to help you perfect that swing or improve that serve. There are eateries, lounges, dance floors, poolside snacks, morning walks and cocktail hours all for you to enjoy.

You can tee off at either of the two Indian Wells Golf Resort's Ted Robinson courses. The East Course plays to 6,227 yards and is rated 69.4 from the regular tees. Greens are beautifully manicured, and the cloudless blue sky seems to make even triple-bogey's trivial.

Sands Hotel at Indian Wells

Surrounded by golf, tennis and the scenic splendor of the Palm Springs area, the Sands Hotel at Indian Wells provides a great vacation escape for families and couples alike. One of the finest resorts in the desert area, it is only minutes away from world-class golf, tennis, exquisite shopping, and fine dining.

All hotel accommodations are suites in a condo like setting. Each suite offers a wet bar, coffee maker, refrigerator, microwave oven, dishes and silverware. A balcony or patio overlooking the desert landscape or the outdoor pool and spa. The studio suite has a queen-size Murphy bed (that pulls down when you are ready to retire), a sofa-sleeper, chair and dining room table with four chairs. The one bedroom suite (for a family of four) has a separate living room with sofa-sleeper, separate bedroom with queen size bed and bar or dining room table with four chairs.

Two Ted Robinson-designed 18-hole championship courses are at your disposal. They have a spacious layout with rolling hills and steep slopes. To make the course challenging there are open fairways, large lakes and many traps. It is the former site of the Bob Hope Chrysler Classic PGA Tour event.

Address: 75-188 Highway 111, Indian Wells, 92210
Phone: 760-346-8113
800-874-8770
Fax: 760-568-3698
E-mail: sandshotel@msn.com
Web site: http://www. sandshotel-indianwells.com
Rates: $
Restaurant: Nest Restaurant (adjacent to resort)
Sports Fac.: Swimming pool and spa, 9 hole miniature golf course, Volleyball court, Table Tennis, Playground
Location: In the heart of Palm Springs area

Courses: Golf resort at Indian Wells, East Course, West Course
No. of Holes: 18
Guest Policy: Open to public
Club House: 760-346-4653
Fees: ↑↑↑
Reservations: Call for reservations
Season: Open allyear
Carts: Carts included in fees

Torrey Pines Inn

Address: 11480 N. Torrey Pines Rd,
La Jolla, 92037
Phone: 858-453-4420
800-995-4507
Fax: 858-488-1387
E-mail: sales@
lodgetorreypines .com
Web site: http://www.
lodgetorreypines.com
No. of Rooms: 75
Rates: $
Restaurant: The Golfers Grill,
Seascape Restaurant
Bar: Lantern Lounge
Sports Fac.: Golf, Outdoor swim-
ming pool
Location: 20 miles from San Diego
Airport

Come and stay at a cozy inn by the sea, Torrey
Pines Inn, where tastefully furnished rooms offer
ocean and golf course vistas. You'll be delighted
with the beauty of golden beaches and the Torrey
Pines State Reserve. And there will be plenty to
do … visit the Del Mar Thoroughbred Club and
golf at the Torrey Pines Golf Course's two 18-hole
courses, that is also the home of the San Diego
Open.

Courses: North (6647), South
Course (7055)
No. of Holes: 36
Club House: 858-452-3226
Reservations: Call for reservations
Season: Open all year

La Quinta Resort & Club

During long treks when California was Spanish and Mexican, travel between settlements and missions was arduous. The fifth day was designated as one for good food, music and conviviality, and known as "La Quinta." Some of Hollywood's biggest names including Bette Davis, Ginger Rogers, Erroll Flynn and Frank Capra were regulars at this California desert hideaway. The small luxurious hotel has been expanded and revitalized without losing any of its charm or original flair. Guests stay in adobe Spanish-style casitas and have 45 acres of meticulously landscaped grounds under the imposing Santa Rosa Mountains to explore. Furnishings are expensive contemporary, with a 20's flair.

Swim in any of forty-one pools scattered about the property.

La Quinta is a top tennis resort, and the reasons are obvious. With a tennis stadium, sunken club court, and 23 immaculate courts, (all 3 surfaces), its an impressive setup.

The resort offers 54 holes of Pete Dye's mastery at its best: La Quinta Resort Mountain, La Quinta Resort Dunes, and the world-famous TPC Stadium Golf Course. Look for typical Dye touches such as railroad ties in the center of fairways, big waste bunkers, elevation changes in unexpected spots (greens), and mirror-smooth water hazards. The Jack Nicklaus Tournament Course is ranked among *Golf Magazine*'s "Top 100 Courses You Can Play" in the United states and recently hosted the 2000 PGA Tour Qualifying School.

Address: 49-499 Eisenhower Drive, La Quinta, 92253
Phone: 760-564-4111
800-598-3828
E-mail: accommodations@ kslmail.com
Web site: http://www. laquintaresort.com
No. of Rooms: 920
Restaurant: Morgans, Adobe Grill, Azur by Le Bernardin, Spa Bistro, Mountain Dunes Clubhouse
Bar: Mulligan's Sports & Spirits
Business Fac.: Conference facilities, Professional conference planning staff, Site services, Transportation arrangement, Audio/visual department
Sports Fac.: 90 holes of golf (36 on property, 54 five miles away); 23 tennis courts of all three playing surfaces; Fitness La Quinta, with state-of-the-art fitness equipment, Mind & Movement Studio, tennis pro shop, bicycle rentals and a variety of fitness classes.
Location: 19 miles from Palm Springs Airport

Courses: TPC Stadium Golf Course at PGA West (7266), Jack Nicklaus Tournament Course at PGA West(7204), Greg Norman Course at PGA West (7156), La Quinta Resort Mountain Course (6756) and La Quinta Resort Dunes Course (6747)
No. of Holes: 90
Club House: 800-PGA-WEST
Fees: 1
Reservations: Call for reservations
Season: Open all year

Mount Shasta Resort

Address: 1000 Siskiyou Lake Blvd, Mount Shasta, 96067
Phone: 530-926-3030
800-958-3363
Fax: 530-926-0333
E-mail: msresort@inreach.com
Web site: http://www.
mountshastaresort.com
Rates: $

Course: Mount Shasta Resort (6065, par 70)
No. of Holes: 18
Guest Policy: Open to public
Club House: 530-926-3052
Fees: |
Reservations: Can make reservations 7 days in advance
Carts: Carts available

Come live a mountain high. All of this is available to you in the Mt. Shasta Alpine Valley at 3,500' feet elevation where seasons are vivid and enjoyable. If you're coming to the Mount Shasta Resort just for golf, think again. Mount Shasta and its immediate vicinity have many recreational activities to offer. Even the most avid golfer will feel obligated to bring more than a set of clubs.

When all the day's rigorous activities leave you in need of a little rest, come home to your own private chalet. Curl up by the fire with a special someone or a good book. Soothe your tired muscles in our outdoor hot tub Each chalet is large enough for an evening entertaining friends, either inside or on the open air deck, yet cozy enough for a quiet time alone reflecting or recuperating.

The clubhouse also offers a lovely restaurant with scrumptious California cuisine and a comfortable lounge. Boasting a menu to please all palettes, you'll always find the perfect answer to your craving at our restaurant. With its tasteful decor and expansive views, the Mount Shasta Resort restaurant is the perfect setting for a business lunch, party among friends and family, or a quiet dinner for two. After dinner, enjoy a nightcap in front of the fire in our cozy lounge.

Mount Shasta Resort's challenging 18-hole golf course is rolling, tree-lined, narrow and demanding. Unlike other new, longer courses, this one is designed to be fun, playable, but challenging to all levels of golfers. This course is a public golf course. But anyone who has played this course will tell you there's one thing that sets it apart from all others: The Beautiful Views.

Silverado Country Club & Resort

All of Silverado centers around an historic mansion which was designed to incorporate adaptations of Italian and French architecture. Its surroundings suggested quiet grandeur, and today, guests gather on the terrace overlooking the creek to behold the maze of vineyards, majestic oak, and magnolia trees and manicured gardens.

Silverado Country Club is comprised of individual studios and suites which are private, low-rise clusters around gardens and swimming pools. Vintner's Court, an elegant chandeliered dining room in dusty rose and sand, is a distinctive setting for classic cuisine. The wine list is exclusively Napa Valley.

Eight swimming pools in varying shapes and sizes dot the grounds of the resort, and you'll find the largest tennis complex in the area. This is jogging country, where it's possible to see as many as twenty wineries on an hour's moderate run if you head towards Oakville.

The area is rich in diversions such as the Napa Valley Wine Library, a substantial collection on wine and gastronomy, much of it drawn from winemaker's personal libraries. The other is one of the three great collections of Robert Louis Stevenson materials, which happens to be within sight of the mountain where Stevenson spent his honeymoon in 1881.

Ready for the golf course? Silverado's two courses are almost a dream come true. Maybe not that hole-in-one fantasy, but here are two challenging courses, both by Robert Trent Jones, Jr. Each bear the mark of their distinguished architect—with gigantic trees arching the fairways, and bunkers and greens placed with the touch of an artist. These are championship layouts which host the Transamerica Seniors Tournament, the Northern Cal Open, and many corporate tourneys.

The South Course is the newest of the two. It's a par 72 nicely contoured design with deceiving side-hill lies and over a dozen water crossings. The North Course, also a par 72, stretches to 6700 yards and is occasionally more forgiving. No matter how you play, you'll be treated to some pretty spectacular scenery on these links which have been honored by the National Groundskeepers Association, and by a staff of top professionals. There are ponds, lakes, even three sweet-water creeks, and always, the mystic of the grape.

Address: 1600 Atlas Peak Rd, Napa, 94558
Phone: 707-257-0200
800-532-0500
Fax: 707-257-5400
E-mail: resv@silveradoresort.com
Web site: http://www.
silveradoresort.com
Rates: $$$
Restaurant: Vintner's Court, Royal Oak, Silverado Bar & Grille
Bar: Silverado Bar & Grille, Main Lounge
Business Fac.: Versatile facilities, State-of-the-art audio/visual equipment, Catering and conferences services department
Sports Fac.: World-class spa, 10 swimming pools, Tennis complex, bicycling, Jogging, Walking

Location: 50 miles from Oakland Airport
Courses: South Course (6500), North Course (6700)
No. of Holes: 36
Guest Policy: Open to public
Club House: 800-362-4727
Fees: ↑↑↑
Reservations: Call for reservations
Season: Open all year

Ojai Valley Inn & Country Club

Address: Country Club Road, P.O. Box 1866, Ojai, 93023
Phone: 805-646-5511
800-422-6524
Fax: 805-646-7969
Web site: http://www.ojairesort.com
No. of Rooms: 206
Rates: $$$
Restaurant: Maravilla, Oak Cafe and Terrace, Club Bar, Poolside Snack Bar
Bar: Club Bar
Business Fac.: Topa Center—state-of-the-art facility, in-room fax, Ballroom, Pavilion, Multitude of outdoor spaces
Sports Fac.: Golf, Tennis, Horseback riding, Hiking, Biking, Outward Bound, 3 swimming pools, Daily power walks, Daily water aerobics, Recreation field with softball, soccer, sand volleyball, Children's jungle gym, Lawn croquet
Location: 73 miles north of Los Angeles near Santa Barbara

The setting always was nothing short of incredible, and after its $35 million expansion and renovation, the exclusive retreat of rambling adobe under the towering Topa Topa Mountains continues to attract the elite. Northwest of Los Angeles and 30 minutes east of Santa Barbara, this new addition to the Hilton Group has pulled out all the stops. A new conference center, 108 new guest rooms and suites, and exquisite regional art are a few highlights. A fantastic tennis center, swimming pools, and a chef brimming with impressive credentials and innovative ideas completes the picture. Wines are carefully chosen—many from neighboring vineyards.

Ojai Country Club was one of the first great California golf courses. The course was designed by George C. Thomas, Jr. and Billy Bell, who also are credited with Riviera Country Club, and Bel-Air. Course historians tell us that throughout his career, Thompson never accepted a fee for his services as designer. The scenic natural contours have been retained in the layout's facelift by Jay Moorish, and today's golfer will find a little bit of everything. The new 18 was made more challenging by rebuilding the greens. Plans are underway to host the Southern California Amateur Championship. Try the new driving range, it's one of the best.

Course: Ojai Course (6235, par 70)
No. of Holes: 18
Guest Policy: Open to public
Club House: 805-646-5511
Fees: ⟦⟧
Reservations: Can make reservations 7 days in advance
Season: Open all year
Carts: Carts included in fees

Resort at Squaw Creek

Situated in the heart of Squaw Valley, California, The Resort at Squaw Creek is a 4-diamond luxury resort with 403 guestrooms, nearly half of them suites. The Resort is just steps from its own chairlift into Squaw Valley USA's 4000 skiable acres. Locals and visitors indulge in rugged mountain sports and the leisurely appreciation of the area's spectacular natural resources, including the gem of the Sierra Mountains, Lake Tahoe.

Enjoy superb comfort and privacy in a guesthouse set among the pines. All guestrooms command breathtaking views—ranging from deep forests of ancient Ponderosa to pristine meadowlands with a backdrop of craggy mountain peaks. Windows open to bring in the fresh pine-scented mountain air. Inside, rooms feature such upscale appointments as custom furnishings, original artwork, speaker phones, refrigerator, mini-bar, and individual heating and cooling controls.

Golf Magazine cites our challenging greens as one of the "Top Ten Courses You Can Play." The Resort at Squaw Creek is committed to promoting a high quality, environmentally conscious golf course. Majestically located at the base of Squaw Valley USA at elevation 6200 ft., the Squaw Creek Championship course is par 71 and measures 6,931 yards from the gold tees. The course is designed in a links-style along the mountain and meadow terrain, offering a narrow field of play. The most ecologically sound maintenance practices to ensure a safe haven for both people and wildlife. Situated in the wetlands of Squaw Valley, the course is the culmination of ten years of extensive planning and careful handling of the environment. The spectacular result is a natural golf course that blends with the beautiful surrounding mountains.

Address: 400 Squaw Creek Rd, Olympic Valley, 96146
Phone: 530-583-6300
800-403-4434
Fax: 530-581-6632
E-mail: info@squawcreek.com
Web site: http://www. squawcreek.com
No. of Rooms: 403
Rates: $$$
Location: Five miles from Lake Tahoe in the heart of Squaw Valley

Course: Squaw Creek (6931, par 71)
No. of Holes: 18
Guest Policy: Open to public
Club House: 530-583-6300
Fees: ↑↑↑
Reservations: Can make reservations 30 days in advance
Season: June to October for golf
Carts: Carts included in fees

Desert Springs Marriott Resort & Spa

Address: 74855 Country Club Drive, Palm Desert, 92260
Phone: 760-341-2211
800-228-9290
Fax: 760-341-1872
No. of Rooms: 884
Rates: $
Restrictions: Guide dogs only
Restaurant: The SeaGrille, Mikado, Ristorante Tuscany, The LakeView Restaurant
Bar: Various Lounges
Business Fac.: 51,000 sq ft total, includes: two grand ballrooms, two superdeluxe boardrooms, and a large collection of smaller salons
Sports Fac.: 20 tennis courts, 5 pools, 30,000 sq ft spa/gym, and settings for croquet, lawn chess, boccie, volleyball, basketball, and badminton
Location: 15 miles Southeast of Palm Springs

Courses: Palms Course (6761, par 72), Valley Course (6645, par 72)
No. of Holes: 36
Guest Policy: Open to public, Hotel guests have priorities
Club House: 760-341-1756
Reservations: Can make reservations 14 days in advance, hotel guests—60 days
Season: Open all year
Carts: Carts required

This is the Marriott's flagship hotel, and the 891-room picture of razzle-dazzle and high tech architecture is delivering what it promised. It was quite an attraction when it opened in 1987, complete with Venice-like waterways and a full-service luxury spa. About 13 miles from the Palm Springs airport, this 400-acre resort features everything anyone could want in the way of amenities. There are water views, even though you are in a desert! Nineteen shopping boutiques, complete concierge service, multilingual staff, grand and intimate restaurants, lounges and places to dance await you. Of course, there are beauty shops, a Hertz desk for car rentals, and lots of choices for amusements.

The spa is gigantic-all 27,000 square feet of it. You can be pampered here with steam baths, underwater massages, loofah buffs and a dietary program. Believe it or not, there's a 12,000 square foot beach here, plus two swimming pools and three whirlpools. If you crave tennis, there are 19 courts, with teaching professionals available for private lessons.

Two courses both designed by Ted Robinson opened within a year of each other. Grand palm trees and plenty of water characterize the Palm. The Slope rating for Men's Regular is 114, and for the Valley Course, it's 109.

Shadow Mountain Resort

Discover the warmth and charm of on of America's most relaxing meeting retreats. Come to Shadow Mountain Golf and Tennis Resort … nestled in a sunny cove in the foothills of the majestic Santa Rosa Mountains. The only desert resort within walking distance to the fine restaurants, art galleries and elegant shops of El Paseo, the "Rodeo Drive of the Desert." There are 120 units offering a total of 170 bedrooms, ranging in size from guestrooms to one, two, or three bedroom suites. Each room features patios or balconies, individually air-conditioned, color cable TV, fully equipped kitchenettes or kitchens, and daily maid service.

Recreational amenities offered at Shadow Mountain include 16 championship tennis courts (6 lighted), the highly acclaimed Desert Tennis Academy, 4 pools (including our signature figure 8), saunas, exercise room, massage studio, spas, volleyball, full-court basketball and more.

For a relaxing day, try golfing on one of the 80 plus courses in the Palm Springs area, the "Golf Capital of the World." Most courses are within 15 minutes of Shadow Mountain. The friendly guest service representatives will gladly arrange tee times. Shadow Mountain maintains golf privileges at championship courses in nearby Indian Wells, Rancho Mirage and La Quita.

Address: 45-750 San Luis Rey, Palm Desert, 92260
Phone: 760-346-6123
800-472-3713
Fax: 760-346-6518
E-mail: res@shadowmountain.com
Web site: http://www.shadow-mountain.com
Rates: $$
Business Fac.: Full service catering and conference services
Sports Fac.: 16 tennis courts, Volleyball, water volleyball/basketball, Desert Tennis Academy, Croquet, Ping-Pong, 5 whirlpools, 2 saunas, Horesback riding, Water aerobics, Fitness training, Yoga/stretch classes, Walking, Hiking, Access to other golf courses
Location: 13 miles from Palm Springs Regional Airport in the heart of Palm Desert

Course: Shadow Mountain Golf Course (5800)
No. of Holes: 18
Club House: 760-346-6123
Fees: ⅠⅠ
Reservations: 800-472-6123
Season: Open all year

Mesquite Country Club

Address: 2700 E Mesquite Ave,
Palm Springs, 92262
Phone: 760-293-9611
800-407-8417
E-mail: vacdep@aol.com
Web site: http://www.
vacationdepot.com/mesquitecc.htm
Rates: $$
Restaurant: Clubhouse—fine
dining
Bar: Clubhouse cocktail lounge
Sports Fac.: 16 Swimming pools, 18
Jacuzzis, 8 tennis courts, air condi-
tioned raquetball courts, biking/
jogging/horseback riding trails
Location: In central Palm Springs
with views of the San Jacinto Moun-
tains and the Santa Rosa Mountains

Course: Mesquite Country Club
(6328, par 72)
No. of Holes: 18
Guest Policy: Open to public
Club House: 800-468-4918
Fees: ⫯⫯
Reservations: Tee times 14 days in
advance
Season: Open all year
Carts: Carts required

Relax in the mountain valley splendor of gorgeous
Palm Springs—with the majestic San Jacinto
Mountains as your backdrop, and 180 lushly land-
scaped acres of the gorgeous Mesquite Country
Club as your own backyard. The Mountain View
Villas at Mesquite Country Club offer you all of
the amenities of a top quality resort at a fraction
of the cost.

These warm and intimate villas feature over
900 square feet of cozy comfort, and each is eclec-
tically decorated with exceptional original art,
beautiful pine armoires, comfortable chairs and
sofas, and unique accessories collected from all
over the country. The 2-bedroom/2-bathroom vil-
las have more than 1200 square feet of living
space. Other features to make you feel at home
include 27" stereo TV's, 2nd TV's in the master
bedrooms, CD and VCR players, cordless digital
answering machines, Hunter ceiling fans and
more!

Guests of the Mesquite Country Club have
access to all of the club's 16 swimming pools, 18
Jacuzzis, 8 tennis courts and air conditioned rac-
quetball courts. The Country Club features a club-
house with a very popular restaurant, cocktail
lounge, pro shop, putting green, driving range,
and championship golf course. The Club also
offers extensive trails throughout its 175 acres for
biking, jogging, and horseback riding.

Inn & Links at Spanish Bay

Just outside Palm Springs, where the resorts are endless and the Rolls Royces long, sits this Hyatt. On 34 acres of natural desert terrain, this European-style resort houses 336 all-suite guestrooms, including 289 split-level suites, penthouse suites and garden villas. Twelve suites are equipped for handicapped, and garden suites have butler service in case you forgot to bring yours. Dining rooms, snack bars, lounges and bars are not in short supply. Naturally, you can be served by the pool as you gaze at the cloudless sky. This is one of the few places in North America where you can play golf in 80-degree temperature and (in January and February) see snow-capped peaks of the Santa Rosa Mountains beyond.

Everything is here-from boutiques and modern spa, to babysitting services and a Japanese translator. This is a major resort for meetings, 7,000 square feet of it. After the meetings are over, guests can partake of the resorts recreational facilities. There are four pools and two spas, twelve tennis courts, including grass, clay and hard surfaces, a 10,500-seat stadium court with private enclosed boxes for tournaments, and all sorts of electronic devices to aid your game.

And the golf rates high. Two 18-hole championship courses designed by Ted Robinson, dubbed East and West courses are adjacent to the Hyatt. The property was owned by members of Bob Hope's family. Though the course lacks mature trees, Ted Robinson routed the holes over man-made lakes and through palm groves. Remember that this is a seasonal resort, with some great golf packages available during the warmer months.

Address: 2700 17-Mile Dr, Pebble Beach, 93953
Phone: 831-647-7500
800-654-9300
Fax: 831-644-7960
E-mail: sales@pebblebeach.com
Web site: http://www.
pebble-beach.com/2b.html
No. of Rooms: 270
Rates: $$$
Restaurant: Roy's at Pebble Beach, The Clubhouse Bar & Grill, Traps
Bar: The Clubhouse Bar & Grill, Traps
Business Fac.: World class meeting facilities, State-of-the-art audio/visual tools, Conference services, Catering Department
Sports Fac.: The Tennis Pavillion, The Spanish Bay Club, Outdoor pool, Jacuzzi, Massage, Spanish Bay nature walks, Horseback riding, Jogging, Hiking
Location: 20 minutes south of Monterey Peninsula Airport

Courses: Spanish Bay (6820), Pebble Beach Links (6799), Spyglass Hill (6859)
No. of Holes: 72
Club House: 800-654-7500
Fees: ⌐ ⌐ ⌐
Reservations: Call for reservations
Season: Open all year

Lodge at Pebble Beach

Address: 17 Mile Dr, Pebble Beach, 93953
800-654-9300
Fax: 831-624-3811
E-mail: sales@pebblebeach.com
Web site: http://www.
pebble-beach.com/2a.html
No. of Rooms: 161
Rates: $$$
Restaurant: The Tap Room, Stillwater Bar & Grill, Club XIX, The Gallery
Business Fac.: Offers a variety of elegant & flexible meeting spaces.
Sports Fac.: Beach & Tennis Club, Tennis, Fitness facility, Freshwater outdoor pool, Jacuzzi, Aerobics, Yoga, Massage, Full spa, Equestrian & hiking trails, Jogging
Location: 20 minutes south of Monterey Peninsula Airport

Courses: Spanish Bay (6820), Spyglass Hill (6855), Del Monte (6339), Pebble Beach Golf Links (6799)
No. of Holes: 72
Club House: 800-654-9300
Fees: ↑↑↑
Reservations: Call for reservations
Season: Open all year

Mention Pebble Beach, and note the reactions. Visions of a rugged stretch of ocean-hugging coast. Gnarled cypress trees and fog rolling in. Samuel F. B. Morse, determined to build a golf course, motoring through windswept Del Monte Forest, attracting celebrity players in tournament-ending dramatics. As a landmark destination on scenic 17-mile Drive, the Lodge since 1919 has been the epitome of tranquil dignity. The architecture is California traditional, c. 1919, and void of any vestiges of commercialism. Eleven rooms are available in the main building, which are unpretentiously elegant. 150 are found in 12 separate 2 and 3-story buildings, each offering stunning views of the ocean, gardens, or fairways. The Cypress Room is the main restaurant. Characterized by bouquets of oversized fresh flowers, light woods, natural fabrics in soft colors, Bauscher china and a panoramic view of the bay, the feeling is that of a grand establishment. The Tap Room, ornamented with a fascinating collection of golf mementos, is the spot for conviviality, afternoon or evening. Guests enjoy full privileges at the Beach and Tennis Club, with fourteen plexi-paved courts (stadium court included), and two paddle tennis courts. Perched just above the surf is a heated pool, children's wading pool, viewing deck, and a spa with massage rooms, saunas and exercise studios. Equestrian trails reach every corner of the forest, sea lions bask on the rocks above pounding surf, and the 16 mile drive south of Carmel to Big Sur is a journey not to be missed.

A round of golf here is special, as these courses are among the most famous, and its unusual for tournament-class courses to be available to the public. Both the challenging Robert Trent Jones-designed Spyglass Hill, which traverses dense pine forests and sand dunes, and the Grand Daddy of them all, Pebble Beach Golf Links, are open to the public. These two beautiful courses, together with private Cypress Point, are the home of the prestigious AT&T National Pro-Am, a premier PGA tournament whose players are household names such as Willie Mays, Peter Ueberroth, and George C. Scott. Pebble Beach course starts out along the ocean, then swings back and forth along the coast for holes 4 through 10. 11 through 16 are inland, and 17 and 18 return to the rugged shoreline are second to none as a finish to this supreme course by the sea.

Rancho Bernardo Inn

When the United States regained control in 1846 of what is now San Diego, they found themselves with rich agricultural valleys, a perfect climate (average annual temperature of 72 degrees), and a Mexican-Spanish cultural tie that has spawned a paradise. Rancho Bernardo Inn, thirty miles northeast of downtown San Diego, is a low-slung, red-tiled rambling beauty of low-beamed ceilings, charming small public rooms, and a beautiful view of the San Pasqual Mountains. Add decorative touches of Indian, Mexican and early California artifacts, first-class accommodations, a championship golf course, a spa, excellent conference facilities, and the bottom line is a resort worthy of its accolades.

Composed of 187 rooms including 55 suites, the Inn is enveloped by gardens, old sycamores and pines, and the meandering golf course with its lush fairways and little lakes. Just off the public foyer are smaller hideaways accented by unusual trinkets. A lute, a zither, an ancient accordion, horns, and cymbals of old brass blend in with assorted memorabilia—all part of the Inn's dedication to hospitality in attractive surroundings. Seven haciendas, of varying types, house guests. Decor is casual, yet spacious, with live plants, original artwork, and sliding doors that seem to bring the gardens to you.

Group facilities are sought after for style, attention to detail, and the expert assistance of an assigned coordinator. The 3600 square feet of the Santiago Room, with its own plaza and surrounding garden, is highlighted by a fountain from Vicenza, Italy.

North County is ideal for year round golf. Here one finds a gem of an eighteen hole par 72 course, and three executive nines. William Frances Bell designed the West Course, and the 27 holes of Oaks North was by Ted Robinson, architect of Tokatee in Oregon, and Sahalee Country Club's links in Washington, both rated as top courses. Home of the Honda Civic Classic, the West's 6,388 yards weave through a long, winding valley, with streams and lakes seeming to be everywhere. On the eighteenth hole you drive from an elevated tee. It's a par 5 and the second shot must be placed between a like on the left, and trees on the right. Your shot to the three-tiered green must clear a cascading waterscape across the center front.

Address: 17550 Bernardo Oaks Dr, Rancho Bernardo, 92128
Phone: 858-675-8500
800-542-6096
Fax: 858-675-8501
E-mail: rbisales@jcresorts.com
Web site: http://www.ranchobernardoinn.com
No. of Rooms: 288
Rates: Inquire
Restaurant: Veranda Grille, El Bizcocho, Sports Grille
Bar: Veranda Bar, La Taberna Lounge
Business Fac.: Business Center, Meeting/Banquet facilities, Administrative services
Sports Fac.: Golf, Tennis, Fitness Center, Massage, 2 outdoor pools, 7 Jacuzzis, Jogging trails, Bicycles, Volleyball, Ping-Pong
Location: 30 minutes north of San Diego

Course: Rancho Bernardo (6468)
No. of Holes: 45 (2
Club House: 800-662-6439
Reservations: Call for reservations
Season: Open all year

Marriott's Rancho Las Palmas Resort

Address: 41000 Bob Hope Dr,
Rancho Mirage, 92270
Phone: 760-568-2727
800-458-8786
Fax: 760-568-5845
Web site: http://www.
marriotthotels.com/PSPCA/
No. of Rooms: 444
Rates: $
Restaurant: Pablos Restaurant
(Spanish), Madeira (Mediterra-
nean), Espresso Bar (Coffee House)
Bar: Tortuga Island Bar & Grille,
Casa Lounge
Business Fac.: 41,000 sq ft, includes
10,000 sq ft Fiesta Ballroom, a dozen
conference suites and full-service
business center
Sports Fac.: 25 tennis courts,
health spa & fitness center, Tortuga
island pool and recreation complex
Location: 13 miles from Palm
Springs
Courses: West/North nines (6113,
par 71), North/South nines (6025,
par 71), West/South nines (6128,
par 70)
No. of Holes: 27
Guest Policy: Reciprocal and resort
guests only
Club House: 760-862-4551
Reservations: Make tee times up to
7 days in advance
Season: Open all year
Carts: Carts are required

Marriott's Rancho Las Palmas Resort and Spa is
the relaxing desert retreat of your dreams, with
240 acres of Spanish style charm, tranquil lakes,
brilliant gardens and swaying palm trees. Accommodations include 450 guestrooms, including 22
suites. All rooms have individual climate control,
telephone with message light, color TV, AM/FM
alarm clock radio, cable channels, in-room pay
movies, mini-bar, heat lamp, balcony/patio, cof-
feemaker, data port, high-speed Internet access
and wall safe. There are several wonderful restaurants from which to choose, including Tapas Bar
and Patio and the Madeira Dining Room.

The Spa Las Palmas is a 20,000-square-foot
European Health Spa with full-service salon, fitness center, private pool and restaurant with spa
cuisine. There are three heated outdoor swimming pools; one is a recreation and pool complex
with a 100-foot water slide, water pop-jets, and
play area, and two hydrotherapy pools. Their 25
court tennis complex includes three clay and
eight lighted courts.

Ted Robinson designed the 27-hole on-site
championship golf course. It has narrow fairways
except on the holes that play over the riverbed.
Water comes into play on seven of the 27 holes.

Mission Hills Resort

They call it Playground of Presidents. Rancho Mirage, in the heart of the world-renowned Palm Springs area, is the ideal desert destination. Its superb climate and stunning natural beauty make it an international favorite. Now there's a resort—The Westin Mission Hills—that lets you enjoy all the desert has to offer. The Resort is a full- scale, full- service resort designed in a classic Moorish style reflective of the natural desert environment with extensive recreational facilities. The property is surrounded by the famous 1,760 acre Mission Hills Country Club, home of the Dinah Shore LPGA Classic. It was specifically designed with your entire family in mind—come and enjoy.

Sixteen two-story guestroom pavilions with charming landscaped courtyards, each house an average of 32 of the 512 rooms and suites. A natural garden environment of extensive landscaping and waterways create a welcome departure from high rise structures. Private patios provide spectacular views of the Pete Dye golf course, pools and the surrounding Little San Bernardino and Santa Rosa Mountain Ranges. Interiors, designed and appointed by Concepts Four of Los Angeles feature fully air-conditioned guestrooms, two direct dial telephones with voice mail, computer data lines, stocked refreshment center, private patios, spacious baths with double and triple vanities, remote control cable televisions with in-room movies, vaulted ceilings, alcoves and extra storage.

Westin Mission Hills Country Club features the first Gary Player course in the desert. Rolling with many bunkers and lakes. Millions were spent landscaping this impressive layout. *Golf Magazine* voted it one of the top ten new resort courses. In addition, Pete Dye course opened in 1987, the Resort course has hosted the California State Open, Senior PGA, LPGA, and Nike Tour Qualifying Schools. Pete Dye's trademark railroad ties and pot bunkers are evident from the first tee to the 18th green.

Address: 71501 Dinah Shore Dr, Rancho Mirage, 92270
Phone: 760-328-5955
800-228-0287
Fax: 760-770-2138
E-mail: rancho@westin.com
Web site: http://www.desertresorts.com/westin/

Courses: North Course (7062, par 72), Resort Course (6706, par 70)
No. of Holes: 36
Guest Policy: Open to public
Club House: 760-328-3198
Fees: ↑↑↑
Reservations: Can make reservations 7 days in advance
Season: Open all year
Carts: Carts included in fees

Inn at Rancho Santa Fe

Address: 5951 Linea del Cielo,
P.O.Box 869, Rancho Santa Fe,
92067
Phone: 858-756-1131
800-843-4661
Fax: 858-759-1604
Web site: http://www.
theinnatranchosantafe.com
No. of Rooms: 89
Rates: $$
Restaurant: The Inn's Restaurant
Business Fac.: Fully equipped
conference rooms and hospitality
suites, Trained staff
Sports Fac.: Croquet, Swimming,
Tennis, Walking, Jogging, Gym
Location: 20 miles north of San
Diego

Course: Rancho Santa Fe Golf Club
No. of Holes: 18
Club House: 800-843-4661
Fees: ⅂⅂
Reservations: Call for reservations
Season: Open all year

Partially hidden among towering eucalyptus and
citrus groves, the low, rambling inn remains one
of those spots to which a loyal clientele returns
year after year to enjoy the gentle climate and
hospitality of a family-owned hostelry. Accommo-
dations are in cottages or the main building,
which houses a lounge furnished with family
antiques, including a collection of models of sail-
ing ships. Cottages have secluded porches or sun
decks, and many have fireplaces, kitchens or wet
bars. Diners find many options in a variety of set-
tings. Choose from The Library, book-lined and
cozy, or the Vintage Room, a replica of an early
California taproom which opens onto a patio for
dining and dancing under the stars in summer.
The Garden Room, festooned in flowers, affords a
sweeping view across emerald lawns and pool.
The 20 acres of landscaped grounds provide a
self-contained community offering leisurely
seclusion with a swimming pool, tennis courts,
and croquet. For ocean swimming and sunning,
the inn maintains a beach cottage with showering
and dressing facilities at nearby Del Mar. Within
an hour's drive are Balboa Park and San Diego's
Zoo, shopping and browsing in La Jolla, Sea
World, and the new waterfront complex at San
Diego's Seaport Village.

Inn guests play at private Rancho Santa Fe
Golf Club, a rolling, wooded, challenge designed
by Max Behr, also credited with Pasadena Golf
Club and Hacienda Country Club, and the first
editor of *Golf Illustrated* magazine. The par 72
design claims #13 as its most noteworthy—no
doubt due to a couple of small lakes to be carried.

Alisal Guest Ranch and Resort

Secluded 40 miles north of Santa Barbara, the West Coast's country club of guest ranches dates back to an 18th century. Today, cattle and deer graze on some of the last real California hill country devoted to cattle ranching, and an air of peaceful tranquility reigns over the manicured estate-like grounds.

At the Alisal, you dine on some of the finest food anywhere and never need reservations (Modified American Plan). The Oak Room Lounge, trimmed with handsome Western appointments and a log fire, is the focal point for socializing, with entertainment nightly.

The Alisal, which in Spanish means "sycamore grove," has 7 tennis courts, a private freshwater lake for fishing, boating, sailboats and windsurfs, plus a heated swimming pool, volleyball and shuffleboard. Spacious lawns surround the guest areas.

The Firestone Vineyard, Gainey Vineyard and Zaca Mesa, both within easy reach of the Alisal, are fine examples of the Santa Ynez Valley's emerging wine industry. Visitors can tour the grounds, taste selected current releases and purchase wine. Take a bottle on your picnic, visit a mission or two, shop in quaint Solvang or hike up a tree-shaded canyon.

As a golf resort, the Alisal ranks high. The Ranch course, blends ideally into the natural surroundings of the rolling terrain, dotted by 300 year old trees. This scenic course features four lakes and several holes which border the Santa Ynez River.

Address: 1054 Alisal Road, Solvang, 93463
Phone: 805-688-6411
800-4-ALISAL
Fax: 805-688-2510
E-mail: sales@alisal.com
Web site: http://www. alisal.com
No. of Rooms: 73
Rates: $$$
Restrictions: No Saturday check-ins or check-outs. Two night minimum
Restaurant: Ranch Room, Ranch Grill, River Grill
Bar: Oak Room 5:00p.m.–1:00p.m.
Business Fac.: Combined meeting space of 6000 sq.feet, Unique meeting locations.
Sports Fac.: Heated pool, Jacuzzi, Horseback riding, Sailing, Windsurfing, Pedal boating, Rowing, Fishing, Volleyball, Shuffleboard, Horseshoes, Badminton, 7 tennis courts, Golf.
Location: In the Santa Ynez Valley, 40 miles northwest of Santa Barbara

Courses: The River Course (6500, par 72), Ranch Course (6830, par 72)
No. of Holes: 36
Guest Policy: Ranch course open to resort guests and members only. River course open to public
Club House: 805-688-4215
Fees: ⌐⌐
Reservations: Call for reservations
Season: Open all year
Carts: $28.00 Walking is permitted

Meadowood Resort & Country Club

Address: 900 Meadowood Ln, St. Helena, 94574
Phone: 707-963-3646
800-458-8080
Fax: 707-963-3532
Web site: http://www. meadowood.com
No. of Rooms: 85
Rates: $$$
Restrictions: No pets allowed
Restaurant: The Restaurant, dress code; The Grill, casual
Bar: The Restaurant Lounge
Business Fac.: Message center, Copiers, Audio-visual, Fax, Computer
Sports Fac.: State-of-the-art Health Spa, Whirlpool, Outdoor swimming pools, 7 tennis courts, Hiking trails, 2 croquet lawns, Bicycling
Location: 1 mile east of St. Helena

Course: Meadowood Resort (3869)
No. of Holes: 9
Club House: 707-963-3646
Reservations: 24 hour advance
Season: Open all year
Carts: Carts are also available

What began as a country club for Napa Valley residents a quarter of a century ago, is now a dreamlike resort where you can share the good life with members and local vintners. Your initial impression as you enter along a vineyard-bordered country lane is that you are a guest at a country home with large verandas, lush lawns and wooded hillsides. You'll feel the pulse of the Napa Valley wine and food world here, sequestered on 250 acres of oak and madrone amid buildings patterned after a 1910 New England lodge.

Gastronomes and neophytes alike will marvel at the immersion into the world of the finest Napa Valley wines, and a chef dedicated to a cuisine reflecting simple, imaginative fresh fare. Overlooking the golf course, the casual bistro-style of the Fairway Grill will tempt you with lighter salads, fresh grilled fish, and a sampling of the neighboring vineyards offered by the glass. As shadows lengthen, you might want to savor the magic of this unhurried paradise with a wedge of Doux de Montagne and a glass of local cabernet. Warm evenings lure diners outside to the terrace for dinner under the stars.

The secluded enclave offers six tennis courts, a swimming pool, miles of walking and jogging trails, a par course and a croquet court built to comply with international standards.

The valley's fame, and thus its drawing card, rests largely with its climate—ideally suited to growing the Cabernet Sauvignon grape, with Pinot Noir not far behind. Meadowood offers unique courses in wine and food appreciation, as well as hosting the annual Napa Valley Wine Auction in June. The concierge will be happy to assist you with arrangements to local wineries, the mud and mineral baths of Calistoga, quaint nearby shops, hot air ballooning, or maybe you deserve a laid back afternoon of gliding over the panoramic valley. If you'd like to explore some of the area's more renowned eateries, the list is mind-boggling.

There's a nine-hole executive course here with four par fours and five par threes. The par 62 layout winds around California Live Oak lined fairways which are tight, but demand accuracy. Players of all levels, genders and ages await the Century Pro-Am, a scratch best-ball 18-hole event in which the combined ages of partners must be at least 100 years.

Northstar-at-Tahoe

Tahoe has long been a destination for those seeking the serenity of the clear deep waters of its large lake, the grand peaks of the Sierra Nevada, and its proximity to the glitter of the Nevada casinos. The development is a year-round mecca for those yearning for a mountain resort with family activities in northern California. Wooden buildings with a rustic flair blend well with the environment, yet lodging facilities, ranging from hotel rooms to condominiums, are comfortable without being cutesy. There are several good restaurants in Truckee, a short drive away, and within the resort there are several choices. A cozy bar serves libations; you could try the Basque club for dinner; there is a good pizza place on the premises; and a fully stocked deli is there to help you fill the refrigerator.

You can play tennis, take off on a hiking trail for vistas without parallel, swim in the Olympic-size pool, or see about tubing down the Truckee, a favorite with kids. The resort's stables could provide a gentle mount, or you could take a picnic and kites to a meadow. Fishing, bicycling, rock climbing, or sailing on the lake are options worth considering. Children thrive here, and there are programs for every age.

As for golf, the older nine meanders through groves of tall pines and aspen, with Martis Creek twisting around to haunt you. The front nine, by Robert Muir Graves, hugs the valley, which was sheep country be developers came. Slope ratings are 130 Championship, and 113 Regular.

The Day Camp offers educational and recreational activities for children 2-10 from late June through Labor Day. The facility is licensed for child care.

Address: P.O. Box 129, Truckee, 96160
Phone: 530-562-1010
800-GO-NORTH
E-mail: northstar@boothcreek.com
Web site: http://www.
skinorthstar.com
No. of Rooms: 250
Rates: $
Restaurant: Timbercreek Restaurant, Martis Valley Grille
Sports Fac.: Moutain Biking, Swim & Raquet Club, 10 tennis courts, Spas, Lap pool, Workout room, Game room, Saunas, Massage therapist, Olympic-size heated pool, Kids activities, Horseback riding, Hiking
Location: Minutes from Lake Tahoe's North Shore

Course: Northstar Course (6897, par 72)
No. of Holes: 18
Guest Policy: Open to public
Club House: 530-562-2490
Fees: ⌐
Reservations: Call for reservations
Season: Open all year
Carts: Can walk 9, must have cart for 18

Hyatt Regency Beaver Creek

Address: P.O. Box 1595, Avon, 81620
Phone: 970-949-1234
800-233-1234
Fax: 970-949-4164
Web site: http://www.hyatt.com/
usa/beaver_creek/hotels/
hotel_beave.html
No. of Rooms: 295
Rates: $$$
Restaurant: Patina, McCoy's,
Crooked Hearth, Double Diamond
Deli
Business Fac.: Business Center,
Meeting & Banquet facilities, Ind. or
master controls for AC/heat, Sound,
Telephones, Multiple electrical/
microphone outlets, Special lighting
effects, Indoor/outdoor fireplaces
Sports Fac.: Allegria Spa, Heated
pool, Indoor/outdoor whirlpools,
Fully-equipped health club, Full-
service spa, Jogging paths, Bicycling
trails, Golf
Location: 8 miles west of Vail

Course: Beaver Creek (6646, par
70)
No. of Holes: 18
Guest Policy: Open to public
Club House: 970-949-7123
Fees: ⏇
Reservations: Reservations avail-
able 90 days in advance
Season: May 1–November 1
Carts: Carts included in fees

Vail is about 100 miles west of Denver, and Beaver Creek is just another 10 miles further. You won't find the crowds of Vail, but rather, a well-designed resort community planned around residences. Best of all, the vertical drops of the Rockys, the aspen glades, and the soothing, clear blue skies add up to the incredible scenery. This resort, finished in 1898, is a meld of Alpine architecture and contemporary high Rocky Mountain style, with regional stone and local pine used throughout, as well as area antiques as accents. The mountain resort has full conference facilities, boutiques, restaurants, health club facilities, and a host of summer activities. Guest rooms have marble baths, oversized beds with airy down comforters, and vistas of the mountains and valleys. If trout fishing is your sport, you're in for a treat. Also activities include whitewater rafting, horseback riding and plenty of tennis. Guests can take the Centennial chairlift up the mountain for a scenic guided tour across and down the slopes, or ride horseback to Beano's Cabin for dinner.

If you can drag yourself out of the "Top Resort Shop in Colorado" (1988 and 1989), you'll agree that the vistas on this Robert Trent Jones, Jr., course are memorable. Located in the upper end of the Beaver Creek Valley, it runs the gamut from alpine wilderness to parkland and meadows, with a meandering stream that beckons those way-ward balls when spring runoff turns quiet brooks into torrents. The narrow terrain dictates keeping the ball in control. Carts are mandatory, and you'll have to leave your pull cart in the closet on this layout where the Slope for Men's Regular is 128.

Omni Interlocken Resort

Gateway to the pristine beauty of the Rocky Mountains with their multitude of recreational opportunities, the first luxury resort in north Denver, the Omni Interlocken Resort is located just outside of Boulder. It is a magnificent 11-story hotel, where the offerings range from a full-service health club and spa to fine dining, first-class accommodations, and a 34,000-square-foot conference center. The outdoor attractions include a sparkling pool and whirlpool, 27-hole championship golf course and driving range, and more than 15 miles of scenic trails for jogging, hiking, and biking.

390 comfortable guestrooms and suites, some guestrooms have balconies offering spectacular views of the mountains or the valley. All rooms are equipped with two-line phones, voice mail and dataports with high-speed Internet access. Other amenities include mini-bar, private safe, ironing board and hair dryer.

For your dining pleasure, The Meritage restaurant features a grand stone fireplace and an outdoor patio. The TapRoom restaurant and bar features classic pub fare in a relaxed atmosphere with game tables and entertainment. Fairways restaurant in the clubhouse offers casual dining complimented by spectacular views of the golf course and mountains. There are beautifully landscaped courtyard areas suitable for dining, entertainment and private functions. The Lobby Bar is a casual gathering spot located just off the lobby atrium serving cocktails, hors d'oeuvres, afternoon tea and evening desserts.

A Grand Ballroom, Junior Ballroom and 7 self-contained meeting rooms meet all conference needs. Ballroom pre-function areas offer spectacular views of the golf course. Three meeting rooms have floor to ceiling windows, creating a harmonious balance between the bright outdoors and the no-nonsense conference environment.

With more than 400 feet in elevation changes, the course offers a stunning panoramic view of the Colorado Rockies. From the Vista's fourth hole, one can see from the Front Range of Pike's Peak in the South to Long's Peak in the North, along with views of downtown Denver and the eastern plains. Stretching over 300 acres, this rolling 7,100 yard, par 72 course provides a truly exceptional experience for the pro or amateur golfer.

Address: 500 Interlocken Blvd, Broomfield, 80021
Phone: 303-438-6600
800-THE-OMNI
Fax: 303-438-7224
Web site: http://www.omnihotels.com
No. of Rooms: 390
Rates: $
Restaurant: Meritage, Fairways Restaurant & Bar
Bar: Lobby Bar, Tap Room
Business Fac.: 34,000 sq ft conference center, includes: two ballrooms, boardroom, 8 breakout rooms, plus full-service business center and up-to-date audiovisual capability
Sports Fac.: driving range, swimming pool, health club and spa, over 15 miles of trails for jogging/biking
Location: 20 minutes from downtown Denver

Courses: Vista Course (3521, par 36), Sunshine (3519, par 36), Eldorado (3436, par 36)
No. of Holes: 27
Guest Policy: Open to public, resort guests get discount
Club House: 303-464-9000
Fees: ⌐
Reservations: Public—14 days in advance, Guests—30 days in advance
Season: Open all year
Carts: Cart included in fees

Broadmoor

Address: PO Box 1439, Colorado
Springs, 80901
Phone: 719-634-7711
800-634-7711
Fax: 719-577-5700
E-mail: info@broadmoor.com
Web site: http://www.
broadmoor.com
No. of Rooms: 700
Rates: $$$
Restaurant: Charles Court, The
Golden Bee, Golf Club Grille, Julie's,
Lake Terrace Dining Room,
Primrose Room
Bar: Stars' Club & Cigar Bar, The
Tavern, Terrace Lounge
Business Fac.: 110,000 sq ft of
meeting space, complete inventory
of high-tech equipment, Skilled
technicians, Conference staff
Sports Fac.: Spa, 12 tennis
courts,90,000 sq ft Fitness Center,
Aerobics,16 massage rooms, 6 facial
rooms, 12 mineral-bath tubs,
Indoor/outdoor pools, Fly fishing,
Biking, Walking, Running trails,
Ballooning, riding stables
Location: Southwestern edge of
Colorado Springs, CO

Courses: East Course (7091, par
72), West Course (6832, par 72),
Mountain/South Course (6781, par
72)
No. of Holes: 54
Guest Policy: Open to guests only
Club House: 719-577-5790
Fees: ↑↑↑
Reservations: Can make reserva-
tions one year in advance
Season: Open all year
Carts: Carts included in fees

Breathe deeply, inhale the rich forest scent of firs
and pines. Contemplate Cheyenne Mountain's
mysteries. At home in the Rockies since 1918, the
Broadmoor is a pivotal landmark of tradition,
offering year round activity in fabulous weather.

The Broadmoor diner enjoys a full circle of
renowned and award-winning restaurants from
the haute cuisine under gilt-encrusted cherubs of
the Penrose Room to the rollicking fun of an
authentically-constructed 18th century English
pub. A new menu promises lighter entrees with a
hint of nouvelle cuisine. A good wine list featuring
some of Napa Valley's and Europe's finest, invites
your deliberation.

There are literally 101 things to do in this
Shangri-la of recreational facilities and contem-
porary comfort. Should I shoot skeet and trap?
Line up a tennis game, swim, rent a paddle boat,
join a bicycling tour, ice skate, go trout fishing,
head for a wicket on the croquet lawn, hike up, or
think about, Pike's Peak, play squash, or try shuf-
fleboard? If you're one for spectator sports, you'll
find everything from the Men's Regional Playdown
in Curling to the Annual Pike's Peak Auto Hill
Climb in July. The resort is crawling with activity
and interests. Where else can you visit an Olympic
Training Center, a Rodeo Hall of Fame, and top it
off with a massage in your room?

Championship golf has had a colorful history
at Broadmoor since the first course, designed by
Donald Ross, opened in 1918. During World War
II, Bing Crosby, Bob Hope, Ed Dudley and L. B.
Maytag played an exhibition match here and all
the proceeds were used to build a driving range at
nearby Peterson Field for military personnel. The
golf is demanding and enjoyably hilly on all three
courses. West Course was designed by Robert
Trent Jones, and completed in 1965, while the
third championship course (South) by Ed Seay,
was ready for play in 1976. The greens on all
courses are treacherously fast, and a subtly undu-
lating requiring deft touch and keen eye.

Morning to evening children's program called
the Bee Bunch for ages 5 through 12. The Toddler
Bee Bunch is designed for ages 3 through 4. There
are zoo trips, games, paddle boating, scavenger
hunts, and for the older children golf and tennis
clinics. There are also evening activities offered.
The Bee Bunch is $40, Toddler Bee is $25 (lunch
is included).

Copper Mountain Resort

Copper mines once dotted the Ten Mile Range peaks, followed by fishermen and sheep herders in search of near-perfect alpine meadows. Today's visitor, hoping to rejuvenate the body and repair the spirit, will find just about everything at this vacation destination 70 miles west of Denver.

Bring your bike, fishing gear, tennis clothes, hiking boots, bathing suit, camera—or leave it behind and breathe in the crisp mountain air as you ponder the activities. This is a family-type development with accommodations ranging from hotel rooms to 4-bedroom townhomes. There are a variety of restaurants, shops and sporting facilities. You can take Jeep tours through the mountain peaks, visit historic sites and old mining camps, or take a whitewater rafting trip through one of Colorado's incredible canyons. The bike trails access some of the nation's most scenic paths with over 40 miles extending west to Vail and east to Breckenbridge, and serious cyclists should check out the week-long cycling camp. Who can resist mid-mountain bicycling that includes a chairlift ride and bike lift? Not enough exercise? Try a pack trip on the gentle horse, a sunrise canoe excursion or an hour or two in the Racquet and Athletic Club.

At an elevation of 9,650 feet, this is the highest 18-hole golf course America offers. The Pete and Perry Dye course follows the natural terrain of the spectacular Rocky Mountain area and wraps its way through wooded pines, ponds, and Ten Mile Creek. It's a par 70 course, short and tight, with the Dye trademarks of railroad-tie lakes, bulkhead tee boxes, and some deep sand and pot bunkers. With a gorgeous view of snowcapped peaks framed by pines, the par 3, 168-yard 17th hole is our favorite. Slope rating is 115 Regular Men's, and the wildflower rating in May is off the charts.

Address: 209 Ten Mile Circle, PO Box 3001, Copper Mountain, 80443
Phone: 970-968-2882
888-219-2441
Fax: 970-968-6227
E-mail: wc@ski-copper.com
Web site: http://www. ski-copper.com/index2.html
Rates: Inquire
Business Fac.: 50,000 sq ft of flexible meeting space, divided among 3 distinct villages suited for different meeting types: Center Village (which includes Copper Conference facility), East Village, and the Preserve at West Village
Sports Fac.: Athletic Club, indoor pool, workout room, Jacuzzi, steam room
Location: Nestled in the Ten Mile and Gore Wilderness ranges

Course: Copper Creek
No. of Holes: 18
Guest Policy: Open to public
Club House: 970-968-2318
Fees: ⸋
Reservations: Call for reservations
Season: June 1–October 15

Tamarron

Address: 40292 US Hwy 550 N, PO
Box 3131, Durango, 81302
Phone: 970-259-2000
800-678-1000
Fax: 970-259-0745
E-mail: info@tamarron.com
Web site: http://www.
tamarron.com
No. of Rooms: 400
Rates: Inquire
Restaurant: San Juan, Le Canyon
Business Fac.: Conference rooms,
capacity 500
Sports Fac.: Tennis courts, Rafting,
Fishing, Swimming pool
Location: 18 miles north of Durango

Course: Tamarron Resort (6885)
No. of Holes: 18
Guest Policy: For owners, members
and resort guests
Club House: 970-259-2000
Reservations: 24 hours in advance
if not on package
Season: May–October

Here are found today's conveniences amidst the
charm and rusticity of a mountain getaway. A scenic 18 miles north of Durango, and tucked away
in a 20-mile valley guarded by the San Juan
National Forest, Tamarron's focal point is a main
lodge perched on a stone cliff overlooking a rolling alpine meadows.

Guest activities center around the main lodge,
and here is where you'll find elegant Le Canyon,
and the San Juan Dining Room, as well as the
Caboose Cafe for afternoon and evening snacks.
Nightly entertainment livens up the San Juan
Lounge. A car isn't a necessity here, as an extensive transportation system services the airport,
local sights such as historic Durango, and shuttles
guests around the property.

A full range of outdoor sports facilities including tennis courts, an indoor swimming pool, plus
horseback riding, jeep tours, and a spa and health
club await family vacationers and those coming
for meetings.

Southwestern Colorado, near the only point in
the country common to four state corners, is ideally situated for exploring the area's history and
culture. A short trip will bring you to Chimney
Rock, and the Navajo State Recreation area. Railroad buffs can journey up the Animas River Gorge
to the mining town of Silverton.

The golf course, an Arthur Hills design, offers
a little of everything. Although the green is large,
it's almost totally surrounded by monstrous sand
traps, plus water to the left and to the left rear.
This is ranked as one of Colorado's more difficult
courses.

Lodge at Cordillera

The Lodge at Cordillera is a place where you'll be awestruck by Nature's power and simplicity. Where you'll see deer and elk move weightlessly through forests of Aspen, Blue Spruce, and Douglas Fir. Where adventure, discovery and extraordinary personal service and comfort combine in a unique and quiet manner to rejuvenate, invigorate, and revive you. The Lodge at Cordillera offers extraordinary vistas from every guestroom and suite. Rooms include direct dial telephones, TV, balcony, fireplace, refrigerators and room service. You can also enjoy a champagne lunch basket for your picnic on the Lodge's private trail, or savor a gourmet meal at Cordillera's Restaurant Picasso.

Challenge the rugged terrain on horseback, mountain bike or Nordic skis. Surrender to the exuberance of white water rafting, or the quiet finesse of fly-fishing on their private reserve. Let the setting sun warm your body as the Spa's masseuse revitalizes you. Then slide into a hot tub under a shower of stars. Highlights of the facility include a 25-meter lap pool, Jacuzzis, steam rooms, sauna, and a fully equipped exercise room.

The Hale Irwin Signature golf course faithfully conforms to its rugged mountain setting. Dramatic changes of elevation test your skills while dazzling you with truly incredible views of the snow-capped Sawatch and Gore mountain ranges.

Address: 2205 Cordilla Way, PO Box 1110, Edwards, 81632
Phone: 970-926-2200
800-87-RELAX
Fax: 970-926-2486
E-mail: thelodgeandspa@cordillera-vail.com
Web site: http://www.cordillera-vail.com
No. of Rooms: 56
Rates: $$$
Restaurant: Restaurante Picasso, Chaparral Steakhouse, Timber Hearth Grille, Grouse-on-the-Green
Bar: Grouse-on-the-Green
Business Fac.: 3 Conference Rooms
Sports Fac.: Indoor/outdoor swimming pools, Jacuzzi, Free weights, Tetrix exercise bicycles, Treadmill, Rowing machine, Pilates room, Paramount lifting equipment, Steam & saunas, Nordic Center, Hiking, Tennis, Mountain Biking
Location: 25 minutes west of Vail & Beaver Creek ski areas

Courses: Mountain Course (7444), Valley Course, Short Course (1252, par 27), Summit Course
No. of Holes: 45
Guest Policy: Open to public
Club House: 970-926-5100
Fees: ⛳⛳
Reservations: Reservations available 1 day in advance
Season: Open all year
Carts: Carts included in fees

Keystone Resort

Address: P.O. Box 38, Keystone, 80435
Phone: 970-496-2316
888-830-SNOW
Fax: 970-756-8844
E-mail: keystoneinfo@ vailresorts.com
Web site: http://www. keystoneresort.com
Rates: Inquire
Restaurant: 24+restaurants, from fine dining to casual, family style.
Bar: Ida Belle's
Business Fac.: Conference Center, award winning facilities, Conference Service Manager on hand for aide.
Sports Fac.: Biking, Hiking, White-water rafting, Tennis courts, Fitness center, Horseback riding
Location: In the heart of the Colorado Rockies

Courses: The Keystone Ranch Golf Course (7090, par 72), The River Course at Keystone (6816, par 71)
No. of Holes: 36
Guest Policy: Open to public
Club House: 970-496-4250
Fees: ↑↑
Reservations: Reservations available 7 days in advance
Season: May–October
Carts: Carts included in fees

Say Keystone and envision one of Colorado's great intermediate ski complexes. However, when it all melts, the terrain presents an entirely different facade. About 75 miles west of Denver, this self-contained resort is set in a boundless valley of green meadows and thick pine forests. The main lodge houses 152 rooms, with more than 900 condominiums nestled among the pines.

Three restaurants are found within the main hotel, and many more are found on the grounds, where visitors can dine on anything from sushi to pizza. The tennis center features 12 courts; two are lighted for night play, and an extensive pro shop for clothing and equipment awaits your plastic. Swimmers can choose from several pools, as well as saunas and Jacuzzis. Summer in Keystone is a time for theater, hiking, family reunions, cycling, sailing on Lake Dillon, and trout fishing.

Discover the dramatic distances of your tee shots on the Robert Trent Jones, Jr., layout that is characterized by an interesting variety of holes. With its dense pines, rolling green hills, blue sagebrush, marshland, high native grasses and a nine-acre lake, this course is reminiscent of legendary English and Scottish courses. Beginning holes are high and windswept, and the fourth drops to the valley floor, where boggy swales, sagebrush and buffalo grass remind one of Carnoustie. The eighth is the hole everyone remembers. The par 4 begins with 175 yards of low scrub, then heads uphill where you have to dodge four bunkers. Several weather-worn abandoned wooden buildings, remnants of an 1870s homestead, stand to remind us of a once-thriving vegetable and cattle operation. Slope rating here is 130.

Snowmass Lodge & Club

While Aspen is chic, sophisticated and caters to jet-setters, its neighbor 8 miles away bills itself as "the perfect family vacation." The Aspen/Snowmass area is a premier ski destination during winter for world-class downhill skiing, but when the snow thaws in spring, the golf is delightful. The three-story 76-room lodge with surrounding golf course and tennis courts has the look of a country club and the atmosphere of an Old World exclusive lodge. Gleaming hardwood floors, exposed beams, historic photographs and pine furniture reflect the western ambiance and the lore of the Rockies. You might prefer the Club Villa condominiums within the resort. Summer visitors can opt for tennis, two outdoor pools, and a full athletic club, while children stay at the on-site nursery and child care center. Aspen, with its shops, eateries and night life is only a short drive away.

Views of majestic Mount Daly provide a backdrop for the Ed Seay designed "thinking man's" golf course. Bentgrass tees and greens, rolling bluegrass fairways, water hazards on hole #13, and 64 sandtraps offer challenge, and your ball really does fly farther at this elevation. At 8,100 feet above sea level, this par 71, 6,894 yard course would be equivalent to about 6,400 yards at a seaside layout. Golf here generally begins in early May and goes until the snow flakes hit the greens (mid to late October). Carts aren't mandatory, but are strongly recommended due to the elevation. This 18 hole test is rated 126 on the USGA Slope System.

Address: 0239 Snowmass Club Dr, Box G-2, Snowmass Village, 81615
Phone: 970-923-5600
800-525-0710
Fax: 970-923-0896
E-mail: amdenney@skiaspen.com
Web site: http://www. snowmasslodge.com
No. of Rooms: 61
Rates: $
Restrictions: No pets allowed
Restaurant: Sage, Racquet Bar, Daly Beach Club/Pool Bar
Business Fac.: Message center, Administrative assistance, Copiers, Audio-visual, Fax
Sports Fac.: 13 outdoor/indoor tennis courts, Outdoor swimming pools, Hiking, Biking, Downhill & Cross-country skiing
Location: Mountain resort, 10 miles west of Aspen

Course: Snowmass (6894)
No. of Holes: 18
Guest Policy: Guests may book 2 weeks in advance
Club House: 970-923-5600
Reservations: Inquire at golf shop
Season: May–October

Sheraton Steamboat Springs Resort

Address: 2200 Village Inn Ct, P.O. Box 774808, Steamboat Springs, 80477
Phone: 970-879-2220
800-848-8878
Fax: 970-879-7686
E-mail: sheraton_steamboat@sheraton.com
Web site: http://www. steamboat-sheraton.com
No. of Rooms: 440
Rates: Inquire
Restrictions: Pets limited
Restaurant: Remington's, 19th Hole Bar & Grill
Bar: H.B.'s
Business Fac.: Administrative assistance, Fax, Conference rooms, capacity 785
Sports Fac.: 2 Swimming pools, Tennis courts, Ice skating, Fitness room
Location: Rocky Mountain Park

Course: Sheraton Steamboat (6276)
No. of Holes: 18
Guest Policy: Call for availability
Club House: 970-879-2220
Reservations: Tee time given with room reservation
Season: Late May–late October

Named for its hissing thermal springs, this family resort area, known primarily as a wintertime haven is now being rediscovered for its summer recreational opportunities. Located 150 miles northwest of Denver, and surrounded by Rocky Mountain National Park, and Routt National Forest, the town, more than 100 years old, attracts those seeking superb conference facilities, and quiet sophistication. This is the perfect place for those seeking dry heat, moderate temperatures, and alpine vistas. Statistic buffs will note that the Continental Divide, separating the river systems which flow to opposite sides of the continent, is a stone's throw away.

There's plenty of room here—400 rooms, 3 suites, and Thunderhead Lodge with 58 rooms plus 75 condominium units. Complete conference facilities and a concierge, 4 lively bars and 5 restaurants insure a good time for everyone. Cipriani's is the signature restaurant and features northern Italian cuisine with specialties such as Funghi Genevese and Salmone Alle Nocciole. Your meal isn't complete without hazel nut souffle with zabaglione.

Hot air balloon enthusiasts can get a bird's eye view of the area, and hikers will have the trails virtually to themselves. Whitewater rafting is at your doorstep, just ask the concierge to arrange it. You'll find 2 outdoor pools, tennis, nearby sailing, hot tubs, sauna and massage, horseback riding and some of the best trout fishing anywhere.

This is mountain high golf for all abilities, designed by Robert Trent Jones, Jr. in 1972. When the wildflowers burst forth in spring, and the only sound is Fish Creek babbling, you'll know the meaning of a Rocky Mountain High. This par 72 course is characterized by some great water holes, large greens, and spectacular fall colors. Greens are bentgrass while fairways and tees are bluegrass. #10 is a par 5, requiring length and accuracy off the tee to reach the green in two. Lay up shot is generally recommended, as a clear Colorado stream protects the green.

Peaks at Telluride

Set at 9,500 feet in the San Juan Mountains, the resort is surrounded by the 14,000 foot plus mountains on three sides. The mountains are the real stars here, and the environment is carefully tended to keep it that way. The lavish rooms have their own private terraces that offer magnificent views of the mountains and surrounding valley. Featured is oak woodwork, large windows with a view, down comforters, and oversized bathrooms with jacuzzi.

The health spa at The Peaks is among the top three in the country. The spa offers programs that you won't find anywhere else, and uses natural products indigenous to Colorado. Among the other spa features are facials, body treatments, different massage techniques, and a full-service beauty salon. Also offered is a rock climbing wall, cardiovascular deck, Cybex weight room, a water slide that connects an indoor lap pool to a lower indoor/outdoor pool, and much, much more!

Dining at Telluride is a wonderful experience with a very innovative kitchen, and Peaks Performance Spa Cuisine for the health conscious as well. Dining on the sun deck and the outdoor pool area, weather permitting, offers marvelous panoramic views of the surrounding mountains.

You've come to the right place if you enjoy the outdoors with skiing, snowshoeing, heli-skiing, cross-country all available in the winter. The summer offers some of the best hiking around, with Mt. Wilson in the background for the accomplished climbers, championship golf and jeep tours.

The golf course is somewhat hilly and heavily lined with aspens. There is some water and a four-tiered green. You should find the mountain views distracting, but on this championship course you really need to pay attention. Telluride Golf Academy offers private and clinic instruction by a PGA professional.

The KidSpa program is for children of all ages and offers exploration and learning as well as fun. The Explorers is for ages 2½ through five, and the Mountaineers is for those six through eleven. The activities are seasonal and make use of the outdoors and well as indoors.

Address: P.O. Box 2702, Telluride, 81435
Phone: 970-728-6800
800-789-2220
Fax: 970-728-6175
E-mail: info@thepeaksresort.com
Web site: http://www.thepeaksresort.com
No. of Rooms: 174
Rates: $$$
Restaurant: The Sundance, Legends
Business Fac.: Audio/visual equipment, Off-property meeting sites, Conference Center
Sports Fac.: Snowmobiling, Horseback riding, Snowshoeing, Dog sledding, Ice skating, Cross-country skiing, Sleigh rides, Air Garden, Skiing, Gold Mine Treks, Mountain biking, Fly-fishing, Hikes, Tennish, Rock climbing, Squash, Pool, Weight room, Fitness classes
Location: 10 minutes from Telluride

Course: Telluride Golf Club (6739, par 71)
No. of Holes: 18
Guest Policy: Open to public
Club House: 970-728-6157
Fees: ↑↑↑
Reservations: 2 days in advance
Season: June–September
Carts: Electric cart included in fees

Sonnenalp Resort of Vail

Address: 20 Vail Rd, Vail, 81657
Phone: 970-476-5656
800-654-8312
Fax: 970-476-1639
E-mail: info@sonnenalp.com
Web site: http://vail.net/lodging/
sonnenalp/index.html
No. of Rooms: 150
Rates: $$
Restaurant: King's Club, Bully
Ranch, Swiss Chalet, Ludwig's
Business Fac.: 7 conference rooms
with state of the art equipment,
Audio/visual
Sports Fac.: Alpine/Nordic skiing,
Snowshoeing, Full service health
spa, Yoga, Indoor/outdoor swim-
ming pools, Hot tubs, Practice
range, Tennis, Hiking, White-water
rafting
Location: 30 minutes from Eagle
County Regional Airport

Course: Sonnenalp (7059, par 71)
No. of Holes: 18
Guest Policy: Open to public
Club House: 970-926-3533
Fees: ↑↑↑
Reservations: Reservations avail-
able 1 day in advance
Season: March–November
Carts: Carts available

A family-owned hotel, the Sonnenalp is a roman-
tic spot with memorably delicious food and the
kind of personal attention conducive to large
numbers of repeat guests. Nestled in Vail Village's
central area are the three separate houses that
comprise the 165-room resort. Nothing is stodgy
here—public areas, rooms and suites are light
and comfortably elegant, ceilings are hand-
painted with carved beams, rooms open onto
flower-filled balconies, and the cushions are
down-filled. Breakfast is included, and what a
sumptuous feast!

There are several options for dining, gathering
for cocktails, or sharing a traditional Swiss
raclette and fondue. There are four bars and four
restaurants within the hotel. Try an hour in the
hotel's sauna, or swim in one of the two outdoor
pools and stop by the cozy bar for a thirst-
quencher.

Sonnenalp Golf Club, rated on of America's top
75 resort courses by *Golf Digest*, is accessible by
hotel van provided for guests. The course lies in
an open, sunny valley, alongside wildflower-cov-
ered foothills, with plenty of sagebrush and rocky
terrain to give you a sense of a Scottish-style
course. Greens are among the finest putting sur-
faces anywhere, and you'll have a driving range,
putting green and sand bunkers on which to prac-
tice. Slope rating here is 134 Regular Men's. If
you've been threatening to lower your handicap,
consider a session at one of the *Golf Digest*
Instructional Schools, held here during the sum-
mer.

Amelia Island Plantation

Imagine a 1250-acre island of undisturbed primeval marshlands and lagoons where egrets and herons nest, towering sand dunes, lush foliage draped in Spanish moss, all bordered by a four mile wide white beach. This is Amelia Island, where Indians fished and hunted, where pirates roamed to bury treasure, and where the flags of eight different nations have flown in the past four hundred years. This unspoiled paradise is the northern most barrier island on Florida's east coast, just twenty-nine miles northwest of Jacksonville.

Dining at Amelia Island Plantation can be as elegant as candlelight, champagne and Pheasant with Wild Mushrooms and Walnut Sauce in the Dune Side Club overlooking the Atlantic, or as casual as a hamburger at the Coop. Should you choose dinner at the Veranda, you'll find the freshest seafood the coastal waters offer. Cocktails and after-dinner drinks are served in the Admiral's Lounge, featuring live music, or try the Beach Club's lively disco.

In addition to the wide, breeze-swept beach, there are twenty-five tennis courts, horseback riding, a fully-equipped Health and Fitness Center, swimming pools, and paddleboats. The island's waters are teeming with gamefish, and arrangements can be made to set up sailing, historical river cruises and fishing trips for sailfish and marlin. Whiting, sea trout and bluefish can be caught from the beach. Jogging trails entice you to explore marsh edges, sea oats and pine forests.

You'll want to combine play at Long Point with a round or two at Amelia Links, Pete Dye's 27-hole masterpiece (its the only resort in the world with golf courses by both Tom Fazio and Dye.) The setting challenges and captivates. Long, winding fairways are framed by vivid moss-draped forests. Paddleboats glide by on mirror-smooth lakes, and holes four, five and six hug the Atlantic to keep you on your tees.

Long Point's eighteen championship holes beckon with unusual natural hazards, highly elevated fairways, large bodies of water and more marshland and beachside play. PGA greats Ben Crenshaw, Davis Love, Mark O'Meara, Hal Sutton and Peter Jacobsen have played the course; and all agree that it's outstanding.

Address: 1501 Lewis St Warehouse, P.O. Box 3000, Amelia Island, 32035 888-261-6161
Fax: 904-277-5945
Web site: http://aipfl.com
No. of Rooms: 249
Rates: $$$
Restaurant: The Amelia Inn Dining Room, The Golf Shop Restaurant, The Verandah Restaurant, The Coop, & more
Business Fac.: Conference space for up to 1,000, Built in state-of-the-art audio/visual equipment, Support professionals, Controlled lighting, Catering, Well-equipped business center
Sports Fac.: Ron Philos' School of Golf, Tennis, Raquet Park Complex, 2 swimming pools, Children's pool, Hot tub, Swim lessons, Kayaking, Guided walks, Pool volleyball, Health & Fitness Center
Location: 45 minute drive from downtown Jacksonville

Courses: Oak Marsh/Oysterbay (6502, par 72), Oceanside/Oakmarsh (6117, par 71), Long Point (6775, par 72), Oysterbay/Oceanside (6003, par 71)
No. of Holes: 45
Guest Policy: Closed, except to resort guests
Club House: 904-277-5907
Fees: ⅋⅋
Reservations: Can make reservations one year in advance
Season: Open all year

Ritz-Carlton, Amelia Island

Address: 4750 Amelia Island Pkwy, Amelia Island, 32034
Phone: 904-277-1100
800-241-3333
Fax: 904-261-9063
Web site: http://www.ritzcarlton.com
No. of Rooms: 449
Rates: $$$
Restaurant: The Grill Room, The Gourmet Shop
Bar: Lobby Lounge, Ocean Bar & Grill
Business Fac.: 32,000 sq ft
Sports Fac.: 9 tennis courts, croquet lawn, fitness center and spa, playground, indoor and outdoor pools
Location: Secluded island just North of Jacksonville, bordered by Atlantic Ocean and inland waterways

Course: Golf Club of Amelia Island
No. of Holes: 18
Guest Policy: Private course for members and resort guests only
Club House: 904-277-8015
Fees: ⅠⅠⅠ
Reservations: 100 days in advance
Season: Open all year

The Ritz-Carlton, Amelia Island offers guests a perfect Floridian getaway with genuine Southern hospitality, award-winning cuisine and the Atlantic Ocean right out the resort's back door. The 449 guestrooms offer private balconies—all with breathtaking coastal and ocean views—marble baths, honor bars and 24-hour in-room dining. Choose the Ritz-Carlton Club and you'll have access to a private lounge with a personal concierge and five complimentary food and beverage presentations daily.

For the ultimate in pampering and revitalization of body and spirit, The Ritz-Carlton, Amelia Island offers The Fitness and Day Spa complete with sauna, indoor and outdoor heated pools with whirlpools, a steam room, weight room featuring Cybex equipment, free weights, stair climbers, treadmills, and stationary bikes. The spa also offers Tai Chi, water aerobics and personal trainers. A world-class tennis facility offers six clay courts and three hard courts for an invigorating game, day or night. After an enjoyable run or walk on the beach, take a dip in the indoor pool and whirlpool or enjoy the outdoor oceanside pool and spa.

Play a challenging round of golf on the PGA 18-hole championship course at The Golf Club of Amelia Island at Summer Beach. Golf enthusiasts will enjoy the meticulously maintained course, which is an iron-shot from the front entrance of the hotel.

Turnberry Isle Resort & Club

Where is there a lush, tropical island of waterways, pools, gardens, a helipad, an unrivaled marina, an extravagant health spa and Country Club? Where is this playground to the wealthy, these four soaring residence towers, and this intimate private hotel? It's all in a private, guarded refuge called Turnberry Isle Yacht and Country Club, along the Intracoastal Waterway in North Miami Beach.

The Country Club dining room, which overlooks the golf course is a favorite for American and Continental specialties, while the Yacht and Racquet Club prides itself on northern Italian and new American cuisine. If you're in the mood for dancing, the Celebrities Lounge has the stars and sounds, and the lively Discotheque is where you'll want to rock out.

Sporting facilities leave no whim unfulfilled. 24 tennis courts featuring four different surfaces are available, as well as a full European spa with Nautilus equipment. You may leave your boat (if it's under 150 feet) berthed at the marina, or charter from a variety of glorious yachts, fully stocked and crewed for an unparalleled adventure on Florida's gleaming waters. Deep-sea fishing is just a marlin away, and water sports are featured on a private beach at the Ocean Club.

Adjacent to the Country Club is Aventura Mall, largest shopping center in Florida. Have a limousine whisk you to Jai Alai, nearby galleries and restaurants, or the ponies.

Julius Boros heads the Professional Golf staff which, combined with the climate and setting, make it the masterpiece that it is. Two of Robert Trent Jones' creations provide 36 challenging holes, featuring the largest triple green in the world. The South course has been the site of the Elizabeth Arden Classic and the PGA Senior Championship, as well as numerous celebrity and private tournaments.

Turnberry Isle offers a Children's Program over the Christmas Holidays and summer vacation season.

Address: 19999 W. Country Club Dr, Aventura, 33180
Phone: 305-932-6200
800-327-7028
Fax: 305-933-6560
E-mail: reservations@turnberryisle.com
Web site: http://www.turnberryisle.com
No. of Rooms: 395
Rates: $$
Restaurant: The Veranda, The Grill, The Signature, Ocean Club, Sunset Cafe, Monaco Dining Room, Club Lounge
Bar: Veranda Bar, Grill Bar, Signature Lounge, Club Lounge, Ocean Club Bar
Business Fac.: 45,000 sq ft of meeting space includes massive conference center, 3,500 sq ft South Courtyard for groups up to 300
Sports Fac.: 30 multi-surfaced tennis courts, pool & cabanas, 117-slip marina, complete spa & fitness center, pirvate beach
Location: In the secluded enclave of Aventura

Courses: South Course (7003, par 72), North Course (6403, par 70)
No. of Holes: 36
Guest Policy: Resort guests only
Club House: 305-932-6200
Fees: ⅂⅂⅂
Reservations: Can make reservations 2 days in advance
Season: Open all year

Boca Raton Resort & Club

Address: 501 E. Camino Real, Boca Raton, 33432
Phone: 561-447-3656
800-327-0101
Fax: 561-447-5888
E-mail: resinfo@bocaresort.com
Web site: http://www.bocaresort.com
No. of Rooms: 963
Rates: $$
Restaurant: The Cabana, Chauncey's Court, Nick's Fishmarket, The Patio, Top of the Tower, Grille Room
Bar: Malone's Magic Bar, Cappy's Bar, Mizner's Monkey Bar, Gazebo Bar
Business Fac.: 128,000 Mizner Conference Center includes 26,037 sq ft Grand Ballroom, 15,027 sq ft Royal Palm Ballroom, 4,726 sq ft Addison Ballroom, 3,895 Estate Ballroom, plus 34 meeting rooms that can support high-tech media productions
Sports Fac.: 30 clay tennis courts, several pools, fitness center, ½ mile private beach, 25-slip marina, croquet
Location: South Florida's Gold Coast

Courses: Resort Course (6253, par 71), Country Club Course (6585, par 72)
No. of Holes: 36
Guest Policy: Open to public
Club House: 800-327-0101
Fees: ↑↑↑
Reservations: Call for reservations
Season: Open all year

Located on southeast Florida's Gold Coast, Boca Raton's distinctive pink color and Spanish-Moorish architecture are the legacy of architect-eccentric Addison Mizner. Built in 1926 as the centerpiece of Mizner's dream city, the resort was restored to its original décor recently. Handmade rugs from India now cover new French terra-cotta floors, and even the Mizner Fountain is again in operation.

Take advantage of Boca's Tennis Center, boasting 22 Har-Tru courts, and The Boca Beach Club, the watersports center providing everything from snorkeling to windsurfing. Or, go Gulf Stream fishing for plentiful sailfish, marlin, tuna barracuda and dolphin.

Enjoy the shopping nearby or participate in the popular tours offered by Boca Raton Historical Society. Explore the Mizner Museum, walk through the giant columns of a 13th-century loggia, and view antiques brought from Spain by Mizner.

The Boca Raton Resort & Club enjoys two 18-hole championship golf courses. The Resort course, which was originally designed by William Flynn in 1926 and recently redesigned by Joe Lee in 1988, has become an attraction for golfers all over the world. The club had only two pros from 1926-1970, but what names: Tommy Armour and Sam Snead. The Resort course winds among a variety of tropical foliage and palms.

The Country Club course, located a short 6 miles northwest of the hotel, presents a true country club atmosphere with all the facilities. This Joe Lee designed championship course has water bordering 12 of the 18 holes and finishes with the spectacular 18th hole, a par 5 onto an island green.

South Seas Plantation Resort

Once the hideaway of 16th-century pirates and, later, a flourishing citrus plantation, South Seas Plantation ranks among today's premier resorts. South Seas sits on 330 acres of unspoiled tropical island on the northern tip of Captiva Island, 3 miles out in the Gulf of Mexico. The tranquility of its two-mile stretch of white beach and the natural beauty of the island has won this resort its reputation as "Florida's Tahiti."

Three award-winning restaurants provide a different dining experience for every meal of your vacation … in surroundings that range from candlelight to casual.

You have access to 22 Laykold tennis courts scattered throughout the resort and 17 freshwater pools—a myriad of water sports that take full advantage of the beautiful surroundings await you at South Seas. Windsurfing, sun canoes, waterskiing, jet skiing, and aqua-cycles are all available to guests, including Steve Colgate's Offshore Sailing School.

Also popular are the many island excursions, including the Captiva Island breakfast cruise, lunch and dinner cruises to Cabbage Key or Useppa Island, cocktail cruises through Pine Island Sound, and sightseeing cruises to Boca Grande and Cayo Costa. And for shoppers, Chadwick's Square Shops, the newly-opened gallery of fine boutiques, is ideal.

You'll have the azure Gulf waters around you as you play this scenic nine holes built in 1973. The course is flat with a couple of lakes and a pretty stretch of fairway bordering the beach.

Address: P.O. Box 194, Captiva Island, 33924
Phone: 941-481-6424
800-237-3102
Fax: 941-481-4947
Web site: http://www.south-seas-resort.com
No. of Rooms: 650
Rates: Inquire
Restrictions: No pets allowed
Restaurant: Chadwicks, King's Crown
Bar: Chadwicks
Business Fac.: Audio-visual, Conference rooms, capacity 625
Sports Fac.: Swimming pool, Tennis courts, Water skiing
Location: Lee County

Course: So. Seas Plantation (2902)
No. of Holes: 9
Guest Policy: Call for availability
Club House: 941-472-5111
Reservations: May be made one day in advance
Season: Open all year
Carts: Carts are also available

Wyndham Bonaventure Resort & Spa

Address: 250 Racquet Club Rd, Fort Lauderdale, 33326
Phone: 954-389-3300
800-225-5331
Web site: http://www.
wyndham.com/
Ft_LauderdaleResort/default.cfm
No. of Rooms: 292
Rates: Inquire
Restaurant: Renaissance, The Garden Restaurant
Bar: Terrace Lounge
Business Fac.: World Conference Center with meeting rooms, board rooms, state-of-the-art equipment
Sports Fac.: Raquetball Club with 24 courts, Saddle Club, Bonaventure Spa & Fitness Center with full spa services, Fitness equipment, 5 outdoor pools
Location: Near Miami & Ft. Lauderdale

Courses: East (7011, par 72), West (6189, par 70)
No. of Holes: 36
Guest Policy: Semi-private, members and hotel guest get priority tee times
Club House: 954-389-2100
Fees: ⏇
Reservations: Call for reservations
Season: Open all year

All nine buildings of this complex, set amid 1,250 lush tropical acres, have elegant guest rooms with spectacular views of the greens and ponds, or the pools and their lush tropical plants. Many of the rooms offer terraces to better enjoy the outdoors, and they all afford all the comforts of home.

You must see the Tropical Waterfall Pool and Rain Forest to believe the beauty of the setting, and the four other pools each have a different atmosphere of their own. This resort is home of the John Jacobs Golf School and the Proserv Sports Academy (where you can work on your tennis game). The Saddle Club offers horseback riding, and you might even meet a member of The American Olympic Equestrian Team because they train here. The Spa and Fitness Center offers state-of-the-art equipment, and every conceivable means of pampering you might desire such as: a classic body massage, hydrotherapy, saunas, steam rooms, whirlpools, herbal wraps and much more. If you're planning a conference the award-winning conference service staff will coordinate meetings from 20 to 2,000 people.

For the shopper, the Bonaventure is close to Worth Avenue, Galleria and Plantation Fashion Malls, Las Olas Boulevard, Sawgrass Mills Outlet, Coconut Grove and Bal Harbour shops. You can really shop 'till you drop. Other adventures that await you include cruising the Intracoastal Waterway, tour of the Everglades, an afternoon at the races of an evening of jai alai.

The East course is one of Florida's top ten courses and hosts the Dixie Amateur each year. There's water on almost every hole and a waterfall across the third green. The West Course will give you a more user-friendly round, but still offers plenty of challenge.

Grenelefe Resort

At the center of Florida's wonderland of world-famous attractions, is the Grenelefe Resort and Conference Center. The resort embraces 1,000 lush, wooded acres along the shores of Lake Marion and remains part of a self-contained community that has its own post office, fire department, service station and convenience store.

Grenelefe dining comes in a variety that will suit every taste. Enjoy Grenelefe's 13-court world-class tennis complex, including the 1,700-seat Centre Court Stadium where national tournaments, as well as the Grand Prix Circuit, take place annually. There are also five pools, plus plentiful water sports and fishing on 6,400-acre Lake Marion, where largemouth bass and speckled perch are abundant.

More non-sport activities have been added recently, including arts and crafts classes, cooking schools and bridge tournaments. There's easier access to Florida's famous attractions as well, with the initiation of daily shuttle bus service from Grenelefe to Walt Disney World's Magic Kingdom/EPCOT Center and Cypress Gardens.

With 54 holes of championship meticulously-landscaped golf on three challenging courses ranking among Florida's best, the Grenelefe Resort and Conference Center offers a varied menu of golfing. The West Course has been ranked number one in Florida consistently, and, like all Robert Trent Jones designs, claims long, tight fairways lined with tall pines and monstrous bunkers. Many players tout the ninth and 14th as being the best holes. They're each a long par 4 with plenty of trees and sand traps, but each is more negotiable from the middle markers.

Ed Seay's East Course is much shorter and tighter at 6802 yards. Depending on your mood or your gall, you'll want to tee off the Championship first tee, positioned on the second story of the Conference Center, just outside the golf pro shop.

The newest course, the South, designed by Ronald Garl and PGA touring pro Andy Bean, is no pushover. It incorporates a variety of length, terrain, and hazards. But between the 8th and 9th hole hydrophobes beware!

Address: 3200 State Rd. 546, Haines City, 33844
Phone: 813-422-7511
800-237-9549 reserva
Fax: 813-421-5025
E-mail: info@grenelefe.com
Web site: http://www.grenelefe.com
No. of Rooms: 850
Rates: $
Restaurant: Grene Heron Steak House, dinner, Camelot Restaurant and Patio, casual breakfast, lunch and dinner
Bar: Lancelot's Sports Bar, The Forest Pub
Business Fac.: 50,000 sq. ft. of meeting space and full business services
Sports Fac.: 20 tennis courts (3 different surfaces), Fitness center, Nature trails, Fishing, 4 pools, 2 Jacuzzis
Location: Conveniently located in the heart of the world's #1 vacation destination

Courses: West Course, East Course, South Course
No. of Holes: 54
Club House: 800-237-9549
Reservations: Call for reservations
Season: Open all year

The Diplomat Resort & Country Club

Address: 3514 S Ocean Dr,
Hollywood, 33019
Phone: 954-457-2000
800-327-1212
Fax: 954-457-2026
E-mail: maryh@diplomatresort.com
Web site: http://www.
diplomatresort.com
No. of Rooms: 1,000
Rates: Inquire
Restaurant: 2 restaurants
Bar: Lounge
Business Fac.: 209,000 sq ft of
meeting space includes 50,000 sq ft
Great Hall, 20,000 sq ft Grand Ball-
room, and 43 breakout rooms
Sports Fac.: Diplomat Spa, whirl-
pools, steam & sauna, fitness center,
yacht slips, tennis club
Location: 10 minutes from Fort
Lauderdale/Hollywood Interna-
tional Airport

Course: Diplomat Golf Course
(6624, par 72)
No. of Holes: 18
Guest Policy: Open to public
Club House: 954-457-2082
Fees: ⌐
Reservations: 3 days in advance
Season: Open all year

Newly renovated, this has been one of Florida's
big resorts for years, and now with millions being
spent on public rooms, landscaping, the pool area,
restaurants, lounges, and meeting rooms, this 300
acre resort offers fun-in-the-sun in a most convenient location. Less than a half hour from Miami's
airport, with the Atlantic's beach on one side, and
the intracoastal waterway on the other, the
spruced-up Diplomat glitters in a world of its own.
With 1,001 rooms and 69 suites, the resort has its
own marina, nine restaurants and lounges, two
health clubs, 12 tennis courts, three swimming
pools, and an arcade of boutiques. Nearby is
another shopping complex, and all the attractions
of this popular stretch of playland fifteen minutes
from Fort Lauderdale. You can bet the ponies or
the greyhounds, watch Jai Alai, visit Lion Country
Safari, the Burt Reynolds Theatre in Jupiter, or
drive south to Miami, all within a short distance.
This is the place to windsurf, rent Hobie Cats,
Aqua Bikes, power boats and water skis, or relax
at the pool and contemplate how many gallons of
water are being recycled through the waterfalls.

The course here is the Diplomat, a par 72 flat
course with plenty of water hazards and bunkers,
built in 1958. Diplomat is the work of Red
Lawrence, credited also with Desert Forest in
Carefree, Arizona, and West Course, The Wigwam
in Litchfield Park, Arizona.

Mission Inn Golf & Tennis Resort

Would you like to know about a secluded, one-of-a-kind family-operated retreat? One whose staff remembers returning guests names, offers a full program of children's activities, and even maintains a restored 1930s river yacht for cocktail cruises? Mission Inn is the place. It's a country-inn hideaway, 45 minutes from Walt Disney World in the foothills of Orlando, and it happens to be sitting on one of Florida's largest lakes, bass-filled Lake Harris. Spanish in style reminiscent of Florida's early days, the Inn has 204 rooms, suites and condominiums. Fountains, gardens, birds and waterfalls line the covered walkways. From screened balconies, rooms overlook velvety fairways, tennis courts, towering palms, and placid Lake Harris. Guests gather at La Margarita for cocktails and conversation, while two dining rooms El Conquistador, and La Hacienda tempt diners with menus featuring continental fare. The Nineteenth Hole also offers lunch and dinner. What to do in a town called Howey-on-the-Hills? Start with fishing, sailing, speedboating, tennis, swimming, or relaxing after a workout in the spa.

This is an older golf course, still in excellent shape. Built in 1924 by Scottish designer, Charles E. Clark, it had a facelift in 1970 by Lloyd Clifton. Florida Mini Tour plays here twice a year, and the Tallahassee Open Qualifier sought this course recently, as did the Florida Junior Invitational. It is a hilly layout—with an 85 feet elevation difference tee-to-green. The fourth hole is billed as "Devil's Delight," with more obstacles than many courses claim on 18. Our favorite is number six, "Pine Valley." At 472 yards, it's a short but extremely tight par five which squeezes in even tighter as you approach the green. Lots of water frames the green, and numerous bunkers starting from 80 yards out create a bottleneck for the second shot. Thirteen of 18 holes have water, and the landscape varies from hole to hole—some are wooded, and some have an abundance of tropical foliage.

Address: 10400 County Rd. 48, Howey-In-The-Hills, 34737
Phone: 352-324-3101
800-523-2289
Fax: 352-324-2350
E-mail: reservations@ missioninnresort.com
Web site: http://www. missioninnresort.com
No. of Rooms: 189
Rates: $$
Restaurant: El Conquistador, La Hacienda, La Chiquita Cabana
Bar: Nickers, La Margarita
Business Fac.: 30,000+ sq ft includes 5,000 sq ft El Nuevo Mundo Conference Center and 3,200 sq ft Los Reyes Foyer
Sports Fac.: 8 tennis courts
Location: 35 minutes Northwest of Orlando

Courses: El Campeon (6850, par 72), Las Colinas (6879, par 72)
No. of Holes: 36
Guest Policy: Open to public
Club House: 352-324-3885
Fees: ↑↑
Reservations: Can make reservations 7 days in advance
Season: Open all year

Indian River Plantation

Address: 585 NE Ocean Blvd,
Hutchinson Island, 34996
Phone: 561-225-0110
800-327-4873
E-mail: irprlty@gate.net
Web site: http://www.
indianriverplantation.com/
home.htm
Rates: Inquire
Restaurant: Golf Club dining
Business Fac.: conference area
Sports Fac.: Aqua pitching range,
fitness center, tennis club with 13
lighted courts, 77 slip full-service
marina, club pools, whirlpools,
children's playground
Location: Florida's East Coast

Course: Indian River Plantation
Club (4048, par 61)
No. of Holes: 18
Guest Policy: Open to public
Club House: 561-225-0110
Reservations: Call for reservations
Season: Open all year

Getting to this 200 acre friendly self-contained resort of secluded beaches, water sports, and great golf and tennis is easy. Drive about forty miles north of Palm Beach, cross the St. Lucie River, and follow signs to Hutchinson Island, or have your private jet land at Stuart's Witham Field, or if you're cruising the Intracoastal Waterway, check Nautical Chart #11472, proceed to Marker 229 and cruise in the St. Lucie Inlet. The Island has conveniences such as a bank, gourmet market, service station, and shops, yet, there are a plenty of diversions within a short distance, should you want to explore Florida's Treasure Coast.

Accommodations are in one and two bedroom suites, all with kitchens, balconies and ocean views. In addition, there's a new 200 room hotel adjacent to the full-service 77-slip marina.

The resort has five restaurants, ranging from the elegant Inlet, whose menu is devoted to International specialties and fresh fish, to the casual Emporium, a turn-of-the-century ice cream parlor.

Recreation at this old pineapple plantation centers on the outdoors—all sorts of water sports, swimming pools, dinner and day cruises, sailing and snorkeling. Marlin, sailfish, and wahoo abound in the ocean while pompano and flounder flourish in rivers, lakes and bays. Elsewhere on the Island are historical attractions, and a museum. Flanked by the ocean and a river, the island is a stopping-off place for migrating birds, and roving security patrols watch for injured fliers so they can be treated.

Those who like a less lengthy round will come back for more on the par 61, 4,042 yard short course designed by Charles Ankrom. River Course, and Plantation Course are both relatively flat (everything is in these parts), have terrific bunkering, undulating greens, ocean breezes, and seem to have water everywhere.

For children 3-12 there is the "Pineapple Bunch Children's Camp" which offers arts and crafts, beach and nature walks, excursions, swimming, field games, and bike hikes. For teenagers there is a game room, movie nights, parties, snorkeling, and golf and tennis instruction.

Admiral Lehigh Golf Resort

The resort is set among more palm trees than you can count. The resort's rooms have recently been refurnished and have spectacular views of the landscaped courtyard or the North Course.

Lehigh has a professional staff whose specialty is recreation. They offer a full range of activities throughout the week and will keep you busy on a full-time basis if that's your desire.

If you want to do your own thing there's fishing, paddle boats, bicycles. The shopping in nearby Ft. Myers is also a must see for the dedicated shopper. If you just want to sit back and relax there's a lending library on-site.

Dining at Lehigh is a rare experience of culinary delights presented by your expert Chefs. Not only is there elegant formal dining, but be sure to try the Sunday Brunch. The Highland Pub dancing, entertainment and a Happy hour.

The conference facilities are beautifully appointed and also have sweeping views of the golf course. Our staff will take all the work out of your next banquet or meeting.

The North Course is demanding, with many trees, narrow fairways, and strategically placed bunkers. Many greens are elevated and somewhat undulating. The Mirror Lakes course is the longer of the two with wide fairways and few trees. Trees don't come into play much on this course, but the lake is in play on the first hole and the rough is heavy. There is a driving range that is lit for day or evening use.

Address: 225 E. Joel Blvd, Lehigh Acres, 33936
Phone: 941-369-2121
888-GOLF-222
Fax: 941-368-1660
E-mail: admiral@peganet.com
Web site: http://www.
admiralhotels.com/lehigh.html
Rates: $
Restaurant: Arbor Grill, Masters Tavern, Mirror Lakes Pub, The Healthy Gourmet
Bar: Highland Pub
Business Fac.: Conference Center for up to 250 people
Sports Fac.: Exercise spa with cardio vascular equipment, aerobics, personal trainers, dance studio, massage and sauna
Location: Just east of Ft. Myers and 20 minutes from Southwest Florida International Airport

Courses: North Course at Mirror Lake (5870, par 70), South Course at Mirror Lake (7017, par 73)
No. of Holes: 36
Guest Policy: Open to public
Club House: 941-369-1322
Fees: ↑
Reservations: Can make reservations 1 day in advance
Season: Open all year
Carts: Carts included with fees

Resort at Longboat Key

Address: 301 Gulf of Mexico Dr,
Longboat Key, 34228
Phone: 941-383-8821
800-237-8821
Fax: 941-383-0359
E-mail: reservations@
longboatkeyclub.com
Web site: http://www.
longboatkeyclub.com
No. of Rooms: 232
Rates: Inquire
Restrictions: No pets allowed
Restaurant: Orchids, The Grille,
The Dining Room
Bar: Orchid's Lounge and Barefoots
(poolside)
Business Fac.: Message center,
Administrative assistance, Copiers,
Audio-visual, Translators, Full-scale
conference facilities
Sports Fac.: Outdoor swimming
pool, Whirlpool, Massage, Steam
rooms, Sailing, Tennis courts,
Jogging path, Bicycling, Golf school
Location: Beachfront

Courses: Islandside (6792),
Harborside, Red/White/Blue
No. of Holes: 45
Guest Policy: Call for availability
Club House: 941-383-8821
Reservations: Hotel guests—2½
days in advance
Season: Open all year

What was once a vision of circus king, John Ringling, who had a view of Longboat Key from his mansion on luxurious Sarasota Bay, is now an island resort amid the many cultural and recreational activities of Florida's west coast. It's off the beaten track, retaining its character of decades ago, yet major attractions are within easy reach.

Sporting facilities include 18 Har-Tru tennis courts, a swimming pool, and twelve miles of unspoiled beach. Explore the deep searching for tarpon, kingfish, and cobia in the Gulf. Don't miss birdwatching along mangrove habitats. The resort is in a wildlife sanctuary, giving it an "away-from-it-all" atmosphere, while affording simple, understated elegance.

You'll have a myriad of choices near the resort. The sumptuous Ringling residence, the Museum of the Circus, the remarkable architectural landmark housing his Baroque art collection. A short excursion to St. Armand's Key reveals a fashionable community of stately homes, international shops, restaurants, and galleries.

The two championship courses at Longboat Key Club, Islandside Course and Harbourside Course, rank among the top. Islandside overlooks the Gulf of Mexico and offers a rolling, palm tree-lined adventure . Designed by Billy Mitchell, the par 72 "watery challenge" is an acknowledged test of accuracy.

The par 72 Harbourside (for member play only) is a somewhat longer layout providing a completely different golfing experience. The course is wrapped around Sarasota Bay. Sixty bunkers await the golfer who also has to negotiate lagoons, canals and the bay itself.

The Doral Hotel & Country Club

The sheer size, scope and pace of this ultra-posh sportsman's paradise bordering the Everglades is enough to boggle the mind. 650 rooms are in eight lodges, including a Corporate Lodge with separate check-in. Consider opulent restaurants, bars and lounges, 2,400 beautifully landscaped acres of tennis courts, a heated Olympic-size pool, an equestrian center, jogging, fishing, bicycling, volleyball and game rooms. Stay here and you'll have privileges next door at the new $28 million Doral Saturnia International Spa, a lavish Tuscan-inspired hedonistic pleasure palace where American techniques are combined with renowned therapies. And if you're yearning for the beach, head for the sister Doral on Miami Beach via shuttle. Don't overlook local attractions such as the Bass Museum of Art with a permanent collection of Old Masters and Impressionists, and the Miami Beach Garden and Conservatory, with its beautiful display of native flora. Art Deco lovers should streak for the southern end of Miami Beach, designated a National Historic District.

Golf is king here, and you have 99 holes including a par 3 executive course at your disposal. The Blue Monster is on everybody's list as the epitome of a challenging course. It's a watery, sandy, long expanse that is the site of the annual PGA Doral-Ryder Open. Billy Casper captured the title in 1962, and the list of winners includes Doug Sanders, Raymond Floyd and Jack Nicklaus. The 18th hole here has been consistently ranked as one of the toughest on the PGA tour, a par 4 unless you're bunkering it or al lago. Count on 22 lakes stocked with large-mouth bass, tarpon and a couple hundred Top-Flite IIs.

Address: 4400 N.W. 87th Ave, Miami, 33178
Phone: 305-592-2000
800-71-DORAL
Fax: 305-594-4682
E-mail: reservations@doralresort.com
Web site: http://www.doralgolf.com
No. of Rooms: 650
Rates: Inquire
Restaurant: Provare, Sandpiper Steak & Seafood, Champions, Staggerbush Bar & Grill, Waterhazard Bar & Grill
Bar: Rousseau's
Sports Fac.: Tennis courts, Swimming pool, Saturnia International Spa
Location: Miami

Courses: Blue (6597), Gold, Red, White
No. of Holes: 99
Guest Policy: Call for availability
Club House: 305-592-2030
Reservations: When you make resort reservations
Season: Open all year

Arnold Palmer's Bay Hill Club & Lodge

Address: 9000 Bay Hill Blvd, Orlando, 32819
Phone: 407-876-2429
800-523-5999
Fax: 407-876-1035
E-mail: bayhill@earthlink.net
Web site: http://www.bayhill.com
No. of Rooms: 64
Rates: Inquire
Restaurant: Dining Room
Bar: Lounge
Business Fac.: Full-service business center, Conferences and catering, capacity 250
Sports Fac.: Fitness center, Salon & Spa, Swimming pool, Tennis courts, Golf Academy
Location: On the shores of the Butler Chain of Lakes

Courses: Challenger Course & Championship Course (7207, par 72), Charger Course (3115, par 36)
No. of Holes: 27
Guest Policy: Reciprocal
Club House: 407-876-2429
Fees: ↑↑↑
Reservations: Reservations available 7 days in advance
Season: Open all year
Carts: Caddies

The Lodge is run more like a private club than a resort, with your every comfort being of prime importance. The rooms are set in two separate buildings, and the atmosphere here is unhurried, quiet and well suited to a family vacation.

Located near Disney World, Sea World and Universal Studios Florida, there is also plenty for the non-golfer to see and do.

Needless to say, being Arnold Palmer's Course and his winter home, the emphasis here is perfect for the serious golfer. The Arnold Palmer Golf Academy is ready and willing to tailor a program specifically to your golfing needs.

The perfect place for your small conference, board meeting, or corporate retreat. For a truly memorable get-together, this is the ideal setting. Every need is cared for from a successful meeting to a spectacular banquet.

Bay Hill Invitational is one of the stops on the PGA tour, as well as the Nestle Invitation. There's plenty of water on the courses and beautiful tree-lined fairways, with large well bunkered greens. But don't let the beauty lull you too much, these are very challenging greens, rated in the "top-100" by *Golf Digest* and *Golf Magazine*, and boosts one of the most difficult par-4 holes on the Pro Tour.

Hyatt Regency Grand Cypress

Discover your own private paradise of timeless beauty in an exclusive 1,500-acre resort. A place where waterfalls cascade along velvety canyon grottos into a spectacular pool. And where tropical blossoms fill the air with sweet fragrance. World-class golf and tennis, golden beaches, sailing on a secluded lake and nearby Orlando's theme parks and attractions await.

From the moment you enter our dramatic Atrium Lobby, you will transcend the ordinary. Here, you will experience tropical ambience, accentuated by live music every evening. Once inside your room, you'll discover why this resort is acclaimed for the drama of its design. From your own private balcony, you will witness the gentle blending of the resort's natural beauty into our design theme. Every detail—from ceiling fans, rattan, rich fabrics and linens—has been selected to embody the carefree vitality of Florida.

When it's time for dining or relaxing, we'll tempt you in five restaurants and four lounges. Try La Coquina for fine fare and panoramic lake views, Cascade for delicious entrées beside a cascading waterfall and Hemingways for Key West-style seafood and steaks served on a grotto porch overlooking the pool. The White Horse Saloon and Steakhouse offers Western classics in a casual setting. Enjoy hot entrées and snacks served indoors or alfresco at the Palm Cafe and general store.

The Hyatt Regency Grand Cypress Health Club offers the latest in computerized exercise equipment. The beautiful recreation area is highlighted by the half-acre, free form swimming pool, which contains 12 waterfalls and three whirlpool spas.

Within the 1,500-acre Grand Cypress Resort, discover a golf experience of the highest caliber, featuring 45 holes of award-winning golf, exclusively designed by Jack Nicklaus, in an environment of privacy and calm. Surrounded by unspoiled natural beauty, we're ranked as one of the country's top golf resorts. The North, South and East courses assure a golfing vacation well spent … and pleasantly challenged. For a bit of sporting history, try our 18-hole New Course, modelled on the Old Course at St Andrews in Scotland.

Address: One Grand Cypress Blvd, Orlando, 32836
Phone: 407-239-1234
800-55-HYATT
Fax: 407-239-3837
E-mail: hrgcinfo@mpinet.net
Web site: http://www.hyattgrandcypress.com/vista/index.html
No. of Rooms: 750
Rates: $$$
Restaurant: La Coquina, Cascade, Hemingways, White Horse Saloon & Steakhouse, Palm Cafe
Bar: Hurricane Lounge, On the Rocks, Trellises Lounge
Business Fac.: 65,000+ sq ft of meeting space, plus 10 conference parlors, a 16,768 sq ft exhibit hall, and the 24,960 sq ft Grand Cypress Ballroom
Sports Fac.: Huge pool with 12 waterfalls, grottos & caves, and a 125 ft water slide; health club, 3 whirlpools, Lake Windsong for boating, biking & hiking trails, Pitch 'n' Putt golf, basketball, scuba program, 12 raquetball courts, Equestrian Center
Location: 4 miles from EPCOT Center at Walt Disney World

Courses: New Course (6773, par 72), South Course (3462, par 36), North Course (3521, par 36), East Course (3434, par 36)
No. of Holes: 45
Guest Policy: Closed to the public
Club House: 407-239-4700
Fees: ↑ ↑ ↑
Reservations: Reservations available 60 days in advance

The Villas of Grand Cypress

Address: One North Jacaranda, Orlando, 32836
Phone: 407-239-4700
800-835-7377
Fax: 407-239-7219
Web site: http://www.
grandcypress.com/villas/home-villas.htm
No. of Rooms: 750
Rates: $$$
Restaurant: The Black Swan, fine dining; Fairways restaurant, all meals; Poolside Snack Bar
Bar: Fairways Lounge
Business Fac.: Executive Meeting Center, 3 soundproof meeting rooms, personalized services
Sports Fac.: Equestrian Center, Racquet Club, a nature area, variety of water sports
Location: Just minutes from Walt Disney World

Courses: North (6773), South Course, East Course, New Course
No. of Holes: 72
Club House: 407-239-3620
Fees: ↑↑↑
Reservations: Call for reservations
Season: Open all year

Orlando, barely more than a mid-size citrus center until Walt Disney's World and Cape Canaveral were launched, is more than the fantasy kingdom that attracts over 25 million visitors annually. Easily, accessible, Orlando's attractions are diverse, well-planned and aesthetically pleasing. The recipient of numerous accolades and awards, this 1500-acre resort offers lodging options in a 750-room Hyatt Regency, and two and four bedroom Mediterranean-style villas nestled among the waterways and fairways. A tour of the extensive grounds turns up a 21-acre lake fringed by a white sandy beach, an Equestrian center, a gargantuan swimming pool, a 45-acre nature preserve, an Executive meeting center, and four turn-of-the-century Belgian trolley cars to whisk guests around.

Guests can unwind in the Regency Health Club, or head for the racquet club which has both clay and hard tennis courts, two racquetball courts, and a proshop. No need to cook if you're staying in a villa. A catering service is ready to do it all, whether it's family breakfast or a lobster dinner poolside. Restaurants run the gamut from the Black Swan in the Gold Clubhouse for steaks and assorted seafood, to Ballybunion, and the Clubhouse Lounge which features live entertainment often, and the Hyatt Regency has six other restaurants. Try The Hurricane Bar in Hemingway's for a tall cool one amidst memorabilia and photos of the late outdoorsman and author.

Drop in to the Morse Gallery of Art in Winter Park, a lovely neighboring suburb, for a glimpse of fine Tiffany stained glass, or sample the five course meal served in Elizabethan style (don't wait for a fork) while Romeo romances Juliet at King Henry's Feast.

Jack Nicklaus designed the courses, and his touch is evident on all 45 holes—shaggy mounds that define the terraced fairways and undulating greens, and visibility of target areas and hazards. The courses appeared in stages, with the North and South opening in 1984, followed by East's nine holes in 1985. The "New Course," an eighteen hole gem, was ready in January, 1988. This is also the home of the Jack Nicklaus Academy of Golf, an instruction center with three Academy holes, bunkers, greens and everything conceivable to aid novice and pro to put that small ball in that very small hole. The Academy retains the services of specialists in golf technology and psychological conditioning to help you to get in shape.

Walt Disney World Resorts

At twice the size of Manhattan Island, this empire is mind boggling in concept, scope, and superlatives. Best part is, it all runs like clockwork. (Minnie never had it so good.) With more than 12,000 suites, rooms, villas, campsites, this fantasy world encompasses 43 square miles—and it's all devoted to the service of pleasure. Highlights include: the turn-of-the-century grandeur of Disney's Grand Floridian Beach Resort, Disney's Caribbean Beach Resort, Disney's Village Resort (with its choice of villas or club suites), the Disney Inn (facing the rolling fairways of Magnolia and Palm Golf Course), the Polynesian Resort, and the Fort Wilderness Resort and Campground (where you can bring your own camper and really hoop-dee-doo it up at Crockett's Tavern.) Maybe you'll want to contemplate the brobdingnagian Swan, or the newly opened Dolphin. Of course, with all these accommodations, the brilliant master planners left plenty of space for recreational pursuits. You can take part in sailing, playing tennis, water skiing, bicycling, fishing, jogging, riding, canoeing, swimming in pools, and even swinging from a rope in River Country. But be sure to leave enough time—it takes four days just to see the parks.

And there's more—night life, day life, and even life beyond—as on the fourth floor of the Contemporary Resort, where monorails glide in and out of the concourse bringing guests to the cavernous 90-foot lobby. Theme parks and hotels have plenty of space between them. The Caribbean Beach Resort, for example, set on 200 acres near EPCOT Center, surrounds a 42-acre lake and is actually comprised of five villages. All of the resorts are self-contained and have an impressive list of amenities and planned activities for both day and night.

Golf is not Mickey Mouse here. Joe Lee designed both the Magnolia (more open) and Palm (tighter). Lake Buena Vista, the newest course, is the host of the Disney World/Oldsmobile Classic, which Tim Simpson won in 1990 with a 24 under par. This 18-hole wooded course is situated away from the Magic Kingdom; about the only buildings you'll see are fairway villas on #17. Greens are all Bermuda, fast and fairly large. Slope rating is 124. Two more courses are being developed over by Fort Wilderness by designers Pete Dye and Tom Fazio. They should be ready for play by January 1992.

Address: 1 Magnolia Palm, P.O. Box 10100, Orlando, 32830
Phone: 407-934-7639
Fax: 407-352-3202
No. of Rooms: 1,300
Rates: Inquire
Restaurant: Numerous
Bar: Several
Business Fac.: Full conference facilities
Sports Fac.: Tennis courts, Fitness centers, Rapid shooting
Location: Orlando area

Courses: Lake Buena Vista (6829), Osprey Ridge, Eagle Pines, Magnolia, Palm, and Oak Trail
No. of Holes: 99
Guest Policy: Resort guest should call for tee times
Club House: 407-824-2270
Reservations: Depends on package, call for reservations
Season: Open all year

The Breakers

Address: One South County Rd, Palm Beach, 33480
Phone: 561-659-8404
800-833-3141
Fax: 561-655-6654
E-mail: sales@thebreakers.com
Web site: http://www.thebreakers.com
No. of Rooms: 572
Rates: $$$
Restaurant: Beach Club Restaurant, Circle Dining Room, Flagler's Steakhouse, The Pasta House, The Florentine, and more.
Bar: The Tapestry, Seafood Bar, Henry's Place, Reef Bar
Business Fac.: 59,000 sq ft of meeting space includes 15,000 sq ft Ponce de Leon Ballroom, The Gold Room, Magnolia Room, Mediterraneam Ballroom, and Venetian Ballroom
Sports Fac.: 14 tennis courts, horseshoe pits, jogging trail, lawn bowling, shuffleboard, beach volleyball, croquet, Oceanfront Spa & Beach Club, Oceanview fitness center, 4 oceanfront pools, luxury spa with 17 private treatment rooms, steam/sauna & outdoor Jacuzzi
Location: On 140 acres of the island of Palm Beach

Courses: Ocean Course (6017, par 70), Breakers West Course (6893, par 71)
No. of Holes: 36
Guest Policy: Open to hotel guests & club members
Club House: 561-659-8407
Fees: ⅼⅼ
Reservations: Reservations available 30 days in advance
Season: Open all year
Carts: Carts included in fees

Palm Beach has, for generations, been synonymous with the socially elite; the playground of the beautiful people, and much of this life centered around the grand old landmark, The Breakers. Designed in the Italian Renaissance style, the exterior, with its Belvedere towers was inspired by Rome's Villa Medici. The main lobby, accented by frescoes and vaulted ceilings overlooks the Mediterranean Courtyard, resplendent with fountains and cascading plants, resembling the inner gardens of an Italian villa. The opulent Mediterranean and Venetian Ballrooms, off the loggias, provide the setting for some of society's most elegant charity and debutante balls. Built by millionaires in 1926, The Breakers, with its Flemish tapestries, crystal chandeliers and marble floors, sits on 140 acres of rambling lush tropical gardens. Guests can enjoy 19 tennis courts, a private beach with cabanas, an Olympic-size swimming pool, fitness center, patio bar and grill, dance studio, shuffleboard, table tennis, sailing, croquet, and a unique kids' summer camp where boys and girls aged 10 to 15 learn the basics of investments and personal finance.

Donald Ross fans will be delighted with the Ocean Course, designed around the turn of the century. A short course with tight fairways and small, elevated greens, this classic is home to many amateur events including American Seniors, International Seniors, and the Winter Gold League and Breakers Seniors. It's also here that many golf celebrities come for the Palm Beach Golf Classic with 4 tour pros. #14, a figure "S" hole uphill, is typical of Ross' designs, with deep bunkers and small elevated greens. The Breakers West championship course, a twenty-five minute drive from the hotel, was originally designed by Willard Byrd in 1971, and has recently been updated by renowned golf course architect Joe Lee. Situated in West Palm Beach, players are promised more challenges, improved drainage, and a re-designed #9. The new hole has a distinct dog leg requiring a second water shot onto the new three-tiered green. The course wasn't changed dramatically, rather, the original layout has been refined to give the course more character and make play more enjoyable. A new clubhouse featuring a golf pro shop, an elegant restaurant, saunas and steam rooms, bar and grill, is the ideal spot to relax while overlooking the course.

PGA National Resort

Here it is, the golf resort that has everything and then some. Serious golf aficionados and/or hedonists will think they've gone to heaven as they immerse themselves in this utopia that is invigorating, exciting, relaxing and luxurious.

This self-contained destination, set amidst towering palms on 2,340 acres fifteen miles north of Palm Beach, is the home of the Professional Golfer's association, with four championship 18-hole courses, pollution-free air and first-rate staff waiting to treat your mind and body with the best of everything.

Don't count on ordinary fare in the Explorer's dining room, as Chef Jeff Summerour, from Hilton Head, SC, has discovered recipes from far-off lands that are both interesting and delectable.

Palm Beach County is the heart of croquet in this country, and the United States Croquet Association's home is here, claiming the largest facility in the western hemisphere. As the home of the Women's Tennis Association, the spirit of Martina Navratilova moves around the 19 Fast Dry clay courts. There's also racquetball, a Nautilis fitness center, and a white sand beach on a 26-acre lake.

Area attractions include Jai Alai, polo, thoroughbred harness and dog racing, horseback riding and charter fishing boats. The fabulous shops of Worth Avenue are a short ten minutes from the resort, in case you forgot your tennis bracelet.

The four courses were designed by top professionals George and Tom Fazio, and legendary Arnold Palmer. While each course is distinctive in design, the longest and most challenging is the par 72 Champion: Home of the Grand Slam, and the PGA Seniors Championship. Palmer gave it a Scottish personality with more than 100 bunkers, long Bahia grass valleys, and water on the 17 holes, which provide hazards to test the most accurate shotmaker.

In addition to daily clinics, individual and group lessons, the resort is celebrated for its Three Day "Killer Golf School." Whether you're new to the game, or a seasoned veteran, this intense golf instruction, grouped by ability levels, is bound to improve your game.

Address: 400 Ave. of the Champions, Palm Beach Gardens, 33418
Phone: 561-627-2000
800-633-9150
Fax: 561-622-0261
E-mail: pgainfo@pga-resorts.com
Web site: http://www. pga-resorts.com
Rates: $$
Restaurant: Citrus Tree Restaurant, Shula's Steakhouse, Arezzo, Ta-Kil-Ya Cafe, Oasis Bar & Grille
Business Fac.: 23 meeting rooms, State-of-the-art audio/visual equipment, Full-service business center, Catering
Sports Fac.: Academy of Golf, 3 driving ranges, 6 putting greens, 19 tennis courts, Croquet, Steam, Sauna, Fitness Center, Raquetball, Whirlpools, Lap pool
Location: 20 minutes from Palm Beach International Airport

Courses: The Champion (7022), The General (6768), The Estates (6784), The Haig (6806) and The Squire (6806)
No. of Holes: 90
Club House: 561-627-7593
Reservations: 800-832-6235
Season: Open all year

Westin Innisbrook Resort

Address: 36750 US Highway 19 N, Palm Harbor, 34884
Phone: 727-942-2000
888-625-5144
Fax: 727-942-5576
E-mail: innis@westin.com
Web site: http://www.westin-innisbrook.com
No. of Rooms: 968
Restaurant: Three restaurants: pub, steakhouse and cantina.
Business Fac.: Business center, cellular phone rental, internet access, conference center, secretarial support, 41 meeting rooms.
Sports Fac.: Health club/Fitness center, spa, 6 outdoor swimming pools, water sports.
Location: On the Gulf Coast of Florida

Courses: Copperhead (7230, par 71), Island (7100, par 72), Highlands North (6405, par 71), Highlands South (6635, par 6635)
No. of Holes: 72
Guest Policy: Closed to the public
Club House: 727-942-2000
Fees: ⅓⅓
Reservations: Reservations available 365 days in advance
Season: Open all year
Carts: Cart included in fees

In the rolling hills of Florida's central Gulf coast, just south of the Greek fishing community of Tarpon Springs and immediately west of Tampa, lies one of America's premier golf, conference and leisure destinations—The Westin Innisbrook Resort. This 1000 acre property features 700 luxurious guest suites; 72 holes of championship golf on four award-winning courses; a complete tennis, racquetball and fitness facility; a sophisticated meeting and convention center; plus gourmet dining! Guests enjoy six swimming pools including the fabulous new Loch Ness Pool and Spa, jogging and cycling trails, wildlife preserve, and complete recreation center.

Guest accommodations are in 28 low-rise lodges, nestled around the golf courses, clubhouses and swimming pools. Innisbrook's accommodations are more than just rooms—they're luxurious suites. From club suites to a deluxe three-bedroom layout, each features a fully equipped kitchen and private patio or balcony. Suites are in low-profile villas linked to dining, recreation, and conference facilities by climate controlled shuttles. And here, you'll discover a staff dedicated to pampering each and every guest with graciousness that is Innisbrook's alone.

At The Westin Innisbrook Resort the guest is king. Your dining experience begins with a staff that is attentive to your every need. In our three clubhouse restaurants, for instance, you'll savor culinary delights and experience a level of service that is distinctly Innisbrook's.

In golf, it's not whether you win or lose, it's where you play the game. And at Innisbrook, you'll play 72 holes of the country's very best. Copperhead enjoys an international reputation for excellence and is on everybody's list of favorites. Island—an equal contender among those who enjoy golf at Innisbrook. Tight fairways, intimidating hazards, abundant bunkers—all designed to test the skills of the most accomplished golfer. Highlands South offers abundant water and other hazards of differing forms including well-bunkered greens and beautification / waste areas reminiscent of Pinehurst. Highlands North with its beautiful 18-hole layout promises tight fairways and well-bunkered greens, placing a costly premium on accuracy from tee to green.

Marriott's Bay Point Resort

There are 1,100 acres of wildlife sanctuary overlooking Florida's beautiful Grand Lagoon awaiting your arrival. The Emerald green waters meet a generous stretch of soft white sand almost at your doorstep. The suites are spacious and have many luxurious extra touches. Bay Point has been awarded Meeting & Convention magazine's "Gold Tee Award and *Golf Illustrated* has named it among the top 25 golf resorts. All this and Southern Hospitality too!

With seven restaurants you're sure to find many wonderful dining experiences, and Stormy's is a favorite place for a cool refreshment after a tough day on the golf course.

Tennis here is not to be overlooked, the resort was awarded the Gold Racquet Award by Racquet Magazine. The 12 Har/Tru tennis courts are top notch, and you can even play at night. There are also five swimming pools and a marina.

You can tour the secluded Gulf Islands, deep sea fish, sail, scuba, or indulge in just about any water sport in the Gulf of Mexico. Or try a romantic moonlight walk on the Boardwalk, then set out for dining adventure with a dinner cruise on the Island Queen, the resort's 85-foot Mississippi River boat.

On the Lagoon Legend water and marshes are in play on fifteen holes, and twice on the last hole. A very demanding course that has humbled many a golfer while giving the appearance of not being a difficult course. There are three island greens that appear to be tiny, but really aren't. The Club Meadows course will be a relaxing change after playing the Legend. The fairways are long and narrow, and beautifully tree-lined. The resort offers many different golf packages, be sure to inquire.

Address: 4200 Marriott Dr, Panama City Beach, 32408
Phone: 850-236-6000
800-874-7105
Fax: 850-234-0305
E-mail: info@marriottbaypoint.com
Web site: http://www. marriottbaypoint.com
No. of Rooms: 355
Rates: Inquire
Restaurant: Bayview Restaurant, Stormy's Steakhouse, Teddy's Back Bay Beach Club
Bar: Lobby Bar
Business Fac.: Comprehensive outdoor/indoor meeting facilities, Skilled staff, Full state-of-the-art audio/visual equippment, Food/beverage capabilities
Sports Fac.: 12 Har-Tru tennis courts, Indoor/outdoor pools, Jogging trails, Whirlpool, 2 workout rooms, Village Explorers, Sauna, Game room, Bicycles, Aquaaerobics, Massage, Basketball
Location: 15 minutes from Panama City

Courses: Lagoon Legend (6885, par 72), Club Meadows (6913, par 72)
No. of Holes: 36
Guest Policy: Open to public
Club House: 850-235-6905
Fees: ⚑⚑
Reservations: Reservations available 14 days in advance
Season: Open all year
Carts: Cart included in fees

Palm Aire Spa Resort

Address: 2601 Palm Aire Dr. North, Pompano Beach, 33069
Phone: 941-972-3300
800-272-5624
Fax: 941-639-3883
Rates: Inquire
Sports Fac.: Tennis courts, Hot tub, Fitness center, Outdoor heated swimming pool
Location: Four miles east of Pompano Beach

Courses: Cypress Course (6868), Oaks Course (6747), The Palms Course (6932), The Pines Course (6610) and Sabals Course (3401— executive par 3)
No. of Holes: 54
Club House: 941-974-7699
Reservations: Call for reservations
Season: Open all year

Palm Aire is a total destination resort, 1,500 acres big 45 minutes north of the Miami International Airport, with an emphasis on golf, tennis and a major world-class fully equipped spa. There are 194 hotel rooms, each having a private terrace, and 21 suites overlooking fairways.

The Peninsula Dining Room, romantic with etched, lighted mirrors, and the Peninsula Bar, mirrored with suede padding, set a tone of tropical opulence, and the Tiki Bar poolside is great for unwinding after a day's activities. Amenities include tennis courts, swimming pool, racquetball courts, a jogging trail, and use of the private beach a couple of blocks away. If you opt for the spa, plan to luxuriate in a sanctuary of total rejuvenation from whirlpools, steam rooms and saunas to massages and the hand-rubbed salts of a loofa scrub.

You can tee up at any of three courses; Palms, Pines or Sabals. Chosen for three Florida Opens, and the Florida PGA in 1978, the courses are first-rate. Palms Course, was designed in 1960 by William Mitchell, an early advocate of courses designed specifically for women. #12 takes a demanding drive, playing about 400 years, with water guarding both sides of the narrow fairway. Second shot is played into a long narrow green surrounded by water and trapped on both sides. Pines is a shorter course, ranked one of the country's best public courses, and Sabals at 3401 yards is an unintimidating "executive course" with all par 3's and 4's.

Ponte Vedra Inn & Club

Come visit 215 acres of ocean front property at the Ponte Vedra Inn & Club. For a relaxing vacation or an event-packed conference, this will be an ideal choice. Two superb 18-hole golf courses, 15 all-weather tennis courts, and 3 swimming pools offer plentiful sources of recreation for the vacationer. Complete meeting facilities, accommodating groups from 20 to 300, and a professional staff will help make your conference a success.

Address: 200 Ponte Vedra Blvd, Ponte Vedra Beach, 32082
Phone: 904-285-1111
800-234-7842
Fax: 904-285-2111
E-mail: reservations@ pvresorts.com
Web site: http://www.pvresorts.com
No. of Rooms: 222
Rates: Inquire
Restaurant: Seafoam Room, Florida Room, Inn Dining Room, The Golf Club, Surf Club Patio & Beach Snack Bar
Bar: Seahorse Lounge, Audobon Lounge, High Tides Lounge, The 19th Hole
Business Fac.: 17,000 sq ft of meeting space includes 17 rooms, two ballrooms, and an elegant boardroom
Sports Fac.: 15 tennis courts, 3 putting greens, 4 swimming pools, full-service spa, fitness center
Location: Along the sparkling blue waters of the Atlantic Ocean

Courses: Ocean Course (6574, par 72), Lagoon Course (5574, par 70)
No. of Holes: 36
Guest Policy: Open to public
Club House: 904-273-7710
Fees: ↑
Reservations: Reservations available 365 days in advance
Season: Open all year
Carts: Carts available

Sawgrass Marriott Resort & Beach Club

Address: 1000 PGA Tour Blvd, Ponte Vedra Beach, 32082
Phone: 904-285-7777
800-457-4653
Web site: http://www. marriotthotels.com/JAXSW/
No. of Rooms: 508
Rates: $$
Restaurant: Augustine Grille, Cafe on the Green, 100th Hole, Sea Porch Bar & Grill, Ocean View
Bar: Champs Lounge, Cascade Lounge
Business Fac.: Full business center, Administrative assistance
Sports Fac.: Outdoor swimming pool, Health club, Whirlpool, Sauna, Jogging, Tennis courts, Beach and sailing 1 mile away
Location: Nestled along Florida's Atlantic coast

Courses: TPC Stadium (6857, par 72), TPC Valley (6838, par 71), Marsh Landing Club (6841, par 72), Oak Bridge Club (6355, par 70)
No. of Holes: 99
Guest Policy: Closed
Club House: 904-273-3720
Fees: ↑↑
Reservations: Reservations available 3 days in advance
Season: Open all year
Carts: Carts available

Here on the white beaches of northern Florida, where sugary dunes are covered with tall sawgrass, wild flowers and sea oats, Marriott presides over a special world of golf and tennis. 650 rooms, plus beach and golf villas overlook a lake or golf course, and the windows actually open! You'll have miles of beach to explore, several swimming pools, and two excellent restaurants. For cocktails, try Cascades in the lobby or Champs, offering live entertainment nightly. The Cabana Club Restaurant serves fresh seafood for lunch or dinner, and for breakfast and lunch you have 4 golf club dining rooms from which to choose. You can play tennis, work out, swing a croquet mallet, ride horseback, fish in 350 acres of lakes stocked for fishing, or charter a boat at a nearby marina. Shopping at Sawgrass Village will certainly help the economy. Jacksonville's International Airport is 37 miles north. If you love challenges on the course, you'll find them here, especially when the winds pick up. There are 99 holes of championship golf, including the famous par 3, 17th floating hole of the PGA Tournament Player's Club. This is the original stadium course designed by Pete Dye. The new TPC Valley Course, with hills, mounds, elevated greens and expansive waste areas is rated as one of the all-time great courses. There's also Ed Seay's Marsh Landing Course, and his Oceanside Course, plus Oak Bridge. This short and narrow course is the most forgiving. Good luck!

Club Med Sandpiper

If you haven't had Club Med experience, this is probably the one to try for golf, and experience also the wonderful feeling knowing every extra is included. The resort is 45 minutes north of the Palm Beach Airport, facing the mile-wide St. Lucie River. Built on 1,000 acres, the village features accommodations in three-story riverfront lodges, a cocktail lounge, five swimming pools, a theater, a disco, and a boutique. Guests can hop aboard the shuttle service to the beach, just twenty minutes away, or choose from all sorts of activities within the village. You could play tennis, loll around the pools, water ski, try the circus workshop, check out the volleyball and basketball, tone up at aerobics and water exercises, go on a river cruise, or try bocce ball. This is the place to bring children; instructors will even teach them scuba diving in the pool.

The central restaurant serving breakfast, lunch and dinner buffets, overlooks the river. There are two specialty restaurants, plus a pub at the clubhouse. Beyond the village, visitors can check out Walt Disney World Resort, Sea World, Kennedy Space Center, the Everglades, and deep-sea fishing in the Atlantic.

Golf is the big attraction here, with many attractive packages and clinics. There are two 18-hole championship courses, Sinners and (you guessed it) Saints, both designed by Mark Mahannah. In addition, there's a driving range, two putting greens, a chipping green, and a practice sand trap.

Address: 3500 SE Morningside Blvd, Port Saint Lucie, 34952
Phone: 561-398-5091
Fax: 561-398-5103
Web site: http://www.clubmed.com/ID-OOFMKdFDAckAACX1j20/Villages/
No. of Rooms: 331
Rates: Inquire
Sports Fac.: 4 swimming pools, driving range, 19 plexipave courts, bocce ball, fitness center
Location: On the Ste. Lucie River, 43 miles north of Palm Beach

Courses: Sinners (6848. par 72), Saints (6478, par 72)
No. of Holes: 36
Guest Policy: Open to public
Club House: 561-337-6638
Fees: ↑
Reservations: Reservations available 1 day in advance
Season: Open all year
Carts: Carts included in fees

Burnt Store Marina Resort

Address: 5000 Burnt Store Rd,
Punta Gorda, 33955
Phone: 813-639-6633
800-237-4255
Fax: 813-639-2993
No. of Rooms: 150
Rates: Inquire
Restaurant: Salty's Harborside
Bar: Castaways Lounge
Business Fac.: Audio-visual,
Copiers, Conference rooms, capacity
250
Sports Fac.: Driving range, Boating,
Bicycling
Location: Charlotte Harbor

Courses: Heron (3709), Pelican,
Osprey
No. of Holes: 27
Guest Policy: Call for availability
Club House: 813-637-1577
Reservations: Call for tee times
Season: Open all year
Carts: Limited

The Marina Inn provides one, two and three bedroom condominiums with full service kitchens, private lanais, and comfortable living and dining rooms. The real lure is the quiet sheltered cove a few miles from the Gulf on Florida's west coast. The password is uncrowded, as in beaches, waterways, even the roads. With golfing, tennis, restaurants, fishing, and all sorts of water activities, life proceeds at a slower pace here. Salty's Harborside is the ideal spot for dinner—try the catch of the day, shrimp, and the melt-in-the-mouth key lime pie, as you watch the dolphins play. Then move into the Oar Room Lounge for live entertainment. The Gasparilla Conference Center has the capacity for up to 300. With the Gulf at your doorstep, you can literally cruise the local scene. Visit Cayo Costa, Cabbage Key and Boca Grand, or charter a boat for deep sea fishing. Landlubbers might want to visit Fisherman's Village with over 40 boutiques and specialty shops.

The 18 hole par 60 executive golf course designed by Ron Garl is a flat layout with plenty of water. You can visit the driving range or putting green before teeing off, and lessons are available from the pro. A second nine, par 29, was designed by Mark McCumber, also credited with Dunes Country Club on neighboring Sanibel Island.

World Golf Village

Relax and enjoy the amenities of World Golf Village from an array of spectacular vacation villas at the Sheraton's Vistana Resort at World Golf Village or the World Golf Village Renaissance Resort.

The Vistana Resort overlooks the 17th and 18th hole of The Slammer & The Squire golf course. Just a chip shot from the Hall of Fame and bordering the 18th fairway of The Slammer and The Squire golf course, is a cloistered resort community of luxurious one- and two-bedroom vacation villas.

At the center of activity is the World Golf Village Renaissance Resort. Appointed with European accents and overlooking the Village lake, the hotel is a leisurely stroll from everything there is to see and do. Adjacent to the hotel is the World Golf Hall of Fame. The World Golf Village Renaissance Resort is just as inspiring on the inside. The hotel's 300 rooms and suites surround a towering atrium rising 10 stories, with lush vegetation and cool streams nestled at the base where guests can relax and enjoy superb food and beverages. World-class amenities include a business center, exercise facilities, a swimming pool, and an expansive gift shop. The St. Johns County Convention Center is adjacent to the World Golf Village Renaissance Resort.

The World Golf Village now features two courses with 36 holes of championship golf. The King & The Bear is now open to the public. The Slammer & The Squire was created with golf legends Sam Snead and Gene Sarazen tapped as player consultants.

Address: 500 South Legacy Trail, St. Augustine, 32092
Phone: 904-940-8000
888-446-5301
Fax: 904-940-8676
Web site: http://www. wgv.com
No. of Rooms: 302
Restaurant: Cypress Pointe, Hall of Fame Cafe, Legends Grille & Tap Room, Mochapelli's Deli & Coffee Shack
Bar: Cypress Point Lounge
Business Fac.: 40,000 sq ft of meeting space at adjacent St. John's County Convention Center
Sports Fac.: 24-hour fitness center, massage services, outdoor pool & whirlpool
Location: In the oldest city in the US

Courses: The Slammer & the Squire, The King & The Bear, 3rd Course under construction
No. of Holes: 54
Club House: 888-955-1234
Reservations: Call for reservations
Season: Open all year

Innisbrook

Address: P.O. Drawer 1088, Tarpon Springs, 34286
Phone: 813-942-2000
800-456-2000
Fax: 813-942-5578
E-mail: innis@westin.com
Web site: http://www.
westin-innisbrook.com
No. of Rooms: 700
Rates: $$$
Restaurant: Copperhead Grille, Toscana, Sandpiper
Bar: Hacker's Pub
Business Fac.: Complete conference facilities
Sports Fac.: Tennis Center, Indoor Racquetball courts, Fitness Center, 6 Swimming pools, Lakes, Jogging & Cycling trails
Location: Tarpon Springs, Tampa

Courses: #1 (7230), #2 (7000), #3 (6550), #4 (6400)
No. of Holes: 72
Club House: 800-456-2000
Fees: ⫙⫙
Reservations: Call for reservations
Season: Open all year

Hills? In this part of Florida? You bet. Innisbrook, sister resort of Durango's Tamarron, also operated by Golf Hosts, is a woodsy kaleidoscope of citrus groves, perfumed hibiscus, lakes and moss-laden pines. It's also a well-respected golf and tennis resort, plus it has a noted health and sports institute where professionals assess your overall athletic abilities, then tailor a program to help you meet your goals. The thousand acre estate is located a few miles south of the fishing and Greek sponge diving town of Tarpon Springs, on the Gulf of Mexico coast. Tampa International Airport is a 25 minute limousine drive away, and for those coming by Amtrak, Clearwater station is closest.

Guests stay in condominium complexes, the largest being a 2,000 square feet two-bedroom suite which can sleep up to six.

Tennis is big here, and the facilities are geared to the serious player, as well as we mortals who love a recreational game or two. 18 tennis courts, 11 of which are Vel-Play composition clay, and 7 faster, firm-surfaced Laykold courts are available. This is the home of the Australian Tennis Institute, featuring an individualized program of small-group clinic instruction. The large tennis and racquetball center has four racquetball courts, and a well-stocked shop carrying every accessory imaginable.

Catfish, blue gill and bass are stocked in the resort's lakes, and you can rent the rods needed to reel in the big ones. Other diversions include a fitness center, miniature golf, bicycles, 6 swimming pools, charter fishing and sailing, and a pretty beach just minutes away. Suggested area attractions include the Dali Art Museum in St. Petersburg, sports events at Tampa Stadium, the live sponge diving show at Spongeorama in Tarpon Springs, and shopping excursions to nearby St. Armand's Key.

Lucky is the golfer who can play all 63 holes here. Copperhead, rated the state's #1 course in 1986, is three nines. A tough tournament course, its fairways are bordered by towering native pines, with plenty of water coming into play. Sandpiper, shortest of the three, requires accurate iron play as each hole is well defined by bunkers and water. Island, first course to open, in the fall of 1970, is a par 72 hilly layout with many heavily wooded areas.

Royal Oak Resort & Golf Club

Royal Oak, may be the "best kept golf secret" in Florida. The Club is located in the town of Titusville, near the Space Center. The lodge, a two-story structure adjacent to the clubhouse, includes 21 spacious and well appointed rooms, owned and operated by the Club. The rooms overlook either the Olympic sized pool or the beautiful ninth fairway and green. Each of these newly renovated guestrooms has two double beds, a refrigerator, cable TV and coffee maker. A laundry and ice machine is located in the building for the convenience of all lodge guests. The restaurant facility is located in the 22,000-square-foot architecturally dramatic clubhouse and features a conference room, banquet facilities, a large main Dining Room, a lounge and snack bar.

The course was designed by Dick Wilson, who was not only the architect for many great courses in Florida, such as Doral and Bay Hill, but others throughout North America and overseas. The 18-hole championship course, rated 70.1, opened for play in 1963. The course is maintained with Bermuda grass and over seeded in early November with rye grass to tees and fairways and poa trivialis on the greens. Many beautiful native birds, including sand hill cranes and other Florida Wildlife have made their home on the 170 acres of picturesque terrain, adding to the enjoyment of playing at Royal Oak.

Address: 2150 Country Club Drive, Titusville, 32780
800-884-2150
E-mail: royal_oak_golf@msn.com
Web site: http://www.royaloakgolfresort.com
No. of Rooms: 40
Rates: Inquire
Restaurant: Royal Oak Restaurant
Business Fac.: Conference room, Banquet facilities
Sports Fac.: Swimming pool
Location: 45 minutes east of Orlando airport

Course: Royal Oak (6709, par 71)
No. of Holes: 18
Guest Policy: Open to public
Club House: 407-268-1550
Fees: ↑
Reservations: Reservations available 6 days in advance
Season: Open all year
Carts: Carts included in fees

Saddlebrook Resort – Tampa

Address: 5700 Saddlebrook Way, Wesley Chapel, 33543
Phone: 813-973-1111
800-729-8383
Fax: 813-973-1312
E-mail: info@ saddlebrookresort.com
Web site: http://www. saddlebrookresort.com
No. of Rooms: 800
Rates: Seasonal
Restaurant: Cypress Restaurant, Terrace on the Green, Dempsey's Steak House, Poolside Cafe
Bar: TD's Sports Bar, Polo Lounge, Poolside Bar
Business Fac.: Resort has 82,000 sq. ft. of versatile function and meeting space in 34 meeting rooms.
Sports Fac.: Two 18-hole golf courses, 45 tennis courts, Sports Village and Fitness Center, 7,000 sq ft European-style spa
Location: On 480 acres of lush Florida countryside, 12 miles north of Tampa

Courses: Saddlebrook—6574–70, Palmer—6469–71
No. of Holes: 18
Guest Policy: Open to public
Club House: 813-973-1111
Fees: Inquire
Reservations: 2 days in advance
Season: Open all year
Carts: Cart included in fees

Saddlebrook Resort is just 35 minutes north of Tampa International Airport.

Saddlebrook has renovated and added to it's meeting services. Through it's group activites department, Saddlebrook offers a variety of team building activities to enhance the themes and goals of meetings. Corporate challenges, team building and sports events, as well as wellness seminars, small group and spouse programs are among the choices offered.

Saddlebrook's unique Walking Village design features 800 guest rooms and one- and two-bedroom suites.

From the Golf Shop, located within the Walking Village, golfers tee off on two 18-hole championship courses designed by Arnold Palmer. Saddlebrook is headquarters of the Arnold Palmer Golf Academy. Tennis at Saddlebrook is unsurpassed. The resort boasts 45 tennis courts; all Grand Slam playing surfaces. World renowned Hopman Tennis Program is available year round. Saddlebrook's Sports Village is anchored by a 3,300 sq. ft. Fitness Center. The 7,000 sq. ft. Spa offers a full array of relaxation and pampering services. There are three pools including the half-million Superpool.

Four star dining is available in a variety of indoor and outdoor restaurants. What was once the Little Club Restaurant is now Dempsey's Steak House. Guests can choose prime beef. The Cypress Restaurant features market fresh seafood. There is a lounge featuring nightly entertainment, a sports bar and a pool bar.

Palm Beach Polo & Country Club

This is the international home of polo: we mean white breeches, mallets, 7½ minute-long chukkers and the Piaget $100,000 World Cup Championships. The Club is recognized as the international headquarters for the sport of kings, with ten polo fields, club house and an equestrian center. Guests stay in contemporary Florida-style condominiums with fairway of lake views, and have the use of a tennis center with 24 courts, (all three surfaces), two croquet lawns, numerous swimming pools and a full health spa. Additional amenities include rowing clinics, bicycle rentals, squash and racquetball. Three clubhouses scattered about the grounds house four dining rooms. Prince Watchers, be alert! Prince Charles has visited here four times, as have other assorted royalty.

Bring your credit cards because Worth Avenue is only 20 minutes away. The ocean is a half hour away, and the concierge will be glad to help you arrange a deep sea fishing excursion.

If you're coming for golf, you won't be disappointed. Three top designers have had a hand here. 1976 U.S. Open winner Jerry Pate teamed up with Ron Garl to design the Dunes—a Scottish style links course with treacherous pot bunkers, extensive mounding, grass traps and fairways full of swales and ripples. There's also Cypress Course by Pete and P. B. Dye. There's still another nine, the fabulous Fazio holes from 1978. Site of the PGA Chrysler Team Championship held annually in December, all 45 holes are in excellent shape.

Address: 13198 Forest Hill Blvd, West Palm Beach, 33414
Phone: 407-798-7000
800-327-4204
Fax: 407-798-7052
E-mail: info@pbpolo.com
Web site: http://www.pbpolo.com
No. of Rooms: 100
Rates: Inquire
Restrictions: No pets allowed
Restaurant: Four dining rooms
Bar: Players Club
Business Fac.: Administrative assistance, Audio-visual, Conference room, capacity 60
Sports Fac.: Tennis courts, Handball courts, Polo, Helath Spa, Croquet, Horseback riding, Swimming pool, Fitness center
Location: Palm Beach County

Courses: Dunes Course (7050), Cypress Course, Olde Course
No. of Holes: 45
Guest Policy: Call for availability
Club House: 407-798-7407
Reservations: Must be made 48 hours in advance
Season: Open all ycarr

Barnsley Inn & Golf

Address: 597 Barnsley Gardens Rd, Adairsville, 30103
Phone: 770-773-7480
Web site: http://www.barnsleyinngolf.com
No. of Rooms: 70
Rates: $$$
Restaurant: The Rice House, Woodlands Grill
Business Fac.: Conference facilities for up to 150
Sports Fac.: Walking/hiking trails, Swimming pool, Tennis courts, Fitness Center, Golf practice facility, Fishing, Sauna, Steam, Whirlpool

Location: One hour north of Atlanta on I-75
Course: Barnsley Gardens
No. of Holes: 18
Guest Policy: Open to public
Club House: 770-773-7480
Fees: TT
Reservations: Call to make reservations
Carts: Cart and range balls included in fees

Destined to be one of the finest resorts in America, Barnsley Inn & Golf will soon be a favorite among those with discriminating taste. A 19th Century inspired village with charming pedestrian streetscapes contain the sumptuously appointed country cottages.

Barnsley's boutique guest cottages feature 70 individually appointed residences with wood-burning fireplaces, 12-foot ceilings, hardwood floors, book cabinets, king-size four-posted and sleigh beds, armories and ceiling fans. Each cottage bathroom features a period-inspired ball-and-claw foot cast iron tub.

Fresh herbs and vegetables grown at the resort heighten the culinary experience enjoyed by each patron. For fine dining, The Rice House features traditional Southern dishes recreated for the contemporary palate. In the tradition of the world's finest steakhouses, there is the Woodlands Grill.

The Spa at Barnsley Gardens offers seven treatment rooms, a ladies' and gentlemen's grooming area with separate sauna, steam room and whirlpool. The facility includes a fitness center and parlor room, where guests can relax and enjoy herbal teas and fresh vegetable and fruit juices.

A golf course crafted in a pristine woodland setting with only golf in mind, it is traditional in design without disturbing the surrounding residences, it was meticulously designed to preserve the natural beauty of the course's wooded surroundings by one of America's foremost golf experts, Jim Fazio. Whether you are here for the day or overnight, Barnsley Inn & Golf offers its' golf patrons the practice green and range facilities at no additional cost. Surrounded by nature at its' best with no two holes alike. Memorable dramatic elevation changes contribute to the creation of one of the best collection of par three's in golf.

Marietta Conference Center and Resort

The moment you enter the marble floor lobby with rich mahogany pillars, you realize you are someplace special. Exquisite area rugs, tasteful crystal chandeliers, privately commissioned wall murals and an outstanding collection of art all contribute to the distinctive ambiance that is the Marietta Conference Center & Resort. Inspired by Greek Revival architecture of the classic South, this 132 acre-resort reflects the historic ground on which it stands. Traditions of the Old South meet modern convenience at the Resort's hilltop setting in historic Marietta.

Mellow golds, deep reds and rich greens are gracefully used throughout the 200 spacious guestrooms, including impressive parlors and a Presidential Suite offering a spectacular view of rolling fairways and Kennesaw Mountain. Traditional furnishings with a rich mahogany finish and reminiscent of the style and elegance of 1850's Georgia.

The Marietta Conference Center & Resort offers guests a fine dining experience in Hamilton's Restaurant, or light fare, billiards and conversation in The Pub. The catering professionals of the Marietta Conference Center & Resort offer exceptional service, impeccable settings, and unparalleled menu selections. The Resort creates experiences appropriate for any size event, for any occasion.

The Marietta Conference Center & Resort provides a fully equipped health club and sauna, and the latest in aerobic and weight equipment. The resort also features lighted tennis courts and an outdoor swimming pool with sauna and sundeck.

The 18-hole par 71, championship golf course, just steps away from meetings, will satisfy even the most demanding enthusiast. Presenting a spectacular view of the lush Georgia countryside, it is an ideal backdrop for outdoor events and networking sessions on the Veranda Lawn. The grounds of the Resort are perfect for a quiet stroll after dinner or a walk through the historic gardens of Brumby Hall.

Address: 2964 Peachtree Road, N.W. Suite 530, Atlanta, 30305
Phone: 404-261-7080
Fax: 404-261-7101
E-mail: info@sentryhospitality.com
Web site: http://www. mariettaresort.com
No. of Rooms: 200
Restrictions: 7 rooms equipped for physically challenged
Restaurant: Hamilton's Restaurant, The Pub, The Veranda
Business Fac.: Conference concierge services, Dedicated conference space, Continous coffee breaks, On-site Audio/visual, Valet Parking, Airport shuttle, Telephone/computer communications
Sports Fac.: Fully equipped health club, Sauna, Aerobic and weight equipment, Lighted tennis courts, Outdoor swimming pool with sauna and deck
Location: 20 minutes from downtown Atlanta

Course: The City Club (5721, par 71)
No. of Holes: 18
Guest Policy: Open to public
Club House: 404-528-4653
Reservations: Call to make reservations

Chateau Elan Golf Club

Address: 100 Rue Charlemagne, Braselton, 30517
Phone: 678-425-0900
800-233-WINE
Fax: 678-425-6000
E-mail: chateau@chateauelan.com
Web site: http://www.chateauelan.com
No. of Rooms: 277
Rates: $$
Restaurant: 7 restaurants
Bar: Irish pub
Business Fac.: 25,000+ sq ft of meeting space, which includes 19 conference rooms, 2 grand ballrooms, 3 boardrooms, and a stepped auditorium (can accomodate up to 60 people). Meeting space comes equipped with complete sound & lighting and audiovisual capabilities
Sports Fac.: Stan Smith Tennis Center, full-service European-style health spa
Location: Just minutes north of Atlanta

Courses: Chateau Course (7030, page 71), Woodlands Course (6851, par 72), Executive Walking Course (9 hole course)
No. of Holes: 45
Guest Policy: Open to public
Club House: 678-425-6050
Fees: ⌐
Reservations: jross@chateauelan.com
Season: Open all year

The pitch roof, wrought-iron exterior detailing, and cornice moldings combine to give this French-style Chateau just north of Atlanta the feel of an authentic French Country Estate. The 277 deluxe guest rooms, 17 of which are ADA accessible, and 20 suites continue the French theme with pastel colors, window shutters, and French Country furnishings.

Relax in the European-style health spa while a massage therapist massages away your tension, have an expert trainer assess your fitness and make a customized exercise program, or take yoga, aerobic or stress management classes. And, of course, the spa offers skin and body treatments. Afterwards, continue on your way to health and wellness with the Fleur-de-Lis Restaurant, serving nutritious and delectable cuisine.

The resort, which was awarded with a Four-Star Award from the Mobil Travel Guide, also features the Stan Smith designed tennis center, winery tour and tasting of the award-winning wines, an equestrian show center, and seven restaurants.

The Golf Academy at Chateau Elan provides a great practice facility, and group tournaments and lessons can be arranged through the pro shop. The club features a covered, climate-controlled outdoor pavilion, perfect for award presentations, meetings, cocktail parties and banquets. In the evening, groups can enjoy the Chateau Elan's Night Golf on the 9-hole Par 2 Course, with lighted flagsticks, glow markers and tiki-torches marking the course, and glow balls, clubs and flashlights for the golfers.

Chateau Elan features 4 golf courses, ranging from 18-hole championship courses to the 9-hole Par 3 course. The championship Chateau Course was designed by Dennis Griffiths with contoured fairways, lakes and ponds on 178 acres. The Woodlands Course, also designed by Griffiths, is an 18-hole course ranging in location from pastureland to forest to water with many elevation changes. The Par 3 Executive Walking Course is a 9-hole course behind the Chateau, perfect for a quick golf game.

Gold Creek Resort & Conference Center

The charm of Gold Creek is seen in the European designed villas that surround the reception and Conference Center. Each two-story villa is comprised of eight individual guestrooms, each with different decor and offering such practical comforts as hairdryers, iron and ironing boards, as well as Jacuzzis in selected rooms. In addition, there are two common gathering rooms in each villa, with fireplaces, full refrigerators, microwaves, coffee makers and wet bars, making your accommodations intimate and private.

Enjoy a round robin, a doubles or singles match on the tennis courts, or relax and unwind poolside while enjoying the sounds of their spectacular 60-foot waterfall. Volleyball, horseback riding, fishing and boating are available, as is a soothing massage given by a trained masseuse.

Golf Digest nominated Gold Creek as Georgia's Best New Course. It's no wonder. The Gold Creek course was shaped from the natural beauty of rolling hills, spring-fed lakes and streams. Featuring fast bent greens, Gold Creek is immaculately maintained, plays to 6921 yards and offers 360-degree views of the magnificent Georgia Mountains. Take pleasure in the gentle breezes, the quiet, and the pure challenge of championship golf. Gold Creek welcomes the opportunity to host corporate golf outings and events.

Address: PO Box 1357, Dawsonville, 30534
Phone: 706-265-2700
800-966-2441
Fax: 706-344-3400
Web site: http://www.goldcreek.com
No. of Rooms: 74
Rates: $
Business Fac.: 3,000 sq ft ballroom, 2 breakout rooms, executive board room, 15 gathering rooms, audiovisual equipment & ergonomic chairs
Sports Fac.: Tennis courts, outdoor pool, volleyball sand court
Location: 50 minutes North of Atlanta

Course: Gold Creek Course (6921, par 72)
No. of Holes: 18
Guest Policy: Open, semi-private
Club House: 706-265-2700
Fees: ††
Reservations: Can make reservations 5 days in advance
Season: Open all year

Reynolds Plantation

Address: 100 Linger Longer Rd,
Greensboro, 30642
Phone: 706-467-3151
800-733-5253
E-mail: holle@
reynoldsplantation.com
Web site: http://www.
reynoldsgolf.com
Restaurant: Elegant cuisine or
casual lounge
Business Fac.: Meeting rooms and
facilities
Sports Fac.: Golf, swim, tennis,
marina
Location: Historic house in GA,
7,000 acres of woodlands

Course: Plantation Course (6656,
par 72)
No. of Holes: 18
Guest Policy: Open to public
(closed on Mondays)
Club House: 706-467-3159
Fees: ⅂⅂
Reservations: Can make reserva-
tions 3 days in advance

About halfway between Atlanta and Augusta is
Lake Oconee and the 5,200-acre Reynolds Plantation, a community of golf courses in the pine forests that wrap around some of the lake's 374-mile
shoreline. If the dozens of species of trees and 50
varieties of birds don't reset your pulse to a slower
rhythm, just give it a few minutes. A community
rich in history and tradition, the gracious grounds
of Reynolds Plantation provide a cool retreat in
the rolling woodlands overlooking magnificent
the lake.

Accommodations will include two- and three-
bedroom cottages with a complimentary breakfast at the club each morning. The other recreational amenities at Reynolds also are superb and
include boating, swimming in the lake or in one of
two club pools, tennis, and fitness facilities.

And if you are looking for a good round of golf,
there are three to choose from here. The Plantation course's layout was immediately honored as
one of *Golf Magazine*'s top 10 new courses in the
country. A delight to golf purists, the course features shapely rolling fairways that produce subtle
lies, with smaller greens framed by the forest's
dogwoods and azaleas. There is no radical contouring, harsh transition areas or artificial landscaping. The Jack Nicklaus-designed Great
Waters course garnered the same honor from *Golf
Magazine*. Great Waters recently hosted to qualifying stages for the Andersen Consulting World
Championship of Golf. The newest course at Reynolds Plantation is the Tom Fazio-designed
National Course. Fazio used the beautiful rolling
terrain and built a course that pleases him particularly for the variety of holes he has been able to
create on elevations that rise and fall anywhere
from 60 to 100 feet, in and around the lakefront's
most dramatic topography.

Renaissance Pineisle Resort

Just south of the Chattahoochee National Forest in northwestern Georgia resides Stouffer PineIsle Resort on sparkling Lake Lanier. This contemporary five story design is perched in a lush pine forest surrounded by this stunning recreational area. The lakeside setting provides a special opportunity for guests, particularly families, to indulge in just about any recreational whim.

You'll find the food at PineIsle lives up to Stouffer's reputation. The Pavilion charms you with seafood and continental favorites while you enjoy Lake Lanier's views. For an informal setting, The Gazebo offers tempting selections ranging from salads to heartier fare. The Clubhouse Restaurant is the spot for a cold beer and a mile-high sandwich after a round of golf or tennis. Kids will want to head for the great hamburgers and cookouts at the scenic Marina Grill. You'll welcome the famed Southern hospitality, and PineIsle knows how to serve it.

If you're an avid fisherman, or have fantasized about Striped Bass, the creeks, quiet coves and inlets of the deep clear lake are waiting for you. Sailboats, dinghies, motor boats, you name it—they're all available at an excellent marina. Don't overlook water skiing, hiking, tennis, horseback riding, and the twin-flume water slides. An unbeatable white sand beach for unlimited castle-building and a special Kids Krew program ensure that children will have the time of their lives.

Listed as one of Georgia's Top Ten, this 12 year old scenic, tough course annually hosts the Nestle World Championship of Women's Golf, a tournament that pays the highest first place money on the LPGA. Gary Player and Ron Kirby and Associates designed the course, which is very tight, with eight holes calling for drives across sections of the lake. Hilly, rolling and pine-scented, with elevated tees and views of the lake and the Blue Ridge Mountains, the course is 6,003 yards from the white tees. #5 is similar in design to Pebble Beach's 18th—a long drive over water, and the second shot is anywhere from a 160-250 yard shot with an inlet guarding the front part of the green. What's guarding the rest of it is more of lovely Lake Lanier.

Address: 900 Holiday Rd, Lake Lanier Island, 30518
Phone: 770-945-8921
800-HOTELS-1
Fax: 770-945-1024
Web site: http://www.renaissancehotels.com/ATLSR
Rates: Inquire
Restaurant: The Breeze Restaurant and Lounge, The Clubhouse, The Marina Grill.
Business Fac.: Business center and 22 indoor business meeting rooms.
Sports Fac.: Exercise/weight room, sauna, pool, challenge ropes course.
Location: Nestled amid a majestic 1200 acre pine forest in the foothills of the Blue Ridge Mountains

Course: Pineisle (6527, par 72)
No. of Holes: 18
Guest Policy: Open to public
Club House: 770-945-8921
Fees: ↑↑
Reservations: Can make reservations 7 days in advance
Season: Open all year
Carts: Gas carts included in green fees

Lake Lanier Islands Hilton Resort

Address: 7000 Holiday Rd, Lake Lanier Islands, 30518
Phone: 770-945-8787
800-932-3322
Fax: 770-932-5471
Web site: http://www.hilton.com/hotels/LKLLHHF/
No. of Rooms: 224
Rates: Inquire
Restaurant: Sylvan's, Emerald Pub, Golf Club Grill
Bar: Emerald Pub
Business Fac.: 16 meeting rooms, largest up to 500 capacity
Sports Fac.: Tennis courts, Swimming pool, Fitness center, Nature/jogging trails
Location: 45 minutes from downtown Atlanta

Course: Lake Lanier Island Resort (6341)
No. of Holes: 18
Guest Policy: Open to public
Club House: 770-945-8787
Reservations: Up to 7 days in advance
Season: Open all year

Set on the shores of Lake Lanier among stately trees, this luxurious facility makes you feel you've left all your cares far behind. All rooms are have spectacular views, some of the forest and others the lake. You'll be pampered in the lap of luxury here. A perfect family resort, the Hilton Family Plan makes no charge for children (regardless of age) when you share the same room, so pack-up your bags and come and see us!

The resorts had something for the whole family from relaxing on the beach to swimming, fishing, water-skiing and boats for rent. You can even enjoy the nearby water park with rides and water slides. Their is also a private pool, tennis courts, horseback riding, a fitness center, biking, nature trails and games for the children.

The conference facilities are top-notch, well worth considering for your next event. Just leave the planning to us!

Lake Lanier Island Hilton Golf Course was designed by Joe Lee, and voted in the top five new resort courses by *Golf Digest* in 1989. Most of the holes on the course run along the lake and are surrounded by stately, mature trees. There are over seventy bunkers, the fairways are hilly and offer many difficult lies. A challenging and beautiful course!

Pine Mountain Callaway Gardens

If flowers, butterflies, flamboyant greenhouse displays, a 175-acre fishing lake, fly fishing and a gun club appeal to you, Callaway Gardens is the place for you. Add 63 holes of golf, tennis, racquetball and a smorgasbord of lakeside activities for all ages, three swimming pools, a variety of restaurants and accommodations and you have the ingredients for a memorable vacation in a horticultural paradise about 70 southeast of Atlanta.

The new Virginia Hand Callaway Discovery Center serves as the welcome center. Adjacent is the Discovery Amphitheater featuring a daily Birds of Prey show, featuring native and exotic raptors. A few items from the resort's calendar show Summer performances by the FSU "Flying High" circus; a hot air balloon festival; a steeplechase; and a spectacular holiday light shows, Fantasy In Lights.

The golf course names are easy to remember: Mountain View, Gardens View, Lake View and Sky View, an easy-going 9-hole executive course. Mountain View hosts the PGA Tours Buick Challenge. Its rating of 74.1 gives one an idea of its difficulty, but no rating can be given the sheer beauty of fairways and wooded glens ablaze with magentas, roses and salmons of azaleas and rhododendrons in bloom. Gardens View features bent grass year round on tees, fairways and greens. Lakes and streams characterize Lake View course, a par 70, 6,006 yard test where #10 is tricky. It's a short par 3 over a lake, but bunkers and the green block entrance to the green.

Address: U.S. Highway 18, PO Box 2000, Pine Mountain, 31822
Phone: 706-663-2281
800-CALLAWAY
Fax: 706-663-5090
E-mail: reservations@ callawaygardens.com
Web site: http://www. callawaygardens.com
No. of Rooms: 800
Rates: Inquire
Restaurant: The Georgia Room, 7 other restaurants
Bar: The Vineyard Green 5:30 pm to Midnight (most days)
Business Fac.: Conference & connvention rooms, capacity 1500, on site food, full service conference staff.
Sports Fac.: Swimming pools, Tennis courts, Water skiing, Sailing, Fitness center, gun club, biking.
Location: World-class garden and resort 60 minutes from Atlanta airport.

Courses: Mountain View (yardage 7057, slope 138, par 72), Lake View (yardage 6006, slope 122, par 70), Gardens View (yardage 6392, slope, 119, par 72), Sky View (9 hole executive course)
No. of Holes: 63
Guest Policy: Open to public
Club House: 800-225-5292
Fees: Inquire
Reservations: Overnight guests can book at anytime, day guests may book 72 hours in advance
Season: Open all year
Carts: Included with most greens fees

The Cloister

Address: 100 First St, Sea Island, 31561
Phone: 912-638-3611
800-732-4752
Fax: 912-638-5159
Web site: http://www.
seaisland.com/
inpage.asp?pid=100&menuid=1
No. of Rooms: 286
Rates: $$$
Restaurant: The Cloister Dining Room, Sea Island Beach Club, Sea Island Golf Club, St. Simon Island Club
Bar: Spanish Lounge
Business Fac.: Business center, Computer service, Copiers, Audiovisual
Sports Fac.: Full service spa, Tennis courts, 2 swimming pools, Horseback riding, Boating, Fishing, Biking, Skeet and trap shooting, Sailing
Location: On 5-mile beach off the southern coast of Georgia

Courses: Plantation, Seaside, Marshside, Retreat
No. of Holes: 36
Guest Policy: Open to public
Club House: 912-638-5118
Fees: ↑↑↑
Reservations: Reservations available 365 days in advance
Season: Open all year
Carts: Carts included in fees

A massive fireplace and a grand piano set in a romantic Spanish-style lounge with chandeliered high ceiling and stained glass windows will greet your arrival at this exclusive island resort. Opened in 1928, The Cloister has maintained its historic charm of years gone by while providing all the modern amenities that guests appreciate.

Southern tradition is nowhere better expressed than in the food served here. An exciting Friday night treat is the plantation supper, lighted by torches and bonfire. Savor steaming clam chowder, hush puppies and picnic favorites Cloister style, to the music of the Sea Island singers.

Or, experience the expertise of chef Franz Buck in the luxury of a plush carpeted dining room overlooking gardens.

You can work off the dessert with an invigorating swim at the Sea Island Beach Club and Spa, or take advantage of the resort's 18 tennis courts. For a more relaxing sport, take a leisurely horseback ride on the beach and trails, or go boating the broad waterways beside River House.

Splashy azaleas, a quaint covered bridge, lagoons guarding tight fairways, sharply elevated greens, gargantuan deep bunkers, unpredictable ocean breezes, holes hemmed by marshes, an insouciant pelican gazing at your grip. These are The Cloister's 54 holes of legendary golf, which include four nines by four different architects at the Sea Island Golf Club, and an additional 18 at adjacent St. Simons Island Club.

Seaside Nine, opened in 1929, plays like the legend it is. #7, at 414 yards requires a powerful carry from the tee across 200 yards of tidal creek and marshes, then a tremendous bunker blocks a shorter drive to require a dogleg. Add a stiff Atlantic prevailing wind, and any birdie here will most likely be in the bush. Plantation Nine is characterized by sweeping fairways and the lagoon that lurks around four holes. Dick Wilson designed Retreat Nine in 1960, emphasizing huge lakes and the Atlantic itself which borders fairways. Marshside Nine was created to be wholly different, yet happily complementing the other Sea Island nines. The name tells you a lot about the layout. Here's hoping you learn about the marsh wrack and ghost crabs from the "Field Guide to Sea Island" instead of figuring out how to play out of it.

Sky Valley Resort

Sky Valley is Georgia's highest city with alpine skiing in winter & championship golf when the snow melts.

The Treed Bear restaurant serves up artful afternoons & elegant evenings with fabulous food & drink.

Sky Valley is a 2300 acre resort with elevations of 3000-4000 feet so you can experience cool breezes all summer long.

Surrounded by national forest, you will never know you are just 2 hours North of ATL, and minutes from Dillard, GA & Highlands, NC.

Address: 696 Sky Valley Way #1, P.O. Box 1, Sky Valley, 30537
Phone: 706-746-5302
800-437-2416
Fax: 706-746-5198
E-mail: info@skyvalley.com
Web site: http://www.skyvalley.com
No. of Rooms: 60
Rates: $
Restaurant: Treed Bear @ the Sky Valley Lodge
Bar: Big Bear Tavern (only for catered parties)
Business Fac.: A relaxed retreat setting—for groups up to 100 people.
Sports Fac.: Championship Golf, GA's only Ski Resort, Swim & Tennis Center, & 2300 acres to explore
Location: 14 miles from Highlands, NC & 4 miles from Dillard, GA—2 hours North of ATL

Course: Sky Valley Course (6452, par 72)
No. of Holes: 18
Guest Policy: Open to public
Club House: 706-746-5303
Fees: ⌐
Reservations: Can make reservations 20 days in advance
Season: year round
Carts: Carts included in fees

Brasstown Valley Resort

Address: Highway 76, Young Harris, 30582
Phone: 706-379-9900
800-201-3205
E-mail: info@brasstownvalley.com
Web site: http://www.
brasstownvalley.com
No. of Rooms: 134
Rates: $$
Restaurant: The Dining Room, McDivets
Bar: The Fireside Lounge
Business Fac.: 14,298 square ft of meeting space, includes: Brasstown Grand Ballroom (3,872ft), Trackrock Amphitheater (1,950ft), Conference Center (6 conference rooms and 2 board rooms), Rear screen projection, Catering staff
Sports Fac.: Tennis, Hiking, Complete fitness center, Heated indoor/outdoor pools, Whirlpool, Steam room, Sauna, Rock climbing, Mountain biking, Boating, Whitewater rafting, Nature walks, Horseshoes, Fishing
Location: In the Blue Ridge Mountains in northern Georgia, 2 hours from Atlanta, Chattanooga and Asheville

Course: Brasstown Valley Golf Club (7100)
No. of Holes: 18
Club House: 706-379-4613
Fees: ⌐
Reservations: Call for reservations
Season: Open all year

Nestled beneath Brasstown Bald, about two hours north of Atlanta, Georgia is the sweeping, forested cove known in old Indian lore as "the Enchanted Valley." Since 1995, this natural sanctuary for birds and travelers has become known as Brasstown Valley Resort. Strolling the valley these days, archeologists would most likely find errant golf balls, lost buttons and contented wildlife in the rolling hills of Brasstown Valley Resort.

The moment you step into the stunning hexagon shaped lodge you'll be enveloped in the soft glow of the massive stone fireplace and oak vaulted ceilings. Turn and look out any floor-to-ceiling window for a panoramic view of exquisite golf links under glorious mountain vistas. Flop into a giant chair and sip hot cider by our 72-foot high fireplace, or settle into a rocker along the verandah and contemplate the stunning view. Wander the grounds, hike a trail or focus your swing on the driving range. It all adds up to your own personal Mountain Retreat experience.

Enjoy a menu of traditional North Georgia favorites and regional game specialties prepared by Chef David Boggs. Dine near a cozy fireplace, out on the spectacular mountain-view verandah, or indoors in the white table-clothed privacy of the Overlook. McDivots Sports Pub is open for lunch, dinner or just a quick bite in-between. Stop by for a drink and a game of darts, billiards or armchair sports viewing on the big-screen TV. The Fireside Lounge is perfect for cocktails and conversations by a crackling fire under natural pine beams.

Ranked by *Golf Digest* as one of the Top Five Best Places to play golf in Georgia, Brasstown Valley is also a member of the prestigious "Leading Golf Courses of America" which is based upon ranking in the top three percent of all golf courses in North America. The championship 7,100-yard Scottish links-style golf course designed by Don Griffiths and Associates with respect to wildlife and mountain terrain, is a true nature-lovers dream. The Brasstown Valley Golf Course plays through tall native grasses, highly manicured fairways, treacherous roughs and water coming into play on 10 holes. Nearby wildlife include black bear, deer, wild turkey and bald eagles.

Hyatt Regency Maui

The Kaanapali strip of hotels, condominiums and cottage colonies was the first planned resort complex on Maui, home of the sweetest onions, biggest protea, and potato chips like no others. Now, more than twenty-five years later, its centerpiece, the Hyatt Regency, is nothing short of spectacular. Tourists flock in droves to gawk at the multi-million dollar's worth of Asian art adorning lobbies and promenades, swans gliding on tranquil waters, and 20 acres of Japanese and tropical gardens. The eye-popper here is a two-acre water garden that incorporates grotto bar, waterfalls, streams, pools, a free-form swinging footbridge, a 130-foot water slide and exotic birds everywhere.

815 luxurious rooms in subdued tones of peach, beige and mauve overlook this jungle kingdom. Recreational diversions include a 55-foot catamaran, health club, tennis courts, popular restaurants and a disco.

The strip hops with activity night and day. Jump on the complimentary Kaanapali trolley that serves the resorts, Whalers Village Museum, shopping complex and golf courses. Join bodies sunning, sip a mai tai in a dazzling Polynesian bar, or sign the kids up for a snorkeling lesson. Hula or go scuba diving, sailing, swimming or visit historic sites.

The Royal Kaanapali Golf Courses, North and South, offer a pair of 18 hole championship courses with sweeping ocean views, blue sky, emerald fairways, and green mountains dominating the verdant landscape. North Course was designed by Robert Trent Jones, the golf course architect who has had more influence over the game than any other man. Bing Crosby played the opening holes here in 1962, and its been attracting celebrities ever since. You'll find undulating elevated greens, and generous bunkers, reflecting Jones' tenet that a well-designed course should be difficult to par, yet easy to bogey.

South Course, an Arthur Jack Snyder design, can be even trickier, with its own quirky hazards. It's a gem imbued with Snyder's strategic approach to the game—narrow fairways and small greens. As it winds from sea to mountain, the player faces a variety of holes, probably the most challenging being the ear-piercing whistle of the turn-of-the-century sugar train whose camera laden sightseers haven't developed an appreciation for concentration on the game.

Address: 200 Nohea Kai Dr, Kaanapali Beach, Maui, 96761
Phone: 808-661-1234
800-233-1234
Fax: 808-667-4498
Web site: http://www.hyatt.com/usa/maui/hotels/hotel_oggrm.html
No. of Rooms: 815
Rates: Inquire
Restaurant: Swan Court, Cascades Grille & Sushi Bar, Spats Trattoria, Pavillion, Weeping Banyan, Sunset Terrace
Bar: Grotto Bar
Business Fac.: Business Center with word processing, typing, faxes, photocopying, computer rental, internet access, shipping, communication equipment rentals, Full food/beverage service, Audio/visual equipment
Sports Fac.: Regency Tennis Center, Swimming pools, Beach Activity Center, Regency Health Club, Snorkeling, Kayaking, Boogie boarding, Windsurfing, Surfing, Parasailing, Scuba diving, Biking
Location: Lahaina

Courses: Ka'anapali—North Course (7179), South Course (6758)
No. of Holes: 36
Club House: 808-661-3691
Reservations: Call for reservations
Season: Open all year

Mauna Kea Beach Hotel

Address: 1 Mauna Kea Beach, P.O. Box 218, Kamuela, The Big Island, 96743
Phone: 808-882-7222
800-882-6060
Fax: 808-882-7657
E-mail: mkrres@ maunakeabeachhotel.com
Web site: http://www. maunakeabeachhotel.com
No. of Rooms: 310
Rates: $$$
Restaurant: The Batik, The Pavilion, The Terrace, Hau Tree/ Gazebo, 19th Hole, Clambake, Luau
Bar: Copper Bar
Business Fac.: North & South Pointe Lawns for outdoor receptions, Lloyd Sexton Gallery and smaller indoor garden rooms
Sports Fac.: Swimming, Snorkeling, Scuba, Sailing, Kayaking, Deep sea fishing, Whale watching
Location: On beautiful Kauna'oa Bay

Course: Mauna Kea (7114)
No. of Holes: 18
Guest Policy: Open to public
Club House: 808-882-1035
Fees: ↑↑↑
Reservations: Can make reservations 4 days in advance
Season: Open all year
Carts: Carts included in fees

A vision of Laurance Rockefeller, and now under the helm of Westin, this splendidly understated vacation destination welcomed its first guests in 1965, as the most luxurious hotel ever constructed in Hawaii. The renowned hotel sits on a hillside overlooking a white sandy beach and crystal waters. Landscaping and architecture are imaginative, with lofty palms towering over public areas where gentle breezes play. But what's most memorable here is the antique art displayed in public areas. A majestic seventh-century Buddha, Japanese tansu chests, and a remarkable collection of Hawaiian quilts are just a few of the treasures from Pacific Islands. Rooms are large, fanned by tradewinds, with attractive wooden shutters, wooden ceiling fans, private lanais, polished brick floors, and wicker furniture. Large floral lithographs in bright island colors by Hawaii's Lloyd Sexton inspire the decor. There are also 10 suites and 8 villas. Expect impeccable service, handsomely appointed tables and an innovative menu in the exotic, split-level Batik Room with its Ceylonese motif. There are five other restaurants, and five lounges scattered about the main building. Don't miss the weekly luau, with traditional roasted pig and local favorites such as guava and poi palau, and the music of Hawaii. There is excellent snorkeling, windsurfing and boogie boarding from the beach. And of course, a beautiful pool, thirteen tennis courts, and badminton courts. Also available are Lasers, and Scuba and deep sea fishing excursions aboard the resort's 58 foot catamaran. Try horseback riding, play volleyball, go hunting, or take a sightseeing helicopter trip and look down on the rivers of lava created by the Kiluea volcano. Or relax under a palm tree and ask yourself where else you can snow ski down a dormant volcano in the morning, and body surf in 75 degree clear water in the afternoon.

The Robert Trent Jones, Sr. 18 hole course is something to behold. Ready for play in 1964, the challenging course has won numerous awards. With lush grass growing on ancient lava that spills dramatically into the sea, the par 72 layout was recently toughened and softened, with four tees to challenge all playing levels. The spectacular par-three third hole carries 200 yards over the ocean from the blue tees. Hook it and you can kiss that little ball good-bye.

Kapalua Bay Hotel & Villas

Nestled in a 23,000 acre plantation on the west coast of Maui is Kapalua, one of Hawaii's most exclusive resorts. You'll get a taste of island luxury the minute you step into the hotel's grand, vaulted main lobby which opens to outdoor ocean vistas and tropical breezes.

Kapalua's variety of restaurants and gourmet menus featuring international cuisine and local specialties will please every palate. Below the hotel lobby, set amid a black marble waterfall and meandering waterways, The Garden offers everything from Maui's most tempting breakfast to gourmet dining with the sunset as its first course. Just a short stroll down the beach is The Bay Club, perched atop the promontory fronting Kapalua Bay. Here, spectacular ocean panoramas and outstanding island cuisine al fresco provide a most pleasurable diversion.

On land and sea, the sporting life is given high priority. Not only is there golf and a complete tennis complex at The Tennis Garden, there are also three secluded white-sand beaches at Kapalua where sailboating, scuba, surfing, and deep-sea fishing are available.

As if the resort's other amenities weren't enough, this is a golfer's Elysium. The Kapalua Golf Club comprises three championship courses illustrating the variety and diversity in the design work of Arnold Palmer, Ed Seay, and Ben Crenshaw/Bill Coore. The Bay Course, with lush tropical vegetation, and ocean vistas framed by historic Cook pines, rewards players of all levels. Village Course climbs higher in the hills, through eucalyptus and ironwood trees, past sparkling lakes and alongside ridges, then plunges dramatically into deep green valleys.

The Plantation Course is a grand-scale layout with strategic design. The fifth is Kapalua's signature hole. The hole will vary in length depending on the tee used, and you may be hitting anything from an 8 iron to a fairway wood. While carrying the blue Pacific is first order of business, the green is well bunkered and offers varying pin placements.

This is the home of big-name tournaments, which the golfing staff handles with ease. The Isuzu Kapalua International happens here as well as The Kirin Cup and the 1987 World Cup of Golf. Golfing greats who have birdied and bogeyed here include Norman, Langer, Simpson, Crenshaw, Nicklaus and Palmer.

Address: One Bay Dr, Kapalua, Maui, 96761
Phone: 808-669-5656
800-367-8000
Fax: 808-669-4694
Web site: http://www.kapaluabay.com
No. of Rooms: 294
Rates: Inquire
Restrictions: No pets allowed
Restaurant: The Bay Club
Bar: Bay Lounge
Business Fac.: Full conference facilities, Conference rooms, capacity 200
Sports Fac.: Swimming pool, Tennis courts, Sailing, Water sports
Location: Northwest corner of Maui

Courses: Bay Course (6731), Plantation Course, Village Course
No. of Holes: 54
Guest Policy: Resort guests have priority
Club House: 808-669-8871
Reservations: One week in advance
Season: Open all year

Ihilani Resort & Spa

Address: 92-1001 Olani St, Ko Olina, Kapolei, 76707
Phone: 808-679-0079
800-626-4446
Fax: 808-679-0080
E-mail: reservations@ihilani.com
Web site: http://www.ihilani.com
No. of Rooms: 387
Rates: Inquire
Restaurant: Spa Dining, Poolside Grill, Naupaka Terrace, Azul, Ushio-tei
Business Fac.: Several conference facilities, Audio/visual equipment
Sports Fac.: Tennis, Golf, Jacuzzi, Steamroom, Dolphin Experience, Scuba & Snorkel Cruise, Massage, Personal fitness & training
Location: 25 minute drive from Honolulu International Airport

Course: Ko Olina Course (6867, par 72)
No. of Holes: 18
Guest Policy: Open to public
Club House: 808-676-5300
Fees: ↑↑↑
Reservations: Reservations available 7 days in advance
Season: Open all year
Carts: Cart included in fees

The Ihilani is set in the 640-acre Ko Olina Resort. It is set on its own lagoon which features a beautiful white sand beach. The setting is quite dramatic and the lagoon gives you the opportunity to see and hear the gentle lapping of the waves.

The guest rooms are extremely large and luxuriously furnished in custom-make teach furniture. They offer deep European style tubs, two pairs of slippers, terry-cloth and Yukata robes, and the finest toiletries. Each room has a private lanai.

The cuisine at Ihilani is unique and uses only the best of local products. The five restaurants offer international and innovative new dishes. The Spa Cafe offers full flavor without the calories. The Spa specializes in an underwater massage that uses warmed seawater, which is uniquely relaxing. Almost every type of massage technique is offered, as well as herbal wraps and seaweed masks. A fitness facility has the latest exercise equipment, yoga, T'ai Chi and Hularobics workouts on the lagoon.

Since the resort is close to Waikiki, you'll have all the sightseeing and shopping readily available. Needless to say, all water sports can also be experienced right here at the resort!

The golf course is a championship layout and has hosted the Seniors Tour, and annually has hosted the LPGA Orix Hawaiian Ladies' Open. Water is the main ingredient to give you difficulty on this course, but don't underestimate the dozens of pot bunkers and split-level greens! Golf packages are available.

The Keiki Beachcomber Club is designed for the kids to have fun. They offer kite-flying, tide pool exploration, international games like Bocce ball, Indian kick ball and Tinikling, the Filipino Bamboo dance. Also offered is a state-of-the-art Computer Learning Center with color printer and scanner. And the kids get a great tour of the kitchens and chocolate shop.

Mauna Lani Bay Hotel & Bungalows

Nestled in a 16th century ebony lava flow, this six-story 351room resort, is the newest of the great golf and tennis destinations along this breathtaking coast. The atrium lobby is the most incredible feature, with six stories of lush rain forest foliage, waterfalls and a fish-filled lagoon. Acres of King Kamehameha I's ancient spring-fed fishponds and gardens provide solitude, picnic grounds and even a private swimming hole. 15th century rock shelters were left untouched during construction.

Ocean and mountain views highlight large light rooms, decorated in tones of burgundy and ivory. The Le Soliel is the signature restaurant here. Opening onto a seaside garden, the casually elegant award-winner boasts one of Hawaii's most extensive and impressive wine cellars. The other eateries, too, deserve applause.

Flanked by the island's four great mountains, the showpiece resort's recreational facilities are excellent. The Tennis Garden, with a five-star rating, has ten 3-speed outdoor courts. A large free-form pool, and jogging and bike trails are guaranteed to tempt a confirmed couch potato. The white sandy beach is slide show perfect, plus you can scuba dive, sail, fish for marlin, snorkel, or try an outrigger canoe.

Address: 68-1400 Mauna Lani Drive, Kohala Coast, 96743
Phone: 808-885-6622
800-367-2323
Fax: 808-885-1484
E-mail:
maunalani@maunalani.com
Web site: http://www.
maunalani.com
No. of Rooms: 350
Rates: $$$
Restaurant: Canoe House, The Bay Terrace Restaurant, Ocean Grill, Gallery Restaurant
Bar: Honu Bar
Business Fac.: Conference and banquet facilities for 10 to 400
Sports Fac.: Golf, 16 tennis courts, Jogging trails, Health club, Swimming pool, Sandy beaches, Diving, Sailing, Windsurfing, Fishing, Aerobics
Location: On the Kohala Coast of Hawaii's Big Island

Courses: South Course (6938, par 72), North Course (5331, par 72)
No. of Holes: 36
Guest Policy: Open to public
Club House: 808-885-6655
Fees: ↑↑↑
Reservations: Reservations available 3 days in advance
Season: Open all year
Carts: Cart included in fees

The magnificence of the Francis H. I'I Brown Course has moved players and naturalists to praise the vast lava sculpture whose green fairways snake through a treasure trove of ancient cave-homes, shrines and petroglyphs as well as the historic King's trail. The Homer Flint design, a 6,259 yard par 72, features four ocean holes, three lakes, 43 fairway bunkers, plenty of green traps, and a spectacular ocean shot from the 6th tee. A second 18 hole just opened in 1991.

Westin Hapuna Beach Prince Hotel

Address: 62-100 Kaua'oa Drive, Kohala Coast, 96743
Phone: 808-880-1111
800-882-6060
Fax: 808-880-3200
E-mail: mkrres@
hapunabeachprincehotel.com
Web site: http://www.
westinhapunabeachprincehotel.
com
No. of Rooms: 350
Rates: $$$
Restaurant: Five restaurants
Bar: Reef Lounge
Business Fac.: Full-service meeting complex, State-of-the-art versatility, Open-air courtyards
Sports Fac.: Golf, Fitness center, Sauna, Massage, Tennis, Seaside pool, Whirlpool spa
Location: Along the Kohala Coast on the big Island of Hawaii

Course: Hapuna Golf Course (6875, par 72)
No. of Holes: 18
Guest Policy: Open to public
Club House: 808-882-1035
Fees: ↑↑
Reservations: Call for reservations
Season: Open all year
Carts: Cart included in fees

Hapuna is a resort that prides itself on caring for the environment, and it shows in the low buildings that blend into the setting and a vastly increased bird population. Set on 32 acres, the paths wander through lush tropical gardens.

All rooms are large and elegantly furnished. There are private lanais with spectacular beach and ocean views.

You can't go wrong holding your convention here, everything is state-of-the-art, and the staff is friendly, attentive, and efficient. The facility even allows networking around the world, with translations services available if needed. A perfect meeting environment.

A fitness center will help to keep you trim, and the resort gives you access to all of Mauna Kea Beach's recreational facilities as well. Hiking trails make a walking tour easy, or go by horseback or bicycle. Helicopter tours are always a fascinating way to see the island, and are available for 30 minutes up to a full day.

With five different restaurants, you're sure to find something new for every meal. The Ocean Terrace offers sweeping ocean views along with its breakfast buffet. If you're looking for entertainment try the Reef Lounge.

The golf course is links-style and is quite hilly. Greens are set right into the landscape and can be tough with plenty of the lush growth coming into play. *Golf Magazine* has rated the course one of the best new courses.

Hyatt Regency Kauai

Of all the places of Paradise, this is perhaps most apparent on the Island of Kauai, and in the classic architecture and serene atmosphere of the Hyatt Regency Kauai Resort and Spa. To begin, a traditional lei welcome inspires your discovery and enjoyment of a culture at once timeless and timely.

Every room is a view room, with sweeping vistas of the ocean, the hotel lagoons, or the Haupu Mountains. Ground floor Garden Rooms are nestled among lush tropical gardens. We remind you that you are here to discover the secrets of the Garden Isle; and not just of your huge, 1,200 square foot room. This fact may escape you, given the ocean or pool view, separate bedroom with king size bed, and living area with remote TV, wet bar and separate dining area. The bath has both a shower and a tub with whirlpool and a remote mini TV.

At the Hyatt Regency Kauai, an extended and tempting menu of five restaurant and five lounge venues will sustain you. Tide Pools is a journey back to a time long ago is nurtured by the chance to feast on foods grown from the traditions and rich culture of the islands. Franciscan murals grace a Romanesque courtyard at Dondero. Antipasto, tiramisu, heavenly pastas and risotto are accented with herbs picked from the garden and complemented by the most extensive wine cellar on the island. Like a rainbow, Ilima offers a multi-hued open-air dining experience. Children love their own special menu. A conch shell sounds and dancers draped in ferns and flowers tell their stories in silence. This is the enchantment of the luau, and no visit to Hawaii is complete without experiencing it.

Perched atop spectacular 80 foot cliffs, and weaving gentle green contours accented by the stone ruins of ancient places of worship called heiaus, our Robert Trent Jones Jr. links-style course plays up to 7000 yards, and is truly one-of-a-kind. Since 1994, the Poipu Bay Resort Golf Course has been the home of the PGA Grand Slam of Golf; an event claimed to be the world's most exclusive golf tournament. Fair warning: your concentration is certain to be tested by distractions including rare Hawaiian monk seals, green sea turtles, humpback whales and native nene geese.

Address: 1571 Poipu Rd, Koloa, 96756
Phone: 808-742-1234
800-55-HYATT
Fax: 808-742-1557
Web site: http://www. kauai-hyatt.com
Restaurant: Llima Terrace, Tidepools, Dondero's, The Dock, Poipua Bay Grill & Bar, Kupono Cafe
Bar: Captain's Bar, Stevenson's Library, Seaview Terrace, Shipwreck Bar, Drums of Paradise Luau
Business Fac.: Over 65,000 sq ft of indoor/outdoor meeting space
Sports Fac.: 2 swimming pools, 5 acre saltwater lagoon, 25,000 sq ft ANARA health & fitness spa, 4 tennis courts, mountain bike rentals, beach access
Location: On 50 acres of oceanfront on Keoneola Bay

Course: Poipu Bay Golf Course (6959, par 72)
No. of Holes: 18
Guest Policy: Open to public
Club House: 808-742-9489
Fees: ↑↑↑
Reservations: Reservations available 30 days in advance
Season: Open all year
Carts: Cart included in fees

Kiahuna Plantation Resort

Address: 2253 Poipu Road, Koloa, Kauai, 96756
Phone: 808-742-6411
800-367-7052
Fax: 808-742-9121
Web site: http://www.outrigger.com/details/property.asp?code=kpr
No. of Rooms: 300
Rates: Inquire
Restaurant: Plantation Gardens
Sports Fac.: Tennis courts, Organized beach activities
Location: South shore Kauai

Course: Kiahuna (5631)
No. of Holes: 18
Guest Policy: Call for availability
Club House: 808-742-9595
Reservations: May be made one week in advance
Season: Open all year

Devotees of Kiahuna, the beautifully landscaped low-key condominium resort on Poipu Beach's sandy shore, have reef-sheltered beaches, long considered the garden island's best for snorkeling and surfing. The resort is plantation-style, with buildings no higher than the coconut palms, blending into the mature tropical gardens which were originally planted in the 1930s.

Dining options range from barbecuing and picnicking to the casual Courtside Bar and Grill and Clubhouse Restaurant. The creme de la creme here is the luxurious Plantation Gardens, where seafood and local delicacies are served in the original charming 19th century plantation house.

10 tennis courts, a large pool with a snack bar and acres of gardens for strolling will keep you busy. Beach sports are fantastic here—if you've never snorkeled, it's a must. Waimea Canyon, a 12-mile long chasm more than 3,000 feet deep is a mind-boggler when viewed through a rainbow spanning the river below. Spouting Horn, and historic Hanalei, too, are worth a visit. Next to the resort is one of the best snorkeling and body surfing beaches anywhere.

The course here is an 18 hole championship Robert Trent Jones, Jr. links course. It covers flat terrain and mingles with several important Historic Hawaiian village sites. A nicely maintained course, the fairways are bordered by lava gardens, and cloud-veiled Mount Waialeale, the world's wettest spot, serves as a backdrop.

Lodge at Koele

Lanai, known as The Pineapple Island created by the Dole dollars, is the least known of the major Hawaiian islands, and certainly the latest to be discovered. Development has been slow, largely because Castle & Cooke, owner of most of the land, is committed to maintaining and preserving the agriculture and wilderness areas.

The luxurious Lodge at Koele is an upscale up-country resort; a blend of an English hunting lodge with the traditions of old Hawaii. This Rockresort, with 102 rooms in garden surroundings, sits at the base of Lanaihales's towering heights, with a mani-cured croquet court facing the wide veranda. If you climb high enough on a clear day, you'll be rewarded by the sight of five other islands, miles of pineapple fields, and perhaps a whale or two in the channel off Maui. Take a stroll around the gardens, stopping for a view of the Great Hall with 50-foot fireplaces, beamed ceilings, overstuffed sofas, and an outstanding collection of Polynesian relics dis-covered on Lanai. The island, untrampled by hordes of visitors, is a perfect getaway for those seeking an adventure without organized tour bus-ses and fast food. While you won't find traffic jams and malls, you'll be offered top-notch horseback riding through the Lodge, you can play tennis, or hike the Munro Trail, up and over the ridge of mountains behind Lanai City (surely one of the most spectacular in Hawaii). The concierge will gladly help you plan day sails to other islands, acquaint you with hunting procedures, provide maps to Hulopoe Bay, and point you in the direc-tion of the Garden of the Gods, and petroglyphs to remember.

This is high country golf at its best—eighteen holes designed by Greg Norman and Ted Robin-son. You'll tee off on a plateau nearly 2,000 feet above sea level, set off by stunning views of Maui and Molokai directly across the channel, and wind through lush, natural terrain. You'll pass thick stands of Norfolk and Cook Island pines, indigenous island plants, and water, which seems to be everywhere; seven lakes, streams, cascading waterfalls and number 17, completely surrounded by a lake. Number eight's a stunner—"from its 250-foot elevation, you're shooting down into a mile-long valley filled with mist rising above the trees," says Robinson. the green is guarded to the right by a 70-foot eucalyptus, so your best bet is to drive to the left. Too bad the trade winds usually blow to the right.

Address: P.O. Box 310, Lanai City, 96763
Phone: 808-565-3800
800-321-4666
Fax: 808-565-3868
E-mail: reservations@
lanairesorts.com
Web site: http://www.
lanai-resorts.com
No. of Rooms: 102
Rates: $$$
Restaurant: Formal Dining Room and Terrace Restaurant, Koele Clubhouse
Bar: English Tea Room & Bar
Sports Fac.: Golf, Croquet, Lawn bowling, Pool & Fitness Center, Putting green, Tennis
Location: Right outside Lana'i City

Course: The Experience at Koele (7014, par 72)
No. of Holes: 18
Guest Policy: Open to public
Club House: 808-565-4653
Fees: ⅠⅠ
Reservations: Reservations avail-able 30 days in advance
Season: Open all year
Carts: Carts included in fees

Manele Bay Hotel

Address: P.O. Box 310, Lanai City, 96763
Phone: 808-565-3800
800-321-4666
Fax: 808-565-3868
Web site: http://www.
lanai-resorts.com
No. of Rooms: 250
Rates: $$$
Restaurant: Hulopo'e Court, Ihilani Restaurant, Pool Grille, The Challenge at Manele Clubhouse
Bar: Hale Ahe Ahe Lounge
Business Fac.: Library
Sports Fac.: Fitness Center, Game room, Introductions to snorkeling/scuba diving, Pool, Putting green, Snorkel & beach activity equiment, Tennis, Fitness hike, Hydro-Tone
Location: Beach at Hulopo'e Bay

Course: Challenge at Manele Golf Course (7039, par 72)
No. of Holes: 18
Guest Policy: Open to public
Club House: 808-565-2222
Fees: ❢❢
Reservations: Reservations available 30 days in advance
Season: Open all year
Carts: Carts included in fees

A grand expression of Hawaii's traditional architecture, the Manele Bay Hotel is set above a spectacular white sand beach. Seclusion, outstanding vistas of the Pacific, a dramatic coastal setting and luxuriant, multilevel gardens with waterfalls offer a colorful diversion. Romance and privacy characterize this special resort. The Manele Bay Hotel is perfect for a private getaway and even a great location for small meetings and conventions. The Lanai Conference Center has six beautifully appointed rooms (a total of 12,000 sq. feet) which boasts panoramic views of Lanai's southern coastline.

Thirty-six holes of golf are available as well as swimming (pool and ocean) fishing, snorkeling and scuba diving. The list of activities is endless. The spectacular tennis complex at the Manele Bay Hotel features six plexi-paved courts managed by a PBI tennis pro.

Carved from lava cliffs, 150 feet above the crashing surf, "The Challenge at Manele" is a Jack Nicklaus masterpiece. *Golf Magazine* honored "The Challenge" with a Gold Medal Award. The course was one of only two Hawaii courses to be ranked in the top 10. The Par 72 course covers 7,039 yards. There are five sets of tees, challenging even the best golfers with precise tee shots over natural lava gorges, while the average golfer will enjoy the beautiful vistas without suffering limitations on distance or accuracy.

Kauai Lagoons Resort

Set on 800 acres of spectacular beach front, the resort is surrounded by its own tropical gardens. Its 26,000 square foot pool is the largest in the Islands and has its own waterfalls. The recent renovation of the resort has created a unique atmosphere of a royal Hawaiian estate, striving to maintain the best from the past. The unmatched beauty has made this island the star of over fifty movies since the 1930's.

A perfect place for relaxation, and if you've had enough of that you can try a ride on an outrigger canoe, scuba dive, explore the island lagoons by boat, try the fishing, kayak on the Kanalei river, windsurfing, snorkeling, or explore the canyons on horseback. The shops and open-air markets are an adventure in themselves, be sure not to miss them.

From Hawaiian specialties, sushi, hamburgers, the restaurants here cater to every taste. The dining is superb, almost reason enough for the trip,

The Spa and Tennis Club will help you to keep in shape after all the wonderful food, and the Aveda Concept Salon will help to keep you looking your very best.

Not to be overlooked here are the two magnificent golf courses, both of which were designed by Jack Nicklaus. The Kiele had been rated the best in Hawaii, and is a course that demands tough nerves and complete control of your game, and not only because of the ravines! The Lagoons is not as tough, but don't let it fool you, it will challenge you more than you expect.

The Kalapaki Kids is for guests ages 5-12. It operates Monday-Saturday from 9am to 3pm. They teach the basics of surfing. Also offered arc swimming almost everyday, tennis, volleyball, arts & crafts, lei making, and hula. An enjoyable and educational vacation for the kids.

Address: Kalapaki Beach, Lihue, 96766
Phone: 808-245-5050
Fax: 808-245-5049
E-mail: jolene.ogle@vacationclub.com
Web site: http://www.marriotthotels.com/LIHHI/
No. of Rooms: 956
Rates: Inquire
Restaurant: 4 restaurants
Bar: Kukui's Restaurant and Bar
Business Fac.: Ten flexible meeting rooms, audio-visual support, professional meeting staff, and catering
Sports Fac.: Fitness center, whirlpool, swimming pool
Location: On Poipu Beach in Kauai

Courses: Kiele (7070, par 72), Lagoons (6942)
No. of Holes: 36
Guest Policy: Open to public
Club House: 808-241-6000
Fees: ↑↑↑
Reservations: Call for reservations
Season: Open all year
Carts: Carts included in fees

Maui Prince Hotel

Address: 5400 Makena Alanui, Makena, Maui, 96753
Phone: 808-874-1111
800-321-MAUI
Fax: 808-879-8763
E-mail: info@princehawaii.com
No. of Rooms: 310
Rates: $$$
Restrictions: no metal spikes
Restaurant: Prince Court
Bar: Moldkini Lounge
Business Fac.: Conference facilities
Sports Fac.: 2 Tennis courts, 2 Swimming pools, 2 Whirlpools
Location: Makena, West Maui

Courses: North Course (6914, par 72), South Course (7017)
No. of Holes: 36
Guest Policy: Open to public
Club House: 808-879-3344
Fees: ↑ ↑ ↑
Reservations: Reservations available 3 days in advance
Season: Open all year
Carts: Carts included in fees

The dry leeward southwestern coast of Maui is the ideal spot for a grand luxury resort—and it's here—the Maui Prince Hotel, located in the 1,000 acre Makena Resort. Opened in 1986 and nestled in a secluded cover south of Wailea, the 300-room resort destination is a modern V-shaped structure of white tile and marble, accented inside with teak, brass and tropical foliage. A creation of Designers of Tokyo, the focal point is the inner courtyard, almost an acre in size, which artfully harmonizes local flora with a traditional Japanese watergarden. The lobby, cool, simple and elegant, is highlighted by massive displays of orchids and palms. Rooms and suites face the ocean, with a rose-toned motif.

Two of the hotel's dining rooms, the Prince Court, and the authentic Japanese Hakone, are listed in *Who's Who in American Restaurants*. The chef's "Menu of the Evening" at the showcase Prince Court is an exercise in wonderfully innovative and eclectic fare combined with the freshest seasonal ingredients. An evening repast might begin with poached fingers of Opakapaka served on corn cakes. For an entree, try the marinated loin of lamb served on grilled pumpkin squash with rosemary potatoes and blueberry relish. Assuming you are still with us, don't pass up the banana bread pudding with Jack Daniels bourbon sauce, and, to top it all off, why not sample a freshly made petit four?

This is sunbathing and swimming territory, with a long stretch of white sand beach fronting the hotel, and fairly good snorkeling grounds near the hotel. Horses are available to rent for an unforgettable beach ride, and the concierge can help you with plans for scuba diving, catamaran sailing, windsurfing, and nearby shopping. Bring your racquet, for you'll find six Laykold tennis courts which have received *Tennis Magazine*'s 5-star award. Or jump in one of the two swimming pools.

Robert Trent Jones, Jr. designed Makena Golf Course, which is built on volcanic cinder and winds around the hilly terrain. This is one of the most beautifully maintained courses anywhere, with 16 ocean view holes and 2 ocean front holes affording spectacular views of outer islands, narrow fairways and some fairly difficult uphill pitches between trees. The fast, velvety greens, often with the sparkling ocean backdrop are not soon to be forgotten.

Ritz-Carlton Kapalua

Set between the West Maui mountain range and the Pacific Ocean, the resort is in the midst of a pineapple plantation. The resort has carefully preserved the century old Cook Pines and Ironwood trees, and has built to blend into the natural landscape. The music of the islands and the native art works in the public areas let you start relaxing, Hawaiian style, right from the start.

The rooms are large and airy, with private balconies for sitting and enjoying the gentle breezes of the island. The terraced pool is a perfect resting place, or take a walk on the beach, or enjoy one of the beach cabanas. And then, of course, from November to May whale watching is a favorite recreation. For the really energetic there's golf and tennis. Nothing is hurried here!

There's plenty of shopping opportunities, and night time entertainment at Lahaina. A hike up to the Haleakala Crater is awe-inspiring, and it's hard to beat a helicopter tour of Maui. Just about any water sport you might want to try is readily available

The Ritz-Carlton prides itself on fine dining, and the Lobby Lounge offers spectacular views and afternoon cocktails, complete with Hawaiian entertainment.

54 holes of golf all in one place is hard to beat! The resort is the home of the Lincoln-Mercury Kapalua International. The bay Course is on the shores of Oneloa Bay. The Plantation Course nestles into the landscape and is quite long but forgiving. The Village course is mountainous and makes for some difficult lies and many spectacular views.

The Ritz Kids, for ages 5 to 12, is offered from 9 a.m. to 4 p.m. at $60 per day, or is included in the Family Fun Package. The program operates 7 days a week and each day has a theme: Volcano Day, Maui Day, Rainbow Day, Plantation Day, Whale Day, Aloha Friday and Ocean Day. Saturday night dinner and videos and games are offered in The Terrace from 6–9 p.m., giving Mom and Dad a chance for a romantic evening!

Address: One Ritz-Carlton Drive, Maui, 96761
Phone: 808-669-6200
800-262-8440
Fax: 808-665-0026
Web site: http://www.ritzcarleton.com
No. of Rooms: 548
Rates: $$$
Restaurant: The Anuenue Room, The Terrace Restaurant, The Lobby Lounge and Library
Bar: The Anuenue Lounge, The Banyan Tree, The Beach House & Bar
Business Fac.: All facilities soundproofed, Indiv. climate and lighting controls, Audio/visual equipment, Easel, Flipcharts, Teleconferencing available, Amphitheatre
Sports Fac.: Swimming, Kapalua Tennis Club, 10 tennis courts, Fitness equipment, Massage, Snorkeling, Scuba diving, Kayaks, Boogie boarding, Sunset sails, Wind-surfing, Deep-sea fishing, Scenic jogging/walking trails
Location: 10 miles north of Lahaina on Maui

Courses: Bay Course (6600), Village Course (6632), Plantation Course (7263)
No. of Holes: 54
Club House: 808-669-8044
Fees: ↑↑↑
Reservations: Call for reservations
Season: Open all year

Kaanapali Shores Resort

Address: 100 Kaanapali Shores Pl,
Maui, Lahaina, 96761
Phone: 808-667-2211
800-92-ASTON
Fax: 808-661-0836
E-mail: info@aston-hotels.com
Web site: http://www.
kaanapalishores-maui.com
Location: Near Lahaina on the
island of Maui

Courses: Tournament North Course
(6994, par 71), Resort South Course
(6555, par 71)
No. of Holes: 36
Guest Policy: Open to public
Club House: 808-661-3691
Fees: ↑ ↑ ↑
Reservations: Call to make reservations
Season: Open all year
Carts: Cart included in fees

Kaanapali Shores enjoys one of Maui's finest
beachfront locations, with spectacular views of
our own lush tropical gardens, the blue Pacific,
and the gorgeous West Maui Mountains. And
we're convenient to world class golf, shopping,
and dining. Aston Kaanapali Shores will pamper
you with the full services of a fine hotel and the
convenience and spaciousness of an elegant condominium resort.

Front desk service is available 24 hours a day.
Our activities desk can help you plan your outings. And we have on-site shops, a fitness center,
and kid's camp which offers year-round activities
such as creative arts, nature walks, hula lessons,
Hawaiian storytelling.

Choose from a wide variety of rooms and
suites, including hotel rooms with refrigerators,
or spacious studio, one- and two-bedroom condominium suites with complete kitchens and plenty
of room to spread out and get comfortable.
Washer/dryers are available in one and two-bedroom suites. All accommodations feature private
lanais (except hotel rooms) and air-conditioning.
All rooms and suites have daily maid service.

Kaanapali Golf Courses is home to the Senior
PGA Tour EMC Kaanapali Classic. The Tournament North and Resort South championship golf
courses at Kaanapali have achieved legendary
status. Maui's idyllic climate and the fabled setting of the West Maui coastline certainly add to
the mystique. The Kaanapali Golf Courses lie at
the heart of Kaanapali Beach Resort. Kaanapali
Visitors also enjoy the use of a comprehensive
clubhouse, whose golf shop stocks a full compliment of top-name golf apparel and equipment for
rental or sale. Kaanapali's resident pros are available for lessons, and there are putting greens and
driving ranges to practice what you have learned.
The clubhouse restaurant, Reilley's, overlooks the
North Course's challenging 18th hole. It's the perfect spot from which to contemplate how you'll
play that fairway … next time.

Kaluakoi Hotel & Golf Club

As Hawaii's last outpost, the "Lonely Isle," was practically ignored after missionaries in the eighteenth century settled. Then came the big pineapple operators and cattle ranchers whose heirs were responsible for preserving the wilderness, glorious west end beached, (often unswimmable) waterfalls and secluded valleys. While the island lacks public transportation and traffic lights, capuccino bars, and Elvis look-alikes hula contests, it offers some spectacular views of deep jungle valleys, good hunting, hiking and bumper stickers asking "Wouldn't you rather be riding a mule on Molokai?"

The 288 rooms, in one and two story clusters, plus condominiums, are furnished with rattan, and are cooled by the trade winds and ceiling fans.

A large free-form swimming pool, four plexipave tennis courts, shops, croquet, and restaurants and lounges are all here for your enjoyment. For a succulent, well-aged melt-in-your-mouth steak, try the Ohia Lodge, where Hawaii's famous Kiawe charcoal imparts its flavor. And if you're on the run, hit the 15-kilometer jogging course, where the scenery, if not your pace, will leave you breathless. This is a marvelous spot for a meeting, as the facilities are well-maintained, and the resort can handle up to 300 in conference rooms. Exploring the oblong-shaped island can be in a rental car, by helicopter, van, or on the back of a mule winding its way down the steep cliffs to the Kalaupapa National Historical Park. See the Molokai Ranch Wildlife Park, where barbary sheep, Rhea, oryx, and other endangered species thrive in the dry brush. The island might be slightly sleepy, but the Ted Robinson 18 hole championship course which opened in 1977 is no sloth. The course has hosted the Kaluakoi Open for four years, the Aloha section of the PGA High School State championships, and the Airline Executives tourney. It's an experience bound by seaside holes, and an inland sojourn where fairways fringe the open rangeland blending with virtually untouched wilderness. You might spot an occasional wild turkey or axis deer. #16 is a thriller from the white tees its 182 yards over a deep gorge for a part three. Contoured greens, deviously placed bunkers, and even lakes contrast with briskly low shrubs, and as your head comes up in the follow-through, you can see Oahu across the channel.

Address: P.O. Box 1977, Maunaloa, Molokai, 96770
Phone: 808-552-2555
888-552-2550
Fax: 808-552-2555
E-mail: kaluakoi@juno.com
Web site: http://www.kaluakoi.com
Rates: Inquire
Restaurant: Ohia Lodge
Sports Fac.: Free golf for hotel guests, Freshwater pool
Location: 20 minutes from Molokai's Hoolehua Airport

Course: Kaluakoi Course (6564)
No. of Holes: 18
Club House: 808-552-2739
Reservations: Call for reservations
Season: Open all year

Princeville Resort

Address: P.O. Box 3040, Princeville, 96722
Phone: 808-826-9644
800-826-4400
Fax: 808-826-1166
E-mail: info@princeville.com
Web site: http://www.
princeville.com
No. of Rooms: 252
Rates: $$$
Restaurant: Cafe Hanalei, La Cascata Restaurant, Beach Restaurant, Beachside Luau
Bar: The Living Room, Pool Bar
Business Fac.: Conference facilities: Grand Ballroom and 5 meeting rooms, capacity up to 500
Sports Fac.: Water sports in Hanalei Bay
Location: On Pu'u Poa Ridge terraced along the bluff facing Hanalei Bay

Courses: Prince Course (7309), Makai (6900, par 72)
No. of Holes: 45
Guest Policy: Open to public
Club House: 800-826-1105
Fees: ↑↑↑
Reservations: Reservations available 14 days in advance
Season: Open all year
Carts: Cart included in fees

Princeville Resort acts as a gateway to the wonders of Kauai's spectacular North Shore. A verdant green promontory with seven miles of coastline, the resort overlooks Hanalei Bay and the Pacific Ocean. The resort features a wide variety of activities from watersports to tennis, horseback riding and even polo during summer months. Accommodations include the luxurious Princeville Hotel, managed by Sheraton, and a variety of condominium complexes and executive homes available for vacation rental. A shopping center and commuter airport complete the resort complex.

Sightseeing is a big attraction here, and what sights! Hiking to Kilauea Point, under the protection of the U.S. Fish and Wildlife Service, visiting Hanalei Valley Lookout to see endangered koot and stilt, helicopter flightseeing, trail riding or raft trips along the Na Pali Coast, checking out the shopping, polo matches, or the occasional hukilau all contribute to the haole's vacation.

Makai, meaning "toward the sea" Golf Course consists of four nine hole courses: Ocean, Lake, Woods, and the newest, which will eventually be a full 18 hole course, Prince Course. Home of the 1978 World Cup, the Kauai Open, and the LPGA Women's Kemper Open, these Robert Trent Jones, Jr. wonders have attained high marks in their 17-year existence, and as such, it is the only course in Hawaii to have been listed within the *Golf Digest*'s Top 100 for the past fifteen years. #3 on the Ocean Course, a par 3, is world-renowned as an achingly beautiful sight, as well as a formidable one. Only 125 yards, with dense grass on the left, a green protected on the left side and rear by threatening sand traps, a placid lake in front, and a thicketed canyon beyond, the player prays for respite from looking for a wayward ball. Lake Course boasts ocean views, jungle caverns and plenty of water coming into play, and Woods Course heads inland, graced with regal Norfolk pines and rock garden bunkers. The Prince, operated as a separate course from the other 27 holes, will offer the golfer natural waterfalls cascading down behind a lush green, deep verdant ravines, jungle, rocks galore, ancient mango trees, and vision of a machete to hack one's way back to the narrow fairway.

Sheraton Makaha Resort and Country Club

Heading out the Farrington Highway on the dry, leeward side of the island, about an hour's drive from Honolulu, you'll find one of the island's most stirring natural wonders, the Makaha Valley. Here on a magnificent plain, reposing in grandeur under Mt. Kaala, the highest peak on Oahu, is a golf and tennis getaway minus the hype of other areas. 189 guest rooms in clusters of wooden low-rise Polynesian-inspired architecture are enveloped by tropical vegetation and well-maintained lawns. History buffs will want to visit the beautifully restored Kaneaki Heiau, a 17th century chief's temple, complete with sacrificial altar and prayer towers. A large swimming pool, four tennis courts, and a croquet lawn provide on-premises recreation. Count on an abundance of beach activities and watersports, even though the ocean is a fair hike from the hotel. If you like to "hang ten," head for the Makaha surfing beach, where world famous surfing contests are held.

Host to the annual Ted Makalena Hawaii State Open in 1983 and 84, and the annual NFL March of Dimes Invitational, the William Bell championship course is practically an old-timer for the islands. Ready for play in 1969, the country-like setting has rolling hills, bermudagrass greens, 107 bunkers, 11 water hazards, and dazzling ocean views. A note from the pro shop reads: "We do our best to accommodate resort guests whenever they want to play, morning or afternoon."

Address: 84-626 Makaha Valley Rd, Waianae, 96792
Phone: 808-695-9511
800-334-8484
Fax: 808-695-5806
No. of Rooms: 200
Rates: Inquire
Restrictions: No pets allowed
Restaurant: Kaala Room
Bar: Lobby Lounge
Business Fac.: Audio-visual, Copiers, Conference rooms, capacity 500
Sports Fac.: Tennis courts, Scuba, Snorkeling, Fishing
Location: Rural setting

Course: West Course (7091)
No. of Holes: 18
Guest Policy: Resort guests have priority tee times
Club House: 808-695-9544
Reservations: Required, check with pro shop
Season: Open all year

Ranaissance Wailea Beach Resort

Address: 3550 Wailea Alanui,
Wailea, Maui, 96753
Phone: 808-879-4900
800-HOTELS-1
Fax: 808-874-5370
No. of Rooms: 347
Rates: Inquire
Restaurant: Raffles, Hana Gion,
Palm Court, Maui Onion
Bar: Sunset Terrace, Wailea Sunset
Luau
Business Fac.: 5 conference rooms
Sports Fac.: Tennis courts, Fitness
center, Swimming, Water sports
Location: Nestled against the
gentle slopes of Mt. Haleakala

Courses: Blue Course (6152), Gold
Course, Emerald Course (6653)
No. of Holes: 54
Guest Policy: Call for availability
Club House: 808-879-2966
Reservations: Hotel guests may
make 2 days in advance
Season: Open all year

In the shadow of the world's largest dormant volcano, Mount Haleakala, lies a 15-acre tropical Eden, home of Stouffer Wailea Beach Resort. Here on the sunny, uncrowded shore of Hawaii's second largest island, is the epitome of luxury and taste in a low-rise destination resort. Views are nonpareil of neighboring Lanai and Molokai, verdant glades and mountain tops peeking out of clouds.

You can expect the exceptional in dining at Raffles', recipient for many years of the Travel/ Holiday award. Patterned after the celebrated Singapore landmark, Raffles' transports you to another world while blending favorites with a touch of Hawaiiana. The fish is fresh, the sauces are light, and the seasonings are delicate. Palm Court serves breakfast and a nightly buffet in an open-air atmosphere. The poolside gazebo called the Maui Onion satisfies your urge for crisp salads and infamous Maui onion rings.

For all its seclusion, Wailea boasts a full complement of superb facilities, including three grass tennis courts. A stadium court for tournament play was noted in *Tennis Magazine* for ranking among the top 50 resorts. Nature has carved five crescent beaches along the shore, perfect for sunbathing and swimming, and a quick catamaran ride away reveals a marine preserve with excellent snorkeling and scuba diving. A real thrill is a bike ride down the crater walls inside Haleakala. Weary tendons can take a van back up! The surrounding slopes offer great hiking, orchid farms, and a National Park to explore. The seascapes, waterfalls, and tropical blossoms are unforgettable.

Dubbed Orange and Blue for the sun and sea colors of Wailea's logo, these two championship courses are the product of Arthur Jack Snyder. The Blue par-72 was designed with rolling, wide fairways, and only two parallel holes. Notice the straight growing trees, a sign of consistently beautiful weather, minus blustery trade winds capable of hampering a near-perfect drive. The 16th hole claims the highest elevation on the course, and the biggest hazard … the view. Ancient stone walls have been left intact, and players consider them a natural hazard. More than half the holes have doglegs, but the 18th, with an extremely narrow fairway has a unique feature. Right in the middle of the green is a natural rock garden.

Coeur d'Alene

Coeur d'Alene is located in Northern Idaho, approximately 31 miles east of Spokane, Washington and 100 miles south of the Canadian border. The Resort is located on the north shore of Lake Coeur d'Alene, where temperatures in the summer average 82 degrees. There's never a lack of activities at The Coeur d'Alene, with a wide range of options for our Guests and their families. The resort's waterfront setting offers a diverse menu of aquatic activities ranging from lake cruises to sailing to jet skis to parasailing. Away from the lake, Guests can play the world's only floating moveable green at The Resort's spectacular new waterfront golf course, or challenge the champagne powder blanketing north facing slopes at Silver Mountain, America's newest ski and summer resort.

The Premier rooms are located above the seventh floor in the Resort's 18-story tower. Each room offers extra large rooms with sunken living area, separate dressing and bath areas and private lanai. Lake accommodations offer terrific views while mountain accommodations offer city and mountain views plus some have a fireplace and lakeside lanai. All rooms include mini-bars, coffeemakers, hairdryers, robes, irons, "lodgenet" movies, and video games. Most rooms include high-speed Internet access.

Experience the Coeur d' Alene Golf Course and the world famous Floating Green signature hole. The Coeur d' Alene Resort was named the top golf facility in Idaho by *Golf Digest* in their ranking of America's 500 Best Places to Play, and was selected among the World's Top 100 Golf Resorts in *The Golfer Magazine* annual travel guide. Golf packages are available and include a choice of accommodations, water taxi service from the Resort's Floating Stage to the Course, a forecaddie with each group, a cart for each twosome and full privileges on the over-the-water driving range.

Address: C-7200, Coeur d'Alene, 83814
Phone: 208-765-4000
800-688-5253
Fax: 208-664-7276
E-mail: resort@cdaresort.com
Web site: http://www.cdaresort.com
No. of Rooms: 337
Rates: $$
Restaurant: Award-winning dining at Beverly's and Dockside, Tito's pizzas and pasta.
Business Fac.: 25,000 sq. ft. of meeting and coference space
Sports Fac.: European-style spa, Access to Idaho's full menu of outdoor adventures
Location: Just minutes from Spokane, WA airport

Course: Coeur d'Alene Resort Golf Course (6309, par 71)
No. of Holes: 18
Guest Policy: Open to public
Club House: 800-688-5253
Fees: ↑↑↑
Reservations: Can make reservations 3 days in advance

Elkhorn Resort at Sun Valley

Address: 100 Elkhorn Road, PO Box 6009, Sun Valley, 83353
Phone: 208-622-4511
800-355-4676
Fax: 208-622-3261
E-mail: ctimme@micron.net
Web site: http://www.elkhornresort.com
No. of Rooms: 229
Rates: Inquire
Restaurant: River Rock Steakhouse, Joe's Southwest Grill, Clubhouse Grill
Sports Fac.: Nordic & downhill skiing, snowmobiling, Sleigh rides, Hiking, Mountain biking, Fishing
Location: At the base of Dollar Mountain

Course: Elkhorn Resort Golf Course (7100)
No. of Holes: 18
Guest Policy: Open to public
Club House: 208-622-6400
Reservations: Call for reservations
Season: Summer and Fall only

A short distance from the world-famous winter playground of Sun Valley, lies Elkhorn Resort—secluded, yet accessible, family-oriented, yet fun and exciting. Elkhorn is like a college town—a self-contained community with every conceivable outlet for self-indulgence. With the mighty Sawtooths as a backdrop, the contemporary Alpine resort has 130 rooms, 12 suites and 136 condominium units. The swinging bar, the Lobby Lounge provides all sorts of entertainment and is a favorite meeting place all year. Tequila Joe's, Papa Din's and Jesse's, all on the premises, offer an array of tempting entrees for every kind of palate.

Five swimming pools, eighteen Laykold tennis courts, croquet, and a spa are among the recreational facilities. Nearby are stables and some great riding trails. Sailing, windsurfing, whitewater rafting, hiking and fishing in some of Idaho's most trout-blessed streams are here to be enjoyed.

This is an outdoorsman's Utopia. The Sun Valley area, part of the Wood River Valley, boasts some magnificent wilderness. Photographers, wildflower enthusiasts and bird watchers will have a field day in these parts, as will Hemingway aficionados. He lived in neighboring Ketchum, hunted in the area, wrote part of *For Whom the Bell Tolls* here, and is buried in the town's cemetery.

Past host to Idaho's Open, Danny Thompson Memorial, and Governor's Cup, the resort's golf course was built n 1973. Robert Trent Jones, Jr. designed this lengthy scenic treat nestled under majestic snow-capped peaks. This top rated course in Idaho is very hilly, with lots of water, antelope, fox, hare, and deer.

Sun Valley Lodge

Sun Valley was a vision of Averell Harriman, who wanted a ski resort accessible by train for the glamorous group of the thirties. It's still exclusive, still a challenge to reach, and enjoys a well-deserved reputation as a family resort with top-notch facilities. The Lodge itself is imposing, conveying an air of genteel luxury and understated elegance. Photographs of the beautiful people who have skied, wined and dined here line corridor walls, and you are aware that the aura of the Hemingway years still lurks. Guests stay in the lodge, an inn, or condominiums. While there are several bars around the premises, the favored one seems to be what returning guests lovingly refer to as the "Doo-Dah Room," known as the Duchin Room in the brochures. The Lodge Dining Room, wood paneled and sedate, serves fresh-from-the-stream trout, inspired desserts, and has an accompanying wine list considered impressive, with a lot of California treasures represented.

A Bavarian-looking mall adjoins the Lodge, offering a lot of irresistible shops and eateries.

The nonstop activities schedule gets an A+ in quality. Wine connoisseurs await the Sun Valley Wine auction every summer, and the month-long Music Festival attracts people from Europe. You might be lucky to be here for the big rodeo, or Wagon Days in nearby Ketchum. Everybody looks healthy and fit here, probably because they've been bicycling, running, swimming, ice skating, or gone to the spa. Or just breathed the clean mountain air. Hiking in the Sawtooths, and white water rafting are activities you won't forget. One can also ride horseback, play tennis or soak up the rays around one of three outdoor pools. Free buses shuttle guests to and from Ketchum, a five minute ride away, where the flavor of the Old West lives in its bars, galleries, shops and laid back attitude.

A round of golf here is visual delight. Originally laid out in 1937 by William Bell, and redesigned by Robert Trent Jones, Jr., the hilly terrain, surrounded by aspen and evergreen, offers unobstructed views of the mogul's mansions. This is one of the west's truly beautiful mountain settings, and has hosted the Idaho Governor's Cup, Danny Thompson Memorial Celebrity Golf Tournament, and numerous others. The fifteenth hole, a 244 yard par 3 is singled out as a challenger.

Address: Sun Valley Rd, Sun Valley, 83353
Phone: 208-622-4111
800-786-8259
Fax: 208-622-3700
E-mail: reservations@sunvalley.com
Web site: http://www.sunvalley.com/lodging.asp
No. of Rooms: 540
Rates: Inquire
Restrictions: No pets allowed
Restaurant: Lodge Dining Room
Bar: Duchin Room
Business Fac.: Full conference facilities, Conference rooms, capacity 1500
Sports Fac.: Health spa, Swimming pool, Horseback riding, Tennis courts, Ice skating, Trap and skeet shooting
Location: Central Idaho

Course: Sun Valley (6057)
No. of Holes: 18
Guest Policy: Call for availability
Club House: 208-622-2251
Reservations: May be made 7 days in advance
Season: April–October
Carts: Carts are also available

Eagle Ridge Inn & Resort

Address: US Route 20, P.O. Box 777, Galena, 61036
Phone: 815-777-2444
800-892-2269
Fax: 815-777-0445
E-mail: res@eagleridge.com
Web site: http://www.eagleridge.com
No. of Rooms: 280
Rates: Inquire
Restrictions: No pets allowed
Restaurant: Woodlands, Shooters, Pro shop Bar & Grill
Bar: Woodlands and Shooters
Business Fac.: Audio-visual, Conference rooms, capacity 200
Sports Fac.: Tennis courts, Fitness center, Volleyball, Swimming
Location: Northwest Illinois, 6 miles from historic Galena

Courses: North (6386), South, East
No. of Holes: 45
Guest Policy: Call for availability
Club House: 815-777-2500
Reservations: 7 days in advance for the public
Season: April–November

Looking for a conference center or family vacation spot a couple of hours from Chicago? Hoping for a quiet rustic retreat coupled with tennis, a lake for fishing and sailing, and two championship golf courses? Search no more. Check out Eagle Ridge Inn & Resort, perched on a bluff above a lake surrounded by rolling hills and valleys, an easy 2 hour drive from the Quad cities through bucolic Illinois farmland and towns.

Lodgings range from inn rooms to 1, 2, and 3 bedroom resort homes scattered among the fairways and tree-covered hills, or townhouses. This is a year-round resort with a range of activities including hay rides nature walks, boating, horseback riding, and cross-country skiing when the time comes. During summer, a children's program offers swimming, arts and crafts, paddleboat rides, and special field trips. You'll find a fine restaurant, a couple of fitness trails, and an indoor pool with sauna and whirlpool in addition to a fitness center.

Galena, a historic lead-mining town, and once home to U.S. Grant, gives you a glimpse of midwest Americana in the 19th century. Visit Victorian mansions, cruise the Mississippi on an old fashioned paddlewheeler, tour a winery, or enjoy a performance at Timber Lake Playhouse.

Golf is two hilly courses with plenty of water, wildlife and isolation. This is no-hassle golf with long wooded fairways, plenty of sand, and courses in top-notch condition. South Course, newer of the two, is an award winner. An innocent meandering stream and thick groves of trees have prompted a time limit of 5 minutes to search for lost balls. Both courses are par 72, with two full service pro shops, full-time professionals, and a large practice fairway and green.

The youth program is offered for ages 3 to 12, and has full- and half-day programs. There is also a Kids Night Klub with a fully equipped playroom, movies, crafts and even sleeping mats. The teens also have group games such as volleyball, boating and horseback riding on site, and Alpine slider outings, movies and bowling off site. The Youth Program is $17 for half day and $25 for full day.

Marriott's Lincolnshire Resort

Situated on 170 wooded acres in Chicago's North Shore suburbs, you will find a tranquil setting for your stay. There's something for the whole family at Lincolnshire.

Lincolnshire Resort offers impeccable facilities for successful conferences and relaxing vacations. With a total of 21 meetings rooms and a spectacular Grand Ballroom, groups of any size will be comfortably accommodated.

Vacationers will be equally pleased with outstanding sports complexes, from the indoor Racquet Club and an 18-hole golf course to two pools, one indoors, one outdoors and a health club.

With the trend toward more frequent and shorter vacations with the entire family, Lincolnshire offers a variety of packages that will have appeal of people of all ages.

Golf at Lincolnshire is on a challenging course designed by George Fazio. The greens are well protect by bunkers. The course is surrounded by mature trees, and water comes into play at every turn, and borders of the Des Plaines River. Company and group outings are a specialty here, and there is a staff member assigned to each group to see that everything runs smoothly. The golf shop offers just about anything you could need and the Club House Bar and Grill can tempt your appetite and quench your thirst.

The Lincolnshire offers a Kid's Crew for ages 5–10. The fee is $10.00 for each session and includes breakfast, lunch, or evening snack. The activities include crafts, cookie decorating, relays, storytime, mini Olympics and much more.

Address: Ten Marriott Drive, Lincolnshire, 60069
Phone: 847-634-0100
800-228-9290
Fax: 847-634-1278
No. of Rooms: 390
Rates: Inquire
Restaurant: Fairfield Inn, King's Wharf
Business Fac.: Full conference facilities
Sports Fac.: Health club, Tennis courts, Swimming, Racquetball, Volleyball, Canoeing
Location: 16 miles to Chicago's O'Hare airport

Course: Marriott's Lincolnshire (6313)
No. of Holes: 18
Guest Policy: Open to public
Club House: 847-634-5935
Reservations: If staying at the resort, up to 3 months in advance
Season: April 15–October 31

Eagle Pointe

Address: 2250 E Point Road, Bloomington, 47401
Phone: 812-824-4040
877-324-7683
E-mail: info@eaglepointe.com
Web site: http://www.eaglepointe.com
No. of Rooms: 100
Rates: $$
Restaurant: Talon's Restaurant, Humuhumu Lounge, Snack Shack,
Bar: Cabana Bar
Business Fac.: 10,500 feet of meeting and banquet space, Fax and photocopy service, Mailing services
Sports Fac.: Outdoor heated swimming pool, Outdoor hot tub, Tennis courts, Bikes
Location: In the rolling hills of Southern Indiana on Lake Monroe

Course: Eagle Pointe (6604, par 72)
No. of Holes: 18
Guest Policy: Open to public
Club House: 877-324-7683
Fees: ⌐
Reservations: Call to make reservations
Season: Open all year
Carts: Cart included in fees

Located 13 miles from downtown Bloomington, Indiana—and The Big 10's Indiana University—Eagle Pointe Golf Resort offers serene setting just minutes away from a world of activities. The resort is located in a picturesque region of rolling wooded hills on the southern edge of Lake Monroe, Indiana's largest man-made lake!

Eagle Pointe offers more than 100 uniquely designed condominiums with choices of lake, golf course, or wooded view. Most condos are furnished and equipped with a full kitchen, TV, VCR, fireplace, and washer/dryer; many have lake view balconies perfect for a relaxing night cap.

Eagle Pointe has over 10,500 square feet of meeting and banquet space, as well as retreat areas including our newly remodeled Lodge. Connected to the Lodge is our covered Terrace. As our largest venue, it is perfect for an outdoor reception, meal, banquet or brainstorming session.

If you enjoy golf, Eagle Pointe is the place to be. The 6,700 yard golf course is known as one of the finest PGA Championship courses in the state, and the sixth most difficult. The challenging course features 100 sand bunkers, tight fairways, paved cart paths and fine carpeted, large greens. Golf lessons are available by appointment.

French Lick Springs Golf Resort

Indians, French, then American explorers followed ancient buffalo through this rich valley of mineral springs. French settlers, in the late 1660s, found their cattle benefitted by licking the mineral deposits at the springs—thus the name given to this part of the Indiana territory by Americans pushing westward. The current hotel, built in the early 1900s became an attraction for prominent visitors who came to take the cure and sip minerals, as well as the rich and famous who visited the opulent casinos and clubs to gamble. In 1986 new ownership acquired the adjoining villas and set about restoring the property to its original grandeur while adding new vitality and modern touches.

The grand lobby has come alive, and the mosaic floor and ceiling moldings, the seating areas overlooking the veranda, and the marbleized columns all recall an era of graciousness and quiet charm. Guests will find five full service dining rooms, and a high tea served in the lobby on Friday and Saturday afternoon. Today's European Mineral spa features a complete beauty and health regimen. Choose from eighteen a la carte treatments—from herbal wraps and facials to a relaxing mineral bath.

This is a popular place for conventions—because of the golf and tennis facilities, and because the Meeting Planners offer a Guarantee of Service. Recreational activities include an indoor and an outdoor swimming pool, croquet, skeet and trap shooting, and six bowling lanes. For video fans, the game room boasts 25 electronic video games and two pool tables. Settle in for an evening of dollar beer, popcorn and sports on the big screen TV. Riders can arrange for horses and a day on the scenic southern Indiana woodlands, and tennis players will be able to play on 10 lighted outdoor courts, or on 8 indoor all lighted.

Golfers look forward to coming here for many reasons, and certainly the Country Club Course is high on the list. Designed by Donald Ross, architect of Pinehurst No. 2, and Oak Hill Country Club, site of the 1989 U.S. Open, this course is extremely hilly, with large undulating greens, and plenty of mature trees. It was here, on a course reminiscent of the Scottish links, that Walter Hagen claimed the 1924 PGA National Championship, and here that the LPGA Championship tournaments of the 1960s were played. Valley Course, the other 18 holes is on more level terrain.

Address: Hwy. 56, French Lick, 47432
Phone: 812-936-9300
800-457-4042
Fax: 812-936-2100
E-mail: daudran@boykin.com
Web site: http://www.frenchlick.com
No. of Rooms: 485
Rates: Inquire
Restrictions: Pets limited
Restaurant: Hoosier Dining Room
Bar: Derby Bar
Business Fac.: Copiers, Audiovisual
Sports Fac.: Swimming pool, Horseback riding, Full mineral spa
Location: Patoka Lake Region

Courses: Country Club (6350), Valley Golf Links
No. of Holes: 36
Guest Policy: Call for tee times
Club House: 812-936-9300
Reservations: Any time up to a year in advance
Season: May 15–November 15
Carts: Walking is permitted

Swan Lake Golf Resort & US Golf Academy

Address: 5203 Plymouth-LaPorte Trail, Plymouth, 46563
Phone: 219-935-5680
800-582-7539
Fax: 219-935-5087
E-mail: info@slresort.com
Web site: http://www.slresort.com
No. of Rooms: 92
Rates: Inquire
Restrictions: Soft-spike facility
Restaurant: On-site restaurant open to the public
Bar: On-site lounge open to the public
Business Fac.: Let our coordinators arrange your meeting facilities, golf activities, meals, and transportation. Swan Lake Resort is large enough to provide a variety of room configurations to match your needs and small enough to maintain the integrity of your group.
Sports Fac.: 36 Championship Holes, Complete Practice Facilities, United States Golf Academy, Indoor & Outdoor Pools, Whirlpools, Sauna, Exercise Room.
Location: We are located in Plymouth, Indiana which is about 30 minutes south of South Bend, Indiana.

Courses: West Course (6942), East Course (6850), 5 hole executive course, 9 hole short game course, and full practice range.
No. of Holes: 36
Guest Policy: Open to public
Club House: 219-936-9798
Fees: Inquire
Reservations: Call for reservations
Season: April–November
Carts: 18-holes: $13.00 & 9-holes: $6.50

Swan Lake Resort offers attractive accommodating facilities to all its guests. Large sleeping rooms have either a king-size or two double beds with in-room cable television. The atmosphere is serene and casual. The location is rural, away from city distractions. You'll find the facilities at Swan Lake Resort relaxing, whether you're here to attend the Academy, to escape for a 'stay & play' golf experience or attend a special event.

The tuition for the Golf Academy includes your lodging, meals, green fees, lessons, practice facilities privileges, videotaping, and use of all recreational facilities. Individuals are grouped by skill level for instruction, with a student to teacher ratio of 4-1.

At Swan Lake Resort we specialize in business retreats and seminars. Our professional staff works with you every step of the way to ensure a perfect meeting environment. Conference facilities will handle 100 people and our full-service dining area will accommodate 200.

Swan Lake Resort offers some of the most beautiful, affordable, and challenging golf in Northern Indiana on 36 Championship holes. The West Course is a great course to start on. The greens are larger and the fairways are wider. The challenge of this course is presented in its distance (6942 yards from pro tees). The East Course will test your accuracy. The layout of the fairways will run you alongside and cross you over numerous streams and ponds.

Amana Colonies Golf Course

Located in the historic Amana colonies of east central Iowa, the Amana Colonies Golf Course was honored with a 4 Star rating in *Golf Digest*'s 1998 list of places to play. Stay in one of the fully equipped condominiums, enjoying the view from the screened-in porch.

Spend time in the dining room overlooking the 18th Hole and Middle Pond or relax in the clubhouse with scenic views of the hills and forest. To enhance the habitat for wildlife on the golf course and preserve the natural resources, Amana Colonies Golf Course has joined the Audobon Cooperative Sanctuary System.

Featuring many different packages and banquet and meeting facilities, the Amana Colonies Golf Course is perfect for all organizations, no matter how large or small.

Opened for play in 1989, the 18-hole golf course was designed to accentuate the features of the land: 300 acres of white oak trees and forests, meandering streams, and ponds. With lush watered bentgrass and strategically placed sand bunkers, the course accommodates all levels of players.

The three PGA golf professionals on staff offer lessons covering posture, grip, alignment, shot making and equipment for all levels of players. Check out the pro shop, awarded "Merchandiser of the Year" in the 1998 and 1997 Iowa Section PGA, featuring the Greg Norman Collection.

Address: 451 27th Avenue, Amana, 52203
Phone: 319-622-6222
800-383-3636
Fax: 319-622-6373
E-mail: golfacgc@netins.net
Web site: http://www.amanagolfcourse.com
Rates: Inquire
Restaurant: Main Dining Room—Family style dining, Concession—lunch, snacks, beverages
Business Fac.: Meeting facilities, Audio-visual, Banquet, capacity 20-150
Sports Fac.: Swimming pool, Exercise room, Sauna, Hydrotherapy pool
Location: East central Iowa

Course: Amana Colonies (6824)
No. of Holes: 18
Guest Policy: Open to public
Club House: 800-383-3636
Fees: ↑
Reservations: 14 days in advance, guaranteed with credit card
Season: Open all year
Carts: Cost includes carts

Terradyne Hotel & Country Club

Address: 1400 Terradyne Road,
Andover, 67002
Phone: 316-733-2582
800-892-4613
E-mail: info@terradyne-resort.com
Web site: http://www.
terradyne-resort.com
No. of Rooms: 53
Rates: $
Restaurant: The Greens—casual
dining, The 19th Hole—casual grill
open to members and guests,
Sunday Brunch
Bar: Lounge
Business Fac.: Complete banquet
and meeting facilities, capacity 400
Sports Fac.: Outdoor swimming
pool, 3 outdoor tennis courts, Indoor
racquetball court, Fully-equipped
exercise room, Sauna
Location: Oasis on the outskirts of
Wichita

From the moment you walk into the mahogany
and marble lobby, with its distinctive fireplace
and rich carpeting, you know this place will be
different. Whether it's for dinner, a business
meeting, a weekend getaway or a round of golf,
this oasis on the outskirts of Wichita, Kansas, will
tempt you back again and again. The 42 uniquely
designed guestrooms include large screen TVs
with HBO/DVD/VCR accessibility, state of the art
touch-tone phones with dual data port, voice mail
and central operator, business work stations, hair
dryers, irons and ironing boards.

In addition to the award-winning Scottish golf
course and pro shop, Terradyne Country Club
offers lighted tennis courts, swimming pool,
sauna, racquetball court and fully-equipped
work-out facilities.

The Don Sechrest design is rated "Four Stars"
by *Golf Digest* and as one of the Top 100 Golf
Resorts in the World by *Golfer Magazine*! The
rolling terrain is a Scottish Links style course
with sand, water, and the unforgettable rough.
The front nine is long and narrow; the back nine
is shorter, but fun to play. There are few trees on
the course, and the main hazards are rough,
water, and sand. Individual lessons, group lessons
and short game clinics are also available.

Course: Terradyne Country Club
(6704)
No. of Holes: 18
Guest Policy: Hotels guests and
members only
Club House: 316-733-5851
Fees: ⌐
Reservations: Call for playing privi-
leges
Season: Open all year
Carts: Cart are also available

Marriott's Griffin Gate Resort

Surrounding Griffin Gate, thoroughbreds graze in lush pasturelands bordered by miles of white rail fences. A tranquil environment, punctuated by the excitement and intrigue of nearby horse-racing parks and world-famous thoroughbred farms are all part of what has been called the "Horse Capital of the World."

From the spectacular, five-story lobby of the main building with its dramatic fountain and cascading walls of water, to the charming, stately mansion, everything at Griffin Gate speaks of the romance of the past.

The Mansion, built in 1873, now houses one of the resort's many fine restaurants. Decorated in 19th century motif, with elegant chandeliers, fireplaces, and rich mahogany furnishings, dining at The Mansion is a classic experience. Begin a perfect meal with escargot and a Caesar salad.

Complete sports facilities are available to all guests. And plenty of sightseeing attractions are nearby at Keeneland and the famed Kentucky Horse Park, home of more than two dozen breeds. There's also Shaker Village and scores of historic homes, including the Mary Todd Lincoln House.

The adjacent Rees Jones 18 hole championship golf course is a rambling, tree-lined layout with large rolling greens, long bluegrass fairways, more than 65 sand bunkers and water coming into play on twelve holes.

Address: 1800 Newtown Pike, Lexington, 40511
Phone: 859-231-5100
800-228-9290
Fax: 859-231-5136
No. of Rooms: 409
Rates: Inquire
Restrictions: Pets limited
Restaurant: Mansion at Griffin Gate, Griffin Gate Gardens, J.W.'s Steakhouse
Bar: Pegasus
Business Fac.: Audio-visual, Conference rooms, capacity 1400
Sports Fac.: Swimming pool, Tennis courts, Volleyball, Exercise room
Location: Fayette County

Course: Griffin Gate Golf Club (6801)
No. of Holes: 18
Guest Policy: Call for availability
Club House: 859-254-4101
Reservations: Can be made up to 1 year
Season: Open all year

Cypress Bend Golf Resort

Address: 2000 Cypress Bend Pkwy, Many, 71449
877-519-1500
Fax: 318-590-0550
E-mail: cbendsales@cp-tel.net
Web site: http://www.cypressbend.com

Course: Cypress Bend (6707, par 72)
No. of Holes: 18
Guest Policy: Open to public
Club House: 318-256-0346
Reservations: Can make reservations 7 days in advance
Season: Open all year
Carts: Carts included in fees

For years, the spectacular beauty of Toledo Bend Lake has belonged to fishermen, hikers, hunters and nature lovers. Now, with the development of Cypress Bend Golf Resort and Conference Center, this remarkable scenic environment is yours. Throughout our design, all aspects of Cypress Bend Resort and Conference Center emphasize harmony with our beautiful surroundings.

To fully enjoy the natural beauty of your surroundings, your accommodations are equally attractive. Cypress Bend Golf Resort and Conference Center features an elegant country inn decor that will please the most discriminating guests. Our attentions to detail, warm Southern hospitality and commitment to service set us apart from other resort hotels.

The Cypress Dining Room serves breakfast, lunch and dinner from extensive buffets or complete menus. Outstanding views over the golf course and lake complement the experience. The Sabine Social Room offers legal beverage service from mid-afternoon through closing. Table games and billiards are available in the adjoining Great Room. The Cypress Café, located in the clubhouse, serves breakfast, lunch and dinner.

More and more businesses and groups are utilizing beautiful natural settings to inspire the relaxation, serenity and focus necessary for the very best conferences and meetings. At Cypress Bend Conference Center, every aspect of our design guarantees that your needs will be met.

Cypress Bend is a championship caliber course strategically designed to challenge all playing levels. Golfers discover spectacular views at every turn. Because it is curled around one of Toledo Bend's many inlets, the 18-hole course features 10 holes along the water and six with shots across water. It is well bunkered and well manicured. Surrounding hardwood forests and undulating greens add to Cypress Bend's challenge and beauty.

Bluffs on Thompson Creek

The Lodge at The Bluffs is a small, exclusive, all-suites facility overlooking the beautifully wooded golf course and Club at The Bluffs on Thompson Creek. The overnight facilities at The Bluffs include 37 one-bedroom suites and two two-bedroom "Conference Suites. The beautiful Plantation style Clubhouse overlooks the spectacular ninth hole and provides the perfect setting for a delicious meal or cocktail.

In addition to the spectacular golf, The Bluffs offers a variety of other activities. Two lighted, hard-surfaced tennis courts are available for use by guests. The pool and sun decks are located adjacent to the Clubhouse, and bicycles are available for rent. Joggers and walkers can enjoy the quiet streets and country lanes surrounding the Bluffs.

An 18-hole round at The Bluffs is a nature walk through all the diverse settings of the Feliciana countryside. Starting and finishing atop the high bluffs along Thompson Creek, playing to a green located adjacent to a white, sand beach, traversing thick forests of mature hardwoods and pines, and attempting a variety of challenging shots over hills, off bluffs, and into hollows. The breathtaking beauty of Arnold Palmer's design makes a round of golf at The Bluffs as much a visual pleasure as a shotmaking challenge.

Address: Freeland Rd at Hwy 965, PO Box 1220, St. Francisville, 70775
Phone: 225-634-3410
888-634-3410
Fax: 225-634-3528
E-mail: info@thebluffs.com
Web site: http://www.thebluffs.com
No. of Rooms: 39
Rates: $$
Restaurant: The Clubhouse Restaurant 7am–9pm – 7 days
Bar: same as restaurant
Business Fac.: State-of-the-art meeting rooms, Flexible seating options, Food services, Computer modem, Fax/copy services, Telephone hook-ups, Conference suites w/conference table, Audio/visual equipment, Wet bar
Sports Fac.: Tennis, Croquet, Swimming pool, Biking, Walking, Jogging
Location: 25 minutes from Baton Rouge Metro Airport
Course: The Bluffs—7154 yds, Par 72—Great Arnold Palmer design
No. of Holes: 18
Guest Policy: Open to public with advance tee times
Club House: 225-634-5551
Fees: ↑ ↑
Reservations: Call for reservations
Season: Open all year
Carts: $12 per person

Point Sebago Golf Resort

Address: 261 Point Sebago Road, Casco, 04015
Phone: 207-655-3821
800-530-1555
Fax: 207-655-3371
E-mail: info@pointsebago.com
Web site: http://www. pointsebago.com
No. of Rooms: 250
Rates: Inquire
Restaurant: Lake View Restaurant, Terrace Room, The Outdoor Cafe, General Store
Bar: Pro Shop Snack Bar, Sebago Lounge
Business Fac.: 9 separate meeting rooms and 17,200 square feet of meeting space. Overnight meetings up to 400. Day outings up to 2,000. Conference Facilites and Business Center.
Sports Fac.: Full-service marina, Watersports, Fitness Center, Tennis, Swimming, Hiking Trails, Miniature golf, Shuffleboard, Volleyball, Horseshoes, Fishing, Bocce Ball, Archery.
Location: On Sebago Lake in southern Maine
Course: Point Sebago Course (7,002)
No. of Holes: 18
Guest Policy: Open to public
Club House: 207-655-2747
Fees: ↑
Reservations: Call for reservations
Season: Late April–Early November
Carts: Included in all fees

The resort is located on Maine's second largest lake and offers Resort Cottage, Park Home & Travel Trailer rentals on 260 sites. Or if you have your own RV, there are 240 sites—many with 50 amp service. All this is set on 775-acres of lakefront!

With beaches, boats, water skiing, tennis, miniature golf, fishing, bingo, horseshoes, softball, shuffleboard, family hayrides and arts & crafts there's more than enough entertainment opportunities for everyone. For the shopping minded there's antiquing and bargain hunting in the surrounding small towns.

The 18-hole championship course was designed by Philip Wogan, and opened in June of 1996. He describes the course as "challenging but fair." The course is dotted with many small ponds and the fairways are bordered with beautiful, stately white birch and mature pines.

Sugarloaf Inn Resort

For some, it's the superb skiing on Sugarloaf Mountain that draws them to the resort that includes 200 contemporary condominiums on the 100 acre high mountain property. For others it's the spectacular Robert Trent Jones Jr. designed Sugarloaf Golf Club. And there are those who come for exciting whitewater rafting on the nearby Kennebec River.

At the Seasons Restaurant, fine dining will be a special treat after a hard day of playing. Amidst spectacular views of Sugarloaf Mountain, you'll feast on prime rib and lamb. And be sure to order their most celebrated desert, Top of Sugarloaf. With a choice of 13 restaurants within the resort complex, there's sure to be something to please any appetite.

Besides golf, swimming, tennis, riding, and fishing are favorite pastimes at Sugarloaf. But for the ultimate adventure, one of the most popular and exciting experiences at Sugarloaf is whitewater rafting down the Kennebec River. For a relaxing wind down after all that activity, take advantage of the exclusive Sugartree Club, one of the most complete facilities of its kind in the East. The 15,000 square foot club features a 20 x 40 lap pool, four hot tubs, two racquetball courts, and a full fitness center that includes an ergometer and bicycle. The Club also offers certified aerobics and swimnastics.

For many who prefer a quieter, relaxing vacation, the mountain air and the peaceful atmosphere of Maine's wilderness are enough to keep them coming back again and again.

Two things come to mind when Sugarloaf Golf Club is mentioned—one is the striking mountainous setting, particularly in full autumn bloom, and the other is its award winning design balance (how well the holes vary in length and configuration).

Robert Trent Jones Jr.'s wilderness golf course was literally carved from the Maine woods, resulting in spectacular holes that begin in the white birch and pine forests and play downhill. Vying for memorability honors is the par-four 10th hole that starts up high and plays up the throat of the Carrabassett River. This is wilderness golf, with the scent of pine wafting through the clear air, Crocker Mountain in the background, and holes separated from each other with tees sitting high above the greens.

Address: Sugarloaf/USA, Kingfield, 04947
Phone: 207-237-2000
800-457-0002
Fax: 207-237-3052
E-mail: info@sugarloaf.com
Web site: http://www.sugarloaf.com/staying/lodging/sugarloaf_inn.html
No. of Rooms: 472
Rates: Inquire
Restrictions: No pets allowed
Restaurant: Seasons
Bar: Cirque Lounge
Business Fac.: Administrative assistance, Copiers, Conference rooms, capacity 750
Sports Fac.: Swimming pool, Tennis courts, Skiing, Full health spa
Location: Maine Mountains

Course: Sugarloaf Inn Resort (6956)
No. of Holes: 18
Guest Policy: Guests at resort have preferred tee time
Club House: 207-237-2000
Reservations: May be made one week in advance
Season: Mid May–mid October
Carts: Carts are also available

Rockport Samoset Resort

Address: 220 Warrenton St,
Rockport, 04856
Phone: 207-594-2511
800-341-1650
Fax: 207-594-0722
E-mail: info@samoset.com
Web site: http://www.samoset.com
No. of Rooms: 178
Rates: $
Restrictions: No smoking,
Handicap accessible
Restaurant: Marcel's, Breakwater
Cafe, Clubhouse Grille
Business Fac.: State-of-the-art
conference facilities
Sports Fac.: Golf simulator, Heated
indoor/outdoor pools, 4 tennis
courts, Fully equipped fitness
center, Children's playground, Shuf-
fleboard, Badminton, Basketball,
Croquet, Horseshoes, Fishing, Teth-
erball, Bicycles, Volleyball
Location: 10 minutes from Knox
County Airport

Course: Samoset Course (6548)
No. of Holes: 18
Club House: 800-341-1650
Fees: ⌐
Reservations: Call for reservations
Season: April–November

The Samoset is a naturally beautiful four-story
cedar resort hugging the Maine coastline in Rockport, about midway up the coast, 81 miles north of
Portland. Its a region of offshore islands, heavily
wooded forests, lobster traps and year-round recreational activities. 150 guest rooms, condominiums and suites with private balconies or patios
overlook rocky seascapes or New England woods.
The main lodge and outlying buildings are rugged
looking, but interiors are comfortable and modern, with floor-to-ceiling windows affording
remarkable vistas.

Marcel's Restaurant is known for relaxed dining, and at cocktail time, enjoy the Breakwater
Lounge as the sun slips over the yardarm.

The Fitness center includes racquetball, an
indoor and outdoor pool, whirlpools, saunas, Nautilus equipment, and a multi-purpose exercise
room for aerobics. You'll also find hot tub, jogging
trails, tennis courts, video game room, children's
playground, shuffleboard, bicycle rentals and a lot
of other diversions. The gift shop features locally
made crafts, and sports accessories. Children
need a vacation, too, and they'll be happy camp-
ers Monday to Saturday at Samo-camp.

While you may want to stay here endlessly,
there are many attractions nearby. There's sightseeing and shopping in Camden, plus the Shakes-
pearean Amphitheater, schooner adventures,
charters and ferry trips to neighboring islands,
and if you like lobster, this is the area to satisfy
the craving.

The course was designed by Bob Elder, and
was ready for play in 1972. With unrivalled views
of sailboats and skiffs on Penobscot Bay, the seaside links has seven holes bordering the bay, and
two double greens, a tradition borrowed from the
Old Course At St. Andrews. The eighth and the fifteenth holes share a large green surrounded by
bunkers on all sides, and the seventh and six-
teenth have their flagsticks on the same green
with the breakwater as a backdrop. Described as
having the potential of becoming the "Pebble
Beach of the East," return players note the addition of numerous bunkers over the past few years.

Sebasco Harbor Resort

Within the 600 acres of Sebasco Harbor Resort, the grounds are naturally and lovingly landscaped with seasonal gardens, Casco Bay island views and pine and white birch groves.

Sebasco Harbor Resort has 115 rooms to choose from. Each unique in its way. Individual room accommodations are available in the 36 room Main Inn, the quaint Early Bird cottage and in the unique Lighthouse. As an alternative, 22 cottages are scattered through out the property.

Meetings and conferences at Sebasco Harbor Resort mean more than sitting in a meeting room. It means a serene backdrop for productive and focussed work, it means being surrounded by water, breezes and Casco Bay islands. While enjoying the diversity of many indoor and outdoor activities and the regional cuisine in the dining facilities, you might find that the fresh air helps fresh ideas and friendships come easily.

Sebasco's sporty nine-hole course has captured attention since it opened in the late 1920's. It's a wonderful course to learn the game and refine your skills as well. Two sets of tees give you 18 holes of variety and scenic beauty. Pars are 33 and 31. This is a course to enjoy. The course is open from late April until early November. The public is welcome on a space available basis.

Address: Sebasco Estates, Sebasco Estates, 04565
800-225-3819
Fax: 207-389-2004
E-mail: info@Sebasco.com
Web site: http://www.sebasco.com
No. of Rooms: 115
Rates: $$
Restaurant: Lobsterbake or cookout
Business Fac.: Versatile meeting spaces, AV equipment, Full business services, Data ports, Spouse and children's programs
Sports Fac.: Candlepin bowling, air hockey, foosball, ping-pong, table shuffleboard, Fishing, Golf, Tennis, Hiking, Croquet, Horseshoes, Health Club, Lawn bowling, Rent kayak, sailing, canoe, or mountain bike, Swimming, Basketball, Softball, Volleyball, Badminton
Location: 48 miles from Portland, ME

Course: Sebasco (par 33)
No. of Holes: 9
Guest Policy: Open to public
Club House: 207-389-9060
Reservations: No reservations, on a space available basis
Season: Golf open April–November
Carts: Walking required

Stage Neck Inn

Address: Route 1A, PO Box 70, York Harbor, 03911
Phone: 207-363-3850
800-340-1130
E-mail: reserve@stageneck.com
Web site: http://www.
stageneck.com
No. of Rooms: 58
Rates: $$
Restaurant: Harbor Porches—breakfast, lunch and dinner, Sandpiper Bar & Grille—2pm–Closing
Bar: Sandpiper Piano Bar
Business Fac.: Complete conference facilities, capacity 5–100
Sports Fac.: Indoor swimming pool, Outdoor oceanside swimming pool, Clay tennis courts
Location: On the Maine coast

Course: The Ledges
No. of Holes: 18
Guest Policy: Open to public
Club House: 207-351-9999
Reservations: Can make reservations 4 days in advance
Season: Open all year

Here on the Maine coast, there is a unique beauty to each season throughout the year. Stage Neck Inn is a complete resort in the New England tradition. Enjoy warm welcoming touches, like our seasonal flower gardens, with breathtaking ocean and harbor views at every turn. While the property is close to the Kittery Outlet Malls and the historic attractions of York, Maine, it's secluded location on an ocean-bound peninsula leads you to a quiet and relaxed vacation.

Each of the Inn's guest rooms was recently redecorated and furnished in a classic oceanfront cottage style with coordinating linens with your choice of two double- or one king-sized bed. Recently added French-door style sliders and in-room stereos with CD players add to your increased relaxation and enjoyment. Each room offers an ever-changing ocean landscape, overlooking the beach, ocean or river from your own terrace or balcony.

Harbor Porches offers casual gourmet dining in a setting reminiscent of the grand hotel style of the Twenties. Or savor a cocktail and dinner in the intimate Sandpiper Bar & Grille, featuring a piano bar on the weekends. Both restaurants offer a wealth of selections from American Bistro to European classics with ever-changing, one-of-a-kind oceanfront landscapes. Be assured fresh Maine lobster is always in season at Stage Neck Inn!

The Ledges Golf Club has rugged, New England terrain framing a setting where your concentration will be broken by spectacular scenery, outstanding course conditions and various woodland inhabitants. York Golf and Tennis Club offers an 18-hole Don Ross golf course and 6 clay tennis courts just 2½ miles from the Inn. While this is a private club, our guests enjoy membership privileges there.

Rocky Gap Lodge & Golf Resort

When you arrive at Rocky Gap Lodge the incredibly blue and tranquil waters of Lake Habeeb to heavily wooded Evitt's Mountain envelop you by nature's peaceful ways. The natural and pleasing tone of the Lodge lends itself to the surrounding landscape.

The spacious guestroom are comfortable and serene. Rooms features custom-made "Shaker-style" furniture and color-coordinated bedding and draperies. Take advantage of the refreshment bar and the 25" remote controlled television. Younger guests enjoy the Nintendo setup in each room. A virtual office is at your fingertips, as each room has two dual line accessory compatible telephones. The lodge also has 18 Junior Suites offering a separate room (with a queen-sized sleeper), making a perfect setting for families.

Among the undulating hills of the ageless Appalachian Mountains and nestled next to the blue waters of Lake Habeeb, the legendary Golden Bear, Jack Nicklaus, has designed a true championship caliber golf course. Golfers of all skill levels are drawn to the challenges and uniqueness that the mountain course provides. Jack and his expert team spent countless hours integrating the natural features of the area into a golf experience without parallel. From the time your ball makes contact at the first tee, this 7000-yard course both teases and soothes, creating an exhilarating and enjoyable experience. Five sets of tees accommodate all levels of play. While the beauty of the course, with lush bent grass from tee to green, can not be disputed, trust that the variety of shots required will find you thinking your way through all 18 holes using every club in your bag.

Address: PO Box 1199, Cumberland, 21501
800-724-0828
Fax: 301-784-8408
E-mail: debbie.mathew@rockygapresort.com
Web site: http://www.rockygapresort.com

Course: Jack Nicklaus signature course (7000, par 72)
No. of Holes: 18
Guest Policy: Open to public
Club House: 301-784-8500
Fees: ⅂⅂
Reservations: Call to make reservations
Carts: Carts included in fees

Turf Valley Resort & Conference Center

Address: 2700 Turf Valley Rd,
Ellicott City, 21042
Phone: 410-465-1500
888-TEE-TURF
E-mail: tvrcc@aol.com
Web site: http://www.turfvalley.com
No. of Rooms: 223
Rates: $$
Restaurant: Alexandra's, The
Terrace on the Green
Bar: The Fairway Lounge
Business Fac.: Professional
Convention Service Managers, 28
Conference rooms, Concierge, Fax,
Photocopying, Tele/video confer-
encing, Transporation available,
Audio/visual, Free parking
Sports Fac.: Pool, Tennis, Whirl-
pool, Steam room, Sand volleyball,
Basketball, Shuffle Board, Chil-
dren's playground
Location: 20 minutes from down-
town Baltimore

Courses: East (6554, par 71), South
(6271, par 70), North (6586, par 71)
No. of Holes: 54
Guest Policy: Open to public
Club House: 888-TEE-TURF
Reservations: Call for reservations
Season: Open all year
Carts: Carts available

A family owned resort, Turf Valley prides itself on
warm, friendly service. The resort is set on over
1,000 acres and the grounds are attractively land-
scaped and lend themselves to pleasant walks.
The area is particularly spectacular in the fall.

The rooms are luxuriously furnished and over-
look the rolling hills of Maryland's hunt country.
The public rooms are elegant, and their are fan-
tastic views from all areas of the establishment.

Turf Valley specializes in fine dining. You'll find
old favorites on the menu as well as new experi-
ences, you can even get your omelettes made-to-
order.

The state-of-the-art conference center even
has an Executive Computer Room. You'll have
your own convention service manager to ensure
that everything is done just the way you want it
with no effort on your part. Whether your group is
large or small, you'll get the best of care and the
best conference ever!

The pool area has a pavilion for parties. And
there's just about every other kind of provision for
sports anyone could want, from softball, baseball
and volleyball field to basketball courts. To help
keep your golf game sharp you can practice on
the lighted driving range and lighted putting
green. A perfect way to work off those extra
pounds you'll be sure to get from the fine dining.

The East Course is the most difficult with nar-
row fairways and bordered by beautiful mature
trees. The South Course offers a more relaxing
round of golf with more open fairways. The front
and back play very differently on the North
Course with target type holes on one nine and lots
of water on the other.

Wisp Resort Hotel

Wisp is a four-season resort located in the panhandle of western Maryland in the Allegheny Mountain Range. The Wisp Mountain Resort Hotel & Conference Center, in the mountains of Western Maryland, is the perfect place to get away from it all-or get down to business.

Ample accommodations include the slopeside hotel complete with an indoor pool and whirlpool. This resort hotel offers 168 rooms including 100 suites with separate sleeping and living areas. Racquetball courts, tennis courts and golf are available. The property features cable TV with movies, exercise room, gift shop, in-room coffee makers, major credit cards accepted, microwaves in rooms, non-smoking units available, and refrigerators.

There are several dining choices at Wisp Mountain Resort. The Place, formerly the Bavarian Room, has been renewed: it is brighter, more contemporary and lighthearted, with a new menu to match. The Place is located at the base of one of our most popular ski runs known as The Face. Pizzaz Pizzeria offers pizzas, sandwiches, salads, and snacks. The Gathering, open during ski season, this lounge offers entertainment on the weekends and boasts a slopeside location that makes it ideal for skiers and snowboarders. 23∫ Below Lounge is a quiet, casual place for retreat, refreshment and conversation.

Bring your sticks to one of Mid-Atlantic's top-rated 18-hole championship golf courses. Tee off onto lush, tree-lined fairways surrounded by beautiful Western Maryland scenery. But beware—it's hard to concentrate on the game with landscapes like this. Each hole has a distinct look and character that makes it singularly captivating and doubly challenging, with 90 bunkers, 4 ponds and 2 lakes in all. Golf at Wisp Mountain Resort isn't just a game, it's a picturesque, par 72 adventure.

Address: Route Box 35, McHenry, 21541
Phone: 301-387-5581
800-462-9477
E-mail: lratliff@wisp-resort.com
Web site: http://www.
wispresort.com
No. of Rooms: 168
Rates: $$
Business Fac.: Conference Center, capacity to 400
Sports Fac.: Indoor swimming pool and whirlpool, Volleyball, basketball, tennis and racquetball courts, horseshoes, Fitness center
Location: In the mountains of Western Maryland

Course: Wisp Resort (6911)
No. of Holes: 18
Club House: 301-387-4911
Fees: ⊺⊺
Reservations: Call for reservations
Season: All year

Chatham Bars Inn & Cottage

Address: Shore Rd, Chatham, 02633
Phone: 508-945-0096
800-527-4884
Fax: 508-945-5491
E-mail: welcome@
chathambarsinn.com
Web site: http://www.
charthambarsinn.com
No. of Rooms: 152
Rates: Inquire
Restrictions: No pets allowed
Restaurant: Main Dining Room,
The Tavern, Beach House Grill
Bar: Inner Bar, Front Terrace,
South Lounge, Pilot House
Business Fac.: Administrative assistance, Audio-visual, Conference rooms, capacity 300
Sports Fac.: Swimming pool, Tennis courts, Sailing, Windsurfing, Fitness room, Deep sea fishing
Location: Cape Cod

Course: Chatham Seaside Links (2490)
No. of Holes: 9
Guest Policy: Register to play
Club House: 508-945-4774
Reservations: Same day except for groups
Season: April–November
Carts: Walking is permitted

Built in 1914 as a hunting lodge for a Boston family, the Inn has received guests continuously, retaining its tradition of service befitting an elegant seaside landmark. The weathered main inn sits high on a knoll and from the wide veranda, guests enjoy views of the Outer Bar and the Atlantic. The lobby and lounges sport soft gray walls, wicker furniture with chintz coverings, and palms in huge Chinese urns. A cozy bar, library, large dining room and a living room that is transformed into a dance floor after dinner, radiate from the lobby. Guests are housed in large traditionally-appointed rooms upstairs, or choose from 26 Cape-Cod style houses dotting the grounds. The guest rooms, recently redone in Laura Ashley soft colors, have fireplaces, antiques, rag rugs and porches overlooking the water so you can sniff that salty air. Awaiting you is a secluded private beach, five tennis courts, heated swimming pool, sailing, windsurfing, clambakes, and water activities for every age and interest group. The Inn is open year-round, and offers an American plan with a traditional menu in the main dining room, and a New England version of nouvelle cuisine in the refurbished Beach House Grill. Can you resist the likes of red pepper pancakes, lobster and seafood sausages? But wait until you sink your teeth in the doughnuts.

In 1914, seven years after Pinehurst Number Two opened, Donald Ross' nine holes here were ready for play. Definitely short, the 2,325 yards are quite challenging as the course winds through rolling terrain, with views of the harbor and the ocean from the 7th and 8th holes. Close to the Inn are two championship courses. Cranberry Valley, is a 1974 creation with credit going to Bornish and Robinson. A par 72 course, the 6300 yard layout is known for large greens and tees. Nearby in Brewster is a superb public course, aptly named Captains Golf Course. This award winning course was designed by Geoffrey Cornish and Brian Silva.

Beach Buddies is a flexible schedule children's program offered from the end of June until Labor day. The program is complimentary and is for children 3-1/2 and up. There are sandcastle contests, arts & crafts, games, movies and magic shows.

Cranwell Resort and Golf Club

Nestled in the Berkshire hills you'll find this jewel of a resort in a 100-year-old country hotel. The individually decorated rooms offer sweeping view of the mountains and fireplaces, for that added extra cozy touch. The rooms are located in the mansion, Beecher's Cottage, The Carriage House and the Cottage Suites, so you certainly won't feel crowded.

You'll find plenty to do here with many sightseeing opportunities, or you can enjoy the many recreational activities at the resort. There are cross-country ski trails, a driving range, an indoor golf facility, and boating, fishing, hot air ballooning and horseback riding nearby. There's even a wildlife sanctuary just a short drive away.

Cranwell is an ideal setting for a luxurious conference. There is a stately Board Room and a grand ballroom. The efficient staff will gladly handle all the details for you, just sit back and enjoy.

The course has many mature trees that line the fairways, so your shot-making abilities will at times be called into service. The greens are small and undulating, and there's plenty of water on the course as well. Set in 380 carefully tended acres, the course makes use of all natural hazards. The views of the surrounding hills can distract you from your game.

Address: 55 Lee Road, Lenox, 01240
Phone: 413-637-1364
800-272-6935
Fax: 413-637-0571
E-mail: info@cranwell.com
Web site: http://www.cranwell.com
Rates: $
Restaurant: Wyndhurst Restaurant, Music Room Grill
Bar: Sloane's Tavern
Business Fac.: Conference facilities, capacity 20-200, Boardroom, Sloane Esq. Ballroom
Sports Fac.: Cross country skiing, Golf School, 4 tennis courts, Outdoor heated swimming pool, Fitness center, Biking
Location: In the Berkshire Hills of western Massachusetts

Course: Cranwell (6346, par 70)
No. of Holes: 18
Guest Policy: Open to public
Club House: 413-637-0441
Fees: ⌐
Reservations: Can make reservations 5 days in advance
Season: Open all year
Carts: Gas carts included in fees

New Seabury Cape Cod

Address: P.O. Box 549, New Seabury, 02649
Phone: 508-477-9400
800-999-9033
Fax: 508-477-9790
E-mail: info@newseabury.com
Web site: http://www.
newseabury.com
No. of Rooms: 291
Rates: Inquire
Restrictions: No pets allowed
Restaurant: New Seabury
Business Fac.: Administrative assistance, Audio-visual, Conference rooms, capacity 125
Sports Fac.: Swimming pool, Tennis courts, Sailing, Nautilus
Location: Upper Cape Cod

Courses: Blue Course (6909), Green Course
No. of Holes: 36
Guest Policy: Limited tee times for non-guests
Club House: 508-477-9110
Reservations: 24 hours in advance
Season: May–October 10
Carts: Carts are also available

An hour and a half from Boston or Providence, on Cape Cod's southern tip, is a family resort comprised of privately owned villas and offering a fantastic New England vacation. From a few model homes begun in 1964, the community has evolved into a 2,000 acre premier recreational resort of where guests may opt for accommodations ranging from oceanfront suites, seaside villas or golf-front patio homes. Full housekeeping services are provided in all of the villas. Decor ranges from 19th century Nantucket style with antiques, wide plank floors and French doors to cool California contemporary. Most have exhilarating ocean and/or golf course views, and all are fully furnished. Restaurants are coordinated under the same management, and each caters to families. The Popponessett Inn is the essence of New England dining, specializing in traditional tureens of chowders, clam and oyster fritters, and succulent lobsters dripping in lemon butter. Who could resist the flavors at the Ice Cream Scoop, a dozen clams at the Raw Bar, or the intimacy of the Gallery?

There's something for every age here, starting with three miles of sandy white beach. Children's activities are numerous—should it be movies, a waterbug slalom race, or beach blanket bingo. Sixteen all-weather tennis courts and expert instruction, in addition to miles of jogging and bicycling trails, plus swimming pools and a health spa with Nautilus equipment add up to variety and healthy appetites.

Boutique shopping is popular during summer months, as well as the Sandwich Glass Museum, and nearby Heritage Plantation. Fishing excursions can be arranged, and the well-known outlets of the Cape are a short drive.

Golf here comes in the form of two championship courses, which are rated among of the best in the nation. Dubbed Oceanfront and Challenger, or Blue and Green, these 36 holes treat golfers to dramatic seascapes, manicured greens, salt marshes splashed with Rugosa roses and the misty expanse of Nantucket Sound. Thanks to the warming Gulf Stream, a Thanksgiving Day round isn't that unusual. Home of the New England Intercollegiate Championship, and the Massachusetts Mid Am Championship, the New Seabury Country Club was called the "Pebble Beach of the East" by Francis Ouimet, the 20-year old winner of the U.S. Open in 1913.

Blue Rock Resort

Situated on the scenic, world renown Blue Rock Golf Course, the Best Western Blue Rock Motor Inn is a seasonal inn operating from April 7, 2000 to October 30, 2000 and offers quality accommodations at affordable prices. If you're looking for a full service golf resort vacation or just a relaxing getaway Best Western Blue Rock Motor Inn provides the perfect setting for a memorable Cape Cod vacation.

After a full day of activities, the peaceful charm of our guestrooms is the perfect setting for total relaxation. All 44 of our guestrooms have a patio or deck that overlooks the golf course, swimming pool or gardens. Each climate-controlled room features a refrigerator and remote controlled color television. The majority of our rooms are equipped with double beds and we also provide Deluxe King Rooms and Queen Jacuzzi Rooms. Our Clubhouse Apartment, overlooking the lush 18th green of Best Western Blue Rock Golf Course, comes complete with a full kitchen and room for up to 6 people.

Blue Rock Golf Course, located in the heart of Cape Cod, was designed by internationally known architect Geoffrey Cornish in 1962. The championship par three course measures 3,000 yards from the professional tees. Blue Rock Golf Course is regarded as the nation's best par three golf course by its design. The holes range in yardage from 103 to 255 yards. With four picturesque water holes, it is often described as a regulation golf course without tee shots. However, bring your driver—You will need it! Blue Rock Golf Course is open year round to the public.

Address: P.O. Box 419, South Yarmouth, 02664
Phone: 508-398-6962
800-237-8887
E-mail: bluerock@redjacketinns.com
Web site: http://www.bluerockgolfcourse.com

Course: Par 3 Golf Course (2923, par 54)
No. of Holes: 18
Guest Policy: Open to public
Club House: 508-398-9295
Fees: †
Reservations: Can make reservations 30 days in advance
Carts: Pull carts available

Hilton Shanty Creek

Address: One Shanty Creek Road, Bellaire, 49615
Phone: 231-533-8621
800-678-4111
E-mail: info@shantycreek.com
Web site: http://www.shantycreek.com
No. of Rooms: 660
Rates: $
Restaurant: Ivans Mountain Grill for family fun and The Lakeview.
Business Fac.: Available for meetings and conferences up to 1,000 people.
Sports Fac.: Fitness center
Location: Picturesque Northern Michigan woodlands

Courses: The Cedar River (6989, par 72), The Legend (6764, par 72), Schuss Mountain (6922, par 72), Summit Golf Club (6260, par 71)
No. of Holes: 72
Guest Policy: Open to public
Club House: 800-678-4111
Fees: ⌐
Reservations: Can make reservations 14 days in advance
Season: April–October
Carts: Cart included in fees

Shanty Creek-Schuss Mountain Resort is owned by Club Resorts, an affiliate of Club Corporations of America, the largest operator of private city and athletic clubs. Bellaire located within northern Michigan's Golf Capital, known for rolling wooded country and a string of lakes known as the chain-of-lakes. Two separate lodging facilities, three miles apart, offers golfers a variety of choices. Shanty Creek offers The Legend and The Deskin, and Schuss Mountain offers the Schuss Mountain Golf Club. Don't be put off by the number of accommodations and facilities-remember that this area isn't densely populated and developers work hard to retain the open space. 640 rooms, suites and condominiums ensure the ideal accommodations for everyone. Both lodges offer restaurants, extensive conference facilities, tennis courts and children's programs with a wide variety of activities.

Bring your hiking boots if you enjoy exploring the trails, as the area that's popular for skiing is even prettier on a summer day. You can fish on Lake Bellaire for perch, or try the trout streams or smelt dipping. Work it all off at the Health Club, rent a bicycle or plunge in one of the outdoor pools, or an indoor one if the weather's inclement. Families congregate for swimming and water sports at the private beach club on Lake Bellaire, sometimes to discuss other nearby activities such as riding, skeet shooting, canoeing, paddlboat cruises, orchard tours, windsurfing and often to rehash that old Midwest favorite, a wagon ride.

Arnold Palmer joined with his partner Ed Seay to create the outstanding "Legend." One of his star creations. Playing the course is like walking solo in the north woods. There are no parallel holes, and each fairway is framed by mature pine and birch. Palmer described the course as "exceptionally pleasureable to play."

The Schuss Mountain Golf Club, home of the ITT Michigan Golf Classic, is noted for its beautiful wooded greens and well manicured fairways. The last three holes are the most challenging finishing holes in northern Michigan.

The Deskin is named after the original Shanty Creek developer Roy Deskin. The 18-hole championship layout was designed by Bill Diddel, who land that was used for farming and an apple orchard, into the course it is today. Bill Diddel mush have had a sense of history because the original Shanty is still standing on the 18th hole.

Caberfae Peaks Ski & Golf Resort

Nestled in the heart of the Manistee National Forest, Caberfae Peaks is a unique world class golf experience located at the base of the Peaks ski runs!

Enjoy the quiet beauty of Caberfae Peaks in hotel rooms overlooking the ski resort. Heated pool and spa on site. The Blackmer Lodge is the perfect location for any event. The cathedral ceilings, stone fireplace, sunny and roomy atmosphere compliment your special gathering. You have to see this lodge to believe it.

The MacKenzie Lodge, a 36-room hotel with an outdoor heated pool and spa, is available for any overnight needs. Caberfae Peaks has been host to numerous outings including weddings, receptions, business conferences, class reunions, and golf outings. We can do it all!

Golf course architect Harry Bowers has done a magnificent job of designing the course to fit with the natural beauty of the surrounding land by using the knowledge and talent gained from his many years tutelage under Robert Trent Jones, Sr. His love of the land and sense of the environment is obvious throughout the course. The golfer crosses 10 bridges as he winds his way through a beautiful two-mile nature trail. Each hole has its own unique personality providing a different and exciting challenge and complete isolation from other holes. All holes have a minimum of four different tee locations. The par-72 course will play 6682 yards from the back tees. The forward tees will play 4372 yards. Striking views, giant 75' trees lining the fairways, miles of forested hills and valleys unblemished by condominium or housing developments, roads or farms, provide only pure wilderness land for the golfer to enjoy. The views are rare and not available from any other golf course in the Midwest.

Address: Caberfae Road, Cadillac, 49601
Phone: 231-862-3000
Fax: 231-862-3302
E-mail: caberfae@michweb.net
Web site: http://www. michiweb.com/cabpeaks/
Restaurant: Caberfeidh Dining Room
Bar: Stagshead Lounge

Course: Peaks (3248, par 36)
No. of Holes: 9
Guest Policy: Open to public
Club House: 231-862-3301
Fees: ┃
Reservations: Can make reservations one year in advance
Season: Golf open May November
Carts: Electric and pull carts available

McGuire's Resort

Address: Mackinaw Trail, Cadillac, 49601
Phone: 231-775-9947
888-MCGUIRES
E-mail: info@mcguiresresort.com
Web site: http://www.
mcguiresresort.com
No. of Rooms: 120
Rates: Inquire
Restaurant: Terrace Dining Room, McGuire's Historic On-site Bakery, Curly's Up North Bar & Grill
Business Fac.: 8 meeting rooms, capacity 250, complete banquet and conference facilities
Sports Fac.: Volleyball, Shuffleboard, ½ court basketball, Horseshoes, Skiing, Vita Trail
Location: Michigan's beautiful lower peninsula

Courses: Spruce Golf Course (6443, par 71), Norway Course (2800, par 36)
No. of Holes: 27
Guest Policy: Open to public
Club House: 888-MCGUIRES
Fees: ⍑
Reservations: Call for reservations
Season: April–October
Carts: Carts are mandatory on Spruce course

Situated 1,462 feet above sea level, the McGuire Resort overlooks the City of Cadillac and Lake Cadillac. Each of the 120 rooms and suites offers great views of the North Country's bounty. Accommodations are contemporary and professionally appointed. Superb meals are a natural element to any North Country experience. The Terrace Room Restaurant offers bountiful meals, while Curly's Up North Bar and Grill offers lighter fare.

The on-site Vita trail has hiking and jogging with exercise points along the way, and two outdoor tennis courts are well lit for evening play. In addition, there's shuffleboard, volleyball, horseshoes, basketball, and miniature golf. After recreation enjoy the indoor pool, sauna and whirlpool, lounge on the tanning deck, or relax in the fireside lounge with bumper pool, table tennis, and game tables. Enjoy on-site cross-country skiing over groomed trails, with lights for night skiing.

The center of summer activity is the 18 hole Championship Spruce Golf Course. Carved through glacier-sculptured hills, the Spruce offers memorable golf holes with plenty of berms, bunkers and hills to challenge the novice player and entertain the avid professional. The nine-hole Norway Course is a fun, sporty play of 2,792 yards at a par of 36. McGuire's golf professional can assist your game with instruction on the driving range and practice greens.

Sugar Loaf Resort

Discover the beauty surrounding you when you stay at Sugar Loaf Resort. Explore unique galleries and shops in the quaint towns and villages on Leelanau Peninsula. Or head for Leland, just 8 miles away, where you'll find historic riverside Fishtown. An 18-hole championship course is always ready for play, and tastefully decorated accommodations are always a comfort at days end.

Address: Route 1, Cedar, 49621
Phone: 616-228-5461
800-748-0117
E-mail: lodging@sugarloaf.com
Web site: http://www.sugarloaf.com
No. of Rooms: 150
Rates: $
Restaurant: The Seasons Restaurant, Double Diamond Restaurant & Pub, Bollwinkle's, Base Lodge, Klister Kitchen, and more
Bar: Shipyards Brewhaus, Widowmaker Lounge
Business Fac.: Complete Conference Center
Sports Fac.: Indoor pool, Spa and Fitness Center, and Outdoor Swimming pool
Location: Leelanau Peninsula

Course: Two 18-hole courses
No. of Holes: 36
Club House: 888-228-0121
Reservations: Call for reservations
Season: Open all year

Eagle Crest Conference Resort

Address: 1275 So. Huron St, Detroit, 48197
Phone: 734-487-2000
800-228-9290
Fax: 734-481-0700
E-mail: hotel@eaglecrestresort.com
Web site: http://www.
eaglecrestresort.com
No. of Rooms: 236
Rates: $$
Restaurant: Bentley's Restaurant

Course: Eagle Crest Course (6750, par 72)
No. of Holes: 18
Guest Policy: Open to public
Club House: 734-487-2441
Fees: ⌐
Reservations: Can make reservations 14 days in advance
Carts: Gas & pull carts available

Three spectacular facilities-the Ypsilanti Marriott Hotel at Eagle Crest, Eastern Michigan University's Eagle Crest Conference Center and Eagle Crest Golf Club-come together in one great location. It's all here for you. No other executive retreat in Southeastern Michigan combines this conference center mentality with resort personality. At Eagle Crest, you can focus on the big picture while you sharpen your skills. You can relax a little, too. It's the place where the dress code is corporate casual and the service is on the mark. Here business and pleasure come together effortlessly-and success is always in sight.

The Ypsilanti Marriott at Eagle Crest features "The Room That Works." Steelcase, AT&T and Marriott have teamed up to create the ultimate guestroom for the business traveler. Among it's many amenities are voice mail, ergonomic chair and a workstation with adjustable desk lamp, electrical outlets and computer modem jack.

The golf club features an 18-hole championship golf course overlooks the picturesque Ford Lake in Ypsilanti Township. The par 72 course provide any golfing buff with one of the most challenging courses in Southeastern Michigan. The layout of the course—designed by Karl Litten of Boca Raton, Florida—dares both novice and seasoned golfers with several holes bordering the banks of Ford Lake and five scenic but challenging water hazards.

Woodmoor Resort

Drummond Island Resort & Conference Center encompasses 2000 beautiful acres of woods, water and wildlife. Accommodations at Drummond Island Resort & Conference Center are unique and plentiful. The Lodge, a forty-room hotel, has unique wood construction rooms with telephone, televisions and small refrigerators. Waterfront cottages and log homes are also available for rent on a nightly or weekly basis. The Bayside Dining is open nightly and serves exceptional gourmet meals.

A small fitness room at the waterfront features free weights, a universal machine, and stairmaster. Other activities include an outdoor pool and whirlpool, a Scandinavian sauna, walking and jogging trails, massage therapy, and tennis. In the winter enjoy guided snowmobiling tours, cross-country skiing and more.

Harry Bowers, who learned at the knee of Robert Trent Jones, designed the course at the Resort. He cut this emerald out of limestone, trimmed by hardwood and cedar, crafting each fairway separately over 400 acres. Play on the Rock is controlled. Each group of golfers is in their own game, unaware of any other golfers on the course except the players ahead or behind. Each hole has four tees and therefore, four choices of challenges on each hole

Address: 33494 S. Maxton Road, Drummond Island, 49726
Phone: 906-493-1000
800-999-6343
E-mail: woodmoor@drummondisland.com
Web site: http://drummondisland.com
No. of Rooms: 41
Rates: Inquire
Restaurant: Bayside Dining, Pins Bar & Grill
Sports Fac.: Bowling Center
Location: Drummond Island—Michigan's Largest Island

Course: The Rock (6837, par 71)
No. of Holes: 18
Guest Policy: Open to public
Club House: 906-493-1006
Fees: ⸂⸂
Reservations: Reservations available 365 days in advance
Season: April–October
Carts: Carts included in fees

Otsego Club

Address: 696 M32 East Main Street, PO Box 556, Gaylord, 49734
Phone: 517-732-5181
877-465-3475
E-mail: reservations@otsegoclub.com
Web site: http://www.otsegoclub.com
No. of Rooms: 105
Rates: Inquire
Restaurant: Pontresina Restaurant—award-winning, Duck Blind Grille, casual dining
Bar: The Logmark
Business Fac.: Meeting and conference facilities, capacity 20-300
Sports Fac.: 22 Ski runs, Cross country skiing, Hiking, Biking,
Location: On the bluffs overlooking Gaylord's Sturgeon Valley

Courses: The Classic (6348, par 72), The Lake (6310, par 71), The Loon (6701, par 71)
No. of Holes: 54
Guest Policy: Open to public
Club House: 517-732-4653
Fees: ❘❘
Reservations: Call for reservations
Season: Open all year—golf only April-September
Carts: Cost includes cart

Opened in 1939, Otsego Club is a wonderful antique, an outpost of casual elegance, near I-75 in Gaylord, Michigan. The Club is comprised of 105 hotel rooms, suites, chalets, and condominiums, with bed and breakfast style rooms for ultimate comfort and utility. If you really want to be spoiled, savor the flavors of the Otsego Club's Pontresina Ristorante, one of Northern Michigan's finest dining experience.

The Otsego Ski Club offers short lift lines, combined with advanced snowmaking capabilities, a Professional Ski Instructor Association P.S.I.A. ski school, a nationally-recognized "all member" ski patrol, an unparalleled ski safety record, and a renowned children's program.

The Otsego Club Collection of Great Golf comprises three, soon to be four, uniquely challenging PGA championship courses—The Loon, The Lake and The Classic. Each course offers scenic beauty in the form of woodlands, water and wildlife. With a plethora of woods, water and wildlife, The Loon was selected as *Golf for Women* magazine's Top 100 Women-Friendly Golf Courses. The Lake's unique Jerry Matthews layout is really three course styles in one: six holes are Alpine traversing up and around ski slopes; six holes are Scottish; and six holes traverse around and over water. The Classic, a traditional, "Country Club" design provides a no gimmicks honest approach to the game.

Treetops Sylvan Resort

Treetops Sylvan is an elegant and affordable resort with spacious guest rooms that are decorated in contemporary and traditional decor, even some four-poster beds! Deluxe rooms have balconies, wet bars and whirlpools. But all are designed with your comfort as the foremost thought!

The sports bar has over 500 different bears and QB1 and interactive sports and trivia game played against people at establishments all over the country. The Horizon Dining room offers fine dining with an extensive menu, even including wild game entrees. The Fairways Grill is cigar friendly and has an assortment of scotches from around the world.

For your conference there is even an elegant board room, and 10,000 square foot convention center. The fine convention staff will handle your event, from start to finish, in an efficient and professional manner that will leave you free to enjoy yourself.

The Rick Smith Golf Academy has tutored the likes of Jack Nicklaus and Lee Janzen and over 100 touring pros. All classes maintain a 2 to 1 student/instructor ratio, so you're sure to get all the attention you want!

The golfing at Treetops is unique in that the courses have been designed by three generations of designers! The Fazio course is tree-lined with wide fairways and difficult greens. The Jones Course is the one that Jones considers his "masterpiece" and is considered the most difficult of the courses here with long narrow fairways and small greens. The Smith Course is tree-lined as well, with player-friendly fairways. Threetops is a par-3, nine hole course that will challenge your short game all the way, sure to give you plenty of practice with your irons!

Address: 3962 Wilkinson Rd, Gaylord, 49735
Phone: 517-732-6711
800-444-6711
Fax: 517-732-6595
Web site: http://www.treetops.com/
No. of Rooms: 254
Rates: $$
Restaurant: Horizon Dining Room, Sports Grille
Bar: Broken Club Pub
Business Fac.: Complete Conference facilities
Sports Fac.: 2 Heated indoor & outdoor pools, Spas, Saunas, Fitness Center, Sand volleyball, Tennis courts
Location: Pigeon River Valley, Gaylord, MI

Courses: #1 (6832, par 72), #2 (6832), #3, #4 and 9 hole course
No. of Holes: 81
Guest Policy: Open to public
Club House: 517-732-6711
Fees: ↑↑↑
Reservations: Reservations available 365 days in advance
Season: Open all year
Carts: Carts included in fees

Grand Traverse Resort Village

Address: P.O. Box 404, Grand Traverse Village, 49610
Phone: 231-938-2100
800-236-1577
Fax: 231-938-2399
E-mail: info@grandtraverseresort.com
Web site: http://www.grandtraverseresort.com
Rates: $$
Restaurant: Trillium, Sweetwater Cafe, The Grille
Business Fac.: Over 49,000 sq ft of meeting space, including private boardrooms, ballrooms, convention centers and outdoor function areas. Area includes 34 meeting rooms and can accomodate groups from 10-2,500 people.
Sports Fac.: 100,000+ sq ft Spa Complex includes indoor/outdoor tennis courts, aquatic facilities, weight room, cardiovascular studio, and spa.
Location: The Northwoods of Northern Michigan

Courses: The Bear (7065, par 72), Spruce Run (6579, par 71), The Wolverine
No. of Holes: 54
Guest Policy: Open to public
Club House: 800-748-0303
Fees: †
Reservations: Reservations available 7 days in advance
Season: April–October
Carts: Carts included in fees

What state has the most golf courses? Michigan claims this distinction, and it is here, on the shores of Grand Traverse Bay, in northwest Lower Michigan that one finds a gem of a resort offering year-round recreational facilities. There are 750 guest accommodations, yet because it's bounded by a bay and two golf courses, a feeling of spaciousness and the pleasures of northern Michigan's forests make it most appealing as a family destination. Choose from suites, hotel rooms, or condominiums facing the bay or along the fairways of a championship course.

The Trillium restaurant offers regional American dishes and a magnificent view of the environs from its glass-enclosed 16th floor setting. The night comes alive in the Trillium Lounge, where live jazz and contemporary sounds round out a fun-filled day.

An indoor sports complex offers tennis and racquetball courts, swimming pool, and a total fitness center. Outdoor sports range from softball, volleyball, and tennis to a multitude of water sports. A lovely private beach is perfect for relaxing, playing with the children or watching the sailboards. Charter fishing expeditions can be arranged for you or your group, or maybe you'll want to test your prowess on a sailboat. Winter provides groomed cross-country trails geared to all levels.

Jack Nicklaus' striking design of The Bear has Scottish touches. The tournament course offers a variety of terrain sculpted from the northern Michigan countryside, terraced fairways and gently tiered greens nestled among lakes, streams and cherry orchards. Home of the AAA Michigan Open, the Cadillac Cup, and the Jack Nicklaus Celebrity Pro-Am. No two holes are similar, presenting a diverse array of targets. The Resort course, designed in 1978 by Bill Newcomb, joins The Bear, and at 6,176 yards offers challenging versatility on a gently rolling landscape.

Boyne Highlands Resort

The picturesque town of Harbor Springs, four miles from Little Traverse Bay and the shores of Lake Michigan, is the backdrop of this retreat, geared to all ages and interests. It's a casual place, lively in summer with festivals, art fairs and water-oriented activities such as sailboat regattas. The resort has touches of a quaint European village, and the amenities today's vacationers seek. You will stay in a hotel room or an elegant suite. The Heather Highlands Inn, close to the main Inn, offers condominium rooms, and has a pool, exercise room, and meeting rooms. A full American plan is offered, always popular with families, and a highlight of summer evenings is the dinner performance of entertainment by Young Americans, complete with costumes, sound, lighting and staging. You can spend your time golfing, sightseeing in neighboring Petoskey, chartering a fishing boat, or playing tennis, swimming or unwinding in the sauna. A sister resort, Boyne Mountain is a short drive away, and offers a wide choice of accommodations, activities and diversions.

Between the two large resorts, golfers have a total of 108 holes. Not just golf, world class golf. Here, carved through forests of birch, maple, beech and cedar, players find undulating greens, tiered fairways, grass and sand traps, ponds, mounds and small lakes. Robert Trent Jones designed the Heather, an award winning par 72 course. It's heavily wooded with blueberry marshes and ponds dotting your scorecard. Greens are vast—ranging from 7,000 to 10,000 square feet. This is a toughie to par. The Moor, also a par 72, plays a little longer with rather wide landing areas and fairways. Don't miss the Donald Ross Memorial Course along with a new clubhouse and driving range. Individual holes have been patterned after one of the Scotsman's most famed creations such as the 14th at Pinehurst, the 17th at Oakland Hills South, and the second at Scioto. Should you play at Boyne Mountain, you'll be teeing off on both courses at 1,150 feet and winding down a wooded mountain.

Address: 600 Highlands Drive, Harbor Springs, 49740
Phone: 616-526-2171
800-GO-BOYNE
Fax: 616-526-5636
E-mail: rooms@boyne.com
Web site: http://www.boynehighlands.com
No. of Rooms: 279
Rates: Inquire
Restaurant: Highlands Lodge Dining Room & Country Club of Boyne
Business Fac.: Administrative assistance, Audio-visual, Conference rooms, capacity 1200
Sports Fac.: Tennis courts, Swimming pool, Skeet shooting, Skiing, Trout pond
Location: Northwest Michigan

Courses: Heather (7210), The Moor, Donald Ross Memorial, Hills (nine)
No. of Holes: 63
Guest Policy: Call for availability
Club House: 616-526-2171
Fees: ⸙
Reservations: May be made with room reservations
Season: May–October

Thunder Bay Golf Resort

Address: 28700 M-32 East, Hillman, 49746
800-729-9375
Fax: 517-742-3380
E-mail: tbg@thunderbaygolf.com
Web site: http://www.
thunderbaygolf.com
Rates: $
Restaurant: Clubhouse Bar & Grill, The Loft
Bar: Clubhouse Bar
Sports Fac.: Tennis courts, Skiing
Location: On the Thunder Bay River

Course: Thunder Bay (6677, Par 73)
No. of Holes: 18
Guest Policy: Open to public
Club House: 517-742-4875
Fees: ↑
Reservations: Call for reservations
Season: Open all year
Carts: Cart are also available

All luxury suites and villas feature living and dining rooms and compact, well-equipped kitchens. Enjoy wooded sites with decks overlooking the golf course. All lodging units will sleep 4 or more people in separate beds—ideal for your foursome or family.

A horse-drawn carriage or sleigh carries you deep into the forest to view the majestic Rocky Mountain Elk. Enjoy the spectacular fall colors or the tranquil blanket of snow in the winter. Through the trees appears the Elkhorn Log Cabin where you will enjoy a 5-course gourmet dinner prepared on antique wood cook-stoves. This wonderful, romantic couples' getaway can be combined with golf during the summer, while winter opens a whole new world of adventure with snowmobiling, ice skating, cross-country skiing & ice fishing.

Carved from mature forest, Thunder Bay's par 73 (with slope ratings form 120 to 313) layout stretches from 5,004 to 6,677 yards. Rolling terrain, ponds and cattail marshes define its Northern Michigan beauty. Thunder Bay now offers 5 sets of tees. Longer and stronger from the back tees, a little easier from the regular tees, new senior men's tees and two new, more user friendly ladies tees make Thunder Bay a fair test for players of all skill levels. Don't miss Joe Libby's School of Golf.

Garland

Garland is 3500 acres of unsurpassed beauty. It is the masterwork and elegance of the largest log lodge east of the Mississippi. It is 72 holes of championship golf, it is world-class dining, it is 1100 acres of premier trophy hunts, Garland is indeed the ultimate four-season retreat.

The main Lodge consists of three types of room styles. Main Lodge queen room consisting of two queen beds, a small sitting area, and a standard shower. Main Lodge king room, consists of one king bed, a small sitting area, and a standard shower. The Garland Penthouse is located above the main lodge. The two bedroom, two bathroom unit, consists of one king bed in the master bedroom and a Jacuzzi tub in the master bathroom. The second room features a double bed and a standard bath. Golf cottages are located on the Fountains golf course and are dynamic for the foursome of golfers or the family getting away for the weekend. Condominiums located on the first hole of the Reflections course are within walking distance from the lodge. At Garland there are three types of villas available. Single Villas, are the most popular accommodations at Garland. Located separate from the Main Lodge, the single villas feature a separate living area with stocked wet bar and gas log fireplace. Double Villas are located separate from the main lodge. They feature a mutual sitting area with a gas log fireplace. French Country Villas are located on the Fountains golf course. They are two story units featuring three bedrooms and 2½ bathrooms.

72 challenging holes of golf and four extraordinary courses to choose from. Each of the four courses: Swampfire, Monarch, Reflections and Fountains feature their own PGA quality challenges.

Address: Route 1, Box 364M, Lewiston, 49756
Phone: 517-786-2211
877-4GARLAND
E-mail: tcampbell@garlandusa.com
Web site: http://www. garlandusa.com
Restaurant: Herman's Dining Room, Herman's Grill, Herman's Patio
Sports Fac.: Heated outdoor pool & pool house, tennis courts, basketball half-court, volleyball court, indoor/outdoor Jacuzzis, nature trails, mountain bike trails, exercise/fitness center, lap pool, sauna, whirlpool

Courses: Swampfire (6854, par 72), Monarch (7188, Par 72), Reflections (6407, par 72), Fountains (6760, par 72)
No. of Holes: 72
Guest Policy: Open to public
Club House: 517-786-2211
Fees: ⌐
Reservations: Can make reservations one year in advance
Carts: Carts included in fees

Lakewood Shores Resort

Address: 7751 Cedar Lake Rd, Oscoda, 48750
Phone: 517-739-2073
800-882-2493
E-mail: info@lakewoodshores.com
Web site: http://www.lakewoodshores.com
Rates: Inquire
Restaurant: Dining Room
Business Fac.: Conference facilities for 10–80
Sports Fac.: Wee links
Location: Northern Michigan

Courses: Gailes Course (6954), Resort Course
No. of Holes: 36
Guest Policy: Open to public
Club House: 517-739-2075
Reservations: Up to a year in advance
Season: April 1–October 31

The resort is set on the shores of Cedar Lake and has its own private beach. A perfect vacation spot for the whole family with its Wee Links course, an 18 hole pitch & putt course that's designed especially with the children in mind, with holes that range from 30 to 100 yards. The practice could do your own short game some good as well! Cedar Lake has recreational opportunities such as jet skiing, swimming, canoeing and fishing.

Lakewood offers a variety of golf packages: Midweek Golf (unlimited golf), Weekend Golf, Family Getaway Packages, Spring/Fall Weekend Golf Package, and Holiday Getaways, so be sure to inquire.

The resort is fully equipped to handle small conferences with the facilities to mix business with pleasure.

The Gailes course is a true Scottish seaside type of course. In 1993 *Golf Digest* voted The Gailes "The Best New Resort Course in the United States," and rated it "The Number One Public and Resort Course in the State of Michigan" in 1996. The course has large double greens, you'll get the feel of playing golf in Scotland without leaving the states! The Resort course is well populated by wildlife and is like a flower garden with plenty of trees.

Crystal Mountain Resort

Crystal Mountain is near the village (population 331) of Thompsonville, in the northwestern part of Michigan, and not far from the national music camp, Interlochen. The resort and conference center has a long history of repeat business with families and business groups, no doubt because it's a friendly place in a scenic part of the state known as the Gold Coast. Lodgings are in condominiums and the main lodge, with amenities such as hot tubs, fieldstone fireplaces, french doors opening onto private decks, vaulted ceilings, and skylights.

The dining room serves breakfast, lunch and dinner, with a full selection of menu items, in addition to a Sunday buffet. Cocktails are served nightly in the Tee-Ville Taproom, where hors d'oeuvres are complimentary, and video highlights of the day's events on the golf course are featured each evening. Sandwiches and snacks are served with indoor and outdoor seating daily at the 19th Hole. Ease into the evening scene with libations at Gregger's, where live entertainment will loosen you up. Bring your racket for tennis, or rent a bicycle and pedal through the countryside, or hike the miles of marked trails. The resort's charter boat hotline gives you access to over 600 captains in the Frankfort/Elberta area for a fishing excursion where not one got away.

The golf course has undergone extensive improvements and alterations during the past two years, and its in top shape now. The course was designed to utilize the area's natural beauty. The front nine fairways are cut through pine forests on rolling hills, and the back nine winds through water hazards and hardwood trees. No two fairways parallel each other, with a choice of tee times to assure that no two holes play alike. Resort guests may also play the Crystal Lake course, featuring panoramic views of hills, orchards and woods. The back 9, completed in 1988, offers doglegs, swales, and links-type roughs to challenge the Sunday golfer, yet make it fair.

Address: 12500 Crystal Mt. Dr, Thompsonville, 49683
Phone: 616-378-2000
800-968-4676
Fax: 616-378-2998
E-mail: info@crystalmtn.com
Web site: http://www. crystalmtn.com
Rates: Inquire
Restaurant: Wildflower Dining Room, MountainFest, The Grill
Business Fac.: Several floors of meeting space includes classrooms, conference rooms, theatre, banquet hall, and exhibit hall. Crystal Center is also equipped with built in video teleconferencing and state-of-the-art projection systems.
Sports Fac.: Outdoor clay tennis courts, indoor & outdoor swimming pools, fitness center, forest trails for hiking, volleyball, children's playground, basketball half court.

Location: Michigan's magnificent north country
Courses: Mountain Ridge Course (6689, par 72), Betsie Valley Course
No. of Holes: 36
Guest Policy: Open to public
Club House: 616-378-2911
Fees: ↑
Reservations: Reservations available 365 days in advance
Season: April–October
Carts: Carts included in fees

Waterfront Inn

Address: PO Box 1736, Traverse City, 49685
Phone: 616-938-1100
800-551-WATER
Web site: http://www.waterfrontinntc.com
No. of Rooms: 127
Rates: $
Restaurant: Reflections restaurant, Clubhouse Deli & Grille Room
Bar: Clubhouse
Business Fac.: Clubhouse available for meeting and weddings, capacity 350
Sports Fac.: Fishing, Watercraft or charter rental, Boat ramp, Whirlpool spa, Indoor pool, Sandy beach, Skiing and snowmobiling at Boardman River Valley
Location: Northern Michigan near Traverse City

Course: High Pointe Golf Club (6881, par 71)
No. of Holes: 18
Guest Policy: Open to public
Club House: 800-753-7888
Fees: ℸ
Reservations: Call for reservations
Season: April- September
Carts: Walking or carts

The Waterfront Inn Hotel and Conference offers 775 feet of shoreline on East Grand Traverse Bay of Lake Michigan. Most of the 127 rooms have a view of the Bay, and all have refrigerators, individually controlled heat and air conditioning, dead bolt locks, remote controlled 25" color TV with cable service and more. The restaurant, Reflections, has views of the Bay and Old Mission Peninsula, and spectacular sunsets are complemented by the attentive service, an attractive informal atmosphere and exceptional food and wine.

Endless recreational activities abound on property and in the surrounding countryside. The Glass enclosed heated pool and whirlpool spa provide year around use regardless of the weather. An exercise room has a Precor treadmill and Precor recumbent bike, and saunas are located on the ground floor of each hotel wing. The sugar sand beach offers excellent sun bathing and swimming opportunities, and the deck over the enclosed pool provides additional sun bathing area.

High Pointe Golf Club was named one of the nation's 100 greatest courses by *Golf Magazine* and is just a scenic ten-minute drive away. Designed by leading architect Tom Doak, High Pointe provides avid golfers with a two-fold golfing experience. The front nine resembles Scottish links, while the back nine features rolling hills lined with northern pines and hardwoods.

Giants Ridge Golf & Ski Resort

A short drive from the Minneapolis area, the Giants Ridge Golf & Ski Resort, originally a local ski area in the 1950s, has expanded into a full resort offering numerous activities. The golf course was selected by *Golf Digest* as one of America's top ten new upscale golf courses in 1998.

Family fun abounds at the Giants Ridge Golf & Ski Resort. Be outfitted for the mountain biking trail system, winding through the Superior National Forest, or, try on a pair of new inline skates and go rollerblading. Canoeing, kayaking, and pontooning are available on Wynne and Sabin Lakes. When you're ready for a break, try one of the eleven restaurants nearby

The resort features 93 suites, many including an oversized whirlpool, fireplace, and view of the Giants Ridge golf course. Permanent vacation home lots arc available in the "Woodlands at Giants Ridge."

Designed by Jeffrey Brauer and PGA Pro Lanny Wadkins, the course was named in May of 1999 as Minnesota's top public golf course. Sculpted out of the beautiful Superior national Forest in northeastern Minnesota, the course is even more beautiful in the fall when the leaves change colors. Facilities include multiple tee boxes, and complete practice and learning facilities, driving range, putting green, and chipping green.

Address: PO Box 190, Biwabik, 55708
Phone: 218-865-7170
800-688-7669
Fax: 218-865-4733
E-mail: info@giantsridge.com
Web site: http://www. giantsridge.com
No. of Rooms: 93
Rates: Inquire
Restaurant: Timbers
Bar: Sticks
Business Fac.: 7,000 sq.ft. of conference space
Sports Fac.: Swimming pool, Mountain biking, Rollerblading, Canoeing, Kayaking, Pontoon boats, Skiing,
Location: Superior National Forest in northeast Minnesota

Course: Giants Ridge (par 72)
No. of Holes: 18
Guest Policy: Open to public
Club House: 800-688-7669
Fees: ⊺⊺
Reservations: Call for reservations
Season: Open all year, Golf May–October
Carts: Cart included in fees

Cragun's Conference & Golf Resort

Address: 11000 Cragun's Drive, Brainerd, 56401
Phone: 218-855-0915
800-272-4867
Fax: 218-825-8271
E-mail: info@craguns.com
Web site: http://www.craguns.com
No. of Rooms: 260
Restrictions: Smoking & non-smoking rooms
Restaurant: The Hungry Grill Restaurant, The Lodge Dining Room, BBQ, Gazebo Snack Bar
Business Fac.: Conference Services, State-of-the-art equipment, Conference planners, 36 meeting rooms
Sports Fac.: Driving Range, Golf, Snowmobiling, Sports Center with swimming, tennis, basketball, volleyball, running track, whirlpool, sauna, golf simulators
Location: Two and one-half hours drive north of Minneapolis/St. Paul

Courses: The Legacy #1 (3405), The Legacy #2 (3465), The Legacy #3 (3275)
No. of Holes: 45
Guest Policy: Open to public
Club House: 800-272-4867
Fees: T
Reservations: Call to make reservations
Season: Open all year

Only Cragun's offers you the complete amenities of Minnesota's largest resort, with a tradition of the best in personal service. Come for a family vacation year-round. Host a business meeting, conference or reunion from four to 1,100. Or golf the incomparable Legacy Courses at Cragun's, a sanctuary for golf and the environment. No matter why you come, you'll leave with a resort experience unmatched in Minnesota.

Comfort comes in all accommodations at Cragun's. They offer several different choices, each with a refrigerator (some include kitchenettes) and balcony or deck overlooking beautiful Gull Lake: Lakeview Rooms, Shoreline Suites, Apartments and Cabins.

Cragun's has the recipe for great food choices at four different eateries. The Hungry Gull Restaurant and the Lodge Dining Room offer panoramic lake views. Or dine poolside at our famous BBQ. For some tasty, quick food try the Gazebo Snack Bar at our outdoor pool.

Cragun's is Minnesota's largest resort and conference center, dedicated to hosting successful meetings in all four seasons. Located on Gull Lake in Minnesota's famed Brainerd Lakes Area, Cragun's specializes in hosting groups large and small, from four to 1,100

Cragun's rich tradition of hospitality is based on treating each guest like a friend. The new Legacy Golf Courses at Cragun's are the perfect complement to that tradition. Robert Trent Jones Jr. designed these golf courses to qualify as an Audubon Signature Sanctuary, which would make them among a select few in the world to be so distinguished. The outstanding natural features include many wetlands, ponds and pristine 100-acre lake. The result is 45 world-class holes of memorable golf.

Madden's on Gull Lake

Three distinctive resorts in one; that's what Madden's on Gull Lake is all about. You'll find 3 times the fun and 3 times the variety, not to mention 3 choices in styles of accommodations, from the classic 1930's charm of Madden Inn & Golf Club and the colonial presence of Madden Lodge, to rustic living at Pine Portage. Six tournament-quality tennis courts, 45 holes of golf, 2 fully-equipped marinas, and 3 beaches.

Address: 8001 Pine Beach Peninsula, Brainerd, 56401
Phone: 218-829-2811
800-642-5363
Fax: 218-829-2811
E-mail: vacations@maddens.com
Web site: http://www.maddens.com

Courses: The Classic (7109, par 72), Pine Beach East (6000, par 72), Pine Beach West (5100, par 67), Social 9 (1341, par 28)
No. of Holes: 63
Guest Policy: Open to public
Club House: 800-642-5363
Reservations: Call to make reservations
Carts: Depends upon which course you choose

Breezy Point Resort Golf Club

Address: HCR2, Box 70, Breezy Point, 56472
800-432-3777
Fax: 218-562-4510
Web site: http://www.breezypt.com
No. of Rooms: 250
Rates: Inquire
Restaurant: Marina Dining Room and Lounge, Antlers Bar and Grill
Business Fac.: State-of-the-art Conference Center, Flexible meeting space for up to 500, Professional staff, Cook out and Banquet service, Catering
Sports Fac.: Golf, Golf lessons, Boating, Canoeing, Kayaking, Paddle boats, Fishing, Pontoons, Hydro bikes, 4 tennis courts, Swimming pool, Children's pool, Jacuzzi, Sauna, Water volleyball, Volleyball, Beach, Horseshoes, Bocce ball, Croquet, Exercise room, Game room
Location: On Pelican Lake

Courses: The Traditional (5192), Whitebirch (6600)
No. of Holes: 36
Club House: 800-950-4960
Fees: ↑
Reservations: Call for reservations
Season: April–November

This Midwestern state with more than 11,000 lakes gets its name from two Sioux words that mean sky-tinted water. With nearby lakes bearing names such as Upper Whitefish, Gull, and Eighth Crow Lake, you get the picture. This is American's breadbasket, the land of the loon, where Longfellow's Song of Hiawatha tells of waterfalls and rivers that rushed through palisades of pine. Here at Breezy; Point on 3,000 acres of Lake Brainerd Lakes area, you'll find lodging and recreation to fit your preference and budget. Over 200 accommodation choices include condominiums, economical motel rooms, beach homes or cabins. Depending on the package you choose, your options might include modified American plan, private jacuzzi, a ten bedroom, 8 bath log mansion which can sleep 38 people, and indoor pools and game rooms.

Saunter around the relaxed grounds, and check out the indoor or outdoor heated pool, the recreation center, spa, tennis courts and horseshoes. Lakeside you'll see the cruiser which takes guests around Pelican Lake, plus other assorted vessels available for a whirl. The beach is sugary-white and the water is refreshing during warmer months. Bicycling, horseback riding, hiking, trap-shooting, and a children's supervised playground completes the list. Of course, should you want to land a lunker from the lake's sparkling waters, boats and guides are available. Dress is casual in the Marina restaurant, the lounge and Dockside, where jazz is heard during summer. If you prefer to lunch poolside, look for Captain's Cove, while ribs and steaks are the specialty at Charlie's, known for family prices and live entertainment.

There are two courses here, the "original" nine holes, and a second course, referred to as Championship Nine, due to have an additional nine constructed. When players are queried as to what's memorable about golf here, the unanimous reply is "trees—millions of them". Norway pines, birch, and maple seem to be everywhere, and scurrying wildlife and watchful birds seem oblivious to the small balls nestling under the needles.

Fair Hills Resort

At Fair Hills Resort, there is always an activity for everyone, with an emphasis on quality family time. Stay in one of the hundred units of different size and variety, from cabins in the traditional northwoods cabin architecture to the cabins with full kitchens.

The bell sounding at the main lodge signals meals the old fashioned way. Breakfast, lunch and dinner are served and the atmosphere is great for family time. When not eating, activities abound! There are activities for all ages, including a water slide, water Olympics and boat rides, tennis, and volleyball, all which are free for the entire family. There is free time for parents while the counselors guide their children on scheduled activities in both the morning and afternoon.

Designed by Joel Goldstrand, the Wildflower golf course was built in the "Prairie Links" style. The course is perfect for all levels of players, with four sets of bent grass tees, 86 bunkers, and expanses of prairie grass.

Address: Route 1, Box 6, Detroit Lakes, 56502
Phone: 218-847-7638
800-323-2849
E-mail: info@fairhillsresort.com
Web site: http://www.fairhillsresort.com
No. of Rooms: 100
Rates: $$$ weekly
Restaurant: Dining Room—Breakfast, lunch and dinner; Tuesday Night Smorgasbord
Business Fac.: Reunion facilities for up to 250.
Sports Fac.: Children's programs, Tennis courts, Volleyball, Swimming, Sailing, Windsurfing
Location: Northwest Minnesota

Course: Wildflower
No. of Holes: 18
Guest Policy: Open to public, guests receive 20% discount
Club House: 888-752-9945
Fees: ⌐
Reservations: Call for reservations
Season: April–October
Carts: Cart are also available

Ruttger's Sugar Lake Lodge

Address: PO Box 847, Grand Rapids, 55744
Phone: 218-327-1853
800-450-4555
E-mail: info@
ruttgerssugarlake.com
Web site: http://www.
ruttgerssugarlake.com
No. of Rooms: 18
Rates: $
Restaurant: Otis'—casual fine
dining, Jack's Grill—pub
atmosphere
Bar: Lodge Bar
Business Fac.: Fully equipped
conference and banquet facilities,
Conference staff on site, capacity
3–300
Sports Fac.: Canoes, Paddleboats,
Row boats, Tennis courts, Outdoor
swimming pool, Sandy beach
Location: In pristine Minnesota
north woods

The Sugar Lake Lodge is set in the northwoods of Minnesota with crystal clear lakes. Come and enjoy the scenic and challenging golf course, uncrowded atmosphere and tons of activities.

Sugar Lake offers numerous packages with accommodations including townhouses alongside the golf course, lakefront rooms with many amenities, and cottages with views of beautiful Lake Siseebakwet. The rate includes use of canoes, paddleboats, rowboats, tennis courts, outdoor heated pool, and sandy beach.

Enjoy Otis' casual fine dining, located in the main lodge of the resort, for delicious, artistically prepared meals. On the Golf Course, try the pub atmosphere of Jack's Grill for burgers, ribs, salads and beverages.

Featuring modern, fully equipped conference and banquet facilities, Sugar Lake is the ideal conference spot, for anywhere from 3 to 300 people. Groups can meet in the conference center, deck, pontoon boat, or lawn. The staff is always available to meet the needs of the group.

The Sugarbrooke Golf Course designed by Goldstrand, features 18 holes and 6,182 middle tees. There is driving range, bar and food available, and pro shop and instruction.

Course: Sugarbrooke Golf Course
(6,182, par 71)
No. of Holes: 18
Guest Policy: Open to the public,
guests get discounted price
Club House: 800-450-4555
Fees: ↑
Reservations: Call for reservations
Season: May–September
Carts: Cart are also available

Grand View Lodge Resort

The resort is in a 1919 lodge that is listed in the National Register of Historic Places. The Lodge prides itself on offering exceptional service. Twelve of the accommodations are in the Lodge, the other sixty are in luxurious lake townhomes and cottages. It is set in a flower filled, garden-like setting with over 15,000 flowers and shrubs, naming them all could be an adventure in itself!

Set on Roy Lake, there is a 1,500 foot sandy beach, and fishing and water sports are greatly to be enjoyed here. There's even a sunken island off-shore!

Grand View takes your dining experience quite seriously, and brings it up to a fine art. The Lodge dining room is rustic, with log walls and the skylight in the Pine dining room helps to bring the outdoors inside. The menu is different every evening.

The Pines is considered by many to be the best course in northern Minnesota. It was rated one of the "Best New Resort Courses" in 1991. A meticulously maintained course, the fairways are lined with mature white birch and pines, set in a 340-acre forest. The natural contour of the land was used here, and the water, sand, rocks and trees will make this a round you'll never forget. The 18th hole offers tilted grass bunkers, forest and a green surrounded by water, trees and traps. Quite a finish. The Gardens Course, as you might suspect from its name, is remarkable for its floral artistry. Every tee box has a different display!

Address: 23521 Nokomis, Nisswa, 56468
Phone: 218-963-2234
800-432-3788
Web site: http://grandviewlodge.com
No. of Rooms: 77
Rates: Inquire
Restaurant: Main Lodge, Sherwood Forest, Freddy's Grille, The Preserve Restaurant, Italian Garden
Business Fac.: 10,600 sq ft of meeting space, divided among 8 meeting rooms ranging from 486-2,800 square feet.
Sports Fac.: Indoor pool & water slide, 2 hot tubs, fitness center, free use of fishing boats, playaks, canoes, and paddle boats, 11 tennis Laykold tennis courts
Location: Gull Lake near Brainerd

Courses: The Pines, The Preserve, Deacon's Lodge, Garden Course
No. of Holes: 54+
Club House: 888-437-4637
Reservations: Call for reservations
Season: April–November

Pines Grand View Lodge

Address: South 134 Nokomis, Nisswa, 56468
Phone: 218-963-2234
800-432-3788
Web site: http://www.thepines.com
No. of Rooms: 77
Rates: $$
Restaurant: The Main Lodge, Sherwood Forest, Freddy's Grill, The Preserve, Italian Garden
Business Fac.: Fully equipped Conference Center & Clubhouse Suites
Sports Fac.: Swimming pool, Fitness Center, Hot Tubs, Water sports, Fishing, Canoes, Kayaking, Paddleboats, Pontoon, Tennis, Horseback riding
Location: On Gull Lake near Brainerd

Courses: Deacons Lodge (7017), The Pines (6837), The Preserves (6601)
No. of Holes: 63
Club House: 888-437-4637
Fees: ↑
Reservations: Call for reservations
Season: April–November

The resort is in a 1919 lodge that is listed in the National Register of Historic Places. The Lodge prides itself on offering exceptional service. Twelve of the accommodations are in the Lodge, the other sixty are in luxurious lake townhomes and cottages. It is set in a flower filled, garden-like setting with over 15,000 flowers and shrubs, naming them all could be an adventure in itself!

Set on Roy Lake, there is a 1,500 foot sandy beach, and fishing and water sports are greatly to be enjoyed here. There's even a sunken island off-shore!

Grand View takes your dining experience quite seriously, and brings it up to a fine art. The Lodge dining room is rustic, with log walls and the skylit in the Pine dining room helps to bring the outdoors inside. The menu is different every evening.

The Pines is considered by many to be the best course in northern Minnesota. It was rated one of the "Best New Resort Courses" in 1991. A meticulously maintained course, the fairways are lined with mature white birch and pines, set in a 340-acre forest. The natural contour of the land was used here, and the water, sand, rocks and trees will make this a round you'll never forget. The 18th hole offers tilted grass bunkers, forest and a green surrounded by water, trees and traps. Quite a finish. The Gardens Course, as you might suspect from its name, is remarkable for its floral artistry. Every tee box has a different display!

There is supervised play and evening programs for guests ages 3 through 12.

Izatys Golf & Yacht Club

Izatys Golf and Yacht Club is located 90 miles north of the Twin Cities on the south shore of Mille Lacs Lake, an ideal location for spectacular sunsetsMille Lacs Lake is the second largest lake within the state of Minnesota. The lake is 20 miles by 14 miles and has earned the nickname "Walleye Factory".

The Stone Lodge is the only remaining building from the original Izatys Lodge. The Stone Lodge was built in 1926 was registered as an historic landmark in the mid 1980's. This building is utilized mainly for group hospitality and meetings today. . Today, Izatys' is the home for 114 shoreline townhomes, complete golf & practice facilities, a Clubhouse, 28 unit hotel complex and activities for all!

Izatys Golf Course is excited about the expansion and remodeling of the existing course into two new golf courses under the guidance of esteemed architect John Harbottle. He combined the existing front nine with nine new holes for a 6,646 yard 18 hole course, The Sanctuary. The existing back nine was upgraded and combined with fourteen new holes for a challenging 6,867 yard 18 hole course, Black Brook, which opened in July of 1999. Izatys offers acres of natural water and marsh hazards, native deciduous trees, and extensive use of wildflowers, and undulating greens. To enhance their golf course, Izatys offers outstanding practice facilities including a driving range, two practice greens, practice bunkers, a chipping green and a three hole Par 3 practice course. Izatys was the 5th golf course in the state of Minnesota to be certified from the National Audubon Society of New York.

Address: Lake Mille Lacs, Onamia, 56359
Phone: 320-829-7051
800-533-1728
Web site: http://www.izatys.com

Course: Izatys Golf Course (6481, par 72)
No. of Holes: 18
Guest Policy: Open to public
Club House: 320-532-4575
Fees: ↑
Reservations: Can make reservations 14 days in advance
Carts: Pull and motorized carts available

The Bridges Golf Resort

Address: 711 Casino Magic Dr, Bay St. Louis, 39520
Phone: 228-467-9257
800-5-MAGIC5 ext 100
E-mail: mblanch@casinomagic.com
Web site: http://www.
casinomagic.com/html/bridges.html
No. of Rooms: 200
Rates: $
Restaurant: The Amazing Randolph's, The Bridges Clubhouse Grill, Abracadabra's, Cafe Magic
Sports Fac.: 4 target greens (including 2 chipping greens and 2 putting greens), over 64,000 sq ft of practice tee surface
Location: 50 miles from downtown New Orleans

Course: The Bridges (6917, par 72)
No. of Holes: 18
Guest Policy: Open to public
Club House: 800-5-MAGIC5
Fees: ⅠⅠ
Reservations: Call to make reservations
Season: Open all year
Carts: Carts included in fees

Whether you're looking for a weekend getaway or a family vacation, you'll find many reasons to plan your next trip to Casino Magic located in quaint Bay St. Louis, just east of New Orleans.

The Casino Magic Hotel features over 200 newly renovated rooms and suites with all the amenities you enjoy at home, including free cable TV, in-room coffee makers, hair dryers, and video games. Be sure to unwind in the soothing whirlpool or relax in the heated outdoor pool.

A spectacular casino awaits with more than 1,100 slots, 40 table games and live Million Dollar Keno. There is big name live entertainment, which changes weekly and four fabulous restaurants for every taste and budget.

And if you're looking for a golf getaway, choose from over 21 golf courses on the Mississippi Gulf Coast, including Casino Magic's own The Bridges Golf Resort. A must-play track on the Mississippi Golf Coast, this Arnold Palmer design is not overwhelming in length but features numerous doglegs, abundant water hazards, strategic bunkering, and more than 20 wooden bridges—hence the course name. And when you are done enjoy great sandwiches and a wide range of beer at the Bridges Clubhouse Grill, 10 feet from the pro shop.

President Casino Broadwater Resort

Drive along the tame water of Mississippi's gulf coast east of Biloxi, where the marriage of ante-bellum and high-tech recreation have produced a balmy sportsman's delight. Meet Broadwater Beach, a tropical garden of magnolias, camellias, wisteria, even a lily pond, surrounding a 360 room resort. Stay in a lanai room, garden cottage, or apartment, while enjoying the stretch of white beach and a complete marina. Biloxi is a shrimp town, and this is the place to feast on local versions of flounder stuffed with crabmeat, and gumbos galore. Restaurants and lounges serve a variety of specialties, and the Lanai Lounge is the Perfect place for cocktails, where bathing suits are proper attire.

Charter a boat if you'd like to go deep-sea fishing, or head for the pool, shuffleboard, badminton or volleyball. Six Omnicourts, lighted for night, will please tennis players, and those with shopping and sightseeing tendencies won't be left in the lurch.

Beauvoir, the last home of Jefferson Davis, is close, as are historic houses, Gulf Islands National Seashore, marine education center and aquarium, and scores of interesting and varied excursions via boats. Space cadets will want to see the NASA Space Technology Laboratories, where all Space Shuttle main engines are tested before launch.

There are two 18 hole courses here, plus a nine-hole, par 3 fun course. The Sea Course—recognized by lofty pines and loads of other trees—is a flat, tight layout, with a really big water hazard (called the Gulf). The Sun Course, a par 72, is more open, but don't be lulled into thinking there's no water. Word has it that the pros agree quietly to play the middle tees so they can save face. Fourteen of its holes traverse water.

Address: 2110 Beach Blvd, Biloxi, 39530
Phone: 228-388-2211
800-THE-PRES
Fax: 228-385-4102
E-mail: presint@presidentbroadwater.com
Web site: http://www.presidentbroadwater.com
No. of Rooms: 500
Rates: $
Restaurant: President's Buffet, Audree's Fine Dining
Bar: Brass Banana Lounge, Vegas Vegas Show Bar
Business Fac.: 50,000 sq ft of meeting/banquet space.
Sports Fac.: 10 tennis courts, 3 tropical swimming pools, large covered marina, shuffleboard, horseshoe pits, jogging trail, playground, exercise & weight room, volleyball, basketball
Location: On the Mississippi Golf Coast

Course: President's (7140, par 72)
No. of Holes: 18
Club House: 800-647-3964
Reservations: Call for reservations
Season: Open all year

Dancing Rabbit Golf Club

Address: PO Box 6048, Philadelphia, 39350
Phone: 601-663-0011
800-557-0711
E-mail: drabbit@netalpha.net
Web site: http://www.dancingrabbitgolf.com
No. of Rooms: 500
Rates: $
Restaurant: Phillip M's, Villa 16 West Steakhouse, Terrace Cafe, Chef's Pavilion Buffet, Dolce, Rally Alley Deli
Business Fac.: Event Coordinator for conferences
Location: Ancient pines and hardwoods of Choctaw lands

Courses: The Azaleas (7128, par 72), The Oaks (7076, par 72)
No. of Holes: 36
Guest Policy: Open only to members and their guests and resort guests
Club House: 800-922-9988
Fees: ⌘⌘⌘
Reservations: Call for reservations
Season: Open all year
Carts: Welcome walkers, caddies also available

Dancing Rabbit Golf Club, is arguably the best course in Mississippi. It is located in Philadelphia, in the red clay hills region of Mississippi on the Choctaw Indian Reservation next to the Silverstar Resort and Casino. Glowing with the gracious spirit of the South, Dancing Rabbit Golf Club offers all the charm and sophistication of a world class resort destination. From the obvious attractions of golfing and gaming to the fine dining and unbelievably courteous and attentive staff, they have created a truly unique resort environment. The golf club, including the picture postcard clubhouse has two wraparound verandas and guest suites on the third floor.

Internationally renowned golf course designer Tom Fazio and PGA great Jerry Pate collaborated to fashion two dramatic golf courses that reveal the terrain's natural contours sand features. Cascading waterfalls. Meandering spring-fed streams. A memorable experience. The Dancing Rabbit Golf Club's par 72 golf courses roll out over 7,000 incredible yards from the back tees. Impeccably maintained Bentgrass greens and grown-in Bermuda fairways enhance the foundation of the golf game. Two miles of creeks weave through the fairways and around the greens. This Tom Fazio/Jerry Pate design offers splendid opportunities to enjoy golf at its finest.

Pointe Royale

Pointe Royale offers condominiums on Branson's premier 18-hole championship golf course in a scenic Ozark Mountain setting below the bluffs of Lake Taneycomo, just downstream from Table Rock Lake Dam. Golf, trout fishing, swimming, tennis and playgrounds are all located in one beautiful, natural and spacious setting right in Branson. Located across from the Lawrence Welk Theater, guests have convenient, low traffic access to all area attractions, theme parks, music shows and marinas.

With a variety of 1, 2 and 3 bedroom condos, Pointe Royale offers affordable, comfortable and beautiful alternatives to the motel room for your Branson vacation. Enjoy the privacy of separate bedrooms and baths while the living and dining areas provide lots of space for gathering with friends and family. Fully equipped kitchens allow you to save on meals. Each condo has a private patio or deck from which you can appreciate our Ozarks scenery.

Pointe Royale Golf Course is a true "shot-maker"course. Lush bent grass greens and Bermuda fairways, with eight water holes, sand and grass bunkers, and tees for all levels of play, Pointe Royale is a world class golfing experience. This challenging 18-hole, 6,067-yard par 70 course is regarded as the original championship course in the Branson area and is maintained to a high level of standards. Overall the rolling fairways and mature trees offer quite a challenge to the average golfer, so remember, club selection and a good golf course strategy are a must.

Address: 158-A Pointe Royale Drive, Branson, 65616
Phone: 417-334-5614
800-962-4710
E-mail: ptroyale@branson.com
Web site: http://www.
pointeroyale.com
Rates: $
Restrictions: No pets
Bar: 19th Hole Deli & Lounge
Business Fac.: Professional staff, Personal service, Outdoor pavilion, Adaptive facilities
Sports Fac.: Golf, 2 outdoor pools, 2 tennis courts, Fishing, Hiking
Location: Across from Lawrence Welk Theater on Highway 165

Course: Pointe Royale Course (6067, par 70)
No. of Holes: 18
Guest Policy: Open to public
Club House: 417-334-4477
Fees: ⌐
Reservations: Can make reservations 7 days in advance
Carts: Cart included in fees

Loma Linda Country Club

Address: 2407 Douglas Fir Rd,
Joplin, 64804
800-633-3543
E-mail: lomalcc@golflink.net
Web site: http://www.golflink.com/
lomalinda

Courses: South Public Course
(6397, par 71), North Country Club
Course (6628, par 71)
No. of Holes: 36
Guest Policy: South is open to
public, North is only for members
and guests
Club House: 417-782-3622
Reservations: Can make
reservations one year in advance
Carts: Motorized carts are available

With two topnotch golf courses, swimming, tennis, croquet, shuffleboard, horseshoes, biking, hiking and fishing all on a 2,300 acre estate, Loma Linda is the place to stay for a night, a few days, or a few months—all at a price below anything comparable—anywhere!

It is the extra large apartments, mini suites and villa rooms that distinguish Loma Linda from most commercial or resort hotels. The apartments are completely furnished with full kitchens, living rooms, bedrooms and a spacious bathroom with Jacuzzi and stall shower. Most units have cathedral ceilings. The mini-suites are smaller complete apartments with kitchen facilities and very distinct, comfortable living and sleeping areas, a stall shower and Jacuzzi, and large walk-in closets. These units are perfect for commercial occupants and travelers, in addition to golfers.

The beauty of the Ozark Hills is enhanced by the vast expanse of green, which distinguishes the fairways. The lush tees and greens are unequalled. These courses are simple in design, varied in their many challenges and totally exciting in every phase of the game. There are no two courses in the country of such quality and quiet beauty in any resort at such incredibly low cost. They are just honest golf courses, completely fair. The North, or Country Club course, accommodates guests or members of other golf clubs. The South, or Resort course, has grown steadily in popularity and challenge. Golfers enjoy superb atmosphere, public golf with country club quality, and green fees which are ever so low.

Lodge of the Four Seasons

Why not a "treetop" getaway? Here, practically mid-way between Kansas City and St. Louis, is an extensive lakeside resort community with excellent recreation facilities. The Lodge overlooks Lake Ozark, and is surrounded by dramatic and intricate Japanese gardens, highlighted by cascading waterfalls. Buildings of stone, glass and wood blend with the surroundings providing sweeping views of densely wooded hills from porches and balconies. Secluded Treetop Village, accommodating up to eight people, is nestled high among the trees, and is available on a time share basis.

French and American fare is served in the white table-clothed Toledo Room, overlooking the lake. Other eateries include HK's for steaks, Casablanca for salads and burgers, The Fish Market, Ted's Cafe, Country Deli, or the Atrium for early morning croissants. The Fifth Season, with nightly entertainment, is a great place to see the action.

Water sports are big here. You'll have all kinds of boating, water skiing, fishing, wind surfing, and good old beach bumming. There's also bowling, billiards, horseback riding, trap-shooting and a jogging path. Tennis players are enroll in the Dennis Van der Meer Tennis University, which offers clinics, lessons and plenty of courts. The sports and social center has additional tennis and racquetball courts, and an indoor golf practice range.

If you're ready to toss the junk food, try the health and fitness evaluation laboratory. You'll receive a fitness prescription and guidelines for improving nutritional habits. You can take advantage of the property's many pools, tone up on all sorts of high-tech exercise equipment, or aerobicize till all hours at the racquet club.

Babysitting is provided, and a host of children's activities are geared for the younger set, such as cookouts, nature walks, and arts and crafts hours.

Golf here is courtesy of Robert Trent Jones' deft hand. The 18 hole course winds around a few lakes, and is quite hilly, and exceptionally colorful in the fall. Golfers praise the variety of holes here; valley ridges, and the lake coming into play, as well as scores of sand traps. Beware Witch's Cover, a 233-yard par 3 requiring a sorcerer's spell to carry the cove. There's also a nine hole executive course here, and a large golf clubhouse with a very good pro shop.

Address: Lake Road HH, Lake Ozark, 65049
Phone: 314-365-3001
800-THE-LAKE
E-mail: reservations@4seasonsresort.com
Web site: http://www.4seasonsresort.com
No. of Rooms: 311
Rates: Inquire
Restaurant: Toledo Room, Ted's Cafe
Business Fac.: Audio-visual, Conference rooms, capacity 1000
Sports Fac.: Tennis courts, Swimming pool, Sailing School, Marina, Bowling, Horseback riding
Location: Nestled in the rolling Ozark Hills

Courses: Seasons Ridge Course (6020), Robert Trent Jones Course, Executive Course
No. of Holes: 45
Guest Policy: Lodge guests, members and property owners
Club House: 314-365-8544
Reservations: Call for availability
Season: March–January

Marriott's Tan-Tar-a Resort

Address: State Rd. K.K., Osage Beach, 65065
Phone: 314-348-3131
800-392-5304
Fax: 314-348-8560
E-mail: ttainfo@lakeozark.net
Web site: http://www.tan-tar-a.com
No. of Rooms: 930
Rates: Inquire
Restrictions: No pets allowed
Restaurant: Windrose, Cliffroom, Oaks, Arrowhead, Nightwinds
Bar: Nightwinds, The Landing, Mr. D's
Business Fac.: Copiers, Audiovisual, Conference rooms, capacity 3750
Sports Fac.: Swimming, Tennis courts, Racquetball, Bowling, Billiards, Ice skating, Mountain biking
Location: Lake of the Ozarks

Courses: The Oaks Course (6442), Hidden Lakes Course
No. of Holes: 27
Guest Policy: Call for availability
Club House: 314-348-8521
Reservations: May be made 7 days in advance
Season: Open all year weather permitting

Tucked in among the fingers of Lake of the Ozarks, near places such as Hurricane Deck, Tightwad, and Climax Springs, is a 420 acre playground carved into the hills where water sports and golf are given top priority. Approximately a three hour drive or a thirty minute flight from Kansas City, or St. Louis, this Marriott's offers 1,000 rooms, of which 250 are suites, in a range of choices. There are dining rooms, lounges, patios and poolside service catering to every whim, depending on the season. For children 5 years and older, an organized recreational program satisfies their cravings for arts and crafts, beach adventures, ice-cream-making and much more. Teens, too can make new friends and enjoy activities planned just for them including mini golf, beach and water volleyball, and video game contests. Evenings aren't dull at Tan-Tar-A; live entertainment awaits you at Nightwinds, and Mr. D's is perfect for a casual drink and watching sports on wide screen T.V.

A glance at the daily activities schedule shows such diversions as aerobic dancing, sailing lessons, teen bowling, nine-tap bowling, an evening excursion boat ride, and twilight tennis. A full health spa is available, as well as indoor and outdoor tennis courts, several swimming pools, jogging trails, fishing, horseback riding, and a variety of shops.

Golfers have two choices—the Hidden Lakes course, a hilly nine holes, and The Oaks, eighteen holes, and the newer of the two. The Club has hosted the Gateway Section PGA Championship in 1983, 1984, and 1985, the Big 8 Conference Championship, Missouri Tiger Invitational Tournament, and the 1988 NCAA Division National Championship. Hidden Lakes winds over the hills and through dogwoods, oaks, and cedars with plenty of water coming into play. The Oaks is enhanced by the beauty of thick woods, gentle hills and the sparkling backdrop of the lake. Demanding approaches, narrow fairways, large challenging greens, and well-placed hazards compel the golfer to concentrate on his game. #13 is tricky and memorable. Its a 413-yard par 4 with a narrow green, and a meandering stream which adds to the Ozark scenery. The course is a beauty in summer, but Spring, with the Dogwoods in bloom is spectacular, and Fall's crisp days and brilliant colors are almost distracting.

Big Sky Resort

The late Chet Huntley loved Big Sky country so much that he retired from NBC to develop what he considered the "ideal resort": a complete mountain hideaway in harmony with nature's endowments. Surrounding the resort are the peaks of the Rockies—snow-clad and majestic at eleven thousand feet; lush meadows bursting with lupine and Indian Paintbrush, and alpine lakes and streams with enough trout to cause a traffic jam. Meadow Village and Mountain Village comprise the two main communities here, with accommodations for every budget at each. The Huntley Lodge, with 204 rooms, an elegant dining room, Chet's Bar, pools, tennis courts, game room and meeting rooms, is a hub of activity in the Mountain Village. A sunken lobby, gigantic stone fireplaces, natural wood interiors and floor-to-ceiling windows offering views of unspoiled pine forests project an informal mood. There are also condominiums and meeting facilities capable of handling groups as large as 600. Next to the Lodge is the Mall which houses the Lookout Cafeteria, several shops, night spots and three restaurants. You might want to head for Whiskey Jack's, the resort's hot spot, serving meals and snacks into the late hours, or catch a friendly poker game.

Kids love it here. During summer, there's swimming, hiking, mountain biking, tennis, horseshoes, croquet, horseback riding, and the thrills of whitewater rafting. The scenic gondola ride gives a full circle tour of Big Sky's panorama, with nearby peaks in Yellowstone standing out. All ages will enjoy exploring the National Park, Lewis and Clark Caverns, Virigina City and Nevada City, and Ennis, a must for art lovers. Late July brings the National College Championships in Bozeman, a first class rodeo where SAT's don't count. Mid-November to mid-April is ski season with an average snowfall over 400 inches of Rockies powder, with 40 slopes covering two separate mountains.

The Arnold Palmer Golf Course, built in 1975, sits in an alpine meadow at 6,500 feet. This is a relatively flat course, where you can't help but get the feeling of wide open spaces. Under jagged mountain peaks, its 6,748 yards meander around the West Fork of the Gallitin River, with water coming into play on six holes. You'll often see beaver, ducks, eagles, and an occasional elk as you pray for a birdie. There's a fully stocked pro shop in Meadow Village, eager to replenish your supply of balls, or rent clubs.

Address: 1 Lone Mountain Tr, PO Box 160001, Big Sky, 59716
Phone: 406-995-5000
800-548-4486
Fax: 406-995-5001
E-mail: reservations@bigskyresort.com
Web site: http://www.bigskyresort.com
Rates: Inquire
Restaurant: Varies, restaurants nearby, hotel has room service.
Business Fac.: Meeting facilities for 25 to 1000 people, catering, group sales.
Sports Fac.: Health club with weights, exercise equipment, pools, saunas, and steam rooms.
Location: Near Yellowstone and Grand Teton National Parks

Course: Arnold Palmer golf course at Big Sky Resort
No. of Holes: 18
Club House: 406-995-5780
Reservations: Call for reservations
Season: April–November
Carts: Golf carts available.

Meadow Lake Resort

Address: 100 St Andrews Dr,
Columbia Falls, 59912
Phone: 406-892-8700
800-321-GOLF
Fax: 406-892-0330
E-mail: vacation@meadowlake.com
Web site: http://www.
meadowlake.com
Rates: $
Restaurant: Sunset Grille—breakfast, lunch and dinner
Bar: Sunset Grille
Sports Fac.: Fly fishing, Horseback riding, Ice skating, Cross country skiing, Hiking, Biking
Location: Northwest Montana's Flathead Valley, minutes from Glacier Park

Course: Meadow Lake (6714, par 72)
No. of Holes: 18
Guest Policy: Open to public
Club House: 800-321-GOLF
Fees: ⌐
Reservations: Resort guests get 25% discount
Season: Open all year
Carts: Carts available

Meadow Lake Resort, located in Northwest Montana, is an internationally recognized, full service golf and ski resort, just minutes from Glacier National Park, The Big Mountain Ski & Summer Resort, Flathead Lake and Whitefish, Montana. Whether you want to golf, ski, fish, snowmobile, go whitewater rafting, cross-country ski, hike, or just relax; Meadow Lake Resort offers luxurious accommodations to stay and play in the Flathead Valley.

At Meadow Lake Resort you will find outstanding amenities. Most accommodations are on the 18-hole championship golf course, which becomes an excellent cross-country ski course when the snows fly. After a day of golf, skiing or relaxing, you can dine at Sunset Grille, the on-site restaurant, or have cocktails in Mulligan's Lounge.

The Recreation Center is where fun and relaxation abound. Take a dip in the indoor or outdoor pool, relax in one of the spas, or watch the kids' splash in the children's pool fountain. If fitness is your thing, try the treadmill, exercise bike or Nautilus equipment. The Recreation Center also has a game room, pool table and massage room, with an on-site certified massage therapist.

Rated sixth in the state by *Golf Digest*, Meadow Lake is the only golf course in the state to be recognized by the Audubon Society for making meaningful contributions to improving environmental quality and wildlife habitat.

Montana Double Arrow Resort

Nestled in the heart of the Seeley-Swan Valley, this 200-acre resort/ranch is open year-round, offering four seasons of fun and adventure. You can enjoy golf, hiking, rafting, fly-fishing, horseback riding, cross-country skiing or snowmobiling, just to name a few. Whether it's a romantic vacation for two or a business conference for a hundred, you'll find the selection of guestrooms and log cabins the perfect accommodations. Each offers peace and quiet, plus cozy comfort and fine cuisine, all amid the picturesque surroundings of mountains and lush forests. Inside the historic 5,000 square foot Main Lodge is the Seasons Restaurant, offering unique "classic country" cuisine and an outstanding wine list, all in warm, comfortable surroundings. Next to Seasons is the Stirrups Lounge, where you can relax and enjoy cocktails in an equally cozy setting.

The 6 year-old Double Arrow Golf Course is a true golfer's paradise right in the heart of the Rockies. This spectacular course is carved among gentle rolling hills and towering ponderosa pines, offering breathtaking views of the Swan Mountains to the east and the Mission Mountains to the west. Each hole is a masterpiece in itself, with Number 6 as the signature hole-featuring an elevated tee and island green.

Address: PO Box 747, Seeley Lake, 59868
Phone: 406-677-2777
800-468-0777
Fax: 406-677-2922
E-mail: doublearrowresort@montana.com
Web site: http://www.doublearrowresort.com
Rates: $
Restaurant: Seasons Restaurant
Bar: Stirrups Lounge
Business Fac.: Complete conference, retreat, reunion and wedding facilities
Sports Fac.: Biking, Hiking, Snowmobiling, Boating, Fishing/Guided River trips, Horseback riding, Wildlife viewing, cross-country skiing, Sleigh rides, Dog sledding
Location: Scenic route between Yellowstone & Glacier National Parks

Course: Double Arrow Resort (6334, par 72)
No. of Holes: 9
Guest Policy: Open, DAL guests given priority
Club House: 406-677-3247
Fees: ⌐
Reservations: Call for reservations
Season: April–October
Carts: Carts available

Grouse Mountain Lodge

Address: 2 Fairway Drive, Whitefish, 59937
Phone: 406-862-3000
800-321-8822
Fax: 406-862-0326
E-mail: gmlodge@digisys.net
Web site: http://www.grmtlodge.com
No. of Rooms: 144
Rates: $
Restaurant: Logan's Bar & Grill
Bar: Logan's Bar
Business Fac.: Accommodate up to 300, Professional catering & banquet staff, A/V and phone/conferencing equipment
Sports Fac.: Volleyball, Tennis, Golf, 10 km Nordic Center, Indoor heated pool, Indoor/outdoor spas, Sauna
Location: 15 minutes from Glacier International Airport

Courses: Whitefish Lake—North (6556, par 72), South (6563, par 71)
No. of Holes: 36
Guest Policy: Open to public
Club House: 406-862-5960
Fees: ┃
Reservations: Can make reservations 2 days in advance
Season: Open all year—golf April–October
Carts: Pull and gas carts are available

A grand Northwest Montana lodge nestled in the heart of a mountain valley. Sunsets over crystal clear lakes. Moose, elk and deer among mature pine and larch forests. This picture comes to life at Grouse Mountain Lodge in Whitefish, Montana, just west of Glacier National Park and minutes from The Big Mountain ski area. Here, every day is a celebration of the great outdoors, with all the luxuries and service of a first-class resort.

Grouse Mountain's sun porch is located off the dining room and has a beautiful view of Whitefish Lake Golf Course, the only 36-hole golf course in Whitefish, Montana. During winter months, the golf course is home to miles of impeccably groomed and lighted cross-country ski trails.

The rooms are spacious. The lofts have enough room for you and the kids or maybe a couple of friends. The whirlpool units are ideal for just the two of you.

Logan's Grill offers the distinctive ambiance of the grand mountain lodges of yesteryear. Logan's was named after William R. Logan, the first appointed superintendent of the Glacier National Park on April 1, 1911. A two-story glass etching located in the restaurant is a pictorial of Glacier National Park. The grandeur of the stone fireplace and our native Montana décor creates a comfortable setting for a fine meal.

Whitefish has plenty to brag about when it comes to golf: two golf courses! *Golf Digest* ranked the top 36 golf retirement counties in America: Flathead County was selected number one under "Four-Season Counties with Great Golf." Whitefish has Montana's only 36-hole golf course with both of its 18s named among the top five in the state. Whitefish is an undiscovered golf mecca, the ultimate golf vacation destination with terrific weather, great prices and 11 outstanding courses within a short drive.

Hyatt Regency Lake Las Vegas Resort

Located on 25 acres of direct waterfront property on Nevada's largest privately owned lake, the "lush Mediterranean-themed oasis" is terraced into the hillside and is surrounded by an 18-hole Jack Nicklaus-designed golf course.

Hyatt Regency Lake Las Vegas Resort's design, landscaping and furnishings reflect the unrivaled charm and beauty of one of the most exquisite desert locations in the world. The architecture boasts two-story arched windows and deep loggias, creating an open-air, Mediterranean atmosphere. The centerpiece of this incredible destination is the sparkling surface of our private, 320-acre lake, one of the largest privately owned lakes in Nevada.

Each of the hotel's 496 tastefully appointed guestrooms, including 47 luxurious suites and 10 Casbah units, features sweeping views of the lake and/or mountains. Standard in-room amenities include hand-painted armoires imported from Morocco.

Hyatt Regency Lake Las Vegas Resort features a European-style casino with popular table games and slot machines. Unlike any other casino in the Las Vegas area, two story windows offer magnificent views of the lake and surrounding mountains.

Overlooking the lake, Japengo offers fine dining and an extensive Pacific Rim-inspired menu in a dramatic setting. Visit our Café Tajine restaurant for breakfast, lunch or dinner. By the poolside enjoy a snack from Sandsabar and Grill.

The Lake, The Land and The Legend—Lake Las Vegas Resort, Reflection Bay Golf Club and the Golden Bear, Jack Nicklaus, have created the ultimate golf challenge for golf enthusiasts. The course at the Reflection Bay Golf Club is a 7,261-yard, par 72 masterpiece—the first signature resort course in Nevada to be designed by the golf legend—and was recently named in *Golf Magazine*'s 1999 "Top Ten You Can Play" list. It is set on the tranquil shores of Lake Las Vegas and is sure to take your breath away while challenging your every golfing instinct and skill.

Address: 101 Montelago Blvd, Henderson, 89011
Phone: 702-567-1234
800-55-HYATT
Fax: 702-567-6112
E-mail: sbingham@lasrlpo.hyatt.com
Web site: http://www.lakelasvegas.hyatt.com
No. of Rooms: 496
Restaurant: Japengo, Cafe Tajine, Sandsa Bar & Grill, Marrakesh Express,
Bar: Arabesque Lounge
Business Fac.: 41,000 sq ft of meeting space
Sports Fac.: 320 acre lake, health club & spa, 2 outdoor swimming pools, whirlpool
Location: On 25 acres of direct waterfront property on Nevada's largest privately owned lake

Course: South Shore (6917, par 71)
No. of Holes: 18
Guest Policy: Closed except for members and hotel guests
Club House: 702-558-0020
Fees: ↑↑↑
Reservations: Call for reservations, closed on Mondays
Season: Open all year
Carts: Carts included in fees

Desert Inn Hotel & Casino

Address: 3145 Las Vegas Blvd. S, Las Vegas, 89114
Phone: 702-733-4434
800-634-6906
Fax: 702-733-4676
E-mail: kgraves@thedi.com
Web site: http://www.
thedesertinn.com
No. of Rooms: 715
Rates: Inquire
Restaurant: Monte Carlo, Portofino, Howan, Terrace Pointe
Business Fac.: 30,000 sq ft of meeting space includes the Grand Ballroom (can accomodate up to 1,000), Veranda Room, and 12-person board room
Sports Fac.: Resort Tennis, World Class spa, swimming pool
Location: Downtown Las Vegas

Course: Desert Inn Golf Course (7193, par 72)
No. of Holes: 18
Guest Policy: Open to public
Club House: 702-733-4290
Reservations: Call for reservations and prices
Season: Open all year
Carts: Pro Link Golf carts included in fees

Desert glamour, big name entertainment, glitter, nightly production spectaculars, the allure of casino action, the Hughes mystique, breakfast and dinner 24 hours a day, sunshine, and a multi-million-dollar redesign concept. The Desert Inn is a Las Vegas landmark where guests experience all of this in a desert resort with luxurious amenities. Located on the Strip not far from the downtown "Glitter Gulch" area, this hotel and casino is the only Nevada property to be a member of the Pre-ferred Hotels network. Step inside and you'll find bars, restaurants and a shopping arcade carrying everything from bathing suits to formal wear. A tour of the grounds reveal ten outdoor hydrowhirl spas scattered about, an Olympic-size pool set amidst gardens of lush foliage, tennis courts, spa, several bars and a casino highlighted by 30 brass chandeliers and some of the most attentive staff in this teeming desert oasis. The 821 rooms, including 95 suites, are housed in two, three, seven, nine and 14-story buildings, each one named after a famous golf or tennis event. St. Andrews and Augusta have glass exteriors, and the seven-storied Wimbledon building is shaped like a modernized Mayan pyramid.

After opening in 1951, the Desert Inn hosted the Tournament of Champions for 13 years, and the golf world will long remember the days when 10,000 silver dollars were wheeled out to the champion in a wheelbarrow! Past winners who received the heavy metal are Gene Littler, Sam Snead, Arnold Palmer, and Jack Nicklaus. Site of PGA Tour and Senior PGA Tour events, the par-72 layout has attracted professionals, entertainers and European royalty, as well as Presidents John Kennedy, Lyndon Johnson, and Gerald Ford. Women who have teed off here during LPGA events are Pat Bradley, Donna Caponi, Nancy Lopez, and Patty Sheehan.

The signature hole is the par-3 seventh, tradi-tionally one of the toughest on the PGA Tour. It stretches out to 209 yards from the championship tees, and looks innocent enough with colorful flowers and railroad ties, but that's when the trou-ble begins. The green is guarded by water and a brick retaining wall to the left and in front, and there are bunkers to the right and behind the dif-ficult two-tiered green. Most players bail out to the right, hoping to make par from the sand.

Mount Washington Hotel & Resort

Designated a National Historic Landmark in 1986, The 1902 Mount Washington Hotel has been host to princes, presidents and countless notables. Nothing could be more grand than this Spanish Renaissance inspired hotel built at the turn of the century. Ringed by Presidential, Dartmouth, and Willey-Rosebrook Ranges the 2,600 acre private preserve has maintained the elegance and graciousness of an era gone by. Step inside and you'll find a doric-columned lobby with soft couches beside a massive fieldstone fireplace.

In the octagonal Main Dining Room and in the opulent 1906 Room, the tradition of service with courtesy and style lives on. Here, the dinner menu—printed on an antique water-powered press—changes daily, but excellent selections from an extensive wine list and an orchestra to accompany your meal are always constants.

Athletic pursuits are varied and plentiful. Their 12 red clay courts were the original site of the Volvo International Tournament. Today, the hotel offers a complete tennis program under the direction of Head Pro Tom Over. The tradition of riding remains at the resort's beautiful Victorian stables building, where trail rides, and beginners' lessons are available.

P.T. Barnum called the view here the "second greatest show on earth", and that's exactly what a round of golf is in the clean mountain air. Donald Ross, who comes in second in number of original routings among *Golf Digest*'s "architects of the 100 greatest courses", has left his mark on this championship thriller.

The Golf Club teems with history, including pros such as Lawson Little, Bill Melhorn and Dave Marr. In 1934 Little won both the British and the U.S. Amateur Championship, and then repeated the same feat the following year! While at The Mount Washington, he won the U.S. Open in 1940, defeating Gene Sarazen in a play-off. The 1965 PGA Tournament was captured by Dave Marr.

After you've learned to spell it, you can concentrate on staying out of the Ammonoosuc River. Holes #2 and #18 require a drive across this gift of nature, and local rules dictate a one stroke penalty should you blow it. The course winds around a fairly flat front nine, with a hillier finish. Who knows, maybe you'll find one of Thomas Edison's or Babe Ruth's balls.

Address: Route 302, Bretton Woods, 03575
Phone: 603-278-1000
800-258-0330
Fax: 603-278-8838
Web site: http://www.mtwashington.com
No. of Rooms: 256
Rates: Inquire
Restrictions: No pets allowed
Restaurant: The Grand Main Dining Room, dress code
Bar: The Princess Lounge, Stickney's, The Cave
Business Fac.: Message center, Copiers, Audio-visual, Teleconferencing, 16 conference rooms, capacity 1000
Sports Fac.: Indoor and outdoor swimming pools, Handball/squash, Croquet, Whirlpool, Sauna, Massage, Weight training, 33 ski trails & 100 km cross-country trails, horseback riding, 12 tennis courts, Bike rentals
Location: Rural—White Mountain National Forest

Courses: Mount Washington (6638), Mount Pleasant (3020)
No. of Holes: 27
Guest Policy: Public welcome with advance tee time
Club House: 603-278-1000
Reservations: Up to 1 year in advance
Season: May–October
Carts: Carts available

Balsams Grand Resort Hotel

Address: Route 26, Dixville Notch, 03576
Phone: 603-255-3400
800-255-0600
E-mail: info@thebalsams.com
Web site: http://www.thebalsams.com
Rates: $$
Restrictions: No pets, Limited smoking areas
Restaurant: BALSAMS Dining Room
Bar: La Cave, Wilderness Lounge
Business Fac.: Meeting planners, Flexible meeting space, Fax, Federal Express, Copier, Administrative assistance
Sports Fac.: Downhill/cross-country skiing, Snowboarding, Telemark skiing, Snow mobiling, Sledding, Wind Whistle Ski School, Tennis, Hiking, Mountain biking, Golf, Swimming pool, Fishing Golf School, Massage, Ice skating, Snowshoeing

Location: High in New Hampshire's White Mountains
Courses: The Panorama (6804, par 72), The Coashaukee (3834, par 64)
No. of Holes: 27
Guest Policy: Open to public
Club House: 603-255-4961
Fees: ↑
Reservations: Reservations available 3 days in advance
Season: May–October
Carts: Carts available

The Dix House opened in 1866 with a capacity of 25 rooms, and by 1918 was enlarged to "grand hotel" status. Today, the 15,000-acre private estate, with a traditional New England clapboard main building, comprises The Balsams. Located in the northern reaches of New Hampshire's White Mountains, the resort's known as the "Switzerland of America." It was named as one of the "The Golf Resorts in America" in 1990 by *Golf Magazine*.

Meals are served in the main dining room where glass chandeliers, lace curtains, linen cloths and mahogany furniture provide the perfect atmosphere to complement Chef Phil Learned's lavish meals. Don't miss his celebrated Veal Saltimbocca alla Romano with Bordelaise, and top it all off with his Chocolate Pate with English Cream. There is entertainment nightly in three rooms.

Activities abound at The Balsams. Try your hand at fly fishing for rainbow trout in nearby Lake Gloriette, and have your catch prepared for dinner by the cooking staff. Or, explore the beautiful countryside along one of the eight Balsams trails that extend from 1.2 to 6.0 miles.

A nine-hole par 32 executive course, the Coashaukee, is very level and flat, making it a perfect place to practice with all your clubs. An unusually scenic 18 hole championship course, The Panorama, has perhaps the most magnificent setting of all the layouts by Scottish master, Donald Ross. Featuring teacup sand traps and bowl-shaped greens, the course affords spectacular views of the entire Upper Connecticut River Valley, Mount Monadnock in Vermont, and Quebec's rolling hills.

Nearly every shot, and especially one's putts, require that the mountainside setting be considered. Players swear their ball breaks up hill until they learn to orient themselves to the slope. Today's layout is almost entirely intact from the 1912 design, although some of the original tee boxes are now designated as ladies tees, because the Scot designed this course to be only slightly over 6,000 yards. Every ability is challenged, and all fourteen clubs will be needed for even the best players. Play as much golf as you like on either course where it's free and unlimited while you are a guest at The Balsams.

Tory Pines Resort

Have you ever wondered what it's like to live in a dairy barn? Tory Pines, now renovated and equipped with all the modern conveniences you expect of a resort, offers you just that opportunity. The rooms all have fireplaces and afford sweeping views. Situated on 780 acres of game sanctuary and forest preserve, you will find breathtaking panoramic views and abundant wildlife.

You'll enjoy fine dining in a 200-year-old Georgian Colonial restaurant that features Continental and New England regional cuisine served with elegance.

The conference facilities can service a group of up to 150 people, all handled by an attentive and professional staff. This is a perfect setting for a relaxing business retreat. Call for the complete "Business is your Pleasure" meeting packet.

There are numerous unique shops in the area, summer theater and concerts, as well as all of the beautiful New Hampshire countryside to explore.

Tory Pines is home to The Roland Staford Golf School where the emphasis is on communication between instructor and student. A wonderful learning experience awaits you.

Tory Pine is a meticulously maintained course that has mountain streams, ponds, rolling hills and elevated greens. The course is sure to provide a wonderful round for any level of golfer. Designed in 1930 by Donald Ross, the course has been renovated with every effort made to maintain the original design.

Address: Route 47, RR1, Box 655, Francestown, 03043
Phone: 603-588-2000
800-227-TORY
Fax: 603-588-2275
E-mail: tp_resort@conknet.com
Web site: http://www.
torypinesresort.com
No. of Rooms: 32
Rates: $
Restaurant: Gibson Tavern Dining Room
Business Fac.: Complete Conference facilities
Sports Fac.: Skiing, Hiking, Mountain bikes
Location: Mount Monadnock

Course: Tory Pines (6004, par 71)
No. of Holes: 18
Guest Policy: Open to public
Club House: 603-588-2923
Fees: ⌐
Reservations: Reservations available 5 days in advance
Season: Open all year
Carts: Carts available

Hanover Inn

Address: P.O. Box 151, Hanover, 03755
Phone: 603-643-4300
1-800-443-7024
Fax: 603-646-3744
E-mail: info@hanoverinn.com
Web site: http://www. hanoverinn.com
Rates: Inquire
Restaurant: Zins Winebistro-contemporary bistro, The Daniel Webster Room-fine dining, The Terrace, catering.
Business Fac.: Many meeting facilities.
Location: On the Darmouth College campus

Course: Hanover Country Club (5876)
No. of Holes: 18
Guest Policy: Guests welcome, it is a public course.
Club House: 603-646-2000
Fees: ‖
Reservations: Call for reservations
Season: Open after about April 15
Carts: Carts available for $3-15.

This is the unspoiled Upper Connecticut River Valley, blessed with photogenic red farmhouses, fields of Queen Anne's lace and black-eyed Susans, panoramic views of green mountains, and almost unbelievable peace and quiet combined with a strong sense of the past. Founded in 1780 by General Ebenezer Brewster, the Hanover Inn occupies the site of his original home. Today's Inn, overlooking the Hanover green and the campus, is a modern, 104 room neo-Georgian brick structure, owned and operated by Dartmouth College. Emphasis is on the traditional—from the canopied beds and highboys to the arched windows and white linen, silver and crystal in the Daniel Webster Room. Menus include hearty New England dishes using regional ingredients, and an impressive and judiciously selected wine list, with offerings from around the world. The Terrace, for alfresco dining is open during warm months, while High Tea and cocktails are served in the Hayward Lounge.

Many guests like taking a picnic and exploring the Appalachian Trail, or fishing the waters of the White River. Cornish, approximately 18 miles south of Hanover, welcomes visitors to the home and gardens of Augustus Saint-Gaudens, one of America's greatest sculptors, and the antiquing locally is worth the time.

The original nine holes at Hanover Country Club was designed in 1899, and later revised and expanded by Geoffrey Cornish and Bill Robinson, designers of noted Cranberry Valley in Harwich, Massachusetts. There's a lot to like about this collegiate course which has hosted state championships, NHPGA events, as well as its own tournament, the annual Tommy Keane Invitational best-ball honoring the late pro and coach. You may reserve a caddie in advance, or you can carry your own bag, and green fees are relatively low, with hotel guests receiving a discount off the weekday fee. An added attraction is the policy of waiving green fees if you book two or more weeks in advance and request the golf package. The Club has one of the most spacious practice areas in New England, including the old "four hole course" for beginners and lessons. The Ski-Jump Hole is the cornerstone of the four "gully holes." The #13 is a 350 yard par four requiring a very accurate drive to avoid "the office" on the left and "Pine Park" on the right. The tee is elevated, and the approach shot is hit into a well-protected green.

Eagle Mountain House

Step back in time to one of New England's last remaining "grand era" hotels nestled among the White Mountains of New Hampshire. A tradition since 1879, guests from all over the world come to the "Eagle" for its picture postcard setting, accommodating staff and delicious New England cuisine.

Charming guestrooms and suites, all with private bathrooms, feature period fixtures, four poster beds dressed with down comforters, cable television and telephone. A two-room suite provides separate living and sleeping areas; perfect for families. Children stay free and enjoy very reasonably priced children's menu. Complimentary coffee and assorted teas (hot cocoa in winter) are served in the lobby each morning.

There are two dining options at Eagle Mountain. Enjoy fine dining in Highfields Restaurant and for lighter fare in the Eagle Landing Tavern.

Outside, you can play tennis on either of two courts—one is lit for night play. Hike and bike on mountain trails surrounding the hotel, then cool off in a nearby cascading waterfall. Better yet, head back to the Eagle for a dip in the outdoor pool. The hotel health club features a spacious weight room overlooking the mountains with treadmill, bike, stair machine and universal gym equipment. Both men's and lady's locker rooms offer full shower facilities and dry saunas. And, don't forget to try the soothing waters of the 10-person Jacuzzi after a busy day. The game room features a billiard table, ping pong, video and arcade games as well as a movie room for feature presentations.

May through October, enjoy golfing on one of New England's most scenic 9-hole mountain courses, or hit a bucket of balls on the driving range. Full time golf pro Julie Rivers-Sena is available for lessons and clinics. Discounted pro shop, gas and pull carts are available. In winter, our golf course becomes part of the 146km cross-country ski trail network meticulously groomed throughout Jackson village by the Jackson Ski Touring Foundation.

Address: Carter Notch Rd, Jackson, 03846
Phone: 603-383-9111
800-966-5779
E-mail: reservations@eaglemt.com
Web site: http://www.eaglemt.com
No. of Rooms: 93
Rates: $
Restaurant: Highlands Restaurant, Eagle Landing Tavern
Business Fac.: From 10-200, Experienced staff and banquet staff
Sports Fac.: Tennis, Hiking, Biking, Health club, Sauna, Jacuzzi, Billiards, Ping-pong, Skiing, Massage
Location: Just above Jackson, NH

Course: Eagle Mountain Course (2126, par 32)
No. of Holes: 9
Guest Policy: Open to public
Club House: 603-383-9111
Fees: ⅂
Reservations: Reservations available 7 days in advance
Season: April–October
Carts: Carts available

Woodbound Inn

Address: 62 Woodbound Road, Rindge, 03461
Phone: 603-532-8341
800-688-7770
E-mail: info@woodboundinn.com
Web site: http://www.woodbound.com
No. of Rooms: 46
Rates: $
Restaurant: Woodbound Inn Restaurant
Bar: Woodbound Inn Lounge 11:00 AM -10:00 PM
Business Fac.: The Woodbound Inn has meeting/banquet facilities for 5-200 people. With 5 different meeting rooms. The Woodbound Inn hosts many weddings, conferences, meetings, Retreats, reunions and more. From very simple to very complex the Woodbound Inn can do it!
Sports Fac.: On the Woodbound inn property we have: Volleyball, Tennis ,Hoseshoes, basketball, trout pond, hiking/cross-country ski trails, beach and lake swimming, shuffle board, ping-pong, putting green.
Location: Off Route #202. Near Intersection of Rt #119. South Central NH

The Woodbound Inn is a Country Inn Resort in South Central, NH. About 65 miles from Boston, MA. Located on 165 beautiful acres with views of Mount Monadnock. The Woodbound Inn has something for everyone.

The Main Inn has classical style "Bed and Breakfast" style rooms. They are individually decorated with antiques scattered among them. Fourteen out of nineteen rooms have private baths (some rooms can be set up to share a bath between two rooms if desired). Staying in the Main Inn is very convenient to the Restaurant, Lounge, Gift Shop and the hub of many activities. The Edgewood Building rooms are a little larger with "Business Class" feel to them. These rooms have two double brass beds and a working desk. The Edgewood rooms are convenient to those attending a function in the Ballroom, which is right downstairs.

The bright and cheerful dining room provides a varied menu, with a unique combination of traditional New England fare, complemented by nouvelle cuisine.

Golf on the Woodbound inn 9 hole par three Golf Course is Free to overnight guests. Woodbound's 1,200 yard, par 3 golf course has nine holes, ranging from 100 to 170 yards, and full size Vesper Bent Greens. Enjoy incredible rustic views and fresh country air, while playing your favorite game. And best of all, our golf course starts right outside the front door. Golf clubs are available for rent. Golf balls and other items are available for sale in our gift shop.

Courses: Woodbound Inn Golf Course, 1100 yards, Par 3, Nearby is the Shattuck Golf Course
No. of Holes: 9
Guest Policy: Open to public
Fees: ↑
Reservations: Sign in at the Front Desk
Season: April 15- October 30
Carts: Pull carts available for rent.

Marriott's Seaview Resort

In 1913 Philadelphia magnate Clarence H. Geist became disenchanted with having to wait to play a round of golf. He decided to build his own course, and the following year the first of his two golf courses opened, as well as the beginnings of his clubhouse. The location, easily accessible from New York and Philadelphia was key, and the quiet retreat for the affluent became quite popular. Today's guests marvel at the well-groomed 670-acre estate, four-story colonial style architecture with porte-cochere, stately lobby with oriental rugs and antiques, brick floored Grill Room, and the serene terraces overlooking Absecon Bay.

Traditional favorites are served in the Main Dining Room, which is decorated in soft green and pink pastels—all with a panoramic view of the fairways. Drop in to the mahogany-lined Grill Room for breakfast or a light snack, or the Oval Lounge with its lively piano bar, where a Transfusion comes in a tall iced glass.

Enjoy pocket billiards, ping pong or a game of five card draw in the classic game room. For recreation, the resort also has a 9-hole putting green, ten outdoor tennis courts (four lighted), an indoor swimming pool, paddle tennis courts, and a hydrotherapy pool. Guests are extended privileges at nearby Health and Racquet Club.

Historic Smithville with tours, shops and restaurants is close, as is the Brigantine Wildlife Refuge, the Lennox China factory, and Noyes Art Museum. The casinos and night life of Atlantic City are a short drive from here.

Serious golfers have always regarded Seaview as legendary. Two 18-hole championship courses, vastly different from each other, make this a golfing paradise. The Bay Course, site of the 1942 PGA Championship, is a Donald Ross "Scottish links" classic featuring windswept bunkers and panoramic seaside views. As with most layouts subjected to buffeting winds, it is relatively short in yardage and has wide openings at the front of the greens to allow run-up shots. The newer and more demanding Pines course, lined with 100 year old Jersey pines, oaks and splashy rhododendron, plays over and around a great maze of fairway and greenside bunkers. Greens are lightning quick, often undulating and do not accommodate poor putters. Due to the bay-front location, golf is available almost all year long.

Address: 401 S. New York Rd, Absecon, 08201
Phone: 609-748-1990
800-932-8000
No. of Rooms: 299
Rates: Inquire
Restrictions: No pets allowed
Restaurant: Main Dining Room, The Grill Room, The Lobby Lounge
Bar: Oval Lounge
Business Fac.: Administrative assistance, Copiers, Conference rooms, capacity 400
Sports Fac.: Swimming pool, Croquet, Tennis courts, Golf School, Sauna, Steam room
Location: Atlantic county

Courses: Pines (6394), Bay
No. of Holes: 36
Guest Policy: Call for available tee times
Club House: 609-748-7680
Reservations: Guests may call 7 days in advance
Season: Open all year

Angel Fire Legend Hotel & Conference Center

Address: Hwy 434, P.O. Drawer B, Angel Fire, 87710
Phone: 505-377-6401
800-633-7463
E-mail: reserve@ angelfireresort.com
Web site: http://www. angelfireresort.com/
No. of Rooms: 139
Rates: $
Restaurant: New Restaurant at the Summitt
Business Fac.: 12 meeting rooms for 20-300 people, Audio/visual equipment, Fax/copy services, Catering
Sports Fac.: Bicycle Tours and Hiking trips, Indoor pool, Hot tub, Massage facility, Ski Board School, Tubing, Snow bikes, Children's Ski and Snowboard School, Terrain Park, Ice fishing, Snow mobiling
Location: 24 miles east of Taos

Set in the Moreno Valley in a perfect alpine setting, Angle Fire offers the 275-room Legends Hotel as well as resort-managed condominiums. Featured here are a spa with an indoor pool and hot tub, and all at a great price.

There's plenty to do here, with horseback riding in the Sangre de Cristo Mountains, gold panning, whitewater rafting, exploring the Taos Pueblo that's over 900 years old, bicycle touring or hiking, even balloon rides.

In the summer Angel Fire has music festivals, beer and wine tastings and many other events. There are even arts and crafts fairs, food fairs and cooking classes!

The Angel Fire course has lots of bunkers and small greens on the front nine, while the back wanders through aspen, pine and spruce in a canyon area. The fairways are narrow, and there's water in play on every hole. The course has been the host of the Premier Invitational and many other important tournaments. There's also a driving range and fully stocked pro shop.

Angel Fire Day Camp offers supervised child care for those 6 weeks to 6 years. Summer Mountain Adventure is designed for the 7–12 set and offers a full day program for the active child.

Course: Angel Fire Course (6600)
No. of Holes: 18
Club House: 505-377-3055
Fees: ⌡
Reservations: 800-633-7463
Season: Open all year

Inn of the Mountain Gods

New Mexico has a lot of wide open spaces, and this stunning mountain resort is surrounded by and engulfed in the serenity of the secluded, heavily forested Mescalero Apache Indian Reservation. At 7,200 feet in the Sacramento Mountains of south central New Mexico a few miles east of White Sands Missile Range, the Inn is a most unique spot. Owned and operated by the Mescalero Apache Tribe, the visitor will find scenic outdoor sports, fine dining and excellent shopping for tribal handcrafts, all on a pristine Alpine lake. With 250 rooms, one still has the feeling of isolation, partly because the surroundings are undeveloped, and its naturally an incredibly quiet place. The lobby is large, with a 50 foot copper sheathed fireplace dominating a warm room filled with Apache artifacts and contemporary furnishings. A lively piano bar which overlooks the mountains, Lake Mescalero and the golf course. Accommodations are shingled chalet-style with large windows facing the lake, and when you depart you have the feeling that all is well-maintained, and surprise! Everything worked!

You might choose archery, badminton, canoeing, lazing poolside, or exploring the forests on horseback. Tennis courts, and trap and skeet shooting are popular pastimes here, as are the big game hunting packages. This is definitely where the antelope play and discouraging words are seldom heard.

Off the reservation, you'll find the White Sands National Monument, art galleries, Alamogordo Space Hall of Fame, and Ruidoso Downs, renowned for the best in quarter horse and thoroughbred racing in the cool pines.

Fans of first-rate home style Mexican food will want to try the Old Road Restaurant nearby.

The golf course here is by Ted Robinson, who also is credited with Sahalee Country Club in Redmond, Washington. It's a rolling layout bordering the lake, with fairly hard fairways, giving the ball a good bounce. With fairways bordered by stands of pinon, cottonwood, aspen and pine, it's more than likely you'll see the trees up close. The front nine is narrower, and you'll need precise shots to carry the water on several holes. The second hole, with its elevated tee and dogleg left can be a devil, especially if you try to cut the corner, where huge trees will hamper progress. Greens are large, well-maintained and undulating, plus pretty slick due to the altitude.

Address: P.O. Box 269, Mescalero, 88340
Phone: 505-257-5141
800-545-9011
Fax: 505-257-6173
E-mail: schino.img@zianet.com
Web site: http://www.innofthe-mountaingods.com
No. of Rooms: 253
Rates: Inquire
Restrictions: No pets allowed
Restaurant: Dan Li Ka Dining Room
Bar: Ina Da Lounge
Business Fac.: Copiers, Audio-visual, Conference rooms, capacity 650
Sports Fac.: Tennis courts, Horseback riding, Canoes & rowboats
Location: Otero County

Course: Inn of the Mountain Gods (6834)
No. of Holes: 18
Guest Policy: Open to public
Club House: 505-257-5141
Reservations: Should reserve tee time
Season: Open year round—weather permitting

Sagamore

Address: On Lake George, PO Box 450, Bolton Landing, 12814
Phone: 518-644-9400
800-THE-OMNI
Fax: 518-644-2626
E-mail: reserve@thesagamore.com
Web site: http://www.thesagamore.com
No. of Rooms: 100
Rates: $$
Restaurant: The Trillium, Sagamore Dining Room, Club Grill, The Morgan
Bar: Mr. Brown's Pub, The Veranda
Business Fac.: Conference center
Sports Fac.: Tennis club, Indoor swimming pool, Water sports
Location: Lake George, Adirondack mountains

Course: Sagamore (par-70 course by Donald Ross)
No. of Holes: 18
Club House: 800-358-3585
Reservations: Call for reservations
Season: Open all year

The Sagamore, with its stately white tower and rambling clapboard wings, is idyllically situated on its own island on one of the cleanest lakes in the United States, Lake George in the Adirondacks. The resort is steeped in local lore and tales of the Northeast's elite vacationing here. Listed in the National Register of Historic Buildings, The Sagamore underwent a $75 million renovation in 1985 and is now a four-star luxury resort and conference center, under the management of Omni Hotels. The main building, well-preserved and dating from 1923, dominates the 72-acre island, and houses 100 rooms and suites. Seven lakeside lodges offer 240 additional rooms and suites with fireplaces and private balconies. A variety of restaurants provide formal and casual dining; cocktails, high tea, late evening coffees and piano music can be enjoyed at the Veranda, a Victorian-style lounge that overlooks Lake George.

Guests can enjoy a host of recreational activities. The resort has indoor and outdoor tennis courts, racquetball, an indoor pool, and a full-treatment spa. Waterskiing, sailing, windsurfing, canoeing and fishing all start at the marina. You can even try parasailing for a unique glimpse of The Sagamore. If that isn't enough, there's also complimentary transportation around the island and to the golf course.

The Sagamore was awarded by *Golf Magazine* a Best Golf Resorts in America Medal. Designed in 1928 by Donald Ross, it is one of American's truly classic championship courses. The course hosted NY PGA Match Play and Challenge Cup Matches in 1986-1988. Your golfing experience starts when you sit in Adirondack rockers overlooking the first hole to put on your golf shoes. Then you play a classic Ross course that winds its way through beautiful mountainside acres of white birches and evergreen trees, punctuated by heather that Ross brought over from Scotland. There are rolling fairways with desired landing areas in order to properly set up your next shot. Deep green-side bunkers catch a stray approach or a missed-hit chip. The 13th hole is considered to be the most breathtaking, but also one of the most difficult. It's a very tight driving hole with water right and woods on the left. The second shot is long and uphill to "one undulating mass," as Ross' description of a very rolling green. After the game, finish your experience at The Club Grille.

Peek'n Peak Resort

Peak'n Peak's stained glass, hand carved wood-work, chandeliers, massive fireplaces, and period artwork add charm to this 1,000 acre resort that prides itself on the individual attention that is paid to guests' needs.

The resort offers rooms and suites varying from a standard room to the Deluxe Jacuzzi Suite, condos, and the privately owned Canterbury Woods Rental Units and also has facilities for conferences. When hungry, try the Tri-State's Premier Steak and Seafood House, the Royal Court Dining Room. Breakfast and lunch are served at the Garden Coffee Shop in the hotel, and afternoon and evening meals can be enjoyed at the Regency Pub. Also, try the seasonal restaurant offerings like the summer Golfers Buffet Breakfast in the hotel, or the casual Winter League Sports Bar

Located in the southwestern corner of New York State, the resort is situated near the Chautauqua Institution, Presque Isle Park, Lake Erie, and Chautauqua Lake. Take a trip to Findley Lake for a quaint village shopping excursion, go skiing on the slopes, or relax by the outdoor pool.

The clubhouses offer a pro-shop, locker storage, cart rental and casual dining for before or after teeing off. The Lower Course, 18 holes, has a par 72 and features many water hazards on the front nine and bunkers on the back nine, which make it beautiful but challenging. The Upper Course also has 18 holes and has amazing views form the rolling terrain that require long shots over deep ravines.

Address: Ye Olde Road, RD 2, Box 135, Clymer, 14724
Phone: 716-355-4141
Fax: 716-355-4542
E-mail: pk-n-pk@travelbase.com
Web site: http://www.pknpk.com/
Rates: $$
Restaurant: Tri-State Premier Steak and Seafood House, the Royal Court Dining Room, Garden Coffee Shop
Bar: Regency Pub
Sports Fac.: Swimming pool, Fitness center, Miniature golf, Tennis courts
Location: Chautauqua County, New York

Courses: Upper Course (6888), Lower Course (6260)
No. of Holes: 36
Guest Policy: Open to public
Club House: 716-355-4141
Fees: 1
Reservations: Call for reservations
Season: Open all year

Otesaga Hotel

Address: 60 Lake St, P.O. Box 311,
Cooperstown, 13326
Phone: 607-547-9931
800-348-6222
Fax: 607-547-9675
E-mail: info@otesaga.com
Web site: http://www.otesaga.com
No. of Rooms: 138
Rates: Inquire
Restrictions: No pets allowed
Restaurant: Main Dining Room,
The Hawkeye Grill, Lakeside Patio
Bar: Templeton Lounge, Colonnade
Verandah
Business Fac.: Full conference
facilities, Conference rooms,
capacity 250
Sports Fac.: 2 Tennis courts,
Outdoor swimming pool, Lake swim-
ming from dock, Game room,
Putting green
Location: Downtown

Course: Leatherstocking (6053)
No. of Holes: 18
Guest Policy: Reserve up to 6 days
in advance
Club House: 607-547-5275
Reservations: As early as desired
Season: April–October
Carts: Walking permitted Monday-
Friday

Commissioned by the Clark family, designer Percy
Griffin chose a Neo-Georgian design for The Otesaga Hotel. This included a stately wood-col-
umned portico as the hotel's signature detail.
Overlooking Lake Otsego—a pristine, deep water
lake immortalized as the "Glimmerglass" in
James Fenimore Cooper's Leatherstocking
Tales—the hotel opened its doors in 1909. Since
1909, The Otesaga has offered distinguished service, dining and amenities to avid golfers and
vacationers from around the world. The hotel
retains the charm and elegance of Colonial yesteryear. Much of the today's interior finishes and
artwork are original.

Besides golf, guests can also enjoy tennis, pool
or lake swimming, sailing, canoeing, and deep
fresh water fishing on Lake Otesaga. There are
also many historical sites nearby, and a short walk
or trolley ride will bring you to the National Baseball Hall of Fame, The Farmer's Museum, and
Fenimore House Museum of the NY State historical Association.

Rates include breakfast and dinner in either
the Main Dining Room or The Hawkeye Bar &
Grill. Both eateries features specialties of New
York State and Otsego county. During the summer, a popular lunch spot is the Lakeside patio,
where a sumptuous noon buffet is served. In the
evening, the Templeton Lounge offers spirits and
nightly music.

The Otesaga offers one of the most scenic and
challenging courses of the Northeast. The 6,324-
yard 72-par course has a rating of 71.0 and slope
of 124.

Nevele Country Club

Ellenville is easily accessible from The Big Apple, the western part of the state and the Philadelphia area. If you're looking for a conference or getaway site in the Catskills, consider a thousand acre resort with a full American plan and Jewish-American cuisine, elegant public areas, nice guest rooms and good recreational facilities. This is a fairly large resort—435 rooms and such amenities as tennis, an Olympic-size outdoor pool, an indoor pool, health clubs, horseback riding, an indoor game room, boating on the lake, fishing, bicycle riding, and racquetball. The main dining room offers special diets as well as an attractive menu featuring seafood and a large variety of home-baked items. A coffee shop, snackquabana at the outdoor pool, loft cafe, safari lounge, aquabar, espresso bar, and stardust room for nightly entertainment round out the picture of restaurants and watering holes.

Children of all ages are pampered here. A day-camp program that runs from breakfast to bed-time stimulates and occupies them, freeing parents to pursue their own diversions. Women love the upscale shopping at the outlet malls nearby. You'll have a pleasant course to play, one that hosts regional amateur tournaments. Look for rolling terrain with a lake and creek running throughout. Tom Fazio redesigned the layout recently, so if your grandfather always birdied the 16th hole, don't count on it running in the family. The lake surrounds the fairway and three sides of the tricky green.

Address: Nevele Rd, Ellenville, 12428
Phone: 914-647-6000
800-647-6000
Fax: 914-647-9884
E-mail: cclub@ulster.net
Web site: http://www.nevele.com
Rates: $
Restaurant: Meal plans
Bar: Lounge
Business Fac.: Conference room
Sports Fac.: Lake with rowboats/paddleboats, 15 indoor/outdoor tennis courts, 2 indoor raquetball courts, 4 indoor/outdoor swimming pools, Jacuzzi, Health Club, Massage, Fitness Center, Ping-Pong, Miniature golf, Downhill/cross-country skiing, Skating rink, Hiking
Location: One mile outside Ellenville

Course: Nevele Grande (6633)
No. of Holes: 27
Club House: 914-647-0000
Fees: 6
Reservations: Call for reservations
Season: March–November

Marriott's Wind Watch Hotel

Address: 1717 Vanderbilt Motor Parkway, Hauppauge, 11788
Phone: 516-232-9800
800-228-9290
Fax: 516-232-9853
No. of Rooms: 360
Rates: Inquire
Restaurant: JW's Sea Grill, The Golf Club Grill
Bar: Atrium Lounge, Tickets Lounge
Business Fac.: Business Center
Sports Fac.: Exercise room, Indoor and outdoor swimming pools, Tennis courts, Volleyball

Location: Long Island
Course: Wind Watch (6425)
No. of Holes: 18
Guest Policy: Open to public
Club House: 516-232-9800
Reservations: Up to 3 days in advance
Season: Open all year

Wind Watch offers a scenic, stately setting for its luxury hotel. You'll feel like you in a secluded place, when you're just minutes from all the action of Long Island and Manhattan. The keynote here is a peaceful and unhurried atmosphere where you can unwind. You'll be as pampered as you'll allow!

The rooms are elegantly furnished, with balconies that overlook the gardens or the golf course.

If you start to get too relaxed, there's plenty of sightseeing, and there's all those beaches to explore along the Atlantic, or visit one of the local wineries. Then a visit to historic Stony Brook Village.

The dining here is unsurpassed with delicious seafood in J.W.'s Sea Grill or the indoor or outdoor dining at the Golf Club Grill.

The resort also has tennis courts, swimming in the indoor or outdoor pools, volleyball, horseshoes or ping pong. Then a nice visit to the whirlpool and sauna!

The Joe Lee designed golf course has more water then you would think possible. In addition to that there dozens of bunkers, with rolling terrain that's likely to make for some very difficult lies. The wind here must be what's given the resort its name, because you sure do have to watch the wind!

Concord Resort Hotel

Set amid 3,000 acres, less than a two hour drive from New York City, the Concord's vacation or conference choices are wide and varied. This is a large resort, with more than a thousand rooms. A conventioneer dream, the Concord offers good value and good entertainment in the heart of the Catskills.

The grounds are like a well-maintained college campus, with varied activities taking place everywhere. You'll find jogging trails, 24 outdoor and 16 indoor tennis courts, horseback riding, indoor and outdoor swimming pools, bowling, exercise classes, an extensive health club, skeet shooting, shuffleboard, volleyball, and that old Italian favorite, bocci ball. It doesn't stop there—look for paddle ball and handball, bicycle riding, miniature golf, a full program for children, softball fields. Boating and fishing on shimmering Lake Kiamesha are favorite pastimes. During winter, the resort offers four ski lifts, and outdoor ice skating.

This is American plan—the room rate includes all meals, and children have their own supervised dining rooms. Entertainment and dancing can be found in The Nite Owl Lounge, as well as numerous other watering holes.

Concord's 45 holes include its infamous "Monster," a 6,793 yard by Joe Finger, wizard of Cedar Ridge in Oklahoma. This par 72 heavily wooded rolling course has hosted many tournaments.

Address: Concord Rd, Kiamesha Lake, 12751
Phone: 914-794-4000
888-448-9686
Fax: 914-794-7471
E-mail: info@concordresort.com
Web site: http://www.concordresort.com
No. of Rooms: 42
Rates: Inquire
Bar: Entertainment Lounge
Business Fac.: Convention Center & Hall, complete facilities
Sports Fac.: Tennis school and courts, Jr. golf school, Swimming pool, Health Club and Spa, Paddle tennis, Indoor/outdoor skating, Fishing, Miniature golf/croquet, Horseback riding, Paddleboats/canoeing
Location: In the Catskill Mountains

Courses: The Monster (7650, par 72), International (6619, par 71), Challenger (2200, par 31)
No. of Holes: 45
Guest Policy: Open to public
Club House: 914-794-4000
Fees: ⅃ ⅃
Reservations: Reservations available 90 days in advance
Season: March–November
Carts: Carts included in fees

Blackhead Mountain Lodge & Country Club

Address: PO Box 96, Round Top, 12473
Phone: 518-622-3157
888-382-7474
Fax: 518-622-2331
E-mail: blackheadm@aol.com
Web site: http://www.thecatskills.com/blackhead.htm
No. of Rooms: 24
Rates: Inquire
Restrictions: Open May through October
Restaurant: Maassmann's Restaurant
Sports Fac.: Swimming pool, Tennis court, Lawn sports and game facilities, Golf Academy

Location: Northern Catskill Mountains
Course: Blackhead Mountain (6242, par 72
No. of Holes: 18
Guest Policy: Open to public
Club House: 518-622-3157
Fees: ↑
Reservations: 3 days in advance
Season: April–November
Carts: Carts available

European charm, American hospitality and Black Forest atmosphere fill this 24 room family-owned German/American Golf Resort located in the heart of the beautiful and majestic Northern Catskill Mountains.

The accommodations are very comfortable. Guestrooms meet today's standards and expectations. They all have air-conditioning, color TV and refrigerators. And most importantly, the housekeeping staff makes certain that they are immaculately clean.

Delicious home cooked breakfasts and dinners make mealtimes memorable occasions. Maassmann's Restaurant features cozy European atmosphere. It is not only the setting for resort guest dining, but is also a local favorite for evening dining. At Maassmann's, daily selections of German & American entrees are tastefully prepared under the supervision of Chef Ewald Maassmann. Everything, including our wonderful desserts, is homemade and only of the best quality. Lunch is also available and is served in the Clubhouse.

"Spectacular" describes the scenery on every one of the 18 holes of our challenging Par 72 Championship Golf Course, which is serenely nestled against the mountainside. USGA Architect Nicholas Psiahas designed this magnificent layout. The golf course and grounds are beautifully maintained and manicured. The additional 9 holes were completed in 1999.

At the Golf Academy, you can learn or improve your game under the expert supervision of Peter Maassmann, PGA Golf Professional & Director of Golf. Peter and his staff of PGA Golf Professionals give lessons on a 4:1 ratio only. Private and semi-private instruction is also available. They feature a full service Pro Shop, as well as a beautiful rustic Clubhouse.

Great Smokies Holiday Inn

One hundred twenty landscaped acres in the Appalachians have been reserved for you at the Great Smokies. The rooms are been fully renovated and are now quite luxurious. Come and enjoy the mountain scenery of the Great Smokies!

The attractions in historic Asheville include the Biltmore estates, a 270-room castle with splendid gardens and its own winery, and the Biltmore Homespun Shops, where you'll see the dyeing, carding and spinning of wool by hand. Then of course there's the home of Thomas Wolfe, or Cherokee Indian Village. The area has some wonderful and unique shops.

The resort offers golf packages which offer play on eight other championship courses as well: Cleghorn Plantation, Connestee Falls, French Broad, Laurel Ridge Country Club, Links of Tryon, Mt. Mitchell, Red Fox and Reems Creek. You'll also have access to an off-property Spa Health Club.

The Great Smokies can arrange a memorable convention for up to 1,000, or a small corporate retreat, just leave all the planning in their able hands.

The Great Smokies course is very hilly, and you'll probably end up with a lot of side-hill lies. Water comes into play everywhere due to the many streams that run through the course. Set amidst the Blue Ridge and Smoky Mountains, the course is very scenic.

Holiday Fun Club is run for the kids 7 days a week from June 1st through Labor Day. In October and special holidays the program runs on weekends only. The program offers arts and crafts, games, carnival night, a Mexican fiesta and much more.

Address: One Hilton Dr, Asheville, 28806
Phone: 828-254-3211
800-733-3211
Fax: 828-254-1603
Web site: http://www.sunspree.com
No. of Rooms: 276
Rates: Inquire
Restaurant: Pro's Table, Market-essen Coffee Shop
Bar: Equinox Lounge
Business Fac.: Meeting and Conference facilities for up to 1000
Sports Fac.: 4 indoor tennis courts, 4 outdoor tennis courts, 2 swimming pools, Basketball, Volleyball, Exercise and Weight rooms
Location: Asheville

Course: Great Smokies (5600)
No. of Holes: 18
Guest Policy: Open to public
Club House: 828-253-5874
Reservations: Up to 2 days in advance
Season: Open all year

Grove Park Inn Resort

Address: 290 Macon Ave, Asheville,
28804
Phone: 828-252-2711
800-438-5800
Fax: 828-253-7053
E-mail: info@groveparkinn.com
Web site: http://www.
groveparkinn.com
No. of Rooms: 510
Rates: $$
Restrictions: Children 16 and under
free, Non-smoking and handicap
equipped rooms available
Restaurant: Horizons
Bar: The Great Hall Bar
Business Fac.: 42 meeting rooms,
totaling 50,000 square feet,
Complete conference facilities
Sports Fac.: Tennis courts, Outdoor
swimming pool, Full Service Spa
Location: In Asheville, convenient
to lots of major cities

Course: Grove Park Course (6520,
par 71)
No. of Holes: 18
Guest Policy: Open to public
Club House: 828-252-2711
Fees: ⅠⅠ
Reservations: Can make reserva-
tions one day in advance
Carts: Carts included in fees

Tucked away neatly in a mountain cove of the
Blue Ridge Mountains in Western North Carolina
is a resort that has hosted the discerning traveler
for nine decades. A grand mountain resort
designed at the turn of the century to lure even
the most well traveled. Beckoning them with pure
mountain air, an awesome spectacle of architec-
ture, the finest service, cuisine, and amenities. A
place to savor as one of the most enduringly origi-
nal and exciting resorts in America. The Grove
Park Inn Resort, one of the American South's old-
est and most famous grand resorts, was built in
1913 overlooking Asheville, North Carolina's sky-
line and the Blue Ridge Mountains. On the
National Register of Historic Places, the Inn is a
favorite year-round destination with its splendid
views, Old World charm, massive fireplaces, and
a long tradition of exceptional service and
hospitality.

Completely renovated and expanded in recent
years, the Inn offers 510 rooms, including 12
suites and 28 oversized Club Floor rooms, 50,000
square feet of meeting space, which includes two
ballrooms and 42 conference rooms. Amenities
include golf, tennis, two pools, Indoor Sports Cen-
ter, 10-station Paramount fitness center, shops,
fine dining and Children's Programs.

First opened for play in 1899, then redesigned
in 1923 by master golf course architect Donald
Ross, the 6,500 yard, par 70 Grove Park golf
course is a shotmaker's challenge with emphasis
on accuracy rather than power. From beneath the
crest of Sunset Mountain, the players' ascent
from the level front nine to the gentle slopes of
the back nine offer spectacular views. This course
is immaculately maintained and is considered
one of the finest conditioned courses in Western
North Carolina.

Bald Head Island Resort

Bald Head Island is a 2,000-acre boat-accessed residential and resort island community located off the southeastern coast of North Carolina at the mouth of the Cape Fear River. It is part of the Smith Island complex, which includes Bluff Island, Middle Island, and a 10,000-acre salt marsh preserve. Bald Head Island accommodations are available in nearly 200 lovely rental homes, cottages and condominiums, and in the 15-room Marsh Harbour Inn. Bald Head Island offers a number of different dining options, from casual open-air eateries to more formal dining.

Bald Head Island's Recreation Department coordinates activities for island residents and resort guests year-round. At the center of social and recreational life on the island is the gracious Bald Head Island Club with its outstanding sports facilities. Yachtsmen enjoy a 10-acre marina that offers quick access to the Intracoastal Waterway, Cape Fear River and Atlantic Ocean.

Bald Head Island's championship 18-hole golf course wraps 6,855 yards around freshwater lagoons, through a spectacular maritime forest and across dunes overlooking the Atlantic Ocean. In the midst of this splendid scenery, most golfers find the biggest challenge is keeping an eye on the ball. A slope rating of 139 and a course rating of 74.3 puts it in the top 20 percent of courses in difficulty. Golf Packages and daily rates are available.

Address: P.O. Box 3069, Bald Head Island, 28461
Phone: 910-457-7270
1-800-234-1666
Fax: 910-457-3703
Web site: http://www.baldheadisland.com
No. of Rooms: 215
Rates: Inquire
Restaurant: The Club Dining Room, River Pilot Cafe & Lounge, Eb & Flo's, The Pelicatessen, Island Chandler Deli
Bar: Lounge
Business Fac.: 7 meeting rooms, 2,500 sq. ft. of meeting rooms, banquet capacity for 120 people.
Sports Fac.: Tennis courts, Boating, Marina, Beach, Swimming pool
Location: Off the coast of North Carolina, it is a 200 acre residential and resort community.

Course: Bald Head Island Golf Course (6855)
No. of Holes: 18
Guest Policy: Guests welcome, Cost of ferry included in fees
Club House: 910-457-7310
Fees: ↑↑
Reservations: Accepts reservations 7 days in advance
Season: Open all year

Hound Ears Club

Address: P.O. Box 188, Blowing Rock, 28605
Phone: 828-963-4321
Fax: 828-963-7566
E-mail: houndears@boone.net
Web site: http://www.houndears.com
No. of Rooms: 28
Rates: $$
Sports Fac.: Heated outdoor pool in secluded natural grotto, Har-Tru tennis courts
Location: A secluded spot in the Blue Ridge Mountains

Course: Hound Ears (6327, par 72)
No. of Holes: 18
Guest Policy: Closed to the public
Club House: 828-963-5831
Fees: ↑↑
Reservations: Reservations available 2 days in advance
Season: April-mid November
Carts: Carts included in fees

Hounds Ears. An intriguing name, an intriguing place. The name comes from a unique rock formation resembling huge ears that dominate the mountain ridge above the club. The Lodge has a cozy, intimate atmosphere, where the Blue Ridge Mountains of Western North Carolina seem to come right to the door. It's a rather small four-season resort, remote and secluded, yet offering an atmosphere where service and comfort are at a premium. Where the staff remembers your name, and your bed is turned down each evening.

Guests in the lodge will enjoy bedrooms opening onto balconies with panoramic views of the golf course and Grandfather Mountain beyond. Longer stays can be arranged for clubhouse suites, chalets and condominiums. The dining room is intimate, done in sea-greens and warm garden colors, but doesn't lack excitement when Gene Fleri plays the organ, and a staff of enthusiastic young people are serving tables. Rainbow trout so fresh it practically quivers is available most evenings, and the ice cream pie is decadent. Piano and organ favorites can be enjoyed in the lively Brown Bagg Lounge, and the dance floor is known as the hot spot of Blowing Rock!

Swimming at Hound Ears is an adventure not to be missed! Just finding the pool is a feat, but you'll understand why it's so remote. The huge rock grotto adjoining the pool and pavilion create a setting of unsurpassed natural beauty, no matter what the hour. Excellent stables and bridle trails, are located in Cone National Park, a few miles from the club.

This is antique and craft country, or if old railroads fascinate you, the Tweetsie but a whistle stop away. Glendale Springs, famous for frescoes, is nearby, as is Crabtree, Tennessee, site of Roan Mountain.

Golf here is on one of the most interesting and scenic mountain courses in America. Water comes into play on seventeen holes—in the form of streams, lakes and rushing waterfalls. Expect a few hills, but it's pretty flat for the area, and thirteen of the holes are dog legs. The 15th is extraordinary—a par 3 of 110 yards with a sixty foot vertical drop, and water everywhere! Four bunkers await your finesse with a sand wedge.

High Hampton Inn & Country Club

Originally the private summer home of the Hamptons, the High Hampton retains a proud history that goes back to the 19th century. Friends of the Hamptons enjoyed hunting, fishing, relaxing, and gracious hospitality on the 1200-acre estate when General Wade Hampton was head of the household. Today, guests from around the world are privy to their private getaway hidden high in the Cashiers Valley of the Blue Ridge Mountains.

Under the protection of Rock Mountain and Chimney Top Mountain, the beauty of North Carolina has been preserved in this lush green valley. Even the way food is prepared is untainted here. High Hampton's menu features American cuisine with selected original recipes from their own kitchen. Breads, rolls, muffins and biscuits are homemade. Even the fresh vegetables and herbs that go into each dish are home grown in the Inn's own gardens.

You'll have plenty of opportunities to enjoy the beautiful outdoors. Not only is golfing plentiful, but there are eight fast-dry tennis courts ready for play. Sweeping vistas and a profusion of wildflowers enhance the joy of hiking on miles of well-marked trails. And water sports such as swimming, sailing, canoeing, rowing and pedal boating on Hampton Lake are always popular. Another favorite is fishing for rainbow trout, bass, and bream. With ample casting areas and a reputation as one of the best fly-fishing areas in the region, Hampton Lake is a mecca for fishing enthusiasts.

This par 71 course with bent grass greens is on a gently rolling plateau at 3600 feet in the Cashiers Valley of the Blue Ridge Mountains. It's one of nature's masterpieces, with a different view of woods, or lakes, or mountains, or of all three, from every hole. And the pleasure of playing it matches its beauty—whether it's spring's blossoms and wildflowers, summer's azure skies or autumn's fiery colors.

A bird's eye view shows the 8th hole as a very narrow finger of land pointing far into a lake. Talk about a water hazard! A shot struck just a shade too lightly or a shade too firmly will drop not into the cup but into the water. The par 3, 137 yard jewel requires intense concentration. You try to ignore the sailboats skimming by like butterflies, but you don't dare admire the scenery until after you've negotiated it.

Address: 138 Hampton Rd, P.O. Box 338, Cashiers, 28717
Phone: 828-743-2411 800-334-2551
E-mail: info@highhamptoninn.com
Web site: http://www.highhamptoninn.com
No. of Rooms: 117
Rates: Inquire
Restrictions: No pets (kennel accommodations available), No smoking in dining room
Restaurant: The Dining Room at High Hampton, The Overlook
Bar: Rock Mountain Tavern
Sports Fac.: Guided walks, Boating, Fishing, Fitness Trail, High Hampton Golf School, 2 putting greens, Practice range, Sailing
Location: 10 miles east of Highlands, North Carolina

Course: High Hampton Golf Course (6012)
No. of Holes: 18
Club House: 800-334-2551
Reservations: Call for reservations
Season: Open all year

Ballantyne Resort

Address: 10000 Ballantyne
Commons Pkwy, Charlotte, 28277
Phone: 704-341-GOLF
Web site: http://www.
ballantyneresort.com
No. of Rooms: 216
Rates: Inquire
Restaurant: Dining Room
Bar: Lobby Bar
Business Fac.: Complete banquet
and conference facilities for up to
500
Sports Fac.: Dana Rader Golf
School, Ballantyne Spa
Location: Just south of Charlotte

Course: Ballantyne (7034, par 72)
No. of Holes: 18
Guest Policy: Private except for
students, members and resort
guests
Club House: 704-544-9755
Fees: ↑↑
Reservations: 2 days in advance
Season: Set to open summer 2001
Carts: Carts included in fees

North Carolina has long been known for its great
golf resorts, and in recent years Charlotte-Dou-
glas International Airport's 500 daily flights have
made Charlotte the major "gateway to the south."
Ballantyne Resort Hotel is scheduled to open the
summer of 2001, and is destined to become a
landmark facility attracting travelers from all corners of the globe. The 216-room hotel is one of the
first "urban resort" concepts in the country which
gives the option of flying in and being on the
course within an hour of landing.

When entering the hotel, guests will be
greeted by an expansive lobby featuring a two-
story palladian window and terrace overlooking
the 18th fairway of the golf course. Each of the
hotel's guestrooms will feature a choice of king or
double bed accommodations, ten-foot ceilings,
and extensive millwork with superlative fabrics
and case pieces. State-of-the-art technology will
be included throughout the building that will
include computer connections, high speed Internet access, direct-dial guestroom phones, as well
as in-room cordless phones for maximum flexibil-
ity. In addition, the hotel will offer 20 suites,
including two magnificent Presidential Suites
with marble entrance halls, antique furnishings
and artwork, lavish baths and spacious accommodations for in-suite dining and entertaining.

Land Design, Inc designed the golf course's
par 71 layout. The only golf course to offer resort
amenities between Asheville and Pinehurst, Ballantyne Resort offers players a choice from five
sets of tees over gently rolling terrain. Water and
winding creeks come into play often. Green fees
for this first-rate facility are amazingly affordable.
In addition to an outstanding golf course, the
resort and recreational complex includes an elegant 30,000-square-foot clubhouse that is filled
with antiques, a golf shop filled with the latest
golf fashions, locker rooms, a lounge, The Grill
Room restaurant for casual dining, and ample
meeting facilities.

Grandover Resort & Conference Center

The Grandover Resort has a broad array of recreational amenities, located on 1,500 acres of oak, pine and dogwood-covered hills, just 10 minutes south of Greensboro.

Elegantly appointed guestrooms and suites offer breathtaking views of our world class golf fairways. All guestrooms have a marble entry foyer, marble bathroom, custom tapestry designed exclusively for Grandover and a warm and eclectic blend of custom furnishing and upholstery. Each room has its own area rug inset in the carpeting to make guests feel more at home.

Relax your mind, tone your body and revitalize your spirit in the soothing Spa at Grandover. Enjoy a Swedish massage, mud wrap, skin care facials, tennis, racquetball, whirlpool, indoor/outdoor pool and a state of the art fitness center.

After a day on one of Grandover Resort & Conference Center's two championship golf courses, guests may enjoy an evening filled with delectable cuisine and views of the resort's golf courses—all in the relaxing, casually-elegant atmosphere of Di Valletta Dining Room.

The resort's two PGA championship courses, which are open for public play, are part of the 1,500-acre Grandover complex just south of Greensboro. The design firm of Graham and Panks International designed both courses. Grandover Resort & Conference Center was off to a great start earlier this year when North Carolina magazine rated its West course among the best new golf courses in the state, and Grandover East among the "Fabulous 40," and the praises keep coming. The East course has recently been named one of the finest public-access courses in the nation—and one of only 11 courses in North Carolina by *Golf Digest's* "The Best of Places to Play". The course received a four-star ranking by *Golf Digest*. Greensboro, NC, was also ranked second in the nation for the best golf in a metropolitan area.

Address: 1000 Club Rd, Greensboro, 27407
Phone: 336-294-1800
800-472-6301
Fax: 336-856-9991
Web site: http://www.grandoverresort.com
Rates: $$$
Restaurant: Di Valletta, Cafe Expresso, Billiard's Room
Bar: Colony Lounge, Raw Bar, Lobby Bar
Business Fac.: 45,000 sq ft of meeting space, includes boardroom and elegant ballroom. Conference Service Staff will assist in planning, and audio visual services area available
Sports Fac.: 4 tennis courts with lights, raquetball facilities, whirlpool, indoor/outdoor pool, state of the art fitness center, the Spa at Grandover
Location: Near almost everything in North Carolina

Courses: East Course (7100, par 72), West Course (6800, par 72)
No. of Holes: 36
Guest Policy: Open to public
Club House: 336-294-1800
Fees: ↑↑↑
Reservations: Call to make reservations
Season: Open all year

Etowah Valley Country Club

Address: P.O. Box 2150,
Hendersonville, 28793
Phone: 704-891-7022
800-451-8174
E-mail: evcc@etowahvalley.com
Web site: http://www.
etowahvalley.com
Rates: $
Restaurant: The Restaurant
Bar: Clubhouse Lodge
Business Fac.: Meeting/event space
for up to 75 people
Sports Fac.: Lighted putting greens,
driving range, heated swimming
pool, fitness center
Location: Western North Carolina

Courses: South (3507, par 36), West
(3601, par 36), North (3404, par 37)
No. of Holes: 27
Guest Policy: Open to public
Club House: 704-891-7141
Fees: ⌐
Reservations: Call for reservations
Season: Open all year
Carts: Carts available

This is a small (70 guests at a time) golf lodge. All the rooms are the same—large, spacious, each with a balcony overlooking the mountains and fairway. The shingled buildings cluster around a central lodge where breakfast and dinner are served. There are three putting greens, (one lighted), driving range, heated pool, clubhouse and meeting facilities for 75 people. As a lodge guest you can enjoy the racquet and health club facilities at a nearby club. The countryside, between the Blue Ridge and Great Smoky Mountains, is fertile and heavily wooded. Spring and fall are extraordinary, as soft blossoms become lush green, then are ablaze with fall color. The bent grass greens are probably some of the largest in the south—some as large as 9,000 feet, as the course winds through rolling valleys. The course is designed to eliminate ball crossover from one fairway to another, insuring uninterrupted play. Golfers encounter a combination of traps and natural hazards, such as meandering streams and duck ponds.

The Eseeola Lodge

This part of Appalachia in the Blue Ridge Mountains is quite picturesque. And, should you be here in late June, you'll be visually assaulted by an incredible display of rhododendrons in bloom. This is a rustic old lodge with a great personality and modern facilities, all in tranquil surroundings. Most rooms have their own porch, and all are tastefully appointed. Days are warm and ideal for sports and relaxation, and at night you'll snuggle under a warm blanket. Bring your tennis racket, hiking boots, bathing suit and a hearty appetite for the exceptional food you'll be served. There's a luncheon room at the Clubhouse, a card room and a recreational program for children during July and August.

Linville's population hovers around the four hundred mark, but fear not, there are some gems to explore. Between Blowing Rock and Boone is the "Tweetsie," a narrow gauge railroad surrounded by a frontier-type village and small amusement park. The Museum of North Carolina Minerals nearby has more than three hundred kinds of gems and minerals found locally.

The 18 hole course was designed by Donald Ross, unequivocally the most prominent golf architect of his day, and one of the most respected. Dating from 1929, the course is one of the highest east of the Mississippi, at 3,800 feet. Burl Dale, the head pro, is available for lessons before or after you tackle the 6, 286 yard challenge.

Address: P.O. Box 98, Linville, 28646
Phone: 828-733-4311
800-742-6717
Fax: 828-733-3227
Web site: http://www.eseeola.com
No. of Rooms: 24
Rates: $$$
Restaurant: Dining Room, dress code
Business Fac.: Pavilion for special occasions complete with catering service
Sports Fac.: Outdoor heated swimming pool, Croquet, Exercise room, 8 tennis courts, Children's playground and day camp, Hiking trails, Fishing
Location: In the heart of the Blue Ridge Mountains

Course: Linville Golf Club (6780, par 72)
No. of Holes: 18
Guest Policy: Call for playing privileges
Club House: 704-733-4363
Fees: ‖
Reservations: Call for reservations
Season: Open all year
Carts: Cart included in fees

Blue Ridge Preserve & Country Club

Address: PO Box 88, Linville Falls, 28647
Phone: 828-756-0020
877-626-0020
Fax: 828-756-4106
E-mail: thelodge@wnclink.com
Web site: http://www.
blueridgecc.com
No. of Rooms: 12
Rates: $
Business Fac.: Conference space, Catered gourmet meals, Business service center
Sports Fac.: Walking trails, White water rafting, Lake/fly fishing, Horseback riding, Hiking, Skiing nearby
Location: Near Linville Falls

Course: Blue Ridge Country Club (6862, par 72)
No. of Holes: 18
Guest Policy: Open to public
Club House: 828-756-7001
Fees: ┃
Reservations: Reservations available 5 days in advance
Season: All year
Carts: Cart included in fees

You enter the Preserve nestled between the Pisgah National Forest and the crystal Catawba River, under the sheltering arm of the Blue Ridge Mountains. Breathtaking natural beauty and moderate year round temperatures provide unlimited leisure pursuits for winter and warm weather sports enthusiasts. Located near Linville Fall's, the Preserve's 556 acres are meticulously planned to safeguard the natural beauty of the environment and to nurture its wildlife habitat. The Blue Ridge Preserve symbolizes the naturalist lifestyle of a community pledged to living in harmony with North Carolina's finest natural resources.

Crowned by the community clock tower, The Inn at Blue Ridge offers luxurious hospitality and amenities for the mountain traveler, the nature lover and the dedicated golfer. Each of the thirteen rooms is generously proportioned, with stone fireplace and private balcony overlooking the Catawba River and the Blue Ridge Preserve & Country Club golf course. The public rooms provide conference facilities, and catered gourmet meals are available for group functions. A variety of recreational opportunities are nearby, including white water rafting, lake fishing, fly fishing, horseback riding, and hiking. The popular winter ski areas of Banner Elk, Sugar and Beech Mountains are also convenient to the Inn.

Inspired by the beauty of the Preserve and with the charge to safeguard and enhance it's many striking natural features, the 6,862 yard, par 72 Championship Golf Course of unqualified appeal. Lloyd Clifton believes Blue Ridge is a strong statement to minimalism, which he practices in golf course design, and states, "the fact that this is a core design is a real plus for golfers to enjoy a pure golf experience in a beautiful, natural, and scenic environment." With the Catawba River in play on 8 of the 18 holes and mountain springs winding around broad curves of white sand, the golfer faces many challenging strategic choices. To play this excellently maintained and managed, semi-private course, open all year, in it's idyllic mountain setting, evokes a strong sense of tranquillity and well being.

Maggie Valley Resort

Bordered by the spectacular Blue Ridge and Great Smokey Mountains, Maggie Valley Resort sits on 35,000 sq. ft. of flower filled gardens. A haven for golfing vacations, the mountains also provide the perfect setting for group meetings and retreats, offering majestic beauty, solitude, and shelter from the temperature extremes. Stay in a quiet and peaceful guestroom with it's own balcony and cable TV, or one of the guest villas on the scenic back nine with 1 or 2 bedrooms, living room, dining area and furnished kitchen,

The resort's Valley Room serves up fine cuisine in a relaxed environment, and tons of fun during the weekend with live entertainment. Dine and converse while overlooking the front nine and the Great Smokey Mountains in the Pin High Lounge where, in season, a full country breakfast is served as well as lunch and cocktails. If you're just looking for a quick bite, try the snack shop for cold sandwiches, snacks, and beverages, or catch the Beverage Cart as it moves throughout the course.

If you're ready to take a break from golfing, spend the day on one of the two hard surface tennis courts adjacent to the golf course, put on your swimsuit and relax in the swimming pool, or have cocktails and snacks in the Chalet Game Room.

Enjoy the year round golf course as it wanders through the valley, rising to nine hundred feet on the back nine, with a breathtaking view of the landscaping. The golf course, rated "One of America's Best" by *Golfweek*, uses cool weather rye and blue grasses on the fairway, so it stays green year round. The golf course was chosen as one of only six courses in North Carolina to be honored as a "Top 50 Southern Resort Course" by *Southern Living Guide*.

Address: 1819 Country Club Road, P.O. Box 126, Maggie Valley, 28751
Phone: 828-926-1616
800-438-3861
E-mail: golf@maggievalleyresort.com
Web site: http://www.maggievalleyresort.com
No. of Rooms: 75
Rates: $
Restaurant: Valley Room
Bar: Pin High Pub
Business Fac.: Meeting and banquet facilities for up to 250, On-site professional sales and catering staff
Sports Fac.: Tennis, Golf, Skiing, Hiking, Putting green, Driving range,
Location: 1½ hours from Knoxville

Course: Maggie Valley Course (6336, par 72)
No. of Holes: 18
Guest Policy: Semi-private
Club House: 828-926-6013
Fees: ↑
Reservations: Book with resort stay or 1 day in advance
Season: Open all year
Carts: Carts included in fee

Pinehurst Hotel & Country Club

Address: P.O. Box 4000, Pinehurst, 28374
Phone: 800-672-4644
800-487-4653
Fax: 910-295-6546
E-mail: pinehurst.info@ourclub.com
Web site: http://www.pinehurst.com
No. of Rooms: 440
Rates: $$$
Restaurant: Carolina Dining Room, Donald Ross Grill, Holly Inn
Bar: Ryder Cup Lounge and Mulligan's sports bar and grill
Business Fac.: 23 meeting rooms, exhibit hall, conference coordinator
Sports Fac.: 18 clay and 6 hard surfacee tennis courts, Lake Pinehurst for swimming, boating and fishing, 5 Swimming pools, Croquet, Biking, Lawn bowling
Location: North Carolina Sandhills

Courses: Pinehurst No.1 (6102, par 73), No. 2 (7041, par 72), No. 3 (5662, par 70), No. 4 (7020, par 72), No. 5 (6827, par 72), No. 6 (7157, par 72), No. 7 (7125, par 72), No. 8 (7092, par 72)
No. of Holes: 144
Guest Policy: Open to public
Club House: 910-295-8141
Fees: ↑↑↑
Reservations: Call for reservations
Season: Open all year
Carts: Cart included in fees

Nestled amidst the tall pines and oaks in the sand hills of North Carolina, the Pinehurst Hotel and Country Club has played host to business and recreation since it opened in 1900. Guests came then, as they do now, to experience the mild climate, the gracious lifestyle, fine dining and their favorite sports. Roosevelt, Rockefeller, DuPont and Morgan found it the ideal place to relax … and so will you.

Recreation is important; you'll choose from sporting options that include exhilarating horseback riding on 75 miles of beautiful Carolina trails, nine shooting ranges for trap or skeet, tennis amid the swaying pines on 28 top courts, sailing and boating on a private 200-acre lake, and a complete health club. Don't miss the Golf Hall of Fame.

To golf enthusiasts, Pinehurst is synonymous with the game, for here in the "Golf Capital of the World," are seven championship courses—among the finest in the world. This celebrated legend, Number 2, features small, sloping greens, deep bunkers, loose sandy soil, and rough accented by "love grass." With new tees, bunkers and water hazards added to Ellis Maples' 1928 design, the 15th hole is perhaps the most pictured hole at Pinehurst.

Mid Pines Resort

Clarion Mid Pines is a full American Plan resort in a stately 66 year-old 3 story hotel flanked by the whispering pines and azaleas which have characterized this area for generations. About 70 miles south of Raleigh-Durham, it's a short 5 miles from the Moore County Airport. There are 118 rooms in the main building, which has a comfortable lounge, and a main dining room. A lovely luncheon buffet is served on the Terrace in warm weather. The Golf Course Villas, ranging from 1 to 10 bedrooms and overlooking the 10th fairway and green are the ideal spot for families.

A variety of shops in Southern Pines and neighboring Pinehurst invites browsers and serious shoppers alike. There are four lighted tennis courts, platform tennis, a driving range, practice greens, outdoor swimming pool, and an indoor game room within the resort.

The course was planned by Donald Ross, golf pro-turned-designer whose genius lay in his ability to adapt his expertise of the wet, windswept rugged links of Scotland to North Carolina's dry sandhills. His masterpiece at Pinehurst having opened in 1907, Ross laid out a narrow, tree-lined course in Southern Pines with small undulating greens. Mid Pines isn't particularly long or strenuous, but often the subtle undulations are difficult to read. The course has played host to several national championships, including the 1980 and 1985 Women's Southern Amateur, the 1986 Women's Western Senior Amateur, and the 1988 Women's Eastern Amateur.

Address: 1010 Midland Rd, Southern Pines, 28387
Phone: 919-692-2114
800-323-2114
Fax: 919-692-4615
E-mail: midpines@golflink.com
Web site: http://www.golflink.com/midpines/
No. of Rooms: 118
Rates: Inquire
Restaurant: Main Dining Room
Bar: Cosgrove's Lounge
Business Fac.: Audio-visual, Conference rooms, capacity 250
Sports Fac.: Tennis courts, Swimming pool, Platform tennis, Game room
Location: 250 acres of beautiful North Carolina countryside

Course: Mid Pines (6515)
No. of Holes: 18
Guest Policy: Open to hotel guests and outside play
Club House: 919-692-9362
Reservations: Advised to book well in advance
Season: Open all year
Carts: Caddies

Quail Hollow Hotel
& Conference Center

Address: 11080 Concord-Hambden
Rd, Painesville, 44077
Phone: 440-497-1100
800-792-0258
Fax: 440-497-1111
No. of Rooms: 167
Rates: Inquire
Restaurant: Formal and informal
dining as well as in-room dining is
availiable.
Business Fac.: Conference Facili-
ties
Sports Fac.: 2 Tennis Courts, indoor
pool, and health club with Cybex
equipment.
Location: Nestled among 700 acres
of wooded countryside

Summer is when Painesville's countryside bursts
to life with new vigor, golf courses turn a bright
green, jogging trails become a wonderland of discovery, and people from all over return to Quail
Hollow for another exciting vacation. Choose one
of 167 spacious accommodations, perhaps your
sentimental favorite, and gear up for good times
... on the tennis courts, 18-hole golf course,
swimming pool, and excellent dining.

Courses: #1 (6700), #2 (7190, par
72)
No. of Holes: 36
Guest Policy: Closed to the public
Club House: 440-552-1726
Fees: ⌐
Reservations: Call for reservations
Season: Open all year
Carts: Carts available

Shangri-La Golf Resort

Arrive at the Shangri-La Resort via your private plane and you'll be whisked to the main lodge by courtesy transportation. In the lobby you'll rind a terraced garden of flowing water fountains, rockeries, tropical plants all giving a peaceful start to your vacation.

Then settle into your home for the stay, be it a comfortable guest room or a 3-bedroom condominium. The rooms are scattered about the grounds in three separate buildings, some with patios or balconies. The perfect setting for a romantic getaway.

Excellent in cuisine is very important here, and there's plenty to choose from on the varied menus. The Greenery, R.D.'s Lobby Bar and Monkey's also have live entertainment during the summer.

Grand Lake O' the Cherokees, at the resort's edge, has 1,300 miles of shoreline, providing parasailing, waverunners, pontoon boat, yachts, ski boats and much more. If you want to explore the lakefront trails and the woods horseback rides and jogging are encouraged.

The Gold course has water in play on ten holes, but the fairways are wide, and the view of Grand Lake fantastic. The Blue Course is considered to be one of the top five courses in the midwest with narrow fairways and difficult greens. Shangri-La hosts the annual Mickey Mantel Celebrity Charity Golf Classic which benefits the Make-A-Wish Foundation.

The kids program here is called the Pirate's Crew, and offers supervised activities.

Address: Route 3, Hwy 125 South, Afton, 74331
Phone: 918-257-4204
800-331-4060
Fax: 918-257-5619
No. of Rooms: 312
Rates: $
Restaurant: Greenery Restaurant, Waters, Pool Hut, Golden Leaf
Bar: Lake View Lounge
Business Fac.: 20 Meeting rooms, Fax, Copy service
Sports Fac.: Exercise Room, Swimming pools, Beach, Marina, Boating
Location: Resort on 650 remote acres of Oklahoma

Courses: Blue (7012, par 72), Gold (5932, par 70)
No. of Holes: 36
Guest Policy: Open to public
Club House: 918-257-4204
Fees: †
Reservations: Reservations available 1 day in advance
Season: Open all year
Carts: Carts included in fees

Bandon Dunes

Address: Round Lake Dr, Bandon, 97411
Phone: 541-347-4380
888-345-6008
E-mail: webmaster@ bandondunesgolf.com
Web site: http://www. bandondunesgolf.com
No. of Rooms: 21
Rates: $$
Restaurant: Bandon Dunes
Bar: The Tufted Puffin Lounge, The Bunker
Sports Fac.: Hot tub, Exercise room, Golf
Location: Two miles north of Bandon, Oregon on the southern Oregon coast

Course: Brandon Dunes (7398)
No. of Holes: 18
Club House: 888-345-6008
Reservations: Call for reservations
Season: Open all year

At Bandon Dunes, not only will you discover golf as it was meant to be, but you'll also enjoy a relaxing resort experience and a wealth of activities. The Lodge includes 15 single rooms, each with one queen bed. Additionally, there are four larger single rooms and two 4-bedroom suites. Some rooms have golf course and ocean views, while others have views of the dunes and surrounding woods. The lodge features spa facilities, sports lounge, complete Pro Shop and the outstanding Gallery Restaurant, serving fresh Pacific Northwest cuisine and the finest cuts of choice beef this side of Kansas City.

Guests have full access to the fitness room, locker rooms, sauna, and Jacuzzi; massages are available upon request. The town of Bandon offers a variety of attractions, including the West Coast Game Park, Bandon Cheese Factory, Cranberry Sweets, horseback riding on the beach, charter boat fishing, windsurfing, kayaking, and scenic Beach Loop Drive.

The course at Bandon Dunes is a links course perched 100 feet above the Pacific Ocean on the Southern Oregon Coast. Designed by Scotsman David McLay Kidd, seven holes run along the edge of the bluff overlooking the beach and all eighteen holes offer breathtaking ocean views. The course tips out at 7,326 yards, with six sets of tees to guarantee golfers of all abilities a challenging and fair experience.

The Riverhouse

At The Riverhouse, you have everything at your fingertips. Nestled along the beautiful Deschutes River in the heart of Bend, The Riverhouse features an array of amenities including recreation, dining and nearby shopping.

Choose from our 220 spacious guestrooms with one or two bedrooms, kitchens, fireplaces and even spas. Room amenities include; cable color TV, VCR, ShowTime, movie video rentals, direct dial phones (free local calls), voice mail, laundry facilities, 24 hr. Front Desk service, Wake-up service, daily housecleaning, in-room coffee, complimentary welcome beverage and room service.

The Riverhouse offers a wide variety of dining choices. Enjoy lunch or your favorite beverage, on our riverview deck. Come experience the best steak money can buy at our premium steak house, "Crossings," Central Oregon's only restaurant using USDA prime beef exclusively. Crossings desserts are prepared fresh in our own bakery and are famous for their quality, uniqueness and use of fresh Oregon ingredients. After dinner, dance the night away to some of the Northwest's best entertainment in our popular Fireside Nightclub. The Fireside also offers a of variety food choices. Also on property is our Poolside Café and a Chinese Restaurant.

Renowned golf course architect, Robert Muir Graves, designed our River's Edge Golf Course. River's Edge is nestled along the beautiful Deschutes River and Awbrey Butte. One of the highest rated courses in Oregon, each hole is unique, offering new and different challenges. With a slope rating of 137 and four sets of tees make this resort course fun for golfers of all skill levels. You'll find breathtaking scenery throughout the course including the Deschutes River & Central Oregon's high deserts, a waterfall on #5 and a spectacular view of Mt. Hood, Mt. Jefferson and Smith Rocks.

Try River's Edge for a unique golfing experience.

Address: 3075 N. Highway 97, Bend, 97701
Phone: 541-389-3111
800-547-3928
E-mail: reservations@ riverhouse.com
Web site: http://www. riverhouse.com
No. of Rooms: 220
Rates: $
Restaurant: Crossings Premium Steakhouse, Poolside Cafe and Lounge, Mai's Chinese Restaurant
Business Fac.: Convention & banquet facilities for up to 400
Sports Fac.: Indoor/outdoor heated pools, Spa, Indoor swim spa, Saunas, Golf, Nautilus exercise room, Jogging trails, Tennis
Location: Nestled along the Deschutes River in the heart of Bend

Course: River's Edge
No. of Holes: 18
Club House: 800-547-3928
Fees: †
Reservations: Call for reservations
Season: Open all year

Lodge at Black Butte Ranch

Address: P.O. Box 8000, Black Butte Ranch, 97759
Phone: 541-595-6211
800-452-7455
E-mail: info@blackbutteranch.com
Web site: http://www.
blackbutteranch.com
Rates: $
Restrictions: no pets
Restaurant: The Restaurant at Black Butte Ranch, open at set times varying from 8 am to 9:30 pm
Sports Fac.: 4 Swimming Pools, 19 Tennis Courts, Equestrian Center, 16 Miles of biking/hiking trails, Trout Pond
Location: 8 miles West of Sisters, Or on Hwy 20

Courses: Big Meadow (6880, par 72), Glaze Meadow
No. of Holes: 18, 1
Guest Policy: Resort guests and guests of property owners only
Club House: 541-595-1500
Fees: ⸙⸙
Reservations: 800-399-2322
Season: Open all year
Carts: Carts available

This is one of those seldom-found treasures that you hope no one else discovers—at least not for a while.

Located amid ponderosa pines in high plateau country a few miles from Sisters, the wood-and-glass resort and residential community is the kind of place people keep returning to year after year. Accommodations are in condominiums or rental homes, many with spectacular views of snow-covered volcanic peaks, a lake or well-kept lawns. Don't miss dinner in the main lodge's dining room, dubbed "most romantic restaurant in central Oregon." Children can't wait to come back—the supervised recreation center and a program in conjunction with nearby Camp Tamarack during summer deserves an A+ in quality. On the premises you'll find a general store, four swimming pools, over 16 miles of paved jogging and biking trails, 19 outdoor tennis courts, and a stable of the ranch's amiable horses.

Golfers love it here—no outside events are held on the two 18 holes course, Big Meadow and Glaze Meadow, and there are various programs available with a staff of four PGA pros. Robert Muir Graves was responsible for Big Meadow, which came after Glaze Meadow, designed by Gene C. "Bunny" Mason. They're gently rolling as they zigzag through tall pines, and aspen, and across water. You'll have ample time to gaze upward for a glimpse of geese in flight and some awesome views of the Sisters.

Westin Salishan Lodge & Golf Resort

The natural beauty of the central Oregon coast, dense forests, lagoons, pounding ocean, rocky beaches, is what makes this naturalist's haven special. No crowds, glitter, high tech or pollution. Salishan comes from salish, ancient Pacific Northwest Indian for "coming together from diverse points to communicate in harmony."

200 rooms in low-rise wooden villas overlook a most stupendous landscape of woods, fairways or the untouched Pacific coast. Rooms are designed for privacy, with fireplaces, balconies, lithographs by local artists, and extra-large bathrooms.

The tri-level dining room is worthy of all accolades, stars, and recognition. Here is Pacific Northwest seafood at its best. The menu is unpretentious, reflecting the freshest and artfully prepared offerings from the sea. Salmon is the name of the game here, you'll find it everywhere, from the breakfast menu's bagels with smoked salmon to barbecued, or baked in a delicate puff pastry. The wine cellar is impressive; lengthy, well-rounded, and reasonably priced. Besides exploring the coves and trails of the property, there are tennis courts, indoor pool and a completely equipped exercise center. In addition, you can try fly fishing, deep sea fishing, shell-collecting, crabbing or clamming. And imagine the thrill of seeing gray whales migrating, or harbor seals sunning themselves. Across the highway is an intriguing assortment of shops, and there are picturesque little towns down the coast.

No earth movers had a hand in this 18 hole course, patterned in the Scottish tradition in harmony with nature. Rugged and challenging, the course winds around, highlighted by ocean views, lofty pines and sparkling lakes. Resort guests have priority tee times on the course. Players who prefer to carry their clubs love to play here, carts aren't mandatory. Number 13, a 402 yard par 4, will take a straight drive between the troublesome dunes on both right and left. The green is guarded by a gargantuan H-shaped trap, and should you hook it, you'll be in Siletz Bay with the seals.

Address: Highway 101, Gleneden Beach, 97388
Phone: 541-764-2321
888-SALISHAN
E-mail: reservation@salishan.com
Web site: http://www.salishan.com
No. of Rooms: 205
Rates: $$$
Restaurant: Cedar Tree Restaurant
Bar: Wine Cellar, Attic Lounge
Business Fac.: conference space available, Outward Bound Professional workshops
Sports Fac.: tennis, swimming pool, jogging/hiking trails, gym
Location: on Hwy 101 between Lincoln City and Newport, about 2 hours from Portland

Course: Salishan Golf Links (6453)
No. of Holes: 18
Guest Policy: Guests and public welcome
Club House: 800-890-0387
Fees: T
Reservations: Call for reservations
Season: Open all year
Carts: Cart rentals available

Running Y Ranch Resort

Address: 5115 Running Y Rd,
Klamath Falls, 97601
Phone: 541-850-5500
888-850-0275
Fax: 541-850-5593
E-mail: webmaster@
eagle-crest.com
Web site: http://www.runningy.com
No. of Rooms: 83
Rates: $
Restaurant: Schatzies on the
Green—fine dining, Sugar Pine
Cafe—breakfast and lunch
Business Fac.: 2,785 square feet of
meeting space
Sports Fac.: 13,000 square foot
sports center includes: pools, tennis,
basketball, fitness center, and
massage
Location: Tucked along Upper
Klamath Lake

Course: Running Y
No. of Holes: 18
Guest Policy: Open to public,
owners and guests
Club House: 888-850-0261
Fees: ⅂
Reservations: Call for reservations
Season: Open all year

High above Payne Canyon overlooking the 10th
fairway and the wetland restoration of Caledonia
Marsh, The Lodge at the Running Y has all the
amenities you'd expect from a world-class estab-
lishment. Comfortable rooms and suites, state-of-
the-art conference and boardrooms, fine dining,
and a tradition of exceptional service. Reasonable
rates and generous amenities make even business stays a pleasure.

Keep fit year round at their extensive sports
facility. Slip into the indoor pool, hot tub, or kids'
pool. Get your heart pounding with weights and
cardio equipment, or take an aerobics class. Hit
the basketball or tennis courts, then wrap it all up
with a massage in the spa. The Sports Center has
a snack bar, arcade, even a Saturday Cub Club
program to keep the kids busy.

Tucked along Upper Klamath Lake's banks in
the shadow of the regal Cascade Range, the Running Y golf course epitomizes Arnold Palmer's
design philosophy of blending the course with the
natural environment. The experience is so spectacular, Running Y has been named by *Golf Digest*
Magazine the Best New Public Course in America.
Amble along meadows and through the restored
wetlands of the front nine. Play beside lakes,
woodlands and into Payne Canyon on the back.
With five tee boxes at each hole, the champion-
ship-caliber course welcomes varied skill levels.

Sunriver Resort

Sunriver Lodge and Resort is the quintessential Oregon High Desert resort. Located about 160 miles southeast of Portland on the sunny side of the Cascade Mountains, guests can arrive by auto, private plane on Sunriver's 5500-foot paved, lighted runway, or commercial airline into Redmond (35 miles north).

Recreational diversions include two swimming pool complexes, 28 plexi-paved tennis courts, indoor racquet club, 26 miles of paved bicycle paths, a marina for whitewater rafting and canoeing, horseback riding, hot tubs and sauna, and the Sunriver Village Mall with a wide variety of shops and restaurants.

You'll find gourmet high desert cuisine and a lavish Sunday champagne brunch in the Meadows Dining Room, one of only two Mobile Four-Star restaurants in the state; casual dining at the Provision Company Restaurant and nightly entertainment at the Owl's Nest Lounge.

The sunny central Oregon climate makes Sunriver an ideal year-round vacation destination, but particularly exciting are the spring and fall when you can combine golf with snow-skiing, biking, tennis. There are endless possibilities for your active lifestyle.

The Sunriver North Course, designed by Robert Trent Jones II, was recently ranked by *Golf Digest* as one of the Top 25 Resort Courses in America. The North Course, visited every year by the pros for the PGA Sunriver Oregon Open, combines the native central Oregon shrubbery and pines with lush fairways, rock outcropping, white sand, lakes and bunkers that hug the edge of the green. Every hole is designed with multi-tees to offer challenge for golfers of all abilities.

Hard against the great meadow is the beginning and ending of the very challenging South Course. The rest of the course meanders through the Lodgepole pine trees, demanding straight, accurate shots. The fast, true, mounded greens will put your putting touch to the test. Along with the fantastic views of Mt. Bachelor, you will enjoy the clean, fresh air and the bright blue skies of the Oregon Cascades while playing the perfectly manicured fairways.

Address: P.O. Box 3609, Sunriver, 97707
Phone: 503-593-1221
800-547-3922
Fax: 503-593-5498
E-mail: info@sunriver-resort.com
Web site: http://www.sunriver-resort.com
Rates: Inquire
Restrictions: No pets
Restaurant: Sunriver Merchant Trader Cafe, Meadows at the Lodge, The Grille
Bar: Owls Nest
Business Fac.: Flexible meeting & banquet space, State-of-the-art equipment
Sports Fac.: Bike trails, 4 swimming pools, Academy of Golf, Hiking, Eco-Tours, Marina, Saddleback Stables, Tennis, White water rafting, Challenge Ropes Course, Snowshoeing, Snowmobiling, Ice skating
Location: 17 miles south of Bend

Courses: Crosswater (7683, par 72), Meadows (7012, par 71), Woodlands (6880, par 72)
No. of Holes: 54
Club House: 503-593-4402
Reservations: Call for reservations
Season: Open all year

Resort at the Mountain

Address: 68010 E. Fairway Ave,
Welches, 97067
Phone: 503-622-3101
800-669-7666
Fax: 503-622-5677
E-mail: information@theresort.com
Web site: http://www.theresort.com
No. of Rooms: 160
Rates: $
Restaurant: The Highlands
Restaurant
Bar: Quiet Bar
Business Fac.: Offers a full range of
meeting services
Sports Fac.: Golf, and full-sized
croquet and lawn bowling greens,
4 tennis courts, Outdoor pool,
Jacuzzi, Fitness Center, Volleyball,
Badminton, Horseshoes
Location: One hour from downtown
Portland

Courses: The Pine Cone Nine
(2822), The Thistle Nine (3480),
The Foxglove Nine (3128)
No. of Holes: 27
Club House: 800-669-4653
Fees: ⅂
Reservations: Call for reservations
Season: Open all year

Set amidst tall Douglas firs and the crystal
Salmon River, this 100 year old resort is at the foot
of Huckleberry Wilderness area in the Mt. Hood
National Forest. Imagine golfing on a finely manicured course in the morning and skiing on the
slopes of Mt. Hood the same afternoon.

Many of the rooms have fireplaces and are luxuriously furnished. A perfect, relaxing atmosphere in which you will be pampered awaits you
at this resort. The scenery is gorgeous and you'll
love the clean mountain air.

The restaurant offers an exquisite dining
experience, and is considered one of the best in
the Northwest.

The area is known for its fishing and river rafting. Horseback riding along the lush trails where
a deer may cross your path, is an especially nice
way to get acquainted with the area. Both summer and winter afford skiing, snowboarding, and
Nordic skiing. Then you can indulge in nature
hikes, picnics and mountain climbing. Plenty to
do here!

If you want a change nearby Columbia Gorge
has world class windsurfing and a sternwheeler.

The three nines are nestled at the base of
Hunchback Mountain, where you'll be able to
hear the river (and retrieve your wayward ball).
The fairways are very, very narrow and the greens
are difficult. Each of the nines has a different personality, but the Foxglove is considered the more
difficult nine.

Seven Springs Mountain Resort

More than 300 rooms and suites await guests in the main lodge, with apartments and townhouses less than a mile away. Its rustic charm and coziness, as well as good hunting, fishing, tennis, and swimming pools keep families returning.

Nearby attractions include Fallingwater, the Frank Lloyd home built over a waterfall, and Fort Necessity National Battlefield.

If you're planning a meeting or a major convention, just relax. The resort's highly proficient Group Sales office works with clients from the initial phone call to the meeting's adjournment. Staff members handles all meeting facilities and equipment needs, schedules recreational activities, and arranges food presentations.

Seven Springs Mountain Resort's spectacular 18-hole golf course stands majestically atop the Laurel Mountains. Tee off into a breathtaking view of the Laurel Highlands countryside while enjoying PA's finest resort experience. After a round of golf, stop in the Tee Top Lounge for a breathtaking two-state vista.

Address: RR#1 Box 110, Champion, 15622
Phone: 814-352-7777
800-452-2223
E-mail: reservations@7springs.com
Web site: http://www.7springs.com
No. of Rooms: 385
Rates: $$
Restaurant: Helen's, Oak Dining Room, Slopeside Grill, The Coffee Shop, The Pizza & Pastry Shop, Adolph's & more
Business Fac.: Versatile conference facilities, Professional planning staff, Multi-media support, State-of-the-art equipment, GO Team
Sports Fac.: Bowling Center, Golf, Massage, Handball/raquetball courts, Hot tubs, Indoor pool, Miniature golf, Mountain Fitness Room, Rollerskating, Swim Program, Sleigh rides, Snow tubing, Skiing
Location: One hour's drive from Pittsburgh, PA

Course: Seven Springs (6360, par 71)
No. of Holes: 18
Guest Policy: Open to public
Club House: 800-452-2223
Fees: 1
Reservations: Can make reservations 2 days in advance
Season: April–November
Carts: Gas or pull carts included in fees

Nemacolin Woodlands Resort & Spa

Address: 1001 LaFayette Dr, Farmington, 15437
Phone: 724-329-6154
800-422-2736
Fax: 724-329-6098
E-mail: reservations@nwlr.com
Web site: http://www.nwlr.com
No. of Rooms: 275
Rates: $$
Restaurant: Golden Trout, Lautrec, Seasons, Caddyshack, Hungry Moose Cafe, Gazebo, Tea Room
Bar: The Tavern, The Lobby Lounge, Diamond Lil's, Hitchin' Post Saloon
Business Fac.: 23,000 sq ft of meeting space includes 2 ballrooms, a 200-seat lecture hall, 23 meeting rooms, and a Business Center. Also available for functions is the LaFayette Gardens, Heritage Court, Sundial Lodge, Panorama Pavilion, and a Polo Field.
Sports Fac.: 4 tennis courts, 5 swimming pools, cross-country and downhill skiing in winter, and an Equestrian Center

Location: Laurel Highlands Mountain Region
Courses: Mystic Rock (6832), The Links (6643)
No. of Holes: 36
Club House: 800-422-2736
Fees: ↑↑↑
Reservations: Call for reservations
Season: April–November

At the spectacular Nemacolin Woodlands Resort & Spa, you'll discover luxurious accommodations and dazzling dining. Choose from the French Renaissance style Chateau LaFayette, the tastefully appointed Lodge, or the roomier accommodations of the one and two bedroom Townhouses. Nemacolin Woodlands Resort & Spa offers an impressive collection of restaurants to satisfy the tastes and moods of casual diners and culinary connoisseurs. From ice cream and sodas in P.J.'s to the fine dining in Lautrec, an array of food and beverage options will make any visit to Nemacolin Woodlands a memorable occasion.

The Activities Center has indoor and outdoor activities for all seasons and all ages. There's swimming, hiking, tennis, fly-fishing, an arcade, a golf simulator, virtual reality, and croquet. Help yourself to footballs, basketballs, soccer balls, bocce balls, horseshoes, volleyballs, badminton sets, shuffleboard equipment, and board games. There is also a shooting academy, an equestrian center and Mystic Mountain skiing. Don't forget to spoil yourself at the Woodlands Spa.

Mystic Rock sprawls majestically throughout Nemacolin's wooded acreage. Designed by the legendary

Pete Dye, this course promises golfers a challenge like no other. The 6,832-yard course was three years in the making, and received top honors from *Golf Magazine* and *Golf Digest* in its opening year. The Golf Academy is equipped with state-of-the-art technology designed to sharpen skills and improve any golfer's game, regardless of handicap.

Felicita Resort

The Inn at Felicita, a converted old barn, has all the charm of a country inn. Each room's décor features a different Waverly fabric, creating a warm and cozy ambiance. With its inviting central living room/breakfast area, the thirteen room Inn is perfect for a group, family reunions, small business retreats, wedding parties or just a get together of good friends. Meals at Felicita are an incomparable delight. Take your pick of The Felicita Room for elegant evening dining; The Grille for lunch and light dinner, the Spa Lounge for continental breakfast and healthy cuisine lunch, or the open-air delight of The Porch and The Patio.

Enjoy a luxurious experience in the spa, where professional technicians will soothe your body from head to toe. The Fitness Center and Spa are conveniently located in the same building and you may complement your workouts by utilizing the sauna and hot tub, or by purchasing relaxing and invigorating spa services such as a massage, body wrap, facial and/or therapeutic bath.

Felicita offers one of the country's most beautiful golf courses. In a mountainside setting, each hole is individually landscaped to represent a different garden scene—Zen (Japanese), Alpine, Topiary, English Park, and Spring. Designed by William and David Gordon, the 6610 yard, par 72 course has a 71.4 rating.

Address: 2201 Fishing Creek Valley Road, Harrisburg, 17112
Phone: 717-599-5301
888-321-3713
Web site: http://www.felicitaresort.com
Rates: Inquire
Restaurant: The Felicita Room, The Grille, The Porch and The Patio, The Pavilion
Bar: The Spa Lounge
Business Fac.: The Inn is perfect for small business retreats—13 rooms
Sports Fac.: The Fitness Center and Spa—complete facilities, Hiking and biking
Location: At the foot of the Blue Mountains

Course: Felicita (6610, par 72)
No. of Holes: 18
Guest Policy: Semi-private
Club House: 717-599-5301
Fees: Inquire
Reservations: Call for reservations
Season: Open all year

Woodloch Pines Resort

Address: 1 Woodloch Drive, Hawley, 18428
Phone: 570-685-2100
800-572-6658
Web site: http://www.woodloch.com
No. of Rooms: 185
Rates: Inquire
Restaurant: Four restaurants with children's menu available, Boat House Restaurant off-site
Bar: Nightclub
Business Fac.: Complete conference facilities with meeting rooms, banquet facilities, and meeting equipment, Weddings
Sports Fac.: Indoor/outdoor swimming pools, Waterskiing, Bikes, Hayrides, Fitness room, Nature trails, Jacuzzi, Massage, Tennis courts
Location: On Lake Wallenpaupack

Course: Woodloch Springs (6579)
No. of Holes: 18
Guest Policy: Open only to resort guests, property owners and renters
Club House: 570-685-2100
Fees: ┃┃
Reservations: Reservations strongly suggested
Season: Open all year
Carts: Cart included in fees

Woodloch Pines, located just 5 minutes from the resort, is a spectacular residential/recreational community built around a nationally acclaimed, 18-hole championship golf course. Open since 1992, Woodloch Springs offers many unique real estate and investment opportunities as well as private golf club memberships, which give access to the magnificent Clubhouse boasting a variety of excellent dining options and a fully-stocked pro shop. Packages include all activities and amenities, entertainment, 3 meals per day and plenty of fun.

Woodloch Pines has a new recreation building that features an indoor multi-purpose room with rubberized floor for basketball, volleyball and other activities. Plus an additional video game room with itneractive games, ping pong tables and pool tables. A number of outdoor activities abound. Enjoy bicycling, boating, fishing, hiking, tennis, and skiing to name a few.

The spectacular championship, 18-hole, par 72 layout winds its challenging way across 6,579 yards of fern-carpeted forests, lush wetlands and broad upland meadows. Four sets of tees on every hole, sculptured bunkers and water holes, miles of cart paths and bridges reflect the attention to detail. The outstanding, signature 14th hole presents a dramatic carry over "Hell's Gate Gorge" carved from the rugged mountainside by a rushing stream 200 feet below. Three PGA pros are available for lessons.

Hotel Hershey

A grand hotel in the finest European tradition, The Hotel Hershey is tailored to American tastes. It's home to two of Central Pennsylvania's most outstanding restaurants, The Circular Dining Room, and The Fountain Café. You'll enjoy perfectly prepared and exquisitely presented food, even at poolside. Elegance and graceful appointments are everywhere, and you can expect impeccable service. Amenities include limousine service 24-hour room service, complete business services, babysitting, valet laundry service, and concierge service.

At the Hotel Hershey, activities are planned with families in mind. The scenic grounds are perfect for a nature hike on winding pathways, bird watching, bicycle riding, or cross-country skiing. There's all day fun at the Hotel Hershey and of course, there's complimentary shuttle service to Hershey Park. Other activities include outdoor/indoor pools, basketball court, carriage rides, a fitness facility, whirlpool and sauna, horseshoes, bocce balls, tennis court and more!

Golf in Hershey is noted for its impeccable greens, mature fairways, and outstanding reputation. At the Hotel Hershey, enjoy the nine holes of this 2,680-yard, par 34 course that winds through a pine forest on the Hotel grounds.

Address: Hotel Road, P.O. Box 400, Hershey, 17033
Phone: 717-533-2171
800-HERSHEY
Fax: 717-534-8888
E-mail: info@herseypa.com
Web site: http://www. HersheyPA.com
No. of Rooms: 235
Rates: $
Restaurant: The Fountain Cafe, Circular Dining Room
Business Fac.: Full-service Business Center, 23,000 sq. feet of meeting space
Sports Fac.: 2 pools, 3 tennis courts, Basketball court, Cycling, Tobagganing, Nordic skiing, Lawn Bowling, Golf
Location: 90 miles east of Philadelphia in Hershey

Courses: West Course (6860, par 73) Private, East Course (7061, par 71) Private, South Course (6146, par 70) Public, Hotel Hershey (2680, par 34) and Spring Creek (2318, par 33)
No. of Holes: 72
Guest Policy: The South Course is public, Guests of Hotel Hershey can use other two course
Club House: 717-533-2464
Fees: ⊺
Reservations: Can make reservations 180 days in advance
Season: April–November
Carts: Carts included in fees

Cliff Park Golf Course and Inn

Address: 155 Cliff Park Road, Milford, 18337
Phone: 570-296-6491
800-225-6535
Fax: 570-296-3982
E-mail: info@cliffparkinn.com
Web site: http://www.cliffparkinn.com
No. of Rooms: 20
Rates: $$
Restaurant: The Restaurant at Cliff Park Inn
Bar: The Bar
Business Fac.: Clubhouse meeting room with both formal and informal meeting areas, Audio-visual equipment, Message center, Copiers, Computers
Sports Fac.: Full service Pro shop, Cross-country ski trails and ski shop
Location: 600 acre estate surrounded by deep woods and cliffs

Course: Cliff Park (3115)
No. of Holes: 9
Guest Policy: Open to public
Club House: 570-296-6491
Fees: ⌐
Reservations: Call for reservations
Season: Open April–October
Carts: Yes, pull carts and carts available

The fifth generation of Buchanan family innkeepers, headed by Harry Buchanan III, continues to lavish Cliff Park Inn with love and attention. The original farmhouse, with its wide floorboards, cozy parlor, and working hearths includes a commodious living room, filled with family heirlooms, and two separate dining rooms. Each of the eighteen guestrooms comes complete with private bath, climate control and private telephone — two feature gas fireplaces — and all truly reflect this classic Inn's long and rich history. Renowned for their fine cuisine and warm atmosphere, Cliff Park is the ideal place for a relaxing romantic getaway, country wedding, or productive business meeting.

Throughout the year, recreational pastimes abound. Golf spring through fall, cross-country ski on the surrounding 500 acres, or hike the seven miles of marked trails. Individual or group instruction, as well as a golf school are provided by the resident golf professional. Nearby you can enjoy hunting, bicycling, and swimming; or fish, canoe and white-water raft on the scenic Delaware River.

The Cliff Park Golf Course was the first golf course in America started by a woman. It has rolling hills, wide fairways and very fast greens. The course is a challenge to experienced golfers, yet isn't too intimidating for the novice. The course is a long 9 holes (3,115 yards), and two of the Par 5's are over 500 yards.

Pocono Manor Resort

Located in a setting of rolling hills, Pocono Manor has constantly striven to maintain its high standard of excellence and elegance. The Manor has been nominated and designated as a National Historic District, and you can certainly enjoy Early American design here.

The Manor prides its on excellence of service. A wonderful place for your next gathering, whether it be a corporate retreat, convention of smaller affair.

The Manor was purchased by Art Wall (won the 1959 Masters) and is a lovingly run family concern. Greg Wall is the director of golf, and you might want to benefit from his golf schools.

The East Course began in 1902, but Donald Ross did the complete design in 1919, then the West Course by George Fazio came along in 1965.

The West Course is the easier playing one here, but whichever one you play (if you're foolish enough not to play both) you'll find lots of water sloping terrain, very narrow fairways, and sloping greens. #7 on the East Course is the signature hole here, only 77 yards and just about the toughest hole anywhere, people come from all over to make a hole-in-one on this hole; hardly any one even makes par!

Address: Pa Hwy. 314, PA Hwy. 314, Pocono Manor, 18349
Phone: 570-839-7111
800-233-8150
Fax: 570-839-0708
E-mail: info@poconomanor.com
Web site: http://www. poconomanor.com
No. of Rooms: 257
Rates: $$
Restrictions: for children 7 years of age and under there is a $25 per day service charge
Bar: available
Business Fac.: board rooms, tiered lecture hall, grand ball room
Sports Fac.: tennis courts, outdoor pool and sauna, gym, ice skating rink, cross country trails, raquetball, volley ball, bocci ball
Location: atop the Pocono Mountains

Courses: East Course (6480, par 72), West Course (6857, par 72)
No. of Holes: 36
Guest Policy: Open to public
Club House: 800-233-8150
Fees: ⌐
Reservations: Reservations available 7 days in advance
Season: Open all year
Carts: Carts available

Shawnee Inn

Address: One River Road, PO Box 67, Shawnee-on-Delaware, 18356
Phone: 570- 424-4000
800-SHAWNEE
Fax: 570-424-9168
E-mail: info@shawneeinn.com
Web site: http://www.
shawneeinn.com
No. of Rooms: 113
Rates: $
Restrictions: Two night minimum on weekends
Restaurant: Dogwood Dining Room, Charlie's Place and Riverdance dining experience, and local dining available
Bar: Charlie's Place—11:00am until 1:00am
Business Fac.: The Fairway House meeting facility, over a dozen conference spaces, computer lab with over 30 work stations.
Sports Fac.: NHL sized indoor ice arena, indoor and outdoor pool, softball field.
Location: On the Delaware River in the Pocono Mountains

Built in 1912 from the beginning, the Inn quickly became a summer retreat for the New York and Philadelphia carriage trade. Overlooking the beautiful Delaware River not far from Strouds-burg, and with the Delaware Water Gap National Recreation Area as its neighbor, this Pocono landmark invites you to enjoy its amenities. The inn offers rooms, suites or one of the 300 two-bed-room villas in the 2,200-acre resort.

For recreational activities during any season, the Shawnee Inn has them all. The river is a playground for rafting, canoeing, or tubing. Or swim in an indoor pool, play tennis day or night, try volleyball or basketball, or putt away on the mini-golf course. In addition, try hiking, horseback riding and fishing. Check out the Shawnee Playhouse featuring popular Broadway shows with a professional New York cast. You'll find a whole complex of Outlet stores 5 miles away, and the Pocono Raceway is half an hour's drive.

A. W. Tillinghast, or Tillie as he was known, designed the original course—many years before his masterpieces at Winged Foot, Quaker Ridge and Baltusrol in New Jersey. This is a course to enjoy the scenery—twenty seven holes with great expanses of forested mountain greenery and the Delaware on both sides. The course is the home of "The Swing's the Thing" Golf School. Arnold Palmer has played many rounds at Shawnee, and it was in the Shawnee Pro Shop that he met his wife.

Courses: Blue (3362, par 36), White (3227, par 36), Red (3438, par 36)
No. of Holes: 27
Guest Policy: Guests of the inn get discounted green fees
Club House: 800-SHAWNEE
Fees: ↑↑↑
Reservations: Call for reservations
Season: End of March through November
Carts: Cart included in fees

Toftrees Resort and Conference Center

Surrounded by its legendary championship golf course, Toftrees rises like a castle from the forest. The resort, nestled in central Pennsylvania's Happy Valley, is a few minutes from Penn State's campus, yet is isolated from city distractions. Featuring a large conference facility, 131 guest rooms (22 of them residence suites), and access to a nearby health club, business travelers and fans of the roaring Nittany Lions will find the resort a welcome respite.

Suites offer views of the tennis courts and the beautiful rolling hills of the valley. A glance at the spacious grounds reveal a heated outdoor pool, four lighted tennis courts, croquet, a parcourse and boat rentals. You can't miss the formal restaurant, Le Papillon, or a more casual eatery perfect for a snack after golf, and two lounges. Night owls will want to hoot it up in the bar with live entertainment, often a two-man combo.

After you've savored the small-town flavor of this college town with 30,000 students strong, you'll want to see some of the sights that have given this area the reputation as a choice retirement spot and one of the least stressful places in the country. You should see the cave at Bellefonte which you can explore by boat, a chapel owned by Christopher Columbus' family, and an incredible military museum.

Toftrees Golf, operated by Marriott, is ranked the #1 resort in Pennsylvania by *Golf Digest*. The course undulates through lovely wooded scenery in the shadows of the Nittany Lion and Allegheny mountain ranges. It's a long course—7,018 yards from the championship tees—and demands a strategic approach to the constant changes of elevation. The signature ninth hole requires a 220-yard carry over water before finding the fairway.

Address: One Country Club Lane, Route 322, State College, 16803
Phone: 814-234-8000
800-458-3602
Fax: 814-238-7093
E-mail: hotel@toftrees.com
Web site: http://www.toftrees.com
Rates: Inquire
Restaurant: Le Papillon, Down Under Steakhouse
Bar: The 19th Hole Bar & Grill
Business Fac.: boardrooms, dining halls for banquets/award ceremonies
Sports Fac.: tennis courts, swimming pool
Location: 3 miles from Penn State University

Course: Toftrees (7018, par 72)
No. of Holes: 18
Guest Policy: Open to public
Club House: 814-234-8000
Fees: ⊺
Reservations: Reservations available 14 days in advance
Season: April–November
Carts: Carts included in fees

Hyatt Regency Cerromar Beach

Address: Highway 693, Dorado, 00646
Phone: 787-796-1234
800-233-1234
Fax: 787-557-5048
Web site: http://www.hyatt.com/puerto_rico/dorado/hotels/hotel_cerro.html
No. of Rooms: 504
Rates: Inquire
Restrictions: No pets allowed
Restaurant: Swan Cafe, Orchid Room
Bar: El Yunque
Business Fac.: Administrative assistance, conference rooms, capacity 1500
Sports Fac.: Swimming pool, Tennis courts, Bicycles, Health spa
Location: North Coast

Courses: North Course (7047), South Course
No. of Holes: 36
Guest Policy: Call for availability
Club House: 787-796-1234
Reservations: May be made two days in advance
Season: Open all year

For some travelers, this mix-and-match sisterhood of two Hyatt resorts adjacent to each other, complete with nine restaurants, casinos, a full range of water sports, 28 tennis courts, gorgeous balmy weather, ocean views, and an incredible state-of-the-art river pool snaking around 4½ acres of tropical Eden isn't enough. But add 4 Robert Trent Jones championship courses, and a chance to explore a 100-mile island with tropical forests, 400 year old towns and a population flavored by Indian, Spanish and African influences, and you have a near-perfect vacation. Dorado Beach, a postcard-like stretch of Pristine coastal property was developed as a grapefruit and coconut plantation in 1905. Featured are 300 rooms and casitas along a two mile white crescent beach. Other attractions include a recreation program offering crab races, samba lessons and mah jongg, a health club, shops, and a full health spa. The piece de resistance at Cerromar Beach is the labyrinthian swimming pool, the world's largest, designed by water swami, Howard Fields.

The courses at Dorado Beach opened in 1958, and East Course has hosted many tournaments such as the 1961 Canada Cup, Pro-Am Invitational since 1963, and Chi Chi's Charity Classic. Some memorable holes: The 10th is a par-5 following the curve of the beach and meandering through forest; but nothing compares to the "Z" hole, that old devil #13. Its a par-5 double-dogleg of 540 yards. Reachable in two by big hitters, but you must play over two ponds to reach the green. The green has a pond in front, and the sparkling Atlantic as a backdrop. The West Course layout bobs in and out of tropical jungle, a constant reminder of plantation days. The second nine has no shortage of water hazards. Hole #15 is a mean 405 yard, par 4 which gives you a chance to carry a lake, avoid a dense jungle and spare the swaying palms on the right from a slice.

Cerromar's North and South Courses are gems built on flat, open land minus the plantation look. Robert Trent Jones returned in the early seventies to produce a par 72 layout with wide fairways ideal for fast play. Hole #7 is a dramatic par 3 175 yard test of skill and concentration. The green sits immediately above the rocky shore, and when the tide's high, too much club will be penalized by a watery grave. This is the host site of the Annual Puerto Rico Golf Classic.

Doral Resort at Palmas Del Mar

In some ways this sprawling Mediterranean-style resort geared to the sports-conscious is reminiscent of a sun-drenched college with an outstanding athletic program. As the Caribbean's most popular destination for tourists, you'll see why, as you head east out of noisy, crowded San Juan for Humacao, which has splendid beaches. Palmas del Mar, which calls itself "Caribbean Side of Puerto Rico" is large—all 2,750 acres of villas, two hotels and condos clustered around a championship golf course, marina, and 20-court tennis center. Conference planners are delighted to find there is a full range of meeting facilities with amenities for every interest group.

For starters, you'll find seven restaurants, a complete water sport center, a casino, an equestrian center, jogging trails, and bars and lounges for relaxing in the cool Caribbean breeze. The beach is uncluttered, long and palm-lined—perfect for children and those who relish romantic sunsets. Be sure to inquire about golf packages—we found some good ones.

Open for play in 1973, the course was designed by Gary Player, and Americans Arthur Davis and Ron Kirby. Winding through coconut groves and cane fields, with heavy tropical rough, lagoons, canals and devilish sand traps, the par 72 layout has the toughest five consecutive holes in the Caribbean, according to the club pro. The 13th is the most difficult par 3 around—uphill against the wind for 250 yards to a two-level green. They make the pin placement so subtle it is almost impossible to par the hole.

Address: P.O. Box 2020, Humacao, 00661
Phone: 787-852-6000
800-468-3331
Fax: 787-852-6320
E-mail: info@palmasdelmar.com
Web site: http://www.palmasdelmar.com
No. of Rooms: 290
Rates: Inquire
Bar: Bar
Business Fac.: Administrative assistance, Audio-visual, Conference rooms, capacity 700
Sports Fac.: Tennis courts, Swimming, Equestrian center
Location: On the island's southeast coast

Course: Palmas del Mar (6803, par 72)
No. of Holes: 18
Club House: 787-285-2255
Reservations: Call for reservations
Season: Open all year
Carts: Carts included in fees

Kiawah Island Resort

Address: P.O. Box 12910, Charleston, 29422
Phone: 843-768-2121
800-654-2924
Fax: 843-768-9339
Web site: http://www.kiawah-island.com
No. of Rooms: 150
Rates: $$$
Restaurant: Jasmine Porch, The Indigo House, Sweetgrass, Night Heron Grill, Dining Room at Osprey, and many more
Bar: The Topsider Lounge, Grandhall Lounge
Business Fac.: Governor's Hall, Brigatine Conference Center, Charleston Gallery, Shipwatch
Sports Fac.: 2 tennis clubs, 3 pool complexes, fitness center
Location: 21 miles from Charleston

Courses: Cougar Point, Turtle Point (5986, par 72), Osprey Point (6678, par 72), The Ocean Course (7296) and Oak Point
No. of Holes: 90
Guest Policy: Open to public
Club House: 803-768-2121
Fees: ↑↑↑
Reservations: Reservations available 5 days in advance
Season: Open all year
Carts: Carts included in fees

You'll be living in the midst of centuries-old buried treasures, a reputedly haunted mansion and one of the most well-preserved natural environments, all with the best that modern resort vacationing can provide at Kiawah Island Resort.

Present-day visitors to Kiawah Island enjoy virtually the same breathtaking first impression that the island's original guests, the Kiawah Indians, did. Only 21 miles from Charleston the semitropical character of this haven has remained virtually undisturbed for millennia. Indeed, many of the magnificent oak trees in Kiawah's dense maritime forest have been here for hundreds of years.

Island dining takes on a unique flavor all its own as outstanding dishes are prepared to complement the island's mild climate. At the Indigo House, American cuisine features excellent shrimp, lobster and succulent beef.

Few resorts sequestered in beautiful settings have been successful in combining aesthetics, a spirit of ecological preservation, and three very different courses offering exhilarating golf. Meet an exception. The first course, Marsh Point, was designed by Gary Player, who felt that a player needs a course where there's a chance to make pars, but will require touch to recover if he goes for the green and misses. The fifth here is a short par-4 bordering the inlet, and the green is waiting for you on a platform island smack in the middle of the marsh.

The Nicklaus course, Turtle Point, is longer, wider, easier to chip to, and every hole with a water hazard has a "bail-out," but it's by no means an easier eighteen. Number 12 is a favorite. It lacks water, but it's long, and rather tight, with a foreboding bunker like a big dog's paw fronting the green.

The scenery on Tom Fazio's Osprey Point Course is absolutely awesome. Sierra Clubbers and John Audubon himself could swap tales of myrtle, magnolias, egrets, otters, deer, and the osprey, a rare hawk who makes this region his home. The course is built on a series of islands, and you cross ten wooden bridges during a round. The last hole is a roller-coaster par-5 monster encompassing water, treacherous bunkers, and a narrow landing area for your second shot that won't be charitable to a hooker.

Inn at Harbour Town

Located adjacent to the world renowned Harbour Town Golf Links in the heart of Sea Pines Resort, the new sixty-room, casually upscale Inn at Harbour Town offers extensive guest services amidst luxurious comfort. Personal butlers are assigned to each floor to arrange any number of personal services, and each room has marble baths with freestanding glass-encased showers, cast iron tubs, two grand bathrobes, dual phone lines, data ports, personalized voice mail and messaging, internet access, refrigerator, coffee bar and 24-hour room service.

Guests of the Inn also receive preferred golf tee times and the lowest available green fees, discounted rates on bike rentals and Sea Pines' summer recreation program, use of Sea Pines Resort swimming pools and complimentary court time at the Sea Pines Racquet Club.

Every year, the top talent in the PGA takes to the fairways of famed Harbour Town Golf Links to vie for the champion's tartan jacket. Nicklaus, Palmer, Love, Norman, Stewart have played here during the more than 25-year history of the MCI Classic—The Heritage of Golf. The panoramic beauty of the course is ample reward for Pete Dye's challenging design. Two other outstanding courses—Ocean and Sea Marsh—bring the total to 54 invigorating holes. Three memorable courses, and three entirely unique experiences.

Address: 32 Greenwood Drive, Hilton Head Island, 29928
Phone: 843-785-3333
888-807-6873
Web site: http://www.innatharbourtown.com
No. of Rooms: 60
Rates: Inquire
Restaurant: Continental breakfast, afternoon tea in Lobby/Lounge, Heritage Grill, Harbour Town Bakery & Cafe
Bar: Happy Hour and Evening Cocktails in the Lobby Lounge
Business Fac.: State-of-the-art Conference Center, Banquets, Ballroom, Meeting rooms, cacacity 400
Sports Fac.: Use of the Sea Pines Resorts swimming pools and Sea Pines Racquet Club, Bike rentals, Sea Pines summer recreation program
Location: Sea Pines, Hilton Head Island

Course: Harbour Town Golf Links (6916, par 71)
No. of Holes: 18
Guest Policy: Open to public, guests and members get discount
Club House: 800-925-4653
Fees: ↑↑↑
Reservations: Reservations available 14 days in advance
Season: Open all year
Carts: Carts included in fees

Palmetto Dunes Resort

Address: P.O. Box 5606, Hilton Head Island, 29938
Phone: 843-785-1161
800-845-6130
Fax: 843-842-4482
E-mail: bborton@ greenwooddevelopment.com
Web site: http://www. palmettodunes.com
No. of Rooms: 500
Rates: Inquire
Restaurant: The Hemmingway, Pralines
Bar: Club Indigo
Business Fac.: Complete business facilities, Conference rooms, capacity 200
Sports Fac.: Tennis courts, Bicycling, Canoes, Swimming pools
Location: Waterfront

Courses: Arthur Hill (6122), George Fazio, Robert Trent Jones
No. of Holes: 54
Guest Policy: Open to public, call for availability
Club House: 803-785-1138
Reservations: May be made 2 months in advance
Season: Open all year

This balmy, 1,800 acre relaxed development represents a unique mingling of residential and resort amenities. The resort area is highlighted by 54 holes of unsurpassed golf, the Rod Laver Tennis Center, a 505 room beachfront Hyatt Regency, and the Mariner's Clarion Inn. Pass the security gates of this attractive lowcountry private environment, and you'll find spacious condominiums and single family vacation homes. Everything is spread out and you get the feeling that the architects weren't sardine-packers. Bicycles paths cross sleepy lagoons, residences are on large lots, dolphins play offshore, while egrets, pipers, and pelicans share the broad hard-packed beach with runners and families. Shelter Cove, bordering a meandering creek, is a self-contained marine community containing shops, restaurants, office condominiums, and boat slips.

You can do as much or as little as you want—there are pages of restaurants from which to choose, nightlife, swimming pools, tennis facilities, canoe rentals, organized nature walks, theater, special events such as tournaments and festivals, and children's programs.

Golf options include three courses designed by three of the game's greatest names. The Robert Trent Jones layout is highlighted by a unique winding lagoon system which comes into play on 11 holes. Bunkers are huge, and greens are built up on the sides and back by rolling mounds. Hole #10 is a long par 5, with a green sitting on the Atlantic's edge. The George Fazio course is a familiar name to followers of *Golf Digest*'s list of America's 100 best. The 16th hole features a few of the course's yawning fairways and greenside bunkers. With only two par 5's, you've got a series of long par 4's that require long accurate second shots to reach the narrow greens. Opened for play in 1986, the Arthur Hills course is characterized by palmettos, dramatic elevation changes, continuous lines of dunes and some stiff ocean breezes. There's a unique seaside character here, complete with beautiful salt marshes, rolling fairways and lagoons which come into play on 10 holes. Be careful looking for your ball on the muddy banks—that placid looking alligator doesn't know a bogey from a birdie.

Westin Resort Hilton Head

No need for devotees of the Inter-Continental on Hilton Head to fret. Only the name's been changed. It's the same charm of Charleston and Beaufort reflected in the lobby design, with lovely antiques, oriental rugs on polished wooden floors, and huge bouquets of fresh flowers.

Set on 24 acres of beachfront inside the gates of Port Royal Plantation, (plantation here is synonymous with development) this luxury horseshoe-shaped hotel has 416 rooms, pool and ocean swimming, a health club, water sports, tennis courts, conference facilities for the multitudes, and a large variety of dining and entertainment facilities. The island is a paradise for sports enthusiasts—not only are there miles of wide white beaches for bike riding, running, and castle building, tennis buffs can choose from any kind of court, shoppers will love exploring a huge outlet mall, and seafood lovers can check the local fleet's catch for shrimp, scallops, bluefish, sea trout and more.

The Kids' Korner, a well-organized complimentary pleasure package for the 5-12 year-old, offers all sorts of activities including kite flying, arts and crafts, alligator races, shell collecting, volleyball and more. For a modest fee, teens can participate in organized activities such as waterskiing, sunset cruises and trips to Harbour Town.

You'll have access to three par 72 championship courses: Barony, Robber's Row, and Planter's Row. Barony has small greens that are well-protected by deep bunkers, lagoons and Bermuda rough that require accurate approach shots with shot and medium irons. Robber's Course is on the marsh side atop what was once Civil War grounds and the historic town of Port Royal. Fairways are oak and magnolia-lined, and approach shots will find relatively large, well-trapped greens. The newest course is Planter's Row, host of the 1985 Hilton Head Seniors International. Greens are large, undulating and sometimes treacherous.

The children's program, "Camp Wackatoo" is for 4–12 year-olds and is a learning based recreational program. Activities include special theme days, beach olympics, giant artistic creations, safety swimmers, earthlings, cooking with kids. On Friday and Saturday night there's "Kids Night Out". The program is offered from May 27th through Labor day and is $40 for a full day ($25 for each additional same family child) or $120/week ($80 for each additional child).

Address: 2 Grasslawn Ave, Hilton Head Island, 29928
Phone: 843-681-4000
800-228-3000
Fax: 843-681-1087
E-mail: hilto@westin.com
No. of Rooms: 412
Rates: $$
Restaurant: 4 Restaurants
Bar: Lounge
Business Fac.: On-site Business Center
Sports Fac.: Health club, 1 indoor/2 outdoor swimming pools, Tennis courts, Water sports
Location: Hilton Head Island

Courses: Port Royal Golf Club #1, #2, #3
No. of Holes: 54
Club House: 843-681-1747
Reservations: Call for reservations
Season: Open all year

Wild Dunes Beach & Racquet Club

Address: P.O. Box 20575, Isle Of Palm, 29451
Phone: 843-886-6000
888-845-8926
Fax: 843-886-2916
Web site: http://www.wilddunes.com
No. of Rooms: 93
Rates: $$
Restaurant: The Grill at Boardwalk Inn, Dunes Deli & Pizzaria
Bar: Edgar's Restaurant & Bar, Cabana Bar & Grill
Business Fac.: 15 separate meeting rooms, banquet facilities, Island House Conference Center, Port O' Call I and II, The Grand Pavillion
Sports Fac.: 17 tennis courts, 20 swimming pools, miles of paved trails for jogging/biking, gym
Location: 20 minutes from Charleston

Courses: The Links (6722, par 72), The Harbor Course (6402, par 70)
No. of Holes: 36
Guest Policy: Open to public
Club House: 888-845-8926
Fees: ↑↑
Reservations: Call for reservations
Season: Open all year

Webster tells us a dune is a hill or ridge of sand piled up by the wind commonly found along shores. The dunes on tiny Isle of Palms just outside Charleston are Tom Fazio's award-winning creation.

Since the island was accessible only by boat until the turn of the century, it became a sanctuary for hundreds of species of birds and animals, and remains so today.

Lodgings are in wind-weathered one, two and three-bedroom villas and houses that look out on the never-ending stretch of sand, waves and dunes. If you've left the cooking behind, there are a myriad of restaurants from which to choose.

Fun for the family comes in the form of Island scavenger hunts, movies, wacky water sports, bingo and much more. Life (for some) centers around the water, and the amenities are first rate. Surf and creek fishing, sailboats and windsurfs are at your disposal. Cottage clusters have pools, and there are two other 25-meter beauties. Tennis is taken seriously here, and the facilities are outstanding.

Nearly three miles of sugar-white beaches, and sprawling marshlands offer an undisturbed glimpse into the habits of Mother Nature's offspring. If you're here between April and August you can see the baby loggerhead turtles trekking to the sea.

Wild Dunes Links is a young course by Tom Fazio where the holes are routed through moss-draped live oaks, exotic palms and magnolias onto severely rolling coastal terrain, then across saltwater marshland before the finishing holes right on the Atlantic. Relentless winds, massive dunes, deep rough and pot bunkers challenge the concentration of the most seasoned golfer. Experts highlight the fact that the course and the weather are so varied that a player can expect to use each club in his bag. Harbor Course, another Fazio layout, features a short narrow front nine holes which play adjacent to the Intracoastal Waterway. The back nine begins at the Yacht Harbor and winds along marshlands and through ancient trees. "Marsh Monster", the doglegged 13th is played from a small island fringed by an expansive marsh, and embodies all the characteristics that have made Fazio holes a true test of a golfer's skill. Sit a spell on the picturesque Clubhouse's spacious decks and ponder the question of which came first, the loggerhead or the egg?

Wyndham Myrtle Beach Resort

Approximately 100 miles north of Historic Charleston lie the Elysian fields of golfdom. Here on South Carolina's Grand Strand, a 60 mile stretch along the Atlantic, golfers will find 44 fabulous courses, with more on the drawing boards. Several things can be attributed to the reign of "King Golf." 241 annual days of sunshine and a year-round mean temperature of 71.1 degrees, well-designed and maintained courses in a bustling seaside resort environment, and first rate accommodations—all halfway between Miami and Manhattan, are what make Myrtle Beach the tourist magnet that it is.

This 14-story 392 room contemporary white hotel is strategically situated in the Arcadian Shores section of the Grand Strand, and offers newly decorated large airy rooms, each with a private balcony and view of the Atlantic.

Restaurants include Alfredo's, an elegant dining room facing the ocean, the Arcadian Gardens Restaurant for casual fare, and sandwiches and salads at the Pool Terrace. The Veranda Bar, and the Wet Whistle Bar, featuring a steel drum band, will wet your whistle, while the rooftop nightclub, Another World is a great spot for dancing and checking out the action.

Step outside to the pool deck and 600 foot beachfront and a world of sunning, sailing, jogging, shelling, biking and sailboarding. Tennis players will find four lighted courts, and kids find so many attractions in Myrtle Beach that they're oblivious to the fact that Dad and Mom are teeing off on a different course every day. Who can resist the outlet malls, an amusement park, mini-auto race track, skating rink, a Ripley's "Believe-it-or-Not" Museum, Guinness Hall of World Records, a wax museum, antique auto museum, and an incredible water park for thrilling, drenching rides?

Designed by Rees Jones, whose company was chosen to redesign Brookline's Country Club for the 1988 U.S. Open. Natural lakes weaving in and out of the fairways, sixty-four white sand bunkers, a variety of trees, and the salty breezes off the Atlantic offer plenty of challenge. When you make your reservation, you'll be able to choose from a slew of nearby courses, and golf package rates. You can indicate your choice of course and tee times from an extensive list which is provided by the hotel.

Address: 10000 Beach Club Drive, Myrtle Beach, 29572
Phone: 843-449-5000
Fax: 843-497-0295
Web site: http://www.wyndham.com/MyrtleBeachResort/
Rates: Inquire
Restrictions: Non-smoking rooms available
Restaurant: Arcadian Steaks & Grill, Beachcomber's
Bar: Veranda Bar
Business Fac.: Conference facilities for 10-1,000 people
Sports Fac.: Golf School, Exercise room, Heated pool, Tennis/volleyball courts, Golf, Golf School, 90 area golf courses
Location: 20 minutes from Myrtle Beach International Airport

Course: Arcadian Shores Golf Club (6938, par 72)
No. of Holes: 18
Guest Policy: Open to public
Club House: 803-449-5217
Fees: ↑
Reservations: Reservations available 365 days in advance
Season: Open all year
Carts: Cart included in fees

Tidewater Golf Club & Plantation

Address: 4901 Little River Neck Road, North Myrtle Beach, 29582
800-788-8433
E-mail: tidewatergolf@navi-gator.com
Web site: http://www.tide-water.com
Rates: Inquire
Restaurant: Clubhouse Grille serving lunch and dinner
Bar: Clubhousse Grille
Business Fac.: Meeting room at the Clubhouse
Sports Fac.: Swim and Racquet Club with Junior Olympic sized pool, Jacuzzi, Kiddie pool, Tennis pavilion, Beach Cabana at Cherry Grove Beach
Location: Grand Strand at Myrtle Beach

Course: Tidewater (7078)
No. of Holes: 18
Guest Policy: Open to public
Club House: 800-446-5363
Fees: ↑↑↑
Reservations: Must make reservations in advance
Season: Open all year

Imagine living in an extraordinary golf community tucked away on over 500 acres of coastal bluffs and pristine forest ... Located between the Atlantic Ocean and Intra-coastal Waterway, Tidewater Golf Club & Plantation is just 25 minutes north of Myrtle Beach, SC. They offer an extensive selection of homes, villas and home sites with enchanting water or fairway views. You'll find fully-appointed two- and three-bedroom villas with a host of outstanding amenities, including the top-ranked course on the Grand Strand, a luxurious clubhouse, lighted tennis courts and a junior Olympic-sized swimming pool ... all just five minutes from the beach!

Ranked by *Golf Digest* as the "Best New Public Golf Course in America" when it opened in 1990, Tidewater continues to maintain a top ranking in Myrtle Beach. *Golf Magazine* has ranked Tidewater as one of the premier golf courses in the country every year since recognizing it as one of the top ten new golf courses built in 1990. Designed and built by native South Carolinian Ken Tomlinson, Tidewater reflects his respect for classic turn-of-the-century golf courses created in harmony with the natural landscape. With its magnificent views of the Intra-coastal Waterway, saltwater marshes and Atlantic Ocean ... and undulating bent-grass greens ... Tidewater has been called as pure as the ocean breezes that blow across it.

Pawley's Plantation Golf & Country Club

Experience the casual elegance of a Pawleys Plantation vacation. This world class golf and resort community is built on the site of a former plantation and set amongst 582 acres of natural wetlands, salt marshes, lakes, live oaks and rolling green fairways. In addition to an outstanding golf course by Jack Nicklaus, you'll find the Phil Ritson-Mel Sole Golf School, a fully-stocked golf pro shop, and countless other amenities.

The spacious, fully equipped accommodations range from one to three-bedroom luxury villas, all nestled along our beautifully-sculpted fairways. In addition to offering beautiful views of the surrounding scenery, luxury villa suites feature individual private entrances, private baths, large living rooms, fully equipped kitchens, dining areas, washer/dryer and screened-in veranda overlooking the fairway. In short, it's an ideal vacation retreat with all the modern comforts and conveniences of home.

It was the exquisite setting that ultimately drew Jack Nicklaus to Pawleys Plantation. With subtle greens enveloped by sand bunkers, challenging fairways dotted with water and unique obstacles evident on every hole, Pawleys Plantation is a player's course that demands strategy, ingenuity and above all, concentration. Pawleys Plantation is one of those rare courses you can play time and time again and never hit the same shot twice. Its subtlety is matched only by its beauty. And best of all as a guest of Pawleys Plantation, you will enjoy special play privileges with guaranteed tee times.

Address: 70 Tanglewood Dr, Pawleys Island, 29585
Phone: 843-237-6009
800-367-9959
E-mail: getgolf@pawleysplantation.com
Web site: http://www.pawleysplantation.com
Rates: $
Restaurant: Oak Grille, Sawgrass Room
Bar: Palmetto Pub
Business Fac.: Conference center with 5 meeting rooms, boardroom, and ballroom, Full service business center, catering, banquets
Sports Fac.: Golf School
Location: On Pawleys Island

Course: Pawleys Plantation (7026, par 72)
No. of Holes: 18
Guest Policy: Reciprocal
Club House: 803-237-6200
Fees: ⏐⏐
Reservations: Reservations available 365 days in advance
Season: Open all year
Carts: Carts included in fees

Seabrook Island Resort

Address: 1002 Landfall Way,
Seabrook Island, 29455
Phone: 803-768-1000
800-845-2475
Web site: http://www.
seabrookresort.com
No. of Rooms: 338
Rates: Inquire
Restaurant: Fine dining on
Carolina seafood
Bar: Bohicket's Lounge with
evening entertainment
Business Fac.: Full service business
facilities, Conference room, capacity
250
Sports Fac.: Pool, 20 lighted tennis
courts, Horses, Fishing and crabbing
equipment
Location: Beach front on private
island, 23 miles to downtown, 30
miles to Charleston

Courses: Crooked Oaks (6759, par
72), Ocean Winds (6805, par 72)
No. of Holes: 36
Guest Policy: Open to public
Club House: 803-768-2529
Fees: ↑↑↑
Reservations: 30 days in advance
Season: Open all year
Carts: Carts included in fees

With a year-round mild climate moderated by the
Gulf Stream, a dedicated commitment to conser-
vation and ecology, and no high-rises to mar the
dazzling views, Seabrook is nearly perfect. This
2,200 acre private island (and they do mean private, as in sentry gates) is 23 miles south of
Charleston, and caters to families, as evidenced
by the numerous organized activities such as
pony rides and treasure hunts.

Condominiums are privately owned, and are
offered in a variety of settings and sizes. Island
House, with a formal dining room featuring savory
Lowcountry Cuisine and a renowned wine list, is
the social center. The names tell it all: Cap's
Sam's, The Half Shell Raw Bar.

There's plenty going on here. You can play tennis, swim in the ocean or pools, or use a wading
pool at the Beach Club, rent a bicycle, go windsurfing, join an exercise class, go fishing or crabbing, rent a Hobie Cat, or swab the decks if you're
tied up at the marina. An equestrian center will
provide a suitable companion for a ride on the
beach.

Conference planners should note that 12 individual meeting rooms, with seating for 10 to 300
eager beavers. Nearby are tours of Fort Sumter,
plantations and garden tours, historic Charleston,
and some upscale shopping with names such as
Banana Republic, Gucci, and Victoria's Secret.
Designer Robert Trent Jones called Crooked Oaks
Course "one of my best." The 18 holes follow a
6880 yard path around moss-draped oaks, and
across treacherous marshlands. Willard Byrd
designed and aptly named 18 hole championship
Ocean Winds Course, the shorter of the two. Mar-
got Walden, 1968 LPGA pro of the year, and
Seabrook's golf director operates three daily clinics. There's a driving range and pro shops ready to
help you.

Cumberland Gardens Resort

Come, relax and just enjoy Tennessee's magnificent Cumberland Plateau. At the Cumberland Garden's, overnight accommodations are available in one- or two-bedroom condominiums. They are tastefully appointed and fully equipped to prepare and serve meals, and they're conveniently located less than a two-minute drive from the golf course.

Sun, swim, play tennis, volleyball, badminton, and horseshoes while the little people enjoy the sandy playground. Children of all ages will enjoy the Sports Park nestled among the trees and only a short hiking distance from your condominium. Golf and family vacation packages are available at Cumberland Gardens, and its location is ideal for off-the-mountain fun, sightseeing, and many other activities.

Golf at Cumberland Gardens is played at Briarwood, an 18-hole championship course, boasting several holes designed only with nature's hazards. Magnetized by its charm, golfers—serious or casual—will be drawn to its repeating challenge of exhilarating play. *Golf Digest* has rated Briarwood a 4-star course, as well as one of the top ten courses in Tennessee.

Address: PO Box 288, Crab Orchard, 37723
Phone: 931-484-5285
Fax: 931-484-9257
E-mail: golf-cgardens@midtenn.net
Rates: Inquire
Sports Fac.: Swimming pool, Tennis courts, Volleyball, Badminton, Horseshoes, Playground, Sports Park nearby
Location: Cumberland Plateau

Course: Briarwood (6341)
No. of Holes: 18
Guest Policy: Open to public
Club House: 931-456-0892
Fees: ⊺
Reservations: Call for reservations
Season: Open all year
Carts: Carts are also available

Fairfield Glade Conference Center

Address: 101 Peavine Rd, P.O. Box 1849, Fairfield Glade, 38555
Phone: 615-484-7521
800-383-7600
Fax: 615-484-3788
E-mail: reservations@ fairfieldglade.com
Web site: http://www. fairfieldglade.com
No. of Rooms: 98
Rates: $$
Restaurant: Sassafras Restaurant, Stonehenge Golf Club & Restaurant, Druid Hills Country Club
Sports Fac.: 10 tennis courts, 11 fishing/boating lakes, miniature golf, horse shoes, gymnasium, fitness center, basketball, billiards, Dorchester Riding Stables

Location: 120 miles from Nashville, 75 miles from Knoxville
Courses: Stonehenge Golf Club (6549, par 72), Cumberland Gardens (par 72), Mountain Ridge (par 36), Deer Creek (par 72), River Run (par 72)
No. of Holes: 81
Guest Policy: Open to public
Club House: 615-484-3731
Fees: ↑↑
Reservations: Can make reservations 30 days in advance
Season: year round
Carts: Cart included in fees

This is an understated place where you can set your own pace. Located between Knoxville and Nashville, Fairfield Glade's next door neighbor is 84,000 acres of protected forest abounding with game. You can stay in the 100 room lodge, or in a condominium. There's a feeling of spaciousness here. No wonder, the resort is on 12,000 acres of Cumberland plateau and includes 4 gold courses, three pools, a full-service marina, tennis facilities, numerous lakes, a children's playground, and miniature golf. This is a wonderful place for bicycling and horseback riding, particularly in spring and fall. Two restaurants and a couple of lively lounges offer a variety of entertainment, and a shopping complex nearby ensures the availability of everything.

Fairfield Glade is the only course in the state claiming bentgrass tees, greens, and fairways, the layout has many elevation changes with lots of natural rock outcroppings, mountain streams and lakes, and maple, laurel and rhododendron lining the fairways. The #14 is a favorite—a par three that drops 90 feet from tee to green with a placid lake as backdrop. Stonehenge is closed January and February, but fear not, the kindly pro assures us that at least two of the four are open all year.

Barton Creek Resort and Country Club

Welcome to Austin … capital of the great state and home of the University of Texas, the LBJ Library and a nationally recognized array of live music featured in the historic Sixth Street district. And Austin is fast acquiring a reputation as a golfer's paradise. Nestled among the hills just west of the Capitol City, Barton Creek Resort is a world of its own, offering 150 guest rooms and suites and a full range of amenities and services.

The resort's rooms are designed with the discriminating guest in mind, offering luxuriously thick bath robes and such amenities as remote color TV and bathroom telephones. Every guest at Barton Creek is a "member," as its staff's impeccable Texas hospitality is the pride of the resort. Interiors reflect the casual, yet up-scale flair of the property's natural surroundings and feature Remington sculpture and dramatic sprays of freshly cut flowers.

For special occasions, The Palm Court features the ambiance of an exclusive club and flambe cuisine prepared tableside. The Tejas Room is more casual for lunch or dinner; The Terrace Room serves a lunch and a breakfast; and The Grille serves lighter fare which may be ordered from the golf course.

During a stay at Barton Creek, take a short drive through the surrounding Texas Hill Country and discover the colorful German town of Fredericksburg, the Bluebonnet Trail and the LBJ Ranch. Forget your image of a flat, barren dusty Texas. The area is a unique region of the state where strange rock formations, live oak, cedar, rugged cliffs and winding rivers abound. Highlighting this dramatic terrain is Barton Creek's resort's Tom Fazio golf course which has quickly acquired the reputation as on of the nation's finest. A second course, designed by Barton Creek's touring professional, Ben Crenshaw and partner Bill Coore, is now in play for resort guests. The Coore & Crenshaw course is a masterpiece of design and integrity as it introduces native grasses, wildflowers and varied elevations. The course reflects Coore & Crenshaw's philosophy of allowing the design to take its natural "course" from the features of the land. Barton Creek's dramatic terrain has lent its hand in the creation of a truly magnificent golf course. Righteous bursts of wildflowers and pleasing, rolling terrain … Hill Country golf has found its showcase.

Address: 8212 Barton Club Dr, Austin, 78735
Phone: 512-329-4000 800-527-3220
Fax: 512-329-4597
E-mail: info@bartoncreek.com
Web site: http://www.bartoncreek.com
No. of Rooms: 147
Rates: Inquire
Restrictions: No pets allowed
Restaurant: The Palm Court
Bar: Jim Bob's
Business Fac.: Full conference facilities, Conference rooms, capacity 320
Sports Fac.: 12 Tennis courts, Swimming pools, Volleyball, Health spa
Location: 15 minutes west of Austin in the Hill Country of central Texas

Courses: Fazio Course (6950), Crenshaw-Coore Course, Palmer-Lakeside Course
No. of Holes: 54
Guest Policy: Reserve tee times through hotel reservations
Club House: 512-329-4001
Reservations: Inquire about tee times when booking
Season: Open all year

Lakeway Inn

Address: 101 Lakeway Dr, Austin, 78734
Phone: 512-261-6600
800-LAKEWAY
Fax: 512-261-7322
E-mail: lakewayinn@dolce.com
Web site: http://www.dolce.com
No. of Rooms: 258
Rates: Inquire
Restaurant: Travis Room Restaurant
Bar: Travis Bar
Business Fac.: 13 meeting rooms, 10 workshop parlors, Soundproof rooms w/ indv. temperature, lighting & sound controls, Ergonomic chairs, Permanent projections capabilities, A/V control room, Computer graphics capability, Multipurpose lighting, Music and sound systems
Sports Fac.: Golf, 26 tennis courts, Full-service marina, Fishing, Boating, Water skiing, 2 swimming pools, Fitness Center, Jogging, Walking, Bicycling
Location: 18 miles west of Austin

Rimmed by 65-mile long Lake Travis, Lakeway Inn is the place to be for water sports activities. Ski, swim, sail, or if you prefer, arrange a party cruise aboard the 101-foot Flagship Texas and enjoy the lake without getting wet. Golfers may have a harder time avoiding water on 36 holes and tennis lovers will love 32 courts and a racquet shaped pool at the World of Tennis. For a Texas-size adventure, ride into the sunset on old Chisholm Trail.

Courses: Live Oak (6643, par 72), Yaupan (par 72)
No. of Holes: 36
Guest Policy: Open to public
Club House: 512-261-7173
Fees: ⌐
Reservations: 7 days in advance
Season: Open all year
Carts: Carts are available

Tapatio Springs Resort & Conference Center

A true luxury resort, built on rolling, tree-filled terrain, the accommodations are elegant. The rooms are housed in low buildings scattered around the resort. The resort has been listed as in "Texas Top 10 Golf Resort" by the *Dallas Morning News* three years in a row.

You're likely to meet as many deer here as people. You can often see the whole family out grazing.

Dining here is done with real class and the cuisine matches. Your table will have a marvelous view overlooking the rolling terrain of the golf course.

If you feel like a change of pace, visit Riverwalk, the shopping mecca in San Antonio. A trip to Seaworld (only 45 minutes away) or to Fiesta Texas, a theme and water park (20 minutes away) are always worth the time.

Both courses have narrow, tree-lined fairways, and are on rolling terrain. The water and strategically places trees can surely change your score on the Eighteen Hole Course. Golf packages are available.

Address: P.O. Box 550, Boerne, 78006
Phone: 830-537-4611
800-999-3299
Fax: 830-537-4962
E-mail: reservations@tapatio.com
Web site: http://www.tapatio.com
No. of Rooms: 148
Rates: $$$
Restaurant: Blue Heron Restaurant & Lounge, The Turn Cafe
Business Fac.: 3000 sq.ft meeting room, 5 breakout rooms, 10,000 sq.ft. conference center with 6,000 sq.ft. ball room
Sports Fac.: Heated swimming pool with built in Jacuzzi, fitness center, tennis, volley ball
Location: not far from San Antonio

Courses: The Lakes, The Valley, The Ridge
No. of Holes: 27
Guest Policy: Guests and public welcome
Club House: 800-999-3299
Fees: ⊤⊤
Reservations: Call for reservations
Season: Open all year
Carts: Carts available

Hyatt Regency – Bear Creek Resort

Address: International Parkway, P.O. Box 619014, DFW Airport, 75261
Phone: 972-453-1234
Fax: 972-456-8668
Web site: http://www.hyatt.com/pages/d/dfwapa.html
No. of Rooms: 1,369
Rates: Inquire
Restaurant: Il Nonno's Italian Bistro, Mr G's Premium Steakhouse, Sullivan O'Shaughnessy's Diner, Papaya's Cafe
Bar: Brighton Taproom, Lobbibar, Sullivan O'Shaughnessy's Sports Bar
Business Fac.: 81 meeting rooms with individual or master controls: AC/heat, Sound, Music, Telephones, Multiple electrical/microphone outlets, Special lighting effects. 2 exhibit halls, 15 pre-set boardrooms with Fax, Flip charts, Screen, Grease board, Concierge servic
Sports Fac.: Heated outdoor pool, Exercise room, Cardio theater, Jogging Track, Hyatt Bear Creek Golf Club, Driving range, Putting green
Location: 20 minutes from downtown Dallas/Ft. Worth

Courses: East Course, West Course
No. of Holes: 36
Club House: 972-615-6800
Fees: ↑
Reservations: Call for reservations
Season: Open all year

As a prominent attraction within the DFW Airport, the twin towers of the 1,390 room Hyatt Regency offer the elegant touches familiar to Hyatt clientele, first rate meeting facilities, and a championship golf course. Recently refurbished, guests will find all the amenities here, in addition to the convenient location. The lobby is Southwestern contemporary in decor, with an earthy palette of teal and peach. Light stained oak, exquisite chandeliers and original Texas artwork complete the picture. Two floors feature Hyatt's Regency Club, with complimentary continental breakfast, and afternoon cocktails in the private lounge. Open 24 hours, Sullivan O'Shaughnessy's Grill is reminiscent of a 1950s corner drugstore. An Irish pub of the same name is nearby, while Brighton's Express Lounge is definitely Victorian. Papayas' welcomes travelers for casual fare, and for hearty steaks, fresh seafood and mesquite-grilled specialties, you might try Mister G's. Care for a taste of northern Italy? Sit back and hear an aria sung by your waiter as you dine on tortellini and veal parmigiana at Il Nonnos, or enjoy the lobby piano bar's offerings.

The environs are worth exploring. You can drive to Southfork, home of the Ewings, or take in Six Flags Over Texas, a theme park. Try Wet 'n Wild, a Texas-sized park of waterslides and inner tube chutes, or head for some legendary names such as Neiman-Marcus, and Bloomingdale's. Old City Park, close to downtown, with its restored Victorian houses, log cabins and an old railroad depot, appeals to all ages.

Hyatt Regency DFW also manages Hyatt Bear Creek Golf & Racquet Club, a 335-acre resort, just a five-minute shuttle ride away. It's a gorgeous layout of rolling hills, mature oak and cottonwood trees, two 18 hole golf courses, a driving range, practice bunkers and 2 putting greens, 2 picnic pavilions, and a snack bar and lounge. Tennis buffs will find 7 Laykold courts. Ted Robinson designed the East Course in 1980, and it has since hosted many tournaments including the PGA Regional Qualifying, National Lefthanders, Texas State Open, National Juniors Championship, and the MDA Gatlin Brothers Tournament. The #5 East Course is a picturesque par-4 that's not long, but requires 2 perfectly placed shots over water to reach the bentgrass greens. Shoppers take note: the Golf Shop is considered one of the best in the country.

Horseshoe Bay Country Club Resort

All the superlatives associated glamour, amenities and service can be applied to this premier golf destination deep in the heart of Texas.

Horseshoe Bay is situated among spring-fed streams, exotic gardens, miles of shoreline and coves on a lake where anglers search out perch and catfish, a fully equipped marina, and 4,000 acres of scenic overlooks and horseback trails. There is an airstrip, should your plans include private flight.

The resort has meeting and group facilities and flaunts a magnificent two-tiered pool fed by a waterfall from granite outcrops. Dining can be elegant at The Captain's Table or the casual touches of The Keel Way at the Yacht Club.

The tennis gardens are four covered courts and eight outdoor courts surrounded by lakes, waterfalls and lush gardens. Within the complex is a fitness program, and two sport courts featuring sports rounding out the tennis program at Horseshoe Bay. The Equestrian Center, under the supervision of a riding master, offers boarding, trail rides and lessons.

This is the spot to live out your golf fantasies on three Robert Trent Jones courses. The courses are well designed and maintained—the PGA have opted to hold tournaments here. Think about the name—Slick Rock—and you'll get a clue about the topography. Arborists will delight at the specimens of trees, plants, and colorful granite. The Ram Rock, built eight years later, plays through brooks, waterfalls and rock gardens, small greens, and much sand.

Address: One Horseshoe Bay Blvd, Box 7766, Horseshoe Bay, 78654
Phone: 800-252-9369 in TX 800-531-5105
Fax: 830-598-5525
E-mail: frontdesk@ horseshoebaytexas.com
Web site: http://www. horseshoe-bay-resort.com
Rates: $$$
Restrictions: NO PETS
Restaurant: Yacht Club, Waterfront Pub & Eatery, Top Side
Bar: Men's Sports Lounge
Business Fac.: Yacht Club Complex & Corporate Meeting Center, Hurd Center.
Sports Fac.: 12 Laykold/6 clay tennis courts, Fitness Spa, Therapy Pool, Putting course, Racquet Club Pro Shop, Sauna, Whirlpool, Marina w/sports equipment, Adult pool, kids pool, Hot tub.
Location: 43 miles from Austin

Courses: Slick Rock (6834, par 72), Ram Rock (6946, par 71), Apple Rock (6999, par 72)
No. of Holes: 54
Guest Policy: Closed to the public/ Lodging required
Club House: 830-598-2561
Fees: ↑↑↑
Reservations: Reservations available 14 days in advance
Season: Open all year
Carts: Carts available

Houstonian Hotel, Club & Spa

Address: 111 North Post Oak Lane, Houston, 77024
Phone: 713-680-2626
800-231-2759
Fax: 713-688-6305
E-mail: hotelgm@houstonian.com
Web site: http://www.houstonian.com
No. of Rooms: 286
Rates: $$$
Restaurant: Olivette, The Manor House and Center Court
Business Fac.: 30,000 sq ft of meeting space
Sports Fac.: Houstonian Club—Health & Fitness Club (One of the top ten in the US), Running track, Horseshoe pit,3 swimming pools, nature/jogging trails, 15 raquet-sport courts, rock-climbing wall, basketball, volleyball, children's activities center
Location: In the Heart of the Galleria area

Course: New Houstonian Golf Club (7100)
No. of Holes: 18
Guest Policy: Closed to the general public
Club House: 713-494-4244
Reservations: Call for reservations
Season: Open all year

In the heart of Houston, nestled amidst towering pines and majestic oaks, where the tranquility of nature prevails over the clamor of the city, is The Houstonian Hotel, Club & Spa … as unique as the people who come here. The grounds are home to squirrels, hundreds of birds, and a wide variety of lush plant life. Among the trees are a 3/4 mile running track and a horseshoe pit built specially for George Bush.

As you enter the hotel you are greeted by the Great Room lobby, what we think of as the world's coziest den. Modern comfort and old-world charm pervade the rich, wooden surroundings, and in the middle of it all a magnificent fireplace to warm both the hearth and the heart. Guests may enjoy one of 277 luxurious guestrooms and nine suites, as well as complimentary access to the nation's only health and fitness country club

Chef Jim Mills' newly renovated restaurant Olivette, offers a marriage of ancient culinary tradition and modern inspiration, featuring the vibrancy of Mediterranean foods reflecting the richness of the earth. Chef Mills' signature style is also evident in The Manor House's American regional cuisine and the lighter fare available at Center Court.

In keeping with the tradition of first class service and facilities of The Houstonian Hotel, Club & Spa, renowned golf course architect Rees Jones designs the Houstonian Golf Club. With 18 magnificent holes and over 7100 championship yards quietly tucked away in Southwest Texas, golfers of all skill levels will find enjoyment in every aspect of their game. With rolling Bermuda fairways and state of the art TifEagle Bermuda grass greens, The Houstonian Golf Club will entice you to come back again and again. The rich and comfortable atmosphere of the 18,000 square foot clubhouse at The Houstonian Golf Club completes the ultimate golf experience.

Del Lago Resort & Conference Center

This is a meeting planners dream come true. Covering more than 300 acres on Lake Conroe's edge 40 miles north of Texas, Del Lago provides complete conference facilities in a tranquil environment. You can survey it all from a one or two bedroom suite twenty-one stories above the lake. There's no lack of recreation. The spa and fitness center offers everything from a workout, tanning bed and massage therapist to work your body over, to racquetball and exercise classes. 13 hard surface tennis courts, and many other additional seasonal activities are available. Start with horseshoes and finish with swimming, a game of softball or volleyball. The marina offers a variety of party boats for private functions or you can sail solo.

Lago Vista is a split-level restaurant overlooking the pool area, marina and lake, and scattered about are several other eateries, as well as a hearty Texas-style barbecue in the pool area in warm months.

Del Lago has recently added 51 golf cottages and 13 lakefront villas available for rent. All units have two bedrooms and feature full kitchens, large living rooms with fireplace, washer-dryers, and private deck areas.

There are local fairs, shopping the Texas Renaissance Festival, hunting, antiquing and historic home tours all nearby, and the local theater and symphony perform in a restored theater nearby.

The championship course, built in concert with the local ecology intact, is a year-round haven. A product of Jay Riviere and Dave Marr, the course hosted the 1987 TPA tour event, Del Lago Classic. You may also remember the Palmer-Lopez vs. Player-Stephenson match here in November of 1984. Signature hole is #9, a 464 yard par 4 with narrow driving fairway. Sounds easy, but you'll need a long second shot over water to a long, narrow green. This is Texas, and everything's long. Hotel guests have priority tee times here amid eleven lakes, more than 80 sand traps, and those long fairways lined with pines and white oaks.

Address: 600 Del Lago Blvd, Montgomery, 77356
Phone: 409-582-6100
800-558-1317
E-mail: info@dellago.com
Web site: http://www.dellago.com
No. of Rooms: 310
Rates: Inquire
Restrictions: Pets limited
Restaurant: Cafe Verde
Bar: Fiddler's
Business Fac.: Complete business facilities, Conference rooms, capacity 1000
Sports Fac.: Tennis courts, Swimming pool, Jogging, Boats, Bicycling
Location: On Lake Conroe

Course: Del Lago (6907)
No. of Holes: 18
Guest Policy: Guests have priority tee times
Club House: 409-582-6100
Reservations: May be made any time for hotel guests
Season: Open all year
Carts: Carts are also available

Westin La Cantera Resort

Address: 16641 La Cantera Pkwy,
San Antonio, 78256
Phone: 210-558-6500
800-WESTIN1
Fax: 210-558-2400
E-mail: info@westinlacantera.com
Web site: http://www.
westinlacantera.com
No. of Rooms: 508
Rates: $$$
Restaurant: Brannon's Cafe,
Francesca's, Grille Restaurant
Bar: cigar bar, lobby bar and lounge
Business Fac.: 39,000 square feet
Sports Fac.: 2 tennis courts, 7,600
sq ft fitness center, lap pool, sports
pool, adult pool, pool with a water-
slide, kiddie pool, and whirlpools
Location: Northwest San Antonio

Course: La Cantera Golf Course
(7001, par 72)
No. of Holes: 18
Guest Policy: Open to public
Club House: 210-558-6500
Fees: ⊺⊺⊺
Reservations: Call for reservations
and specials
Season: Open all year
Carts: Cart and range balls included
in fees

The General Manager's note reads—"Resort to
the Best of Texas!" Located on Lake Livingston in
the heart of East Texas hill country, Waterwood is
a world of clean air, tall pines and plenty of recre-
ation opportunities. Accommodations are in
beautifully appointed guest rooms, including four
suites with patios and balconies overlooking the
golf course. There are also forest lodge rooms
which are a bit more secluded. The Garden Room
and its adjacent Garden Court Lounge set the
pace for leisurely meals and entertainment.

Lake Livingston, with a full service marine is
just the spot for bass fishing, sailing or simply con-
templating. Tennis players will have four lighted
Laykold courts, and four swimming pools scat-
tered about the resort await the serious lap-
counters and sun-bathers. Bicycle through the
pines or visit the Health Club with weight equip-
ment, saunas and aerobics classes.

An impressive selection of meeting rooms,
banquet areas and services are available to the
conference planner.

Carved from the deep East Texas Piney Woods,
the Pete Dye course abounds in long vistas of roll-
ing, narrow tree-lined fairways, natural rough,
deep bunkers and small well placed greens. This
is the site of the PGA tour qualifying school in
1978, '79, and '81; the Women's Western Amateur
in 1982, and the Women's Southern Amateur in
1984. Tall Texas tales recount #14, a par three
that requires a 225 yard carry over water from
championship tees to a small cliffside green.
There's a sizeable practice and teaching area
including driving range, putting greens and sand
chipping area.

Homestead Resort

The Homestead Resort's landmark mineral hot springs crater was the resort's main attraction over 100 years ago. From its humble beginnings, the Homestead has grown in size and reputation to establish itself as a gracious world-class resort featuring a championship golf course, luxurious accommodations, fine dining and an array of activities to suit each of our guests.

The Homestead encompasses approximately 200 acres in a spectacular mountain valley setting. National forests, State Park land and several reservoirs provide scenic surroundings and a plethora of sporting opportunities. Lush grounds encourage guests to relax in the outdoor environment and enjoy the peacefulness the Homestead offers.

You'll be impressed with the sheer number of fun activities the resort has to offer. There are at least six ways to get wet, like the one-of-a-kind experience of floating in the Homestead Crater and ten ways to get around, including horseback, golf carts, tandems, snowmobiles, snowshoes and horse-drawn buggies. Even basic yard games like croquet, sand volleyball, tennis, horseshoes and shuffleboard get full play.

The Homestead offers over 150 lodging rooms, condominiums and homes in an eclectic mix of sizes and styles. Choose from vintage Victorian to ranch-style comfort to executive suites and cottages.

With everything the Homestead offers, you can do anything you want or nothing at all!

Address: 700 N. Homestead Dr, P.O. Box 99, Midway, 84049
Phone: 435-654-1102
800-327-7220
Fax: 435-654-5087
E-mail: info@homesteadresort.com
Web site: http://www.homesteadresort.com
No. of Rooms: 150
Rates: Inquire
Restaurant: Simon's Restaurant, Fanny's Grill, The Snack Shack
Bar: Fanny's Grill, 12pm to 10pm daily; Simon's Pub, 5:30pm–10pm daily
Business Fac.: Complete Conference and Banquet Services, Flexible Breakout Space, State-of-the-Art Conference Equipment, Team-building Activities, Seasoned Staff, Unique Catering Menus; Capacity: Multiple Groups of up to 300.
Sports Fac.: Summer: Golf, Tennis, Volleyball, Shuffleboard, Croquet, Horseback Riding, Bike Rentals; Year-Round: Swimming, Scuba Diving, Snorkeling, Mineral Baths; Winter: Snowmobiling, Cross-Country Skiing, Snowshoeing, Nearby Downhill Skiing.
Location: 20 minutes from Park City, UT
Course: Homestead Golf Course (7017, par 72)
No. of Holes: 18
Guest Policy: Open to public
Club House: 800-327-7220
Fees: ⌐
Reservations: Public reservations available 7 days in advance, lodging guest reservations 30 days in advance
Season: April–November
Carts: Carts available, included in greens fee

The Equinox

Address: Historic Rte. 7A, Manchester Village, 05254
Phone: 802-362-4700
800-362-4747
Fax: 802-362-1595
E-mail: reservations@equinoxresort.com
Web site: http://www.equinoxresort.com
No. of Rooms: 183
Rates: $$$
Restaurant: The Colonnade, The Marsh Tavern, The Dormy Grill
Business Fac.: Charles Orvis Inn has recessed audio/visual equipment.
Sports Fac.: Equinox Fitness Spa, Sauna, Steam room, Falconrey school, Land Rover Driving School, Ski Center, Indoor/outdoor pools, Ice skating, Snowmobile tour, Horseback riding, Fishing
Location: One hour from Brattleboro

Course: Gleneagles Golf Course (6423, par 71)
No. of Holes: 18
Guest Policy: Open to public
Club House: 800-362-4747
Fees: ↑↑↑
Reservations: Can make reservations 2 days in advance
Season: May–November
Carts: Carts available

Nestled between the Taconic and Green Mountain ranges, The Equinox has been serving travelers and neighbors sincec 1769. The Equinox, a national landmark is listed in the National Register of Historic Places.

The tiny village of Manchester, renowned for its outlet shopping has one of the finest collections of designer outlets in the northeast, including Esprit, Brooks Brothers, Donna Karan, Calvin Klein, and J. Crew to name a few.

Manchester is also home of the world-famous Orvis Company, the hunting and fishing outfitter and country clothier. Exploring old country stores and scores of antique shops is also a favorite pastime while at the Equinox. You can rent a bike or a canoe, take a drive in the country, or hike in the nearby Green Mountain National Forest.

The Equinox features a full health club with indoor and outdoor pools, saunas, steam and daily aerobics. Nautilus and cardio-vascular equipment are also available. Massages and herbal wraps are available with 24-hours notice. The hotel is managed by Guinness Enterprises who own and operate the famed Gleneagles Hotel in Scotland.

The golf course has a spectacular setting. Nestled between 2 mountain ranges and rolling green hills, it is beautifully groomed. The 13th hole is known as the "Snake Pit" and features unusually high/elevated green with a severe drop into "the snake pit on the right." In 1991 The Equinox Country Club underwent a $3 million total restoration by renowned golf architect Rees Jones.

Mount Mansfield Resort

Mount Mansfield is Vermont's highest peak, and from its summit you can peer into 3 states and Canada. In this charming New England village you'll see a traditional way of life where friendliness and family activity are stressed.

The resort consists of an Inn and condominiums in varying settings. Stowe Village offers every kind of eatery imaginable—from sundaes to sushi. Guests at the resort have access to a complete Fitness Center, and the amenities at Stowe Country Club, which is operated by the resort. The Club has tennis courts, a first-rate golf shop, and an attractive New England-y Clubhouse with a dining room, luncheon patio, and meeting areas.

This is one of New England's more scenic courses, where the clear blue sky and crisp, clean air heightens the pleasure of carrying a mountain stream. It's not unusual to see a mama fox and a youngster playing on the green, or chasing a fallen crabapple. Plan on thrills in the hills here, as well as several ponds. It's spectacular here in the fall.

Address: Mountain Rd, Route 108, Stowe, 05672
Phone: 802-253-7311
800-253-4SKI
No. of Rooms: 100
Rates: Inquire
Restrictions: Pets limited
Restaurant: Toll House
Bar: Fireside Tavern
Business Fac.: Complete business facilities, Conference rooms, capacity 200
Sports Fac.: Tennis courts, Swimming pools, Health spa, Bicycling
Location: Mountain setting

Course: Stowe Country Club (6163)
No. of Holes: 18
Guest Policy: Open to guests and public
Club House: 802-253-7321
Reservations: May be made 3 weeks in advance
Season: End of May–mid October

Topnotch at Stowe

Address: 4000 Mountain Road,
Stowe, 05672
Phone: 802-253-8585
800-451-8686
Fax: 802-253-9263
E-mail: info@topnotch-resort.com
Web site: http://www.
topnotch-resort.com
No. of Rooms: 90
Rates: Vary
Restaurant: Maxwell's at Topnotch
Open Daily for Bkft & Dinner
Bar: Buttertub Bistro Open Daily
for Lunch & Dinner
Business Fac.: Topnotch features
7,000 ft of meeting space and can
host meetings of up to 200 people.
Topnotch also provides and ideal
setting for weddings.
Sports Fac.: Full equestrian center,
5.3 mile paved recreation path,
bicycle rentals, cross country skiing,
downhill skiing, tennis, weight
room, fitness classes, aerobics
studio and much more!
Location: Located in Stowe Village
at the base of Vermont's tallest
mountain

Topnotch is a four star, four diamond property
and a member of Preferred Hotels and Resort
Worldwide. Vermont's premier resort, Topnotch
features a 23,000 square foot European Spa and a
nationally acclaimed Tennis Program with both
indoor and outdoor courts. Golf packages are
available and may be arranged by contacting
hotel Reservations Department.

Courses: Stowe Country Club, 18
holes, par 72, Sugarbush, Vermont
National Country Club
Guest Policy: Open to public
Fees: ↑↑
Reservations: Call to make reserva-
tions
Season: May–October
Carts: Price quoted includes cart

Stratton Mountain Resort

Stratton Mountain Resort is located on 4,000 acres of Green Mountain beauty in southern Vermont, just 35 miles north of Brattleboro. With a summit elevation of 3,875 feet, it is the perfect four-season setting for a successful working retreat. The Stratton Village Square, a colorful pedestrian street lined with fine shops and restaurants, begins right at the base of the mountain.

There is a wide range of lodging accommodations to choose from, including Stratton's one to four bedroom Mountain Villas, country inns, lodges, hotels and motor inns. Stratton Mountain Inn is a full service hotel with 119 air-conditioned guestrooms and suites. Village Lodge, located in the heart of the Village Square, offers 91 spacious air-conditioned rooms including 25 two-story loft units. All amenities at Stratton Mountain Inn available to guests at Stratton Village Lodge on space available basis.

Stratton Mountain Inn houses Sage Hill Restaurant for breakfast and candlelight dining with a New England flair, as well as The Tavern with its firelit lounge, light fare menu, and bar.

Stratton offers some of Vermont's best recreation. The Stratton Mountain golf course is actually comprised of three, nine-hole layouts—Lake, Mountain and Forest. Lake and Mountain were opened in 1965; Forest in 1986. One of the big pluses to Stratton is that the golfer experiences noticeable variations in design approach from one nine to the next with each having a distinct feel of its own. The noted course architect, Geoffrey Cornish, designed all of the courses. As with his other Vermont courses, the holes are solid and enjoyable across the board. A golfer will readily understand why this course was considered to be of a caliber high enough to host an LPGA tournament for many years. We have yet to encounter any golfer with very much in the way of disparaging remarks to say about this resort venue.

Address: Stratton Mountain Rd, Stratton Mountain, 05155
Phone: 802-297-2500
800-843-6867
E-mail: sales@strattonmountain.com
Web site: http://www.strattonmountain.com
No. of Rooms: 200
Rates: $
Restaurant: Sage Hill Restaurant
Bar: The Tavern
Sports Fac.: Stratton's Golf School, Hiking, Snowboarding, Snowshoeing, Ice skating, Tennis, Hot tubs, Co-ed sauna, Seasonal outdoor heated pool, Stratton Sports Center
Location: 35 miles north of Brattleboro

Courses: Lake/Mountain Course (6602, par 72), Forest/Lake Course (6526, par 72)
No. of Holes: 27
Guest Policy: Open to public
Club House: 802-297-4115
Fees: ↑
Reservations: Can make reservations 7 days in advance
Season: April–October

The Woodstock Inn & Resort

Address: 14 The Green, Woodstock, 05091
Phone: 802-457-1100
800-448-7900
Fax: 802-457-6699
E-mail: email@woodstockinn.com
Web site: http://www.
woodstockinn.com
No. of Rooms: 144
Rates: $$
Restaurant: Dining room
Bar: Richardson's Tavern
Location: Woodstock, VT

Course: Woodstock (6001, par 69, Robert Trent Jones Course)
No. of Holes: 18
Guest Policy: Open to public
Club House: 802-457-6674
Fees: ⊺⊺
Reservations: Reservations available 1 day in advance
Season: Open all year
Carts: Carts available

Close your eyes and imagine a small New England town whose village green is surrounded by a beautifully preserved landmark village of red and white clapboard and brick houses. The original Inn burned and a new handsome Woodstock Inn emerged in 1969. Handcut stone, weathered timbers, patchwork quilts and a staff renowned for service are what guests will remember. Historians have noted that Woodstock has four church bells forged by patriotic night rider and hero, Paul Revere.

Not too big, this gracious 143-room establishment includes suites and three guest houses. A ten foot fireplace dominates the hospitable lobby which is filled with antiques, seasonal floral arrangements and touches of New England. An afternoon tea is served for guests. Rooms are furnished in modern oak, and many have views of surrounding hills, ablaze with russets and golds of the changing seasons.

Guests can partake in a myriad of activities. Choose from indoor or outdoor swimming and tennis, handball and squash, croquet, racquetball, paddle tennis, or hiking in surrounding hills. A full health spa includes the works from whirlpool to massage to weight training.

Dinner is an occasion in the Dining Room, and gentlemen are expected to don a jacket. Guests congregate in Richardson's Tavern for cocktails or after dinner libations.

Exploring historic Woodstock, shopping for antiques and crafts, and the Billings Farm Museum, are all favorite pastimes of returning guests.

Come winter, guests can enjoy the snow either on cross-country skis or at the resort's slopes. Or try ice skating and sleigh rides.

Robert Trent Jones redesigned this narrow course here which was originally built in 1895. A brook meanders throughout the holes in this picturesque valley adding variety and interest to your game.

Carambola Beach Resort Golf Club

On the north side of the 84 square mile island in surroundings evocative of a classic Carribbean Great House, sits the first Rockresort to open in the area since the sixties. Carambola, names for a star-shaped fruit from a tree cultivated in East India, is modeled after a traditional fishing village with red roofs, high dormered windows, raftered ceilings, and private screened porches that beckon cooling trade winds.

Your room is in a tropical garden by the sea, perhaps in the superb Davis Bay Suite, housed in its own sugar mill. Separate sleeping and sitting areas in the luxurious guest rooms blend colorful fabrics with rattan to give a feeling of spaciousness and tropical elegance. Consistent with Rockresorts' philosophy for a Carribbean resort, guest accommodations have no televisions. The restaurants here offer West Indies cuisine minus excessive spices and fats. Produce is brought from the resort's own farm, and what isn't grown here comes from local sources.

Guests can play tennis, soak up rays at the gorgeous beach, swim in the pool, relax in the Jacuzzis, snorkel, scuba dive, or explore some of the sights on the island.

Golf is fabulous here on a Robert Trent Jones, Jr. course that opened in 1966 under the name Fountain Valley. Rolling past ancient stone sugar ruins deep in a lush valley of tall bamboo, enormous saman trees and endless varieties of palms, it's like playing in a botanical garden. Those in the know claim its string of par three holes is the best in the tropics. The par-5 13th is only 458 yards, but a sharp dogleg, a sparkling pond and a steep ravine will test your finesse. This is the home of the Annual Queen Louise Charity Classic (major league baseball players), Shell's Wonderful World of Golf, the Eastern Caribbean Championship, and the future site of the Club Champions Championship. *Golf Magazine* awarded Carambola its prestigious Golf Medal in 1990.

Address: Kingshill, P.O. Box 3031, St. Croix, 00851
Phone: 809-778-3800
800-447-9503
Fax: 809-778-1682
No. of Rooms: 157
Rates: Inquire
Restrictions: No pets allowed
Restaurant: Saman & Mahogany Rooms, Golf Club Terrace
Bar: Flamboyant
Business Fac.: Audio-visual, Copiers, Conference rooms, capacity 200
Sports Fac.: Tennis courts, Scuba, Sailing, Horseback riding
Location: Edge of Rain Forest on Davis Beach

Course: Carambola Beach Golf Club (6181)
No. of Holes: 18
Guest Policy: Reservations made through golf shop
Club House: 809-778-5638
Reservations: Tee time 2 days in advance for guests
Season: Open all year

The Buccaneer Hotel

Address: P.O. Box 218, St. Croix, 00821
Phone: 340-773-2100
800-255-3881
Fax: 340-778-8215
E-mail: mango@thebuccaneer.com
Web site: http://www.
thebuccaneer.com
No. of Rooms: 147
Rates: Inquire
Restrictions: No pets allowed
Restaurant: Terrace, Mermaid, Brass Parrot, Grotto
Bar: Terrace Lounge
Business Fac.: Large screen TV, Slide projector, Podium & Microphone, Overhead projector and flip charts, 2 conference rooms
Sports Fac.: 3 beahces, Snorkeling, Health spa, Fitness center, Tennis courts, Exercise circuit, 2 swimming pools
Location: Caribbean Sea

Course: Buccaneer (5504)
No. of Holes: 18
Guest Policy: Call for availability
Club House: 340-763-5526
Reservations: May be made with room reservation
Season: Open all year
Carts: Limited

What a history this family-owned and operated hotel has had. Hugging 248 acres of shore with vistas of Christiansted's harbor to the west, St. Thomas and St. John to the north, and Buck Island National Park to the east, the resort is a place where returning families are remembered and pampered. During the mid-1600s it was a hospice, under the Danes, a sugar factory, later a cotton plantation, and subsequent owners bred cattle here. De Luxe beachside rooms with private patios to "no frills" rooms (perfect for extra children provided that they are over four years) in a wide range of settings are available. The open-air Terrace Restaurant with its unimpaired view of the harbor, the beaches, tennis courts, lounges, spa, watersports, horseback riding, shopping arcade, all add up to a vacation you'll never forget. A glance at the Coconut Grapevine keeps guests apprised of such earth-shattering events such as croquet games, Jimmy Hamilton playing jazz, island tours, a scuba or kayak demonstration, and should you be the lucky winner of the "World Class Hermit Crab Races" you'll win a free seaplane trip to St. Thomas for a day of duty-free shopping. Don't miss the excursion to Buck Island Underwater National Park—truly unique and worth the trip.

Tim Johnston, an amiable golf pro, gives tips on how to play the 18 hole course. An excerpt reads: "Hole #12—the island hole—this hole looks like a monster, but is actually a birdie hole! The directional flag is 165 yards from the tee. Should your tee shot "splash," the drop area is the rear of the ladies' tee. This is an enjoyable course occasionally featuring a tail wind as bonus!"

During all holiday periods The Buccaneer features a special complementary children's program with such enjoyable activities as sandcastle building contests, water games, treasure hunts, snorkeling parties, tropical arts and crafts, and remote car races. For the older kids (at a separate fee), some of the pioneering environmental programs may be of interest, such as a rain forest walk, a salt river hike, or a grotto beach walk.

The Homestead 1766

Since 1766, The Homestead has offered visitors an incomparable retreat, located amidst the beauty of Virginia's Allegheny Mountains. When you visit, you will find 500 luxuriously appointed rooms and suites, superb dining (more than 9 restaurants to choose from), and exquisite shopping, in addition to traditional Southern hospitality in a gracious atmosphere.

The Homestead is 15,000 acres of relaxation and recreation for the whole family. Enjoy horseback and carriage rides, shooting sports, 100 miles of hiking and biking trails, fly fishing, falconry, bowling, skiing, ice-skating, snowboarding, and children's program. The Fitness Center comes complete with Cybex equipment, treadmills, steppers and stationary cycles, aerobics and yoga classes. On the ground floor are the spectacular indoor pool and the heated outdoor pool. And don't forget to pamper yourself at the renowned Homestead Spa.

If golf is your game, you are in for a treat. The Cascades Course touts a nearly incomparable tradition of championship golf, and is the jewel in the trio of Homestead courses. The Old Course—boasting the oldest first tee in continuous use in the U.S.—dates back to 1892 and is an original Donald Ross design, while the Lower Cascades Course features the work of Robert Trent Jones, Sr. Each course presents golfers with unique challenges, characteristics and breathtaking scenery.

Address: US Hwy 20 N, Hot Springs, 24445
Phone: 540-839-1766
800-838-1766
E-mail: homestead.info@ourclub.com
Web site: http://www.thehomestead.com
No. of Rooms: 510
Rates: Inquire
Restaurant: Ten restaurants including: Sports Bar, Sam Snead's Tavern, The Grille, Cafe Albert, Casino Club
Business Fac.: 60,000 sq. ft. of meeting space, full conference equipment and facilities, Theater
Sports Fac.: European spa, 9 run ski area, Ice skating, Snowboarding, Snow tubing, Gun Club, Horseback riding, Mountain biking, 100 miles of hiking/riding trails, Bowling, Tennis, Falconry
Location: Surrounded by the Virginia Allegheny Mountains
Courses: The Cascades (6566), Lower Cascades (6619), Old Course (6211)
No. of Holes: 54
Club House: 540-839-1766
Reservations: Call for reservations
Season: April–October

The Tides

Address: King Carter Drive, P.O.
Box 480, Irvington, 22480
Phone: 804-438-5000
800-873-3746
Fax: 804-438-5222
Web site: http://www.the-tides.com
No. of Rooms: 110
Rates: Inquire
Restaurant: Rappahannock Dining
Room, Cap'N B's, Summer House,
The Tides Lodge
Bar: Chesapeake Club
Business Fac.: Conference Rooms
Sports Fac.: Tennis courts, Boating,
Health club, Swimming
Location: Rappahannock River

Courses: Golden Eagle (6511),
Executive 9 Hole Course
No. of Holes: 27
Guest Policy: Call for tee time,
guests have priority
Club House: 804-438-5501
Reservations: Telephone for reser-
vations
Season: Open all year
Carts: Carts are also available

Poised on the shores of historic Carter's Creek
and the Rappahannock River, The Tides Inn is a
small family resort whose main attraction is its
idyllic setting. Just an hour's drive north of Williamsburg and three hours south of Washington,
DC, this forty-year-old rambling clapboard Inn
hosts many returning guests who seek the relaxed
pace, amenities and climate of Virginia's Northern Neck.

Most rooms have spectacular water views and
many have balconies. The Lee Suite, with 2 canopied beds, jacuzzi and marble counters, is
accented with lovely antiques.

Lunch and cocktails are served at the Summer
House, aboard the yachts, at the Beach Pavilion
or at Cap'n B's at the Golden Eagle. Dinner in the
Rappahannock Dining Room overlooking the
river, might begin with a hot oyster cocktail and
be followed by luscious sauteed soft shell crab.
The Inn's policy is to offer activities on a complimentary basis, except for golf, mid-April to
November. This includes yacht cruises, paddleboats, oyster roasts, bicycles, and canoes. History
buffs can explore the birthplaces of Washington
and Lee, the shops and lore of colonial Williamsburg, and the backroads of Lancaster County.

Two eighteen-hole courses are available for
guests, the Golden Eagle, and Tartan Golf Course.
The Golden Eagle, designed by George Cobb, was
chosen in 1989 by *Golf Digest* as one of the Top 3
Courses in Virginia, and is the site of the Virginia
State Amateur Golf Tournament for 1991. Several
holes play over the lake on a course that's fairly
hilly considering this is a fairly flat part of Virginia. The #5 is the one to write home about—a
great par 4 experience! The tee shot is difficult
because the player must bite off only what he
thinks he can carry on the fly. Water, again, but
the carry is a shorter one—and then the green.
It's guarded by water on the left and two large
bunkers on the right, sloping gently towards the
water. Good shots are rewarded, and poor ones
penalized.

Tartan is noted for narrow tree-lined fairways,
water on 10 holes, and numerous twists, dog-legs
and dips. Greens are large, and a gurgling stream
seems to be everywhere.

Kingsmill Resort

There are a few places that each of us should visit during our lifetime, and Williamsburg, swathed in history, and basking in glorious restoration heads the list. Developed by Anheuser-Busch, this meticulously-planned conference center/resort reeks of quality in concept, design, and amenities. Lodging is in condominiums which vary in size. The 60,000 square foot conference center can accommodate large and small meetings, and offers state-of-the-art facilities. There are several fine restaurants on the premises, all offering expansive views of the historic James. Don't miss the colonial atmosphere at Moody's Tavern—a paneled cozy gathering place. The Sports Club is fully equipped with indoor and outdoor pools, saunas and racquetball courts, even a grill, while a game room for billiards, cards and chess occupies the top floor. Tennis buffs appreciate a complete shop and 12 all-weather courts, plus use of a ball machine. The marina's gorgeous—in a protected harbor with picnic and beach area. It's here that you'll get everything you need for saltwater and freshwater fishing, or tie up if you're cruising the area.

You'll have all of historic Williamsburg to devour, plus the wonders of adjacent Busch Gardens, a re-creation of eight European villages. In addition, there are more than 30 rides, shopping and live entertainment.

The accolades accorded golf facilities here are well-deserved. Challenge yourself to Pete Dye's River Course, home of the PGA Anheuser Busch Golf Classic. Walk the fairways where Tom Sieckmann, after overshooting the 18th green, took home the money in 1988. Plenty of big rolls and swells on the greens. Or tee off on Arnold Palmer's Plantation Course, around ponds, lakes and river views. Curtis Strange, a familiar figure especially after the 1988 U.S. Open, is the Touring Pro; he frequently conducts clinics and exhibitions here. As if all this isn't enough the Golf Shop heads the list of "friendliest and most helpful anywhere."

Address: 1010 Kingsmill Road, Williamsburg, 23185
Phone: 757-253-1703
800-832-5665
Fax: 757-253-8237
Web site: http://www.kingsmill.com
No. of Rooms: 400
Rates: $$
Restaurant: The Bray Dining Room, Regattas' Cafe & Market, Eagles' at the Golf Club, The Deck
Bar: Moody's Tavern
Business Fac.: Fully staffed modern Conference Center with expansive meeting and ballrooms
Sports Fac.: State-of-the-art sports club, 15 tennis courts, Billiards, Indoor/outdoor pools, Biking, Boating, Fishing
Location: On the James River in Williamsburg, VA

Courses: The River Course (6853, par 71), The Plantation (6543, par 71), The Woods (6784, par 71)
No. of Holes: 54
Guest Policy: Open to public
Club House: 757-253-3906
Fees: ↑↑↑
Reservations: Can make reservations 300 days in advance
Season: April–October
Carts: Cart included in fees

Williamsburg Inn

Address: Francis Street, P.O. Box 1176, Williamsburg, 23187
Phone: 757-229-1000
800-962-6770
Fax: 757-220-7729
Web site: http://www.colonialwilliamsburg.com
No. of Rooms: 39
Rates: $$$
Restaurant: Regency Dining Room, Gold & Green Clubhouse Grills
Bar: Regency Lounge
Sports Fac.: Fitness center, Indoor swimming pool, Outdoor swimming pool, Tennis courts, Croquet/lawn bowling
Location: Colonial Williamsburg

Courses: Gold Course (6700, par 71), Green Course (7120, par 72)
No. of Holes: 45
Guest Policy: Open to public
Club House: 757-220-7696
Fees: ↑↑↑
Reservations: Reservations available 14 days in advance
Season: April–October
Carts: Cart included in fees

The restoration of Virginia's 18th century capital, where George Washington, Patrick Henry and Thomas Jefferson plotted revolution, is an exercise in authenticity not to be missed. Located adjacent to the 173-acre Historic Area, the whitewashed brick rambling Regency style Inn, built in 1937, is furnished with antiques and faithful reproductions. Owned and operated by the Colonial Williamsburg Foundation, the Inn also offers accommodations in taverns and colonial homes within the Historic Area. Providence Hall, a restored home, is available for special events.

The Inn's guest list is long and impressive, and includes Queen Elizabeth II and Prince Philip, the Emperor and Empress of Japan, Sir Winston Churchill, movie personalities such as Elizabeth Taylor, John Wayne, and Ronald Reagan.

The Regency Dining Room, a study in tranquil green, Empire accents, and Chinoiserie, reflects the quiet elegance of the landed gentry of 19th century England. An exquisite afternoon tea is served daily in the East Lounge, while the Regency Lounge is a comfortable meeting spot, complete with piano music.

Recreational and sports facilities include 4 clay and 4 Hartru tennis courts, an indoor and an outdoor swimming pool, lawn bowling, croquet, and a full health spa.

Golfers will find 27 holes of challenging Robert Trent Jones' design here in Virginia's picturesque Tidewater area. Each August, the course hosts the Middle Atlantic PGA Championship, but other times guests have no trouble getting a tee time. Opened in 1963, the Golden Horseshoe Golf Course spreads over 125 acres of rolling terrain, with fairways stretching over a five-acre lake, up densely wooded ravines, and through glades of flowering trees and bushes, culminating in large sculptured greens. The hole that seems to fascinate the most is the 16th—"island green". The par-three, 168-yard hole plays without fairway to a green completely surrounded by water. As if the water isn't enough, Jones tempts the wayward ball with three menacing bunkers at water's edge. Jack Nicklaus established the course record—67 from the championship tees, in 1967. An additional nine holes, the par-31 Spotswood Course, also by Jones, has plenty of doglegs, lakes, and cushioned turf.

Wintergreen Resort

High in Virginia's Blue Ridge Mountains lies Wintergreen, an 11,000-acre, four season resort that is fast becoming recognized as one of the nation's premier vacation destinations. The resort encompasses both the beauty of its Blue Ridge Mountain setting as well as 2,000 acres in the valley below known as Stoney Creek. Located just 43 miles southwest of Charlottesville, VA, Wintergreen Resort offers a setting of rare natural beauty and year-round fun for the whole family.

Wintergreen has received numerous accolades. It was selected as one of *Golf Magazine*'s "Best Golf Resorts in America." *Golf Digest* recently named Wintergreen's new Stoney Creek Golf course the "Best New Resort Course in the Continental U.S." *Tennis Magazine* selected the resort as one of the "Top 50 Tennis Resorts in the Country." *Family Circle Magazine* named it one of the Top Ten "Family Mountain Resorts in the U.S." *USA Today* called Wintergreen "the best ski resort experience in the South." The resort was also recognized as "one of the most environmentally sensitive resort communities in the country" as winners of the National Environment Achievement Award presented by the American Hotel & Motel Association.

The resort also features luxurious accommodations in mountain villas, fine dining from continental cuisine to family style, 25 miles of marked hiking trails, 25 tennis courts, 10 ski slopes, horseback riding, swimming in 6 outdoor and one indoor pool, fishing, swimming and canoeing in 20-acre Lake Monocan, a Spa that features a swimming, Jacuzzi, exercise room and sauna, a conference center that can accommodate groups from 10 to 650, and year round innovative children's programs.

However, most of all, the resort offers a unique, first-rate golf experience with its mountain and valley setting. In fact, the 3,000-foot difference in elevations between mountain and valley creates a 15 degree temperature difference so that weather permitting, guests can ski in the morning and play golf in the afternoon, all on the same day from December through March.

The resort's four-season appeal offers something for everyone in the family. With such a diversification of activities, it is no wonder the resorts tag line is "never the same vacation twice".

Address: P.O. Box 706, Wintergreen, 22958
Phone: 804-325-2200
800-266-2444
Fax: 804-325-7448
Web site: http://www.wintergreenresort.com
No. of Rooms: 291
Rates: $$
Restaurant: Copper Mine, Devils Grill, The Edge at Cooper's Vantage, Cafe Verandah at Stoney Creek, Pryors
Bar: Copper Mine Lounge, Devils Grill Lounge
Business Fac.: 14 meeting rooms, Skyline Pavilion, Banquet facilities, capacity 10-650
Sports Fac.: Horseback riding, Spa & Fitness center, Canoeing/boating/kayaking, Rock climbing, Biking, Fishing, Skiing, Game room
Location: Perched above the Shenandoah Valley in the Blue Ridge Mountains of Virginia

Course: Stoney Creek (7005, par 72)
No. of Holes: 18
Guest Policy: Open to public
Club House: 804-325-2200
Fees: ↑↑
Reservations: Reservations available 90 days in advance
Season: April–October
Carts: Carts included in fees

Resort Semiahmoo

Address: 9565 Semiahmoo Pkwy,
Blaine, 98230
Phone: 360-371-2000
800-770-7992
Fax: 360-371-5490
E-mail: info@semiahmoo.com
Web site: http://www.
semiahmoo.com
No. of Rooms: 198
Rates: Inquire
Restaurant: Stars, Pierside,
Packers Oyster Bar, Great Blue
Heron Bar & Grill, Palmers, Gift
shop Cafe
Bar: Packers Lounge, Great Blue
Heron Bar
Business Fac.: 20,000 sq. ft. confer-
ence facilites, ballrooms, theater,
exhibit hall, boardroom, parlors
Sports Fac.: Complete Spa, 1100
acre wildlife preserve, Tennis,
Health club, Biking and walking
trails
Location: On a scenic peninsula,
surrounded by the pristine northern
waters of Puget Sound

Course: Semi-ah-moo (6435)
No. of Holes: 18
Guest Policy: Dress code strictly
enforced, open to the public
Club House: 800-231-4425
Reservations: Call for reservations
Season: Open all year
Carts: Carts are available, but
walking is permitted

Washington's newest and finest destination resort
hotel, Resort Semi-ah-moo, is located on the site
of the historic Semi-ah-moo Salmon Cannery, at
the far Northwest corner of the Continental U.S.
At this natural wildlife refuge, you'll be sharing
the beaches with seals, shorebirds and migratory
ducks and geese. Here, great bald eagles soar
overhead, and deer step lightly through the
underbrush.

The elegant Stars restaurant highlights the
inn's seafront location, with two levels facing the
water and an open-aired decor accented by natural fir and hemlock. Under the direction of Chef
David Benot, you'll experience the delights of specialties like Baked Salmon Wrapped in Parch-
ment, accompanied by a fine Northwest wine.

Plenty of area attractions will keep the non-
golfer busy. Nearly every imaginable sporting
diversion is available on the resort premises,
including indoor tennis, racquetball, squash and
programmed conditioning. Outdoors, enjoy jogging trails, cycling lanes and paths which wind
along the beach and up through majestic firs.

But, Semi-ah-moo's historic marina is probably most popular of all. A seafaring place since the
1880s when the Star Fleet sailed from the cannery docks and gold seeker shipped off to Alaska,
today's Semi-ah-moo offers new excitement with
summer cruises to the nearby American San Juan
Islands, the Canadian Channel Islands and Old
English Victoria.

The championship Arnold Palmer-designed
golf course opened to rave reviews in July, 1986.
The 7000 yards of cedar, hemlock and fir have
been sculpted from the uplands forest. Generous
landing areas, a profusion of white sand bunkers,
and rolling fairways test every golfing ability, with
water coming into play on seven holes, necessitat-
ing precise shot-making from start to finish. Bent
grass has been used on tees, greens and fairways
for a premium playing surface.

Resort at Port Ludlow

To spend time at Port Ludlow on Puget Sound is to escape to an azure-colored water wonderland with snow-capped Mount Baker in the background, rugged pine and cedar forests, and cool, clear lakes. Designed for family enjoyment, recreational activities include a heated outdoor pool in summer (indoor pool and jacuzzi fall through spring), a squash court, 7 plexipave tennis courts, saunas, a pitch and putt area, bicycles, and a supervised children's game room. Join the sailboats on Puget Sound—you can rent one or join a sight-seeing tour at the 300-slip saltwater marina, and should you be anchoring here and want to play golf, the resort maintains a fleet of vans to take marina guests to the links.

The Harbormaster Restaurant, overlooking the Sound, is popular with visitors and locals. We begin our feast with stuffed shrimp before digging into a fresh whole dungeness crab for two, and finished with a luscious raspberry and chocolate truffle. The Wreckroom Lounge livened up the evening with strains of live 50's, 60's and 70's tunes. Many guests enjoy the solitude of the 3500 acres, but should you yearn to explore the environs, you'll find nature hikes, raft trips, charter fishing, and poking around historic Port Townsend.

The piece de resistance here is the magnificent golf course. Home of the annual Pro-Am tournament, the Pac Rim tournament, and the St. Patricks Day Couples Classic, the course is rarely crowded despite its notoriety. The American Society of Golf Course Architects ranks the ten year old layout in the top one percent of the best designed courses in the nation on the basis of natural beauty, design aesthetics, drama and subtlety, fairness, and how well it plays.

Designed by Robert Muir Graves the course sits on high ground, and was created to preserve the natural beauty of the forest, streams and lakes, and above all, to take advantage of the vistas across the bay. Voted "Best in the Northwest" consistently, the course was carved from a dense forest, with towering firs flanking its fairways, and wild rhododendrons bursting forth in spring. The par-4 thirteenth hole will cause the player to exercise his patience, and certainly test his skills. The U.S.G.A. has rated the course 138 on the SLOPE system, compared to a national average of 113, giving you an idea of its difficulty.

Address: 200 Olympic Place, Port Ludlow, 98365
Phone: 360-437-2222
800-732-1239
Fax: 360-437-2482
E-mail: resort@ portludlowresort.com
Web site: http://www. portludlowresort.com
No. of Rooms: 140
Rates: $
Restrictions: No pets, no smoking
Restaurant: The Harbormaster Restaurant, The Wreckroom Lounge & Sundeck
Bar: The Lounge
Business Fac.: Conference facilities for up to 250
Sports Fac.: Swimming, Golf, Jacuzzi, Sauna, Kayaking, The Beach Club, Water sports
Location: 28 miles from Seattle by car, 1/2 hour by ferry

Course: Port Ludlow Golf Course
No. of Holes: 27
Club House: 800-455-0272
Fees: ⏐
Reservations: Call for reservations
Season: Open all year

The Greenbrier

Address: 300 West Main Street, White Sulphur Springs, 24986
Phone: 304-536-1110
800-624-6070
Fax: 304-536-7834
Web site: http://www. greenbrier.com
No. of Rooms: 650
Rates: Inquire
Restrictions: No pets allowed
Restaurant: Ryder Cup Grille, Main Dining Room, Old White Club, Tavern Room, Golf Club Dining Room, Drapers Cafe
Bar: Rhododendron Cocktail Lounge
Business Fac.: 30 meeting rooms and an exhibit hall
Sports Fac.: Tennis courts, Swimming pools, Bowling alley, Horseback riding, Billiards, Ice skating, Croquet, Shuffleboard, Par-course fitness trails
Location: On 6500 acres in the scenic Allegheny Mountains

Course: Greenbrier (6311)
No. of Holes: 54
Guest Policy: Call for availability
Club House: 304-536-1110
Reservations: May be made with hotel
Season: April–mid November
Carts: Caddies

This is the Grande Dame of American tradition, rich in history and nostalgia. Long a spa for those seeking a panacea for plowman's knee or tinker's elbow, tales of miraculous recoveries spread, and it became a mecca for wealthy Southern patrons. Today's Greenbrier looks like an elegant hybrid of the White House, surrounded by 6500 acres of broad lawns, a profusion of gardens, and acres of eastern deciduous forests. Add the Allegheny Mountains as a backdrop, parlors glowing with antiques and Oriental art, and a dedication to service often touted by rarely delivered, and you won't want to leave. Guests can stay in a variety of accommodations, ranging from traditional hotel rooms and suites, to cottages and estate houses. Each is individually decorated, no two are alike.

Upon waking, your biggest problem will be choosing from the plethora of activities available. Horseback riding along miles of wooded trails, jogging, fishing for trout and bass, golf (of course), indoor or outdoor tennis, shuffleboard, table tennis, lawn bowling, bicycling, swimming, inside or out, or an invigorating hike, to name a few. Don't forget to take the horse-drawn carriage ride through the grounds. The spa beckons, and such a spa! Daylong pampering sessions offering mineral baths and the works are available to all guests. Breakfast and a six-course dinner are included in the room rate, and a lavish luncheon buffet in the Golf Club Dining Room will leave you sated. For lighter fare, try the Golf Club or the coffee shop.

The resort is a National Historic landmark, and for those curious about other historic spots, head out to some of the Civil War battlefields, such as Droop Mountain. Pearl Buck's birthplace isn't far, or you might want to check the action at Organ Caves.

Three scenic championship courses are available. Lakeside opened in 1910. Old White, was next, designed in 1914 by Charles Blair Macdonald, who had learned the game in Scotland as a youngster, and his partner Seth Raynor. Jack Nicklaus redesigned what had been a somewhat flat Greenbrier course in 1976. Carved in a valley, with Kates Mountain as a backdrop, the course is heavily wooded with oak and maple. One course stays open all year, so if you should want to play a round in January, it's yours!

Maxwelton Braes Resort

A historic resort nestled on the quiet side of the Door County peninsula. The 18 hole championship course is par 70 with a USGA rating of 68.7 and slope of 114. The resort includes suites and lodge rooms, McArdle's Casual Fine Dining Restaurant, Droves Sports Bar & Grill, and a heated outdoor pool all on premise.

Address: 7670 Highway 57, Baileys Harbor, 54202
Phone: 920-839-2321
Fax: 920-839-2729
E-mail: information@maxwelton-braes.com
Web site: http://www.maxwelton-braes.com
No. of Rooms: 24
Rates: $
Restrictions: No pets allowed, Non-smoking resort, No charge for children under 6
Restaurant: McArdle's Casual Fine Dining
Bar: Droves Sports Bar & Grill
Business Fac.: Banquet hall which comfortably holds groups up to 200. Can also do smaller functions and group outings.
Sports Fac.: Heated outdoor swimming pool, horseshoe pit, badmiton, volleyball, croquet.
Location: Set in the heart of Door County on the quiet side

Course: Maxwelton Braes (6041, par 70)
No. of Holes: 18
Guest Policy: Open to public
Club House: 920-839-2321
Fees:
Reservations: Call to make reservations
Season: Golf—April–November
Carts: Pull and gas carts available

Lakewoods Resort

Address: HC73 Box 715, Cable, 54821
Phone: 715-794-2561
800-255-5937
E-mail: info@lakewoodsresort.com
Web site: http://www.
lakewoodsresort.com
Rates: $
Restaurant: Dining Room, live music and entertainment on weekends and holidays
Bar: Cocktail bar
Business Fac.: Conference space for 3-300
Sports Fac.: Tennis courts, Indoor and outdoor swimming pool, Boating, Fishing, Golf teaching center, Hiking, Biking, Snowmobiling, Birdwatching, cross-country skiing, Volleyball, Horseshoes
Location: In the Chequamegon National Forest

Course: Forest Ridges Golf Course (6066)
No. of Holes: 18
Guest Policy: Open to the public, guests get discounted fees
Club House: 715-794-2561
Fees: ⌐
Reservations: Call for reservation information
Season: Open all year—golf only March–October
Carts: GPS power carts

From the warmth of the Northwoods lodge rooms and luxurious condominiums to the fantastic views from the cottages, settle into comfort at Lakewoods Resort. Enjoy a warming fire in the fireplace while you savor the beauty of Lake Namakagon and northern Wisconsin. For the ultimate experience, stay in their private island cabin. The 82 lodge rooms offer extended cable TV, free movies, dataports and free local calls.

The 18-hole golf course is an addition to the already complete resort facility, which includes tennis, boating, fishing, indoor and outdoor pools. Gorgeous fall panoramas can be viewed from the 3200-acre Lake Namakagon, and Chequamegon National Forest offers nature, biking, hiking paths, trails, and gleaming glacial lakes. At Lakewoods they've got the best in winter activities with snowmobiling, cross-country skiing, ice-skating, sledding, and snow-shoeing right from your door.

Golf architect Joel Goldstrand designed the Forest Ridges championship, 18-hole golf course. The Northwoods course is 6,066 yards with four tee positions, three water holes, and eleven carries. The bent grass tees and greens with intermediate cut and groomed roughs are all immaculately maintained. Forest Ridges has a separate teaching center and pro shop buildings, driving range and practice putting area. Lakewoods Golf Academy offers golf schools and vacation trips in a variety of sizes and lengths. The Blue Course has a rating of 70.9.

Coachman's Inn

Coachman's Golf Resort is located in the heartland of Southern Wisconsin, just southeast of Madison. The beautiful, golf-side rooms have a private whirlpool for two, fireplace, TV and VCR, refrigerator, microwave and coffee maker. The Resort offers casual dining, lounges, and banquet facilities for up to 200, and they provide everything you need for a wonderful golf vacation or just a pleasant day on the links.

The dining room at Coachman's Golf Resort serves many gourmet specialties in an English country inn setting. Coachman's wine list is nationally acclaimed. Prices are quite reasonable and the food is prepared with the finest quality, freshest ingredients! Come for the golf; stay for the food!

The 27-hole regulation course is fun and challenging. Located on a gently rolling landscape lined with oaks and willows, Coachman's course holds several water hazards, as well as a 503-yard hole. They are a spikeless facility with a pro shop, on-site lockers, and cart rentals available. Be sure to ask about their fabulous golf packages like the Great Escape, which includes unlimited golf, lodging Friday and Saturday nights, Friday evening fish fry dinner, Saturday breakfast or lunch, & dinner, Sunday brunch, and use of their outdoor pool.

Address: 984 County A, Edgerton, 53534
Phone: 608-884-8484
800-940-8485
Fax: 608-884-7720
E-mail: coachman@coachmans.com
Web site: http://www.coachmans.com
Rates: $
Restaurant: Dining Room—breakfast, lunch and dinner
Bar: Coachman's Bar
Business Fac.: Banquet and meeting facilities, 3 meeting rooms, capacity 200
Location: In the heartland of Souhtern Wisconsin

Courses: Red (2975, par 35), White (3205, par 36), Blue (3215, par 36)
No. of Holes: 27
Guest Policy: Open to public
Club House: 800-940-8485
Fees: ↑
Reservations: Guests can make tee times after reservations confirmed
Season: Open all year
Carts: Cart available

Teal Wing Golf Club
at Ross' Teal Lake Lodge

Address: 12425 N Ross Rd,
Hayward, 54843
Phone: 715-462-3631
E-mail: rossteal@win.bright.net
Web site: http://www.rossteal.com
Rates: Inquire
Restaurant: Dining Room
Sports Fac.: Fishing, Boating,
Swimming, Hiking, Biking, Tennis
courts
Location: 8 hours from Chicago-
land, 3 hours from Minneapolis/St.
Paul

While the golf course is now in its fifth year, the
resort has been here, in the very same family, for
80 years and is just entering the fourth generation
of proud ownership and family management.

With 24 lakeside guesthomes that range from
older style log cabins to new style log homes, from
one bedroom to four bedrooms, from romantic
homes for two to spacious homes for 14 for family
reunions, this is a happy and relaxed place. Fish a
little, golf a little, dine a little, swim a little and
never get into your car! Pets are welcome too!
This is truly a rare vacation.

Course: Teal Wing (6379, par 72)
No. of Holes: 18
Guest Policy: Open to public
Club House: 715-462-9051
Fees: ⌐
Reservations: Call for reservations
Season: May–November
Carts: Carts available

The American Club

Built in 1918 as housing for immigrant Kohler Company employees, The American Club has been transformed into one of the Midwest's favorite hotels and conference centers. Set in a quiet village atmosphere, the English Tudor style building is just as breathtaking inside as outside.

Their four sumptuous restaurants also reflect the Club's history. The Immigrant, their showcase restaurant, features such gourmet delights as smoked Irish lamb, fresh Dover sole and delicate white medallions of veal, all complemented by an impressive selection of fine wines from their own cellars.

Take advantage of the Club's Sports Core, one of the country's finest and most complete health and racquet facilities. The Parcourse, a 2.2 mile woodchip jogging and exercise trail, provides for a lovely walk or jog. And to relax, try a refreshing whirlpool soak or an invigorating sauna.

Rediscover nature at River Wildlife, Kohler's unique 800-acre wilderness preserve. Charter a boat on Lake Michigan or paddle your course on the Sheboygan River; the fishing's great. Along the banks of the Sheboygan River a few miles upstream, is a true Pete Dye masterpiece. It's a rugged, natural course with plenty of mounds, moguls, deep bunkers, a gorgeous pond, wild grasses. Three nines—River, Valleys and Meadows give the player plenty of chance to see the water. For the average player, accuracy is the challenge. In Pete Dye's words, "There could not be a better natural setting for golf."

Address: Highland Dr, Kohler, 53044
Phone: 920-457-8000
800-344-2838
Fax: 920-457-0299
Web site: http://www.americanclub.com
No. of Rooms: 236
Rates: $$$
Restaurant: The Immigrant, Wisconsin Room, The Greenhouse, River Wildlife, Cucina, Jumpin' Jacks, Woodlake Cafe
Bar: Horse & Plow, The Winery, Blackwolf Run, River Bar & Cucina
Business Fac.: Complete Business Service center, Full-service audio-visual dept., Confernece facilities for up to 998
Sports Fac.: Sports Core—complete fitness center, River Wildlife game preserve, hunting, fishing, hiking, canoeing, horseback riding, cross-country skiing, trap shooting
Location: East Central Wisconsin

Courses: River Course at Blackwolf Run (6991, par 72), Whistling Straits (7288, par 72)
No. of Holes: 36
Guest Policy: Open to public
Club House: 800 618 5535
Fees: ⅠⅠⅠ
Reservations: Reservations available 14 days in advance
Season: April–November
Carts: Carts available for those unable to walk; caddies available

Grand Geneva Resort & Spa

Address: Hwy 50 & US 12, Lake Geneva, 53147
Phone: 414-248-8811
800-558-3417
Fax: 414-249-4763
E-mail: info@grandgeneva.com
Web site: http://www.grandgeneva.com
No. of Rooms: 355
Rates: Inquire
Restaurant: Newport Grill, Ristorante Brissago, The Grand Cafe
Business Fac.: 50,000 sq ft of meeting space includes 13,500 sq ft Convention Center, 7,680 sq ft Grand Ballroom, 22 meeting and board rooms. Business services include lighting, teleprompting, and audiovisuals.
Sports Fac.: Indoor/outdoor swimming pools, Dan Patch Stables
Location: On Lake Geneva

Courses: The Brute (7528, par 72), The Highlands (6633, par 71)
No. of Holes: 36
Club House: 800-558-3417
Reservations: Call for reservations
Season: April–November

Americana bought the former Playboy Hotel in 1982, poured millions into it, and eureka! Today's resort pulls out all the stops with conference facilities and recreational and fitness amenities. About an hour and a half's drive from O'Hare of Milwaukee, the resort resembles a modern college campus—lots of trees, walkways and cement buildings on 1,400 acres of wooded rolling countryside—all perched on the shores of Lake Geneva. There are rooms, suites and condominiums here—over 350 of them. After you've checked in, take time to stroll the grounds and acclimate yourself to the many diversions. You'll find two pools, indoors and outdoors, 8 outdoor and 4 indoor tennis courts, racquet ball courts, horse stables, miniature golf, rental boats, and a skeet and trap-shooting range. Don't miss the Nautilus-equipped Fitness Center.

Wine and dine in the lavish Americana Steakhouse, Annie's Country Kitchen and the Sidewalk Cafe—two lounges and Sweet Tooth, an ice cream parlor.

Downtown Lake Geneva has recently undergone a restoration, and its unique blend of rural charm, historical significance and retail endeavors make it an attractive destination.

Two distinctively different courses comprise golf here. Briar Patch, the last course Pete Dye and Jack Nicklaus did together is typical Scottish style with small greens, (some double), deep rough, and little rolling hills. There are five sets of tees on this championship layout. A lot of celebrity tournaments are played here, plus state PGA functions. The aptly-named Brute, with a rating of 74.5, is a longer course, with water on twelve holes, and typically American in design. Big long holes, big bunkers, big greens, big tees, and big scores characterize this Robert B. Harris course. With lots of acreage, you won't find parallel fairways or crowds—just unimpaired vistas of the lake and Paul Bunyan's greens.

The Grand Adventure Club is for kids 4-12, and there's the Teen Club for the older children. There are treasure hunts, baking cookies with the resort chef, paint t-shirts, create computer art graphics, or a magic show. The clubs operate 7 days a week in summer, otherwise on weekends and Thanksgiving, Christmas, New Year's and Easter break. The fee is $15 for a half day and $40 for a full day (includes lunch).

Scharenberg's White Lake Golf Resort

Scharenberg's White Lake Golf Resort has something for everyone: golfing, lake sports, lounging, and sightseeing. And there is a place for everyone too: 17 cottages and homes where pets are welcome, 12 guest units, 6 chalets, and homesite building lots. Prepare to be in awe from the two-dozen peacocks that roam free on the scenic grounds, a staple on the country estate for over 70 years.

Enjoy the view at the full-service restaurant and be sure to try the famous chuck wagon buffet, duck and wild rice specialty, nightly specials and original recipe corn fritters. While the parents are in the cocktail bar, the kids can be in the children's rec room, complete with pool table, ping pong, jukebox, and video games.

When not golfing, go water skiing, tubing, sailing, diving, or boating on the White Lake. Fish for Bass, Bluegill, Perch and Crappie. Or, enjoy the beach with a water slide, two rafts and playground equipment, and floating rope protection while swimming. Tired of water activities? Take a nature hike, bike or peacock watch, see the memorial parks, historic rivers, museums, flea markets, and trout streams.

The golf course, a Par 72, 18-hole course, has been carved out of the 200 acres of ancient glacier lands and is accented by hills, woods, and ponds. Open to the public, the course has several elevation changes, dog legs, sand traps and water hazards. There is a clubhouse pro shop and practice green as well as a cocktail bar and sandwich shop for snacks.

Address: N4785 19th Avenue, Montello, 53949
Phone: 608-297-2278
Web site: http://www. wisvacations.com/scharenbergs
No. of Rooms: 35
Rates: Inquire
Restrictions: Pets welcome
Restaurant: The Restaurant
Bar: Cocktail lounge
Sports Fac.: Water skiing, Tubing, Sailing, Scuba diving, Fishing, Boating, Sandy beach, Water slide, Playground equipment
Location: Off Hwy 23 between Montello & Princeton

Course: Scharenberg's White Lake Golf Course (par 72)
No. of Holes: 18
Guest Policy: Open to public
Club House: 608-297-2255
Fees: |
Reservations: Call for reservations
Season: Not open in winter
Carts: Cart are also available

Olympia Resort & Spa

Address: 1350 Royale Mile Rd,
Oconomowoc, 53066
Phone: 414-567-0311
800-558-9573
Fax: 414-567-5934
E-mail: pkrejci@execpc.com
Web site: http://www.
olympiaresort.com
No. of Rooms: 391
Rates: Inquire
Restrictions: No pets allowed
Restaurant: Terrace Dining Room
Bar: Polo Lounge
Business Fac.: Administrative assistance, Copiers, Conference rooms,
capacity 3900
Sports Fac.: Swimming pool, Tennis
courts, Handball, Skiing, Polo
Location: Waukesha County

Course: Olympic Village Resort
(6458)
No. of Holes: 18
Guest Policy: Call for availability
Club House: 414-567-0311
Reservations: Resort guests have
priority
Season: April–October

Carefully designed to blend with its dramatic 400-acre setting of forest, hills, rivers, and lakes, this complete luxury resort of stunning modern beauty lies in southern Wisconsin lake country. The resort's decor allows nature to come inside, as you'll see when you arrive in the lobby that features a fireplace wall that sweeps to the sky, celestial windows that are massive skylights, and handsomely beamed ceilings that add a finishing touch.

The Terrace is Olympia's main dining room, where international dishes are prepared with flair and served at a leisurely pace. Candlelight makes the atmosphere elegant and glass window walls that reveal a panoramic view of spectacular sunsets and the green countryside beyond make it all the more relaxing. Don't miss the Sunday Brunch here; it's a favorite with everyone. A charming alternative is The Beach House at Silver Lake, an informal restaurant featuring fresh seafood and perfectly prepared steaks and chops.

If tennis is your game, play year round on excellent indoor and outdoor facilities at the Country Club. Racquetball, volleyball, badminton, softball, and shuffleboard are also available. After the workout, pamper yourself at Olympia's Spa, where you can relax in their magnificent Roman pools, indulge in a luxurious massage or an herbal wrap, and enjoy a tingling loofa treatment.

While the Spa rejuvenates, relaxes and pampers your body, the eighteen holes here will challenge your lower body action in another way—into the downswing for more power with your driver. This course, most of which is level or gently rolling with many crisscrossing small lakes and streams, plays longer than the yardage indicates. Both nines are very different, with the front characterized by long, narrow holes and rolling tree-lined fairways. The back is more open and flat, but water awaits you on seven holes.

The golfing facilities are pros at handling tournaments, as well as catering to many large corporate and national meetings. Its unique combination of exhilarating golf and a "full-service" health spa put it in a special class.

More
Golf Resorts

---------------------------ALABAMA---------------------------

Willow Point Golf & CC, One Willow Point Road, 35010   Alexander City
Ph: 256-329-9091

Point Aquarius, Box 110A, 35014 Ph: 256-268-9411   Alpine

Still Waters Resort, 1000 Still Waters Dr, 36853 Ph: 256-825-7021   Dadeville

Lakepoint Resort, Box 94, 36027 Ph: 334-687-8011   Eufaula

Gulf State Park Resort Hotel, P.O. Box 437, 36542 Ph: 334-948-4853   Gulf Shores

Lake Guntersville State Park, Box 224, 35976 Ph: 256-582-2061   Guntersville

Sky Center, 10001 Hwy 20, 35806 Ph: 256-772-9661   Huntsville

Cloudmont Golf & Ski Resort, Box 435, 35984 Ph: 256-634-4344   Mentone

Legends at Capital Hills, 2500 Legends Circle, 36066 Ph: 334-290-1235 Prattville

Joe Wheeler State Park Resort, Box 369A, 35652 Ph: 256-247-5461   Rogersville

North River Yacht Club, Box 3199, 35404 Ph: 205-345-0202   Tuscaloosa

---------------------------ARIZONA---------------------------

Franscisco Grande Resort, P.O. Box 326, 85222 Ph: 602-836-6444   Casa Grande

Miraval Resort, 5000 E. Via Estancia Miraval, 85739 Ph: 800-232-3969   Catalina

Concho Valley Country Club, PO Box 57, 85924 Ph: 520-337-4644   Concho Valley

Fairfield Flagstaff Resort, 1900 N Country Club Dr, 86001   Flagstaff
Ph: 602-526-3232

Gold Canyon Golf Resort, 6210 S Kings Ranch Rd, 85219   Gold Canyon
Ph: 480-982-9090

Fairfield Green Valley Lodge, P.O. Box 587, 85622 Ph: 602-625-4441   Green Valley

Nautical Inn, 1000 McCulloch Blvd, 86403 Ph: 602-855-2141   Lake Havasu City

The London Bridge Resort, 1477 Queens Bay, 86403 Ph: 602-855-0888   Lake Havasu City

Beaver Creek Golf Resort, Box 248, 86342 Ph: 602-567-4487   Lake Montezuma

Hilton Pavilion, 1011 W. Holmes Ave, 85210 Ph: 800-544-5866   Mesa

Painted Mountain Golf Resort, 6302 E McKellips Road, 85215   Mesa
Ph: 480-218-2684

The Golf Villas at Oro Valley, 10950 N. La Canada Drive, 85737   Oro Valley
Ph: 877-845-5288

Embassy Suites Scottsdale, 5001 N. Scottsdale Rd, 85253   Paradise Valley
Ph: 602-949-1414

Pointe at South Mountain, 777 S. Pointe Pkwy, 85004, Ph: 602-438-9000   Phoenix
800-947-9784

Sheraton San Marcos Resort, 1 San Marcos Place, 85224,   Phoenix
Ph: 480-812-0900 800-528-8071

Rio Rico Resort & Country Club, 1550 Camino Ala Posada, 85621   Rio Rico
Ph: 602-281-1901

Four Seasons Scottsdale Troon North, 10600 East Crescent Moon   Scottsdale
Drive, 85255 Ph: 480-515-5700

Marriott's Mountain Shadows Resort, 5641 E. Lincoln Dr, 85253   Scottsdale
Ph: 480-948-7111

McCormich Ranch Resort, 7505 McCormick Parkway, 85258   Scottsdale
Ph: 480-948-0260

Pima Golf Resort, 7330 N. Pima Rd, 85258 Ph: 480-948-3800   Scottsdale

Scottsdale Conference Resort, 7700 E. McCormick Parkway, 85258   Scottsdale
Ph: 800-528-0293

Scottsdale Marriott McDowell Mountain, 16770 North Perimeter   Scottsdale
Drive, 85260 Ph: 480-502-3836

L'Auberge de Sedona, PO Box B, 96336 Ph: 520-282-1661   Sedona

Poco Diablo Resort, 1752 South Highway 179, P.O. Box 1709, 86336   Sedona
Ph: 520-282-7333 800-528-4275

Tubac Valley Country Club, P.O. Box 1358, 85640 Ph: 602-398-2211   Tubac

Omni Tucson Golf Resort & Spa, 2727 West Club Drive, 85742   Tucson
Ph: 520-297-2271

Cocopah Bend RV Resort, 6800 S Strand Ave, 85364 Ph: 602-343-9300   Yuma

──────────────────── ARKANSAS ────────────────────

Degray State Park, Box 375, 71923 Ph: 870-865-4591   Arkadelphia

Fairfield Bay Resort, P.O. Box 3008, 72088 Ph: 501-884-3333   Fairfield Bay

Mountain Ranch Country Club, P.O. Box 1008, 72088 Ph: 501-884-3333   Fairfield Bay

Red Apple Inn, P.O. Box 192, 72543 Ph: 501-362-3111   Heber Springs

Hillhigh Hotel, 900 4th St, 72512 Ph: 870-670-5141   Horseshoe Bend

Hot Springs Village, Box 5, 71909 Ph: 501-922-0303   Hot Springs

Arlington Resort Hotel, 239 Central Avenue, 71901 Ph: 501-623-7771   Hot Springs National
Park

Dawn Hill Resort, P.O. Box 1289, 72761 Ph: 501-524-2341   Siloam Springs

──────────────────── CALIFORNIA ────────────────────

Greenhorn Creek, 711 McCauley Ranch Road, 95222 Ph: 209-736-6200   Angels Camp

Seascape Resort, 1 Seascape Resort Drive, 95003 Ph: 800-929-7727   Aptos

San Luis Bay Inn, P.O. Box 189, 93424 Ph: 805-595-2333   Avila Beach

Big Bear Mountain Resort, PO Box 6812, 92315 Ph: 909-585-2519   Big Bear Lake

Bodega Bay Lodge, Coast Hwy #1, 94923 Ph: 707-875-3525   Bodega Bay

San Luis Rey Downs Golf Club, 31474 Golf Club Dr, 92003   Bonsall
Ph: 619-758-3762

Club Circle, Box 306, 92004 Ph: 760-767-5944   Borrego Springs

La Casa Del Zorro, 3845 Yaqui Pass Road, 92004 Ph: 760-767-5323   Borrego Springs

Rams Hill, Box 664, 92004 Ph: 760-767-5028   Borrego Springs

Highlands Inn, Box 1700, 93921 Ph: 831-624-3801   Carmel

Hotel del Coronado, 1500 Orange Ave, 92118 Ph: 619-435-6611   Coronado

Embassy Suites Hotel, 8425 Firestone Blvd, 90241 Ph: 213-861-1900   Downey

Singing Hills Country Club, 3007 Dehesa Rd, 92019, Ph: 800-457-5568   El Cajon

Castle Creek Inn Resort & Spa, 29850 Circle R Way, 92026   Escondido
Ph: 760-751-8800

Lawrence Welk Resort, 8860 Lawrence Welk Dr, 92026 Ph: 760-749-3000   Escondido

Pala Mesa Resort, 2001 Old Hwy. 395, 92028 Ph: 619-728-5881   Fallbrook

The Residence Inn, 5400 Farwell Place, 94536 Ph: 415-794-5900   Fremont

Benbow Inn, 445 Lake Benbow Dr, 95440 Ph: 707-923-2124   Garberville

Pine Mountain Condo, Box PMLA, 95321 Ph: 209-962-7471   Groveland

Half Moon Bay Lodge, 2400 Cabrillo Hwy, 94019 Ph: 415-726-9000   Half Moon Bay
Inn At Silverlakes, 14818 Clubhouse Dr, 92342 Ph: 619-243-4800   Helendale
Ridgemark Country Club Resort, 3800 Airline Highway, 95023   Hollister
Ph: 408-637-8151
Barbara Worth Resort, 2050 Country Club Dr, 92250 Ph: 619-356-2806   Holtville
Miramonte Resort, 45-500 Indian Wells Lane, 92210 Ph: 760-341-2200   Indian Wells
Indian Palms Country Club, 48-630 Monroe St, 92201 Ph: 760-347-0688   Indio
La Jolla Beach and Tennis Club, 2000 Spindrift Drive, 92037   La Jolla
Ph: 858-454-7126
Aliso Creek Inn, 31106 S. Pacific Coast Hwy, 92677 Ph: 707-937-5942   Laguna Beach
Lake Shastina Golf Resort, 5925 Country Club Dr, 96094   Lake Shastina
Ph: 916-938-3201
Little River Inn, Box 627, 95456 Ph: 707-937-5667   Little River
Westwood Marquis Hotel, 930 Hilgard Avenue, 90024 Ph: 213-208-8765   Los Angeles
Snowcreek Resort, PO Box 1647, 93546 Ph: 760-934-6633   Mammoth Lakes
Radisson Plaza Hotel, 1400 Parkview Ave, 90266 Ph: 213-546-7511   Manhattan Beach
Hyatt Regency Monterey, One Old Golf Course Rd, 93940   Monterey
Ph: 408-372-1234
Hyatt Newporter, 1107 Jamboree Road, 92660 Ph: 949-729-1234   Newport Beach
Blacklake Resort, 1490 Golf Course Lane, 93444 Ph: 800-423-0981   Nipomo
El Camino Inn, 3170 Vista Way, 92056 Ph: 619-757-2200   Oceanside
Lexington Hotel Suites, 231 N. Vineyard, 91764 Ph: 714-983-8484   Ontario
Embassy Suites Mandalay Beach Resort, 2101 Mandalay Beach Road,   Oxnard
93030 Ph: 805-984-2500
Radisson Suite Hotel at River Ridge, 2102 West Vineyard Ave, 93030   Oxnard
Ph: 805-988-0130
Embassy Suites Palm Desert Resort, 74-700 Highway 111, 92260   Palm Desert
Ph: 760-340-6600
Ironwood Country Club, 49-200 Mariposa Dr, 92260 Ph: 760-346-0551   Palm Desert
Lakes Country Club, 75-375 Country Club Dr, 92260 Ph: 760-568-4321   Palm Desert
Monterey Country Club, 41500 Monterey Ave, 92260 Ph: 760-568-9311   Palm Desert
Palm Desert Resort, 77-333 Country Club Dr, 92260 Ph: 760-345-2781   Palm Desert
Palm Valley Country Club, 39205 Palm Valley Drive, 92211   Palm Desert
Ph: 760-345-2737
Villas Desert Falls, 102 Desert Falls Dr. E, 92260 Ph: 760-346-3803   Palm Desert
Canyon Resort, 2850 South Palm Canyon Dr, 99226 Ph: 760-327-2019   Palm Springs
Cathedral Canyon Resort, 34567 Cathedral Canyon Dr, 92264   Palm Springs
Ph: 760-321-9000
Gene Autry Hotel, 4200 Palm Canyon Dr. East, 92264 Ph: 800-443-6328   Palm Springs
Casa Palmero, 17 Mile Drive, 93953 Ph: 800-654-9300   Pebble Beach
Aetna Springs, 1600 Aetna Springs Rd, 94567 Ph: 707-965-2115   Pope Valley
San Vicente Resort, 24157 San Vicente Rd, 92065 Ph: 760-789-8290   Ramona
Westin Mission Hills Resort, 71333 Dinah Shore Dr, 92270   Rancho Mirage
Ph: 760-328-5955
Rancho Murieta Country Club, P.O. Box 980, 95683 Ph: 916-354-3400   Rancho Murieta
Morgan Run Resort and Club, 5690 Cancha de Golf, 92091   Rancho Santa Fe
Ph: 858-756-2471
Rancho Valencia Resort, PO Box 9126, 92067 Ph: 858-756-1123   Rancho Santa Fe

Red Lion Hotel, One Red Lion Dr, 94928 Ph: 707-584-LION   Rohnert Park
Carmel Highland Golf Resort, PO Box 28565, 92128 Ph: 619-672-2200   San Diego
Handlery Hotel & Country Club, 950 Hotel Circle North, 92108   San Diego
Ph: 619-298-0511
Park Suite Hotel, 333 Madonna Road, 93401 Ph: 805-549-0800   San Luis Obispo
San Simeon Pines Seaside Resort, Moonstone Beach Dr, 93452   San Simeon
Ph: 805-927-4648
Bacara Resort & Spa, 8301 Hollister Ave, 93117 Ph: 805-968-0100   Santa Barbara
El Encanto Hotel and Garden Villas, 1900 Lasuen Road, 93103   Santa Barbara
Ph: 805-687-5000
Four Seasons Biltmore, 1260 Channel Dr, 93108 Ph: 805-969-2261   Santa Barbara
Four Seasons Santa Barbara, 1260 Channel Drive, 93108   Santa Barbara
Ph: 805-969-2261
Embassy Suites Hotel, 2885 Lakeside Drive, 95051 Ph: 408-496-6400   Santa Clara
Inn at Pasatiempo, 555 Hwy 17, 95060 Ph: 408-423-5000   Santa Cruz
Hilton Round Barn Inn, 3555 Round Barn Blvd, 95403 Ph: 707-523-7555   Santa Rosa
Carlton Oaks Lodge, 9200 Inwood Dr, 92071 Ph: 619-448-4242   Santee
Sea Ranch Lodge, Box 1, 95497 Ph: 707-785-2371   Sea Ranch
Sonoma Mission Inn & Spa, P.O. Box 1447, 95476 Ph: 707-938-9000   Sonoma
Resort at Stallion Springs, 18100 Lucaya Way, 93561 Ph: 661-822-5581   Tehachapi
Temecula Creek Inn, 44501 Rainbow Canyon Rd, 92592 Ph: 909-676-2405   Temecula
800-439-7529
Residence Inn, 3701 Torrance Blvd, 90503 Ph: 213-543-4566   Torrance
The Spa at Warner Springs, PO Box 399, 92086 Ph: 760-782-4255   Warner Springs
Wawona Hotel, P.O. Box 2005, 95389 Ph: 209-252-4848   Yosemite National
                                                                            Park

———————————————————————COLORADO———————————————————————
Doubletree Hotel, 13696 E. Iliff Pl, 80014 Ph: 303-337-2800   Aurora
Charter at Beaver Creek, 120 Offerson Rd, 81620 Ph: 303-949-6660   Beaver Creek
Beaver Run Resort, P.O. Box 2115, 80424 Ph: 303-453-6000   Breckenridge
Cheyenne Mountain Inn, 3225 Broadmoor Valley Rd, 80906   Colorado Springs
Ph: 719-576-4600
Colorado Springs Hilton Inn, 505 Popes Bluff Trail, 80907   Colorado Springs
Ph: 719-598-7656
Skyland Lodge, P.O. Box 1549, 81224 Ph: 303-343-7541   Crested Butte
Skyland Resort & Country Club, P.O. Box 879, 81224 Ph: 303-349-6131   Crested Butte
The Plaza, P.O. Box 5159, 81225 Ph: 303-349-2130   Crested Butte
Inverness Hotel & Golf Club, 200 Inverness Drive W, 80112   Englewood
Ph: 303-799-5800
Scanticon Denver, 200 Inverness Dr W, 80112 Ph: 303-799-5800   Englewood
The Inn at Estes Park, 1701 North Lake Avenue, 80517   Estes Park
Ph: 970-586-5363
Fairfield Pagosa, P.O. Box 4010, 81157 Ph: 303-731-4141   Pagosa Springs
Best Western Pueblo, Box 7125, 71007 Ph: 719-547-2111   Pueblo
Sol Vista Golf & Ski Ranch, PO Box 1110, 80446 Ph: 970-887-3384   Silver Creek
The Ranch At Steamboat Springs, 1 Ranch Rd, 80487 Ph: 970-879-3000   Steamboat Springs

Antlers At Vail Lions Head, 680 W. Lions Head Pl, 81657   Vail
Ph: 970-476-2471
The Lodge at Vail, 174 E. Gore Creek Dr, 81657 Ph: 970-476-5011   Vail
Iron Horse Resort Retreat, P.O. Box 1286, 80482 Ph: 303-726-8851   Winter Park
Lodge High Mountain, P.O. Box 177, 80482 Ph: 303-726-9266   Winter Park

————————————————CONNECTICUT————————————————
Banner Lodge, Banner Road, 06469 Ph: 203-873-8652   Moodus
The Spa at Norwich Inn, Route 32, 06360 Ph: 203-886-1303   Norwich

————————————————————FLORIDA————————————————————
Summer Beach Resort, 5456 First Coast Hwy, 32034 Ph: 904-277-0905   Amelia Island
Atlantis Country Club and Inn, 331 Orange Tree Dr, 33462   Atlantis
Ph: 407-968-4000
Gasparilla Inn & Cottages, Gasparilla Island, 33921 Ph: 813-964-2201   Boca Grande
Holiday Inn Lakeside, 8144 Glades Rd, 33434 Ph: 561-482-7070   Boca Raton
Inn at Boca Teeca, 5800 NW 2nd Ave, 33431 Ph: 561-994-0400   Boca Raton
Cape Coral Golf Resort, 4003 Palm Tree Blvd, 33904 Ph: 813-542-3191   Cape Coral
Belleview Biltmore Resort & Spa, 25 Belleview Blvd, 33756   Clearwater
Ph: 727-442-6171
Belleview Mido Resort, 25 Belleview Blvd, 34617 Ph: 727-442-6171   Clearwater
Biltmore Hotel, 1200 Anastasia Avenue, 33134 Ph: 800-727-1926   Coral Gables
The Biltmore Hotel, 1200 Anastasia Avenue, 33134 Ph: 305-445-8066   Coral Gables
Plantation Inn, P.O. Box 1116, 32629 Ph: 904-795-4211   Crystal River
Holiday Inn Indigo Lakes Resort, 2620 W. International Speedway,   Daytona Beach
32114 Ph: 904-258-6333
Hamlet, 3203 West Atlantic Ave, 33444 Ph: 305-276-3444   Delray Beach
Emerald Bay, 40001 Emerald Coast Pkwy, 32541 Ph: 850-837-5197   Destin
Sandestin Beach Resort, 5500 Hwy 98 East, 32541 Ph: 850-267-8000   Destin
Seascape Resort, 100 Seascape Dr, 32541 Ph: 850-837-9181   Destin
Fisher Island Club, 1 Fisher Island Drive, 33109 Ph: 305-535-6020   Fisher Island
Hyatt Regency Pier 66, Drawer 9177, 33316 Ph: 954-524-0566   Fort Lauderdale
Marriott's Harbour Beach, 3030 Holiday Dr, 33316 Ph: 954-525-4000   Fort Lauderdale
Resort at Bonaventure Country Club, 200 Bonaventure Blvd, 33326   Fort Lauderdale
Ph: 954-389-8000
Rolling Hills Golf Resort, 3501 W. Rolling Hills, 33328 Ph: 954-475-0400   Fort Lauderdale
Sonesta Sanibel Harbour, 15610 McGregor Blvd, 33908   Fort Myers
Ph: 813-466-4000
Plantation Beach Club, 329 NE Tradewind Lane, Stuart, 33494   Hutchinson Island
Ph: 561-225-0074
Cheeca Lodge, Route 1, Box 527, 33036 Ph: 305-664-4651   Islamorada
Fairfield Inn, 8050 Baymeadow Circle West, 32216 Ph: 904-739-0739   Jacksonville
Jupiter Beach Resort, 5 North A1A, 33477 Ph: 800-228-8810   Jupiter
Orange Lake Country Club, 8505 W. Space Coast Pkwy, 34786   Kissimmee
Ph: 407-239-0000
Poinciana Golf Resort, 500 E. Cypress Parkway, 34759 Ph: 407-933-0700   Kissimmee
Quail Heights Country Club, Box 1073, 82055 Ph: 904-752-3339   Lake City
Placid Lakes Inn, 111 Club Road Circle NW, 33852 Ph: 813-465-4333   Lake Placid

Inverrary Hotel, 3501 Inverrary Blvd, 33319 Ph: 954-485-0500	Lauderhill
Marriott's Marco Island Resort, 400 South Collier Blvd, 34145 Ph: 941-394-2511	Marco Island
Golden Strand International, 17901 Collins Avenue, 33160 Ph: 305-931-7000	Miami Beach
Don Shula's Hotel and Golf Club, 7601 Miami Lakes Dr, 33014 Ph: 305-820-8101	Miami Lakes
Ravines, Box 950, 32068 Ph: 904-282-2701	Middleburg
The Moors Golf Club & Lodge, 3220 Avalon Blvd, 32583 Ph: 850-995-4653	Milton
Naples Beach Hotel, 851 Gulf Shore Blvd, 33940 Ph: 941-261-2222	Naples
Quality Inn & Suites Golf Resort, 4100 Golden Gate Pkwy, 33999 Ph: 813-455-1010	Naples
Registry Resort, 475 Seagate Drive, 34102 Ph: 800-247-9810	Naples
Sugar Mill Country Club, 100 Club House Circle, 32168 Ph: 904-426-5200	New Smyrna
Bluewater Bay, PO Box 247, 32578 Ph: 805-897-3613	Niceville
Silver Springs Knights Inn, 5565 Silver Road, 32672 Ph: 904-687-2135	Ocala
Marriott'S Orlando World Center, 8701 World Center Dr, 32821 Ph: 407-239-4200	Orlando
Quality Suites at Parc Corniche, 6300 Parc Corniche Dr, 32821 Ph: 407-239-7100	Orlando
Sonesta Village Hotel, 10000 Turkey Lake Rd, 32819 Ph: 407-352-8051	Orlando
Stouffer Orlando Resort, 6677 Sea Harbor Dr, 32821 Ph: 407-351-5555	Orlando
Ventura Country Club Condos, 3333 Woodgate Blvd #100, 32822 Ph: 407-273-8770	Orlando
Palm Coast Golf Resort, P.O. Box 400, 32135 Ph: 904-445-3000	Palm Coast
Best Western Casa Loma, 13615 West 98, 32407 Ph: 904-234-1100	Panama City Beach
Best Western Del Coronado, 11815 West 98, 32407 Ph: 904-234-1600	Panama City Beach
Edgewater Beach Resort, 11212 Front Beach Rd, 32407 Ph: 800-874-8686	Panama City Beach
Holiday Inn Beach Resort, 12907 West 98, 32407 Ph: 904-234-1111	Panama City Beach
Grand Palms Country Club, 110 Grand Palms Dr, 33027 Ph: 305-431-8800	Pembroke Pines
Raintree Golf Resort, 1600 South Hiatus Rd, 33025 Ph: 305-432-4400	Pembroke Pines
Cottage on the Green, 1 Doug Ford Dr, 32507 Ph: 904-492-1204	Pensacola
Port LaBelle Inn, One Oxford Dr, 33935 Ph: 813-675-4411	Port LaBelle
Marina Inn, 1 Matacumbe Key Rd, 33952 Ph: 813-693-8666	Punta Gorda
The Meadows Golf Resort, 3101 Longmeadow Dr, 33580 Ph: 941-378-6660	Sarasota
Sun 'n Lake Resort, 4101 Sun 'n Lake Blvd, 33872 Ph: 813-385-2561	Sebring
Ponce De Leon Resort, P.O. Box 98, 32085 Ph: 904-824-2821	St. Augustine
Renaissance Vinoy Resort, 501 5th North East, 33701 Ph: 727-894-1000	St. Petersburg
Killearn Country Club, 100 Tyron Circle, 32308 Ph: 904-893-2186	Tallahassee
Plantation Golf Club, 500 Rockley Blvd, 33598 Ph: 813-493-2146	Venice

───────────────────── GEORGIA ─────────────────────

Rivermont Golf Resort, 3130 Rivermont Parkway, 30201 Ph: 404-993-2124	Alpharetta

Fairfield Plantation, P.O. Drawer 1369, 30117 Ph: 404-834-7781	Carrollton
The Port Armor Club, 105 Anchor Bay Circle, 30642 Ph: 706-453-4564	Greensboro
Innsbruck Golf Club Resort, PO Box 845, 30545 Ph: 706-878-2400	Helen
Jekyll Island Club Hotel, 371 Riverview Dr, 31520 Ph: 912-635-2600	Jekyll Island
Callaway Gardens, PO Box 2000, 31822 Ph: 800-CALLAWAY	Pine Mountain
King & Prince Hotel, 201 Arnold Rd. at Downing St, 31522, Ph: 912-638-3631 800-342-0212	St. Simons Island
Sea Palms Golf Resort, 5445 Frederica Rd, 31522, Ph: 912-638-3351 800-841-6268	St. Simons Island
Westin Savannah Harbor Resort, One Resort Drive, 31421 Ph: 912-201-2000	Savannah
Evergreen Resort, 4021 Lakeview Drive, 30083 Ph: 770-879-9900	Stone Mountain
Stone Mountain Inn, P.O. Box 778, 33086 Ph: 770-498-5725	Stone Mountain
Lake Arrowhead Resort, P.O. Station 25, 30183 Ph: 404-681-2230	Waleska

―――――――――――――――― HAWAII ――――――――――――――――

Hotel Hana-Maui at Hana Ranch, P.O. Box 8(I), 96713 Ph: 808-248-8211	Hana, Maui
Hanalei Bay Resort, P.O. Box 220, 96714 Ph: 808-826-6522	Hanalei, Kauai
Hawaii Naniloa Hotel, 93 Banyan Dr, 96720 Ph: 808-969-3333	Hilo
Shores at Waikoloa, 2255 Kuhio Avenue, 96815 Ph: 808-922-3368	Honolulu
Royal Lahaina Resort, 2780 Kekaa Drive, 96761 Ph: 805-497-7934	Kaanapali Beach, Maui
Turtle Bay Hilton, P.O. Box 187, 96731 Ph: 808-293-8811	Kahuku, Oahu
Waikoloa Villas, Box 3066, 96743 Ph: 808-883-9588	Kamuela
Sheraton Royal Waikoloan, P.O. Box 5300, 96743 Ph: 808-885-6789	Kohala Coast
Kiahuna Beachside Hawaiiana, P.O. Box 369, 96756 Ph: 808-742-7262	Koloa, Kauai
Aston Kaanapali Shores, 3445 Honoapiilani Hwy, 96761 Ph: 808-667-2211	Lahaina, Maui
Maui Marriott Resort, 100 Noheakai Kai Dr, 96761 Ph: 808-667-1200	Lahaina, Maui
Sheraton Maui Hotel, 2605 Kaanapali Parkway, 96761 Ph: 808-661-0031	Lahaina, Maui
The Napili Point Resort, 5295 Honoapiilani Hwy, 96761 Ph: 800-669-6252	Lahaina, Maui
Westin Maui, 2365 Kaanapali Parkway, 96761 Ph: 808-667-2525	Lahaina, Maui
Maui El Dorado, Kaanapali Beach, 96761 Ph: 800-367-7052	Maui
Kaanapali Royal, 2560 Kekaa Drive, 96761 Ph: 808-667-7200	Maui, Lahaina
Marc Ke Nani Kai Resort, PO Box 289, 96770 Ph: 808-552-2761	Maunaka, Molokai
Sheraton Molokai, Kepuhi Beach, 96770 Ph: 808-552-2555	Molokai
Sea Mountain at Punalu'u, P.O. Box 70, 96777 Ph: 808-928-6222	Pahala
Cliffs at Princeville, 3811 Edward Rd, P.O. Box 1005, 96714 Ph: 808-826-6219 800-622-6219	Princeville, Kauai
Mirage Princeville Resort, Box 3040, 96722 Ph: 808-826-3580	Princeville, Kauai
Royal Waikoloan, 69-275 Waikoloa Beach Dr, 96743 Ph: 808-885-6789	Waikoloa
The Shores at Waikoloa, Star Route 5200, 96743 Ph: 808-885-5001	Waikoloa
Outrigger Wailea Resort, 3700 Wailea Alanui, 96753 Ph: 808-879-1922	Wailea, Kihei, Maui
Grand Champions Golf, 161 Wailea Ike Pl, 96753 Ph: 808-879-1996	Wailea, Maui

───────────────────IDAHO───────────────────

Warm Springs Resort, 119 Lloyd Dr, 83340 Ph: 208-392-4437	Ketchum
Hill's Resort, Box 162A, 83856 Ph: 208-443-2551	Priest Lake
Twin Lakes Village, 5416 W. Village Blvd., 83858 Ph: 208-687-1312	Rathdrum

───────────────────ILLINOIS───────────────────

Indian Lakes Resort, 250 W. Schick Rd, 60108 Ph: 630-529-0200	Bloomingdale
Inn At Eagle Creek Resort & Conf. Center, Eagle Creek State Park Rd, 62534 Ph: 217-756-3456	Findlay
Nordic Hills Resort, 1401 Nordic Road, 60143 Ph: 630-773-2750	Itasca
Drake Oakbrook, 2301 York Rd, 60521 Ph: 800-334-9895	Oak Brook
Oak Brook Hills Hotel, 3500 Midwest Road, 60522 Ph: 708-850-5555	Oak Brook
Oak Terrace Resort, 100 Beyers Lake, 62557 Ph: 800-577-5798	Pana
Quail Creek CC & Resort, 1010 E. Highland Ave., 62454 Ph: 618-544-8674	Robinson
Pheasant Run Resort, P.O. Box 164, 60174 Ph: 708-584-6300	Saint Charles

───────────────────INDIANA───────────────────

Four Winds–A Clarion Resort, P.O. Box 160, 47402 Ph: 812-824-9904	Bloomington

───────────────────IOWA───────────────────

Proky's Red Carpet Club, 1409 Newell Street, 50704 Ph: 319-234-5595	Waterloo

───────────────────KANSAS───────────────────

Inn At Tallgrass, 2280 N. Tara, 67226 Ph: 316-684-2222	Wichita
Inn at Willowbend, 3939 N. Comotara, 67226 Ph: 316-636-4032	Wichita

───────────────────KENTUCKY───────────────────

Woodson Bend Resort, 14 Woodson Bend Rd, 42518 Ph: 606-561-5311	Burnside
Lake Barkley State Park, P.O. Box 790, 42211 Ph: 502-924-1131	Cadiz
General Butler Resort, Hwy 227., 41008 Ph: 502-732-4384	Carrollton
Pennyrile Forest Resort, 20781 Pennyrile Lodge Rd, 42408 Ph: 502-797-3421	Dawson Springs
Pine Valley Golf Resort, 850 Pine Valley Dr, 42701 Ph: 502-737-8300	Elizabethtown
Rough River Dam Resort, Rural Route 1, Box 1, 40119 Ph: 502-257-2311	Falls of Rough
Kenlake Dam Village State Park, General Delivery, 42044 Ph: 502-362-7271	Gilbertsville
Ramada Inn Resort, US Highway 62, 42044 Ph: 502-362-4278	Gilbertsville
Kenlake State Resort Park, 542 Kenlake Road, 42048 Ph: 270-474-2211	Hardin
Bright Leaf Resort, Highway 127 South, 40330 Ph: 606-734-5481	Harrodsburg
Barren River Lake State Park, 1149 State Park Road, 42156 Ph: 502-646-2151	Lucas
Carter Cave Resort, Box 1120, 41164 Ph: 606-286-4411	Olive Hill
Park Mammoth Resort, I-65 & 31 W, 42160 Ph: 502-749-4101	Park City
Jenny Wiley State Park, HC 66, Box 200, 41653 Ph: 606-886-2711	Prestonsburg

───────────────────LOUISIANA───────────────────

Emerald Hill Resort, P.O. Box 369, 71439 Ph: 318-586-4661	Florien
The Bluffs, PO Box 1220, 70775 Ph: 888-634-3410	St. Francisville

————————————————————MAINE————————————————————

Bethel Inn & Country Club, P.O. Box 49, 04217 Ph: 207-824-2175   Bethel
800-654-0125
Squaw Mountain Resort, Box D, 04441 Ph: 207-695-3049   Greenville Junction
Inn at Poland Springs, Route 26, 04274 Ph: 207-998-4351   Poland Springs
Country Club Inn, Box 680, 04970 Ph: 207-864-3831   Rangeley
Portland Marriott Sable Oaks, 200 Sable Oaks Dr, 04106   South Portland
Ph: 207-871-8000

————————————————————MARYLAND————————————————————

Tidewater Inn, Dover & Harrison Sts., 21601 Ph: 410-822-1300   Easton
Harbourtowne Golf Resort, Miles River & Eastern Bay, P.O. Box 126,   Saint Michaels
21663 Ph: 410-745-9066 800-446-9066

————————————————————MASSACHUSETTS————————————————————

Ocean Edge Resort, 2907 Main Street, 02631 Ph: 508-896-9000   Brewster
Wequassett Inn, One Pleasant Bay, 02633 Ph: 800-225-7125   Chatham
Ferncroft, Rt 1 & I-95, 01923 Ph: 508-777-2500   Danvers
Tara Hyannis Hotel & Resort, West End Circle, 02601 Ph: 508-775-7775   Hyannis
Oak N' Spruce Resort, Rt. 102, 01260 Ph: 413-528-0434   South Lee
Riverview Resort, 37 Neptune Lane, 02664 Ph: 617-394-9801   South Yarmouth
Colonial Hilton Resort, Audubon Rd, 01880 Ph: 617-245-9300   Wakefield

————————————————————MICHIGAN————————————————————

Gull Lake View Golf Club, North 38th St, 49012 Ph: 616-731-4148   Augusta
Bay Valley Hotel & Resort, 2470 Old Bridge Rd, 48706 Ph: 517-686-3500   Bay City
The Lodge at Cedar River, One Shanty Creek Road, 49615   Belaire
Ph: 800-678-4111
Shanty Creek Resort, One Shanty Creek Road, Bellaire, 49615   Bellaire
Ph: 231-533-8621 800 678 4111
Double R Ranch, 4424 Whites Bridge Road, 48809 Ph: 877-794-0520   Belding
Drummond Island Resort, 33494 S. Maxton Road, 49726   Drummond Island
Ph: 906-493-1000
Kellogg Center, South Harrison Road, 48824 Ph: 517-432-4000   East Lansing
Black Forest Wilderness Valley, 7519 Mancelona Rd, 49735   Gaylord
Ph: 517-585-7090
Hidden Valley Resort, P.O. Box 556, 49735 Ph: 517-732-5181   Gaylord
Marsh Ridge, 4815 Old 27 South, PO Box 1367, 49735 Ph: 800-743-7529   Gaylord
Michaywe Resort, 1535 Opal Lake Road, 49735 Ph: 800-322-6636   Gaylord
Heather Highlands Inn, Boyne Highlands, 49740 Ph: 616-526-2171   Harbor Springs
Grand Hotel, General Delivery, 49757 Ph: 906-847-3331   Mackinac Island
Schuss Village Resort, Schuss Mountain Rd, 49659 Ph: 616-533-6356   Mancelona
St. Clair Inn, 500 N. River Side Ave, 48079 Ph: 313-329-2222   St. Clair

————————————————————MINNESOTA————————————————————

Arrowwood, A Radisson Resort, PO Box 639, 56308 Ph: 320-762-1124   Alexandria
Ruttger's Bay Lake Lodge, P.O. Box 400, 56444 Ph: 218-678-2885   Deerwood
800-328-0312

Mille Lacs Lake Golf Resort, 18517 Captive Lake Road, 56450   Garrison
Ph: 612-692-4325
Quadna Mountain Resort, 100 Quanda Rd, 55748 Ph: 218-697-2324   Hill City
Chippewa Pines Resrot, Cass Lake Chain, 56663 Ph: 218-335-6531   Pennington

───────────────────MISSISSIPPI───────────────────

Grand Biloxi Beach Resort, 2060 Beach Blvd, 39531 Ph: 228-388-7000   Biloxi
Royal Gulf Hills Resort, 13701 Paso Rd, 39564 Ph: 601-875-4211   Ocean Springs
Saint Andrews On The Gulf, Golfing Green Dr, 39564 Ph: 601-872-1000   Ocean Springs
Grand Casino Hotel Tunica, 13615 Old Highway 61N, 38664   Robinsonville
Ph: 800-946-4946

───────────────────MISSOURI───────────────────

Thousand Hills Golf Resort, 245 South Wildwood Drive, 65616   Branson
Ph: 800-846-4145
Four Seasons Lodge & Country Club, P.O. Box 437, 65049   Lake Ozark
Ph: 314-365-3001

───────────────────MONTANA───────────────────

Fairmont Hot Springs Resort, 1500 Fairmont Road, 59711   Anaconda
Ph: 406-797-3241
Red Lodge Resort, P.O. Box 650, 59068 Ph: 406-446-3949   Red Lodge

───────────────────NEVADA───────────────────

The Mirage, 3400 Las Vegas Blvd. S, 89109 Ph: 702-791-7111   Las Vegas
The Resort at Summerlin, 221 N Rampart Blvd, 89145 Ph: 702-869-7777   Las Vegas
Casablanca Resort Hotel, 950 W Mesquite Blvd, 89027   Mesquite
Ph: 702-346-7529
Peppermill Resort, P.O. Box 360, 89024 Ph: 702-346-5232   Mesquite

───────────────────NEW HAMPSHIRE───────────────────

Attitash Mt. Village, Route 32, 03812 Ph: 603-374-6500   Bartlett
Maplewood Resort, Box 462, 03574 Ph: 603-869-3335   Bethlehem
Bretton Woods Resort, Route 302, 03573 Ph: 603-278-1000   Bretton Woods
Province Lake Country Club, Route 153, 03830 Ph: 603-793-9577   East Wakefield
Wentworth Resort Hotel, P.O. Box M, 03846 Ph: 603-383-9700   Jackson
Waumbek Inn & Country Club, P.O. Box 40, 03583 Ph: 603-586-4311   Jefferson
Lake Sunapee CC & Inn, Rt 11, 03257 Ph: 603-526-6040   New London
Eastern Slope Inn Resort, P.O. Box 359, 03860 Ph: 603-356-6321   North Conway
Five Chimneys Resort, Rt. 153, E. Wakefield, 03830 Ph: 603-793-9577   Province Lake
Waterville Valley Resort, PO Box 540, 03215 Ph: 603-236-8311   Waterville Valley
Spalding Inn & Club, RR1 Box 57, 03598 Ph: 603-837-2572   Whitefield
Jack O'Lantern, I-93, Exit 30, 03293 Ph: 603-745-8121 800-227-4454   Woodstock

───────────────────NEW JERSEY───────────────────

Crystal Springs Golf Resort, 105-137 Wheatsworth Road, 07419   Hamburg
Ph: 973-827-2222
Legends Resort & Country Club, Route 517, 07428 Ph: 973-827-6000   McAfee
Tennanah Lake Resort, 118 Mill Road, 07656 Ph: 914-794-2900   Park Ridge
Atlantis Country Club, Country Club Blvd, 08087 Ph: 609-296-2444   Tuckerton

────────────── NEW MEXICO ──────────────

Inn at Paradise, 10035 Country Club Lane NW, 87114 Ph: 505-898-0966   Albuquerque

────────────── NEW YORK ──────────────

Villa Roma Country Club, RD 1, 12723 Ph: 845-887-4880   Callicoon
Bristol Harbour Golf Club, 5500 Seneca Point Rd, 14424   Canandaigua
Ph: 716-396-2460
Bewt Western University Inn, 90 East Main Street, 13617   Canton
Ph: 315-386-8522
Athenaeum Hotel, PO Box 66, 14722 Ph: 716-357-4444   Chautauqua
C-Way Inn Resort & Golf Club, Route 12, 13664 Ph: 315-686-4214   Clayton
Scott's Oquaga Lake House, Oquaga Lake Box 47, 13754   Deposit
Ph: 607-467-3094
Pleasant View Lodge, Gayhead Rd, 12431 Ph: 518-634-2523   Freehold
Tamarack Lodge, Route 52, 12435 Ph: 845-647-3500   Greenfield Park
Rainbow Golf Club, 3822 Rt. 26, 12083 Ph: 518-966-5343   Greenville
Wakely Lodge, Cedar River Road, 12842 Ph: 518-648-5011   Indian Lake
Granit Hotel, Granit Rd, 12446 Ph: 914-626-3141   Kerhonkson
Lake Placid Resort, One Olympic Drive, 12946 Ph: 518-523-2556   Lake Placid
Whiteface Resort, P.O. Box 231, 12946 Ph: 518-523-2551   Lake Placid
Inn at Loon Lake, HCR #1 Box 136, 12989 Ph: 518-891-6464   Loon Lake
Hanah Country Inn, Route 30, 12455 Ph: 845-586-2100   Margaretville
Kutsher's Country Club, Route 17, Exit 105B, 12701 Ph: 845-794-6000   Monticello
Mohonk Mountain House, Lake Mohonk, 12561 Ph: 845-255-1000   New Paltz
Bluff Point Golf Club & Resort, 75 Bluff Point Drive, 12901   Plattsburg
Ph: 518-563-3420
Tennanah Lake Golf and Tennis Club, 100 Belle Road, Suite #2, 12776   Roscoe
Ph: 607-498-5502
Saranac Inn, HC1 Box 16, 12983 Ph: 518-891-1402   Saranac Lake
Gideon Putnam Hotel, 24 Gideon Putnam Road, 12866 Ph: 518-584-3000   Saratoga Springs
Pines Hotel, Laurel Ave, 12779 Ph: 914-434-6000   South Fallsburg
The Pines Resort Hotel, Laurel Avenue, 12779 Ph: 914-434-6000   South Fallsburg
Eddy Farm Hotel, Box 500 P.C., 12780 Ph: 914-856-5266   Sparrow Bush
Davidman'S Homowack Hotel, P.O. Box 369, 12483 Ph: 914-647-6800   Spring Glen
Thousand Acres, Route 418, 12878 Ph: 518-696-2444   Stoney Creek
Swan Lake Resort Hotel, P.O. Box 155, 12783 Ph: 914-292-0748   Swan Lake
Byrncliff Resort and Conference Center, Route 20A, 14167   Varysburg
Ph: 716-535-7300
Christman's Windham House Resort, RR1, Box 36, 12496   Windham
Ph: 518-734-4230

────────────── NORTH CAROLINA ──────────────

Minnesott Golf Resort, Box 234, 28510 Ph: 919-249-0813   Arapahoe
Sugar Mountain Resort, P.O. Box 369, 28604 Ph: 704-898-4521   Banner Elk
Hanging Rock Golf Club, P.O. Box 628 DTS, 28607 Ph: 704-963-6565   Boone
Sherwood Forest Golf Club, Hwy 276 S, 28718 Ph: 704-885-2091   Cedar Mountain
Tanglewood Park, P.O. Box 1018, 27012 Ph: 919-766-0591   Clemmons
Washington Duke Inn, 3001 Cameron Blvd, 27706 Ph: 919-490-0999   Durham

Holly Springs Golf Resort, 110 Holly Springs Golf Village, 28734   Franklin
Ph: 704 524 7792
Fairfield Mountains, Route 1, 28746 Ph: 828-625-9111   Lake Lure
Lake Lure Golf & Resort, 112 Mountains Blvd, 28746 Ph: 828-625-3016   Lake Lure
Greystone Inn, P.O. Box 6, 28747 Ph: 704-966-4700   Lake Toxaway
Magnolia Greens Golf Plantation, 9049 Ocean Hwy, 28451   Leland
Ph: 910-383-0990
Village at Nags Head, P.O. Box 1807, 27959 Ph: 919-480-2224   Nags Head
Brick Landing Plantation, 1900 Goose Creek Road, 28469   Ocean Isle Beach
Ph: 919-754-5545
The Winds Inns and Suites, 310 E. First St, 28459 Ph: 919-579-6275   Ocean Isle Beach
The Pines Golf & Resort Club, P.O. Box 427, 28373 Ph: 919-281-3165   Pine Bluff
Holly Inn, P.O. Box 2300, 28374 Ph: 919-295-2300   Pinehurst
Hyland Hills Golf Resort, 4100 US 1 North, 28387 Ph: 919-692-7111   Pinehurst
Longleaf Country Club Resort, Box 3819, 28374 Ph: 919-692-5522   Pinehurst
Pine Crest Inn, Box 879, 28374 Ph: 919-295-6121   Pinehurst
High Meadows Inn, P.O. Box 22, 28668 Ph: 919-363-2445   Roaring Gap
Palomino Hotel, PO Box 777, 27330 Ph: 919-776-7531   Sanford
Fairfield Sapphire Valley, Box 80, 28774 Ph: 704-743-3441   Sapphire
Hawk'S Nest Golf Resort, 1800 Skyland, 28604 Ph: 704-963-6565   Seven Devils
St. Regis Resort, P.O. Box 4000, 28460 Ph: 919-328-0778   Sneads Ferry
Pine Needles Resort, P.O. Box 88, 28388 Ph: 910-692-7111 800-747-7272   Southern Pines
Sea Trail Plantation, 301 Clubhouse Rd, 28459 Ph: 919-579-7740   Sunset Beach
Woodlake Country Club, Box 66A, 28394 Ph: 919-245-4031   Vass
Waynesville Country Club Inn, Box 390, 28786 Ph: 828-452-2258   Waynesville
Whispering Pines Resort, 2 Clubhouse Blvd, 28327 Ph: 910-949-2311   Whispering Pines
Wolf Laurel Resort, Route 3, 28754 Ph: 704-689-4111   Wolf Laurel

———————————————————OHIO———————————————————
Aqua Marine Resort, 216 Miller Road, 44012 Ph: 440-933-2000   Avon Lake
Salt Fork Resort, Box 550, 43725 Ph: 614-439-4406   Cambridge
Glenmoor Country Club, 4191 Glenmoor Road, 44718 Ph: 330-966-3600   Canton
Hueston Woods State Park, RFD #1, 45003 Ph: 513-523-6347   College Corner
Atwood Lake Resort, PO Box 96, 44620 Ph: 216-735-2211   Dellroy
Shawnee State Park, Box 98, 45630 Ph: 614-858-6652   Friendship
Sawmill Creek Resort, 2401 Cleveland Rd W, 44839 Ph: 419-433-3800   Huron
Deer Creek Lodge, P.O. Box 127, 43143 Ph: 614-869-2020   Mount Sterling
Punderson State Park, Route 87, 44065 Ph: 614-439-4406   Newberry
Maumee Bay State Park, 1750 Park Road #2, 43618 Ph: 419-836-1466   Oregon
Wooster Inn, Wayne Ave. & Gasche Street, 44691 Ph: 216-264-2341   Wooster

———————————————————OKLAHOMA———————————————————
Lake Murray Resort Park, 3310 South Lake Murray Dr #12A, 73401   Ardmore
Ph: 580-223-6600
Falconhead Ranch, Falconhead Dr, 73430 Ph: 405-276-9411   Burneyville
Choctaw Nations Arrowhead Resort, HC 67, Box 5, 74425   Canadian
Ph: 918-339-2711

Fountainhead Resort, HC 60, Box 453, 74426 Ph: 918-689-9173   Checotah
Quartz Mountain State Park, Route 1, Box 40, 73655 Ph: 580-563-2424   Lone Wolf
Oklahoma State Park, 500 Will Rogers Building, 73165   Oklahoma City
Ph: 405-521-2464
Western Hills Guest Ranch, P.O. Box 509, 74477 Ph: 918-772-2545   Wagoner
Roman Nose State Park, Route 1, 73772 Ph: 580-623-7281   Watonga

─────────────────────────OREGON─────────────────────────

Inn of the Seventh Mountain, 18575 SW Century Drive, 97702   Bend
Ph: 800-452-6810
Mount Bachelor Village Resort, 19717 Mount Bachelor Drive, 97702   Bend
Ph: 541-389-5900
Emerald Valley Resort, 83293 Dale Kuni Rd, 97426 Ph: 503-895-2147 Creswell
Gearhart By The Sea Resort, P.O. Box 2700, 97138 Ph: 503-738-8331 Gearhart
Eagle Crest Resort, 1522 Cline Falls Highway, 97756 Ph: 541-923-2453 Redmond
Kah-Nee-Tah Hotel Resort, PO Box K, 97761 Ph: 541-553-1112   Warm Springs

─────────────────────────PENNSYLVANIA─────────────────────────

Penn Hills Resort, PO Box 309, 18320 Ph: 570-421-6464   Analomink
Bedford Springs Hotel, P.O. Box 639, 15522 Ph: 814-623-8999   Bedford
Mill Race Golf Resort, Box 81B, 17814 Ph: 570-925-2040   Benton
Fernwood Mountain Resort, Route 209, 18324 Ph: 570-588-9500   Bushkill
Conley Country Club Resort, Route 8, 16001 Ph: 724-586-7711   Butler
Riverside Inn, One Fountain St, 16403 Ph: 814-398-4645   Cambridge Springs
Brandywine Hotel and Resort, Route 30, 19335 Ph: 215-269-2000   Downingtown
Downingtown Inn & Resort, P.O. Box 408, 19335 Ph: 215-269-2000   Downingtown
Carroll Valley Resort Hotel, PO Box 715, 17320 Ph: 717-642-8212   Fairfield
Four Points Greensburg, 100 Sheraton Dr, 15601 Ph: 412-836-6060   Greensburg
Hershey Lodge and Convention Ctr, PO Box 446, 17033   Hershey
Ph: 717-533-3311
Hidden Valley Resort, 1 Craighead Dr, 15502 Ph: 814-443-6454   Hidden Valley
Lancaster Host Golf Resort, 2300 Lincoln Highway E, 17602   Lancaster
Ph: 717-299-5500
Mountain Manor Inn, Golf Course Drive, 18335 Ph: 570-223-8098   Marshalls Creek
Mount Airy Lodge, Woodland Rd, 18344 Ph: 717-839-8811   Mount Pocono
Skytop Lodge, Route 390, 18357 Ph: 570-595-7401   Skytop
Tamiment Resort, Bushkill Falls Road, 18371 Ph: 570-588-6652   Tamiment
Cross Creek Resort, P.O. Box 432, 16354 Ph: 814-827-9611   Titusville
Shadow Brook Resort, Route 6, 18657 Ph: 717-836-2151   Tunkhannock
Venango Valley Inn, Box 216, 16440 Ph: 814-398-4330   Venango
Water Gap Country Club, P.O. Box 188 Delaware, 18327   Water Gap
Ph: 717-416-0300
Hershey Pocono Resort, P.O. Box 126, 18661 Ph: 717-443-8411   White Haven
The Mountain Laurel Resort, P.O. Box 126, 18661 Ph: 570-443-8411   White Haven

─────────────────────────PUERTO RICO─────────────────────────

Hyatt Dorado Beach Hotel, Highway 693, 00646 Ph: 787-796-1234   Dorado

Westin Rio Mar Beach Resort & Country Club, 6000 Rio Mar Blvd,   Rio Grande
00745 Ph: 787-888-6000

———————————— SOUTH CAROLINA ————————————

Houndslake Country Club, 1900 Houndslake Drive, 29803   Aiken
Ph: 803-648-6805

Fripp Island Resort, One Tarpon Blvd, 29920 Ph: 803-838-2411   Fripp Island

Wedgefield Plantation, ST 701N, 29440 Ph: 803-448-2124   Georgetown

Daufuskie Island Club & Resort, PO Box 23285, 29925   Hilton Head Island
Ph: 843-842-2000

Hilton Head Island Resort, 40 Folly Field Rd, 29928 Ph: 843-842-4402   Hilton Head Island

Hilton Oceanfront Resort, P.O. Box 6165, 29928 Ph: 843-842-8000   Hilton Head Island

Hyatt Regency on Hilton Head, P.O. Box 6167, 29928 Ph: 843-785-1234   Hilton Head Island

Marriotts Monarch at Sea Pines, P.O. Box 6959, 29938   Hilton Head Island
Ph: 843-785-2040

Moss Creek Plantation, Box 1697, 29925 Ph: 843-785-4488   Hilton Head Island

Hickory Knob State Resort Park, Box 199-B, 29835 Ph: 803-443-2151   McCormick

Charleston Harbor Hilton Resort, 20 Patriots Point Road, 29464   Mt. Pleasant
Ph: 843-856-6028

Breakers North Tower Hotel, P.O. Box 485, 29578 Ph: 843-626-5000   Myrtle Beach

Captain's Quarters, 901 S. Ocean Blvd, 29578 Ph: 843-448-1404   Myrtle Beach

Caravelle Resort Hotel, Oceanfront at 6900 N. Ocean Blvd, 29572   Myrtle Beach
Ph: 843-449-3331

Defender Resort, P.O. Box 3849, 29578 Ph: 843-449-1354   Myrtle Beach

Ocean Forest Villa Resort, 5601 N. Ocean Blvd, 29577 Ph: 800-845-0347   Myrtle Beach

Golf Colony at Bay Tree, 123 Golf Club Lane, 29578 Ph: 843-449-1354   North Myrtle Beach

Marion Earl Oceanfront Resort, 1401 S. Ocean Blvd, 29582   North Myrtle Beach
Ph: 843-272-5181

Litchfield Beach and Golf Resort, PO Drawer 320, 29585   Pawleys Island
Ph: 888-766-4633

Golf Colony at Deer Track, 888 Golf Colony Dr, 29578 Ph: 803-449-1354   Surfside Beach

———————————————— TENNESSEE ————————————————

Paris Landing State Park, Route 1, 38222 Ph: 901-642-4311   Buchanan

Montgomery Bell State Park, Route 1, 37029 Ph: 615-797-3101   Burns

Henry Horton State Park, P.O. Box 128, 37034 Ph: 615-364-2222   Chapel Hill

Fairfield Glade Lodge, P. O. Box 1500, 38555 Ph: 615-484-7521   Fairfield Glade

Bent Creek Golf Resort, P.O. Box 1190, 37738 Ph: 615-436-2875   Gatlinburg

Roan Valley Golf Estates, Box 138, 37683 Ph: 615-727-7931   Mountain City

Pickwick Landing State Park, P.O. Box 10, 38365 Ph: 901-689-3135   Pickwick Dam

Gatlinburg Country Club, P.O. Box 1170, 37868 Ph: 615-453-3912   Pigeon Forge

Bays Mountain Country Club, 685 Chrishaven Dr, 37865   Seymour
Ph: 615-577-8172

Buffalo Valley Resort, Route 2, 37692 Ph: 615-743-9181   Unicoi

Baneberry Resort, Route 2 Harrison Ferry RC, 37890 Ph: 615-674-2500   White Pine

——————————————————— TEXAS ———————————————————

Flying L Ranch, HCR 1, Box 32, 78003 Ph: 512-796-3001   Bandera

Rancho Viejo Resort, 1 Rancho Viejo Dr, 78520 Ph: 956-350-4000   Brownsville

Valley Inn & Country Club, P.O. Box 3850, 78521 Ph: 956-546-5331   Brownsville
Fortuna Bay B&B, 15405 Fortuna Bay Dr, 78418 Ph: 361-949-7554   Corpus Christi
Horizon Lodge, 13781 Horizon Blvd, 79927 Ph: 915-852-9141   El Paso
Tremont House Hotel, 2300 Ship Mechanic Row, 77550   Galveston
Ph: 409-763-0300
Hotel Galvez, 2024 Seawall Blvd, 77551 Ph: 409-765-7721   Galveston Island
South Shore Harbour, Box 58368, 77258 Ph: 713-334-1000   Houston
Four Seasons Resort and Club, 4150 No. MacArthur Blvd, 75038   Irving
Ph: 972-717-0700
Rayburn Country Club & Resort, P.O. Box 36, 75951 Ph: 409-698-2444   Jasper
Riverhill Club, 100 Riverhill Club Lane, 78028 Ph: 210-896-1400   Kerrville
Vista Grande Resort, P.O. Box 4826, 78645 Ph: 512-267-1161   Lago Vista
April Sound Country Club, 1000 April Sound Blvd, 77356   Montgomery
Ph: 409-588-1101
Tanglewood On Texoma Resort, P.O. Box 265, 75076 Ph: 903-786-2968   Pottsboro
Hyatt Regency Hill Country Resort, 9800 Hyatt Resort Drive, 78251   San Antonio
Ph: 210-647-1234
Sheraton North Hotel, 1400 Austin Highway, 78209 Ph: 210-824-5371   San Antonio
Woodlands Inn Resort & Conf. Center, 2301 N. Millbend Dr, 77380   The Woodlands
Ph: 713-367-1100
Columbia Lakes, 188 Freeman Blvd, 77486 Ph: 409-345-5151   West Columbia
Woodcreek Resort, One Woodcreek Dr, 78676 Ph: 512-847-7176   Wimberley

──────────────────────UTAH──────────────────────

Mount Snow Resort Center, 89 Mountain Rd, 05356 Ph: 800-451-4211   Mount Snow
Aston-Genesis Resort Hotel, P.O. Box 1698, 84060 Ph: 801-649-7100   Park City
Wasatch Mountain, 1390 S. 1100 E., Ste 103, 84105 Ph: 801-463-9842   Salt Lake City
Green Valley Spa & Tennis Resort, 1871 W Canyon View Drive, 84770   St. George
Ph: 435-628-8060

────────────────────── VERMONT──────────────────────

Lake Morey Inn Resort, Lake Morey Road, 05045 Ph: 802-333-4311   Fairlee
Cortina Inn, 103 US Route 4, 05751 Ph: 802-773-3333   Killington
Killington Grand Resort Hotel & Conference Ctr., 228 E. Mountain   Killington
Road, 05751 Ph: 800-621-6867
Mountain Green Ski & Golf Resort, 1333 East Mountain Road, 05751   Killington
Ph: 802-422-3000
Quechee Lakes, P.O. Box 85, 05059 Ph: 802-295-7525   Quechee
Basin Harbor Club, On Lake Champlain, 05491 Ph: 802-475-2311   Vergennes
Mount Snow Resort, Route 100, 05356 Ph: 802-464-3333   West Dover

────────────────────── VIRGINIA──────────────────────

Boar's Head Inn & Sports Club, P.O. Box 5307, 22905 Ph: 804-296-2181   Charlottesville
Dan Hall Mountain Resort, 5560 Dan Hall Mountain Dr, 24230   Coeburn
Ph: 540-395-2487
Summit Golf Resort, Box 250, 22625 Ph: 703-888-4188   Cross Junction
Sheraton-Fredericksburg Resort, P.O. Box 618, 22404 Ph: 703-786-8321   Fredericksburg
Keswick Hall, Box 48, 22947 Ph: 804-295-1972   Keswick
Landsdowne Resort, 44050 Woodridge Parkway, 22075 Ph: 703-729-8400   Lansdowne

Olde Mill Golf Resort, Box 84, 24352 Ph: 703-398-2638 — Laurel Fork
Leesburg Westpark Hotel, 59 Clubhouse Dr. SW, 22075 — Leesburg
Ph: 703-777-1910
Shenvalee Lodge, P.O. Box 930, 22844 Ph: 703-740-3181 — New Market
Quality Inn Lake Wright Resort, 6280 Northampton Blvd, 23502 — Norfolk
Ph: 804-461-6251
Ingleside Resort, 1410 Commers Road, 24401 Ph: 540-248-1201 — Staunton
Bow Creek Motel, 3429 Club House Rd, 23452 Ph: 804-340-1222 — Virginia Beach
1776 Resort, General Delivery, 23185 Ph: 804-222-1776 — Waynesboro
Golden Horseshoe Golf Resort, 5 England Street, 23185 — Williamsburg
Ph: 757-229-1000
Marriott's Manor Club at Ford's Colony, 101 St. Andrews Drive, 23188 — Williamsburg
Ph: 757-258-1120

—————————————WASHINGTON—————————————
Alderbrook Inn Resort, E 7101 Hwy 106, 98592 Ph: 206-898-2200 — Union

—————————————WEST VIRGINIA—————————————
Cacapon Resort, Route 1, 25411 Ph: 304-258-1022 — Berkeley Springs
Glade Springs Resort, 3000 Lake Dr, 25832 Ph: 304-763-2000 — Daniels
Canaan Valley Resort, Box 330, 26260 Ph: 304-866-4121 — Davis
Lakeview Resort, Box 88A, 26505 Ph: 800-624-8300 — Morgantown
Twin Falls State Park Resort, P.O. Box 1023, 25881 Ph: 304-294-4000 — Mullens
Pipestem Resort State Park, PO Box 150, 25979 Ph: 304-466-1800 — Pipestem
Alpine Lake Resort, Rt. 2, 26764 Ph: 304-789-2481 — Terra Alta
Oglebay Resort, Route 88 North, 26003 Ph: 304-243-4000 — Wheeling

—————————————WISCONSIN—————————————
Lake Lawn Lodge, Highway 50 East, 53115 Ph: 414-728-7950 — Delavan
Alpine Resort & Inn, P.O. Box 200, 54209 Ph: 414-868-3000 — Egg Harbor
Nippersink Manor Resort, General Delivery, 53128 Ph: 414-279-5281 — Genoa City
Gateway Lodge, PO Box 596, 54540 Ph: 715-547-3321 — Land O' Lakes
Devil's Head Resort, 56330 Bluff Rd, 53561 Ph: 608-493-2251 — Merrimac
800-338-4579
Fox Hills Resort, P.O. Box 129, 54228 Ph: 414-755-2376 — Mishicot
Whitecap Mountains Resort, Hwy 77, 54550 Ph: 715-561-2776 — Montreal
SentryWorld Sports Center, 601 North Michigan Avenue, 54481 — Stevens Point
Ph: 715-345-1600
Lodge at Cherry Hills, 5905 Dunn Rd, 54234 Ph: 414-743-4222 — Sturgeon Bay

—————————————WYOMING—————————————
Little America, P.O. Box 1529, 82003 Ph: 307-775-8400 — Cheyenne
Teton Pines Resort, PO Box 14090, 83001 Ph: 307-733-1005 — Jackson
Grand Teton Lodge, PO Box 250, 83013 Ph: 307-543-3100 — Moran

BOOKS FROM LANIER

The Complete Guide to Bed & Breakfasts, Inns & Guesthouses – 19th Edition
With over 10,000 listings, this is the one annual source preferred by experienced travelers who love the warmth and intimacy of this style of accommodation. Over 2 million copies in print. Rated #1 guide by innkeepers nationwide.

Elegant Small Hotels—A Connoisseur's Guide – 16th Edition
A tradition in the capital cities of Europe, these exquisite hotels can be found today throughout the United States. Each of the 220 great American hotels described in this guide is unique. Over 50,000 copies in print.

Elegant Hotels of the Pacific Rim, A Connoisseur's Guide – 1st Edition
This is a guide to the finest lodging in the Pacific area, from California to Bangkok. Each of the 200 hotels described in highly rated.

All-Suite Hotel Guide – 10th Edition
This guide is an indispensable aid for the business traveler, listing over 1,400 all-suite hotels in the United States and around the world.

Golf Courses—The Complete Guide – 5th Edition
A definitive directory and travel guide for the nation's 20 million avid golf players. This comprehensive guide includes over 14,000 golf courses in the United States that are open to the public.

Golf Resorts—The Complete Guide – 7th Edition
This is a complete update to over 1,000 golf resorts and is certain to be a hit with the millions of devotees of the game.

Golf Resorts International – 3rd Edition
This wish book and travel guide for the wandering golfer reviews the creme de la creme of golf resorts all over the world.

Condo Vacations—The Complete Guide – 7th Edition
An extensive revision and updating of the first ever national guide to condominium vacations, just as this form of vacation is growing ever more popular.

The Back Almanac
The best new thinking on an age old problem. 25 chapters packed with easy to read information about back problems.

Cinnamon Mornings & Raspberry Teas
This gracefully illustrated cookbook brings to your home outstanding regional cuisine from more than 150 of America's finest bed and breakfasts.

Bed & Breakfast—Australia's Best
A compendium of the best B&Bs "Down Under" reflecting the spirit and atmosphere of their regions.

Sweets & Treats
This delightful cookbook features over 100 of the most requested, cherished, and best-loved sweets and treats recipes from the chefs of America's finest Bed & Breakfast Inns and Guesthouses.

LANIER GUIDES
ORDER FORM

QTY	TITLE	EACH	TOTAL
	Golf Courses—The Complete Guide	$19.95	
	Golf Resorts—The Complete Guide	$14.95	
	Golf Resorts International	$19.95	
	Condo Vacations—The Complete Guide	$14.95	
	Elegant Small Hotels	$19.95	
	Elegant Hotels of the Pacific Rim	$14.95	
	All-Suite Hotel Guide	$14.95	
	The Complete Guide to Bed & Breakfasts, Inns & Guesthouses	$16.95	
	Family Travel—The Complete Guide	$19.95	
	Cinnamon Mornings & Raspberry Teas	$17.95	
	The Back Almanac	$14.95	
	Sweets & Treats	$14.95	
	Bed & Breakast—Australia's Best	$14.95	
		Sub-Total	$
		Shipping U.S.A.	$3.00 each
		Shipping Int'l.	$5.00 each
		TOTAL ENCLOSED	$

Send your order to:

LANIER PUBLISHING,   P.O. Drawer D,   Petaluma, CA 94953

Order Books online by going to http://www.TravelGuideS.com/store

- -

Allow 3 to 4 weeks for delivery

Please send my order to:

NAME _____

ADDRESS _____

CITY _____ STATE _____ ZIP _____